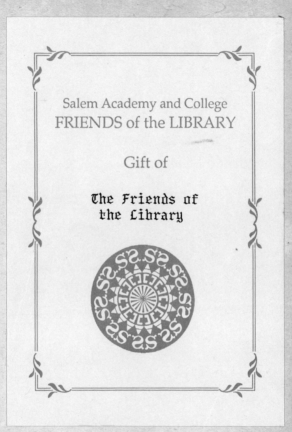

EDGAR ALLAN POE

EDGAR ALLAN POE:

His Life, Letters, and Opinions.

WITHDRAWN

BY

JOHN H. INGRAM.

"Unhappy Master, whom unmerciful Disaster
Followed fast and followed faster till his Songs one burden bore—
Till the dirges of his Hope that melancholy burden bore
Of 'Never,—nevermore.'"

PUBLISHED BY

THE GRAND COLOSSEUM WAREHOUSE CO.

(Founded by Mr. Walter Wilson in 1869.)

GENERAL OFFICES AND WHOLESALE WAREHOUSES:

60 & 70, JAMAICA STREET, GLASGOW.

Branches in all the Principal Towns in Scotland.

EDGAR ALLAN POE.

CHAPTER I.

PARENTAGE.

EDGAR ALLAN POE was of gentle birth.* His paternal grandfather, General David Poe, the descendant of an ancient and highly connected family, was born in Ireland, but, taken at a very early age by his parents to the United States, became a patriotic citizen of his adopted country, and greatly distinguished himself during the War of Independence. The General's eldest son, David, was destined for the law, and after receiving the usual quantum of education then afforded by the schools of Baltimore—his birthplace — was placed under Mr. William Gwynn, barrister-at-law, to read for the bar.

The youthful student, the future poet's father, would appear to have found greater attraction in the drama than in jurisprudence, and, according to the testimony of a fellow-townsman,† " young Poe and several of his gay companions formed an association called the ' Thespian Club,' for the promotion of a taste for the drama. They met in a large room, in a house belonging to General Poe. . . . Here, at

* *Vide* Appendix A, for *Ancestry*.
† E. L. Didier, *Life of Edgar A. Poe*, pp. 23, 24.

A

their weekly meetings, they recited passages from the old dramatists, and performed the popular plays of the day, for the entertainment of themselves and their friends." According to the same authority, "David Poe became so infatuated with the stage that he secretly left his home in Baltimore, and went to Charleston, where he was announced to make his 'first appearance on any stage.' One of his uncles, William Poe, . . . saw the announcement in the newspapers; he went to Charleston, took David off the stage, and put him in the law office of the Honourable John Forsyth of Augusta," Georgia, his own (William Poe's) brother-in-law.

The veritable cause of David's escapade would appear to have been something even stronger than an infatuation for the stage. Whilst still studying law under Mr. Gwynn, young Poe was sent to Norfolk, Virginia, upon professional business, and there saw and became deeply enamoured of Elizabeth Arnold, a youthful and beautiful English actress. From Norfolk the company to which Miss Arnold was attached migrated to Charleston, whither, apparently, it was followed by the young lady's admirer. Different reasons have been given to account for the youthful couple's temporary and compulsory separation; but, whatever may have been the facts, they speedily met again, and ultimately were married, the bridegroom being but nineteen, and the bride about the same age. David Poe's parents were incensed at the imprudent match, and forbade him the house; and as neither he nor his wife possessed any means of subsistence, they turned to the stage in search of a livelihood.

Many absurd stories have been retailed as to the

parentage of Elizabeth Arnold, one widely-circulated rumour declaring her to have been the daughter of General Benedict Arnold, the American traitor. The facts are not yet thoroughly known, but it is believed that her father was an Englishman of very good family, though in impoverished circumstances, who sought refuge in the United States, where he endeavoured to support himself by literature. Elizabeth Arnold herself was born at sea, where her mother is supposed to have died at, or directly after, the child's birth. The little girl being left fatherless, as well as motherless, whilst still an infant, was, apparently, adopted by some compassionate stranger, and carefully educated for the stage. Eventually the poor little orphaned foreigner made her appearance in public, her *début* as an actress taking place on August 18th, 1797, at the old John Street Theatre, New York, in the juvenile character of " Maria," in the farce of *The Spoiled Child.*[*] Two nights later she appeared as " Agnes," in the tragedy of *The Mountaineers,* and is recorded to have made a very favourable impression by her youth, her beauty, and her precocious ability. Mr. Solee, a well-known *impresario* of the period, engaged the juvenile *débutante* for a company he was forming, and under his management, and that of his successors, Messrs. Williamson, Placide, and others, the young English girl became an accomplished actress, ultimately appearing in the leading *rôles* of the tragic drama. Between her first appearance on the New York stage, and her reappearance there in 1806 as Mrs. David Poe, Miss Arnold's career may be traced at the various theatres of New York, Phila-

* Ireland, *Records of the New York Stage,* vol. i. p. 42.

delphia, Norfolk, and Charleston; and it is pleasant to hear her talented son, in the brightest epoch of his own short life, when alluding to his mother's profession, declare that "no earl was ever prouder of his earldom than he of his descent from a woman, who, although well born, hesitated not to consecrate to the drama her brief career of genius and beauty."

In 1806, when Mrs. Poe reappeared in New York, she was accompanied by her husband. The youthful couple were engaged at the new Vauxhall Garden, where the lady made her *entrée*, on the 16th of July, as "Priscilla," in *The Tomboy*, whilst Mr. Poe made his first appearance on the New York stage on the 18th, as "Frank," in *Fortune's Frolic.* "The lady was young and pretty," remarks Ireland, "and evinced talent both as singer and actress; the gentleman was literally nothing." * Eventually the Poes removed from New York to Boston, where they frequently performed. Their various appearances on the stage at the latter city may be traced in 1808 from the commencement of April until the 3rd of June, the theatre having been opened on the latter date for "one night only," in honour of the time-renowned "Artillery Election." A noteworthy circumstance, both for the calculators of prenatal influences and the analytic student of Poe's works, is that on the 18th of April 1808—just nine months before the poet's birth—Mr. and Mrs. Poe appeared in Schiller's ominous tragedy of *The Robbers*, and were assisted by their old friends, Mr. and Mrs. Usher. Their thoughts are likely to have been more than usually occupied with the selection of the piece for performance, as it

* *Records of the New York Stage.*

was their benefit night, and, apparently their own
speculation, they having announced, "That from the
great failure and severe losses sustained by their
former attempts, they [the Poes and the Ushers]
have been induced to make a joint effort." The *rôle*
of "Amelia" was assigned to Mrs. Poe, who, towards
the end of her brief career, almost invariably undertook the chief female characters, whilst her husband's
impersonations strangely varied from the leading male
down to the most minor personages of the drama.

What became of the Poes during the summer, or
what they did for a livelihood until the winter season
of 1808–9 commenced, can only be conjectured.
Other means of subsistence than those derived from
their dramatic labours may have been provided by
Mrs. Poe's abilities : she was an accomplished artist,
and left one or two sketches that have been much
admired. One of her paintings, that ultimately came
into the possession of her celebrated son, was a view
of "Boston Harbour: Morning, 1808;" and upon
the back of it was inscribed, in a neatly-written round
hand, not very dissimilar from the poet's own beautiful
caligraphy, a description ending with the words, "For
my little son Edgar, who should ever love Boston,
the place of his birth, and where his mother found
her best and most sympathetic friends."

During the winter of 1808–9 the Poes frequently
appeared on the Boston boards. On the 17th of
January, Mrs. Poe was absent from the performance,
and on the 19th, her second son, Edgar, was born.
In less than a month the young mother reappeared,
and continued playing in Boston until the 19th of
April, when she took her benefit, assuming the Shake-

sperian *rôles* of "Ophelia" and "Cordelia," whilst her husband, whose health was probably breaking, had to content himself with the minor character of "Laertes." Upon this occasion, as also upon many others, Mrs. Poe sang "a favourite song."

At the close of the Boston season the young couple, after paying a short visit to Baltimore in order to fetch their little boy from General Poe's, where he was staying, flitted back to New York. On the 6th of September they appeared at the Park Theatre of that city, in *The Castle Spectre*, as "Hassan and Angela." * They wintered in New York, remaining there until the beginning of July, when they removed to Richmond, Virginia, where, it is believed, early in 1811, David Poe died of consumption. Some months after their father's decease, a third child, Rosalie, was born. Mrs. Poe's own health now began to fail rapidly, and in consequence of her inability to continue her professional engagements, her circumstances became truly deplorable. These facts becoming known, certain ladies interested themselves on her behalf, and ministered to her wants. A Mrs. Richards and other Richmond ladies who visited the dying actress, frequently commented, in a manner that has left a lasting impression, upon Mrs. Poe's evident refinement of manner; and, despite her poverty and sickness, the exquisite neatness of herself and her surroundings. All help, however, was now of slight avail, for on Sunday the 8th of December, the unfortunate lady followed her husband to the tomb, like him dying of decline. On the Tuesday following her death, the *Richmond Enquirer* contained this announcement:—

* Dunlop, *History of the American Stage*, vol. ii. p. 265.

"DIED.—On Sunday last, Mrs. Poe, one of the actresses of the company at present playing on the Richmond Boards. By the death of this Lady the Stage has been deprived of one of its chief ornaments. And to say the least of her, she was an interesting Actress, and never failed to catch the applause, and command the admiration, of the beholder."

Beyond the fleeting memory of her beauty and talent, Mrs. Poe left little for her three fatherless children ; but, in after years, the sketches above referred to, and a parcel of her letters, were cherished by her illustrious son among his most highly-valued treasures. Evidently she was a woman of great intellectual capacity, as is indeed displayed in her portrait by a breadth of brow similar to that possessed by Edgar Poe, and to conceal the masculine appearance of which she was accustomed to wear her hair low down over her forehead.*

Upon the death of their surviving parent, David Poe's three children—in accordance with a custom not unusual in republican countries—were adopted by comparative strangers. Edgar was taken by Mr. John Allan, a wealthy Scotch merchant, married to an American lady and settled in Virginia; William Henry Leonard, the date and place of whose birth is still uncertain, by some relative or friend in Baltimore ;† and Rosalie, by the family of another Scotchman named McKenzie.‡

* A miniature of his mother accompanied the poet through all his wanderings. Shortly before his death he gave it to a very valued friend, from whom we received it. A second portrait of Mrs. Poe, it may be remarked, remained in the possession of her famous son until his decease, but its subsequent fate is unknown to us.—J. H. I.

† *Vide* Appendix B.   ‡ *Vide* Appendix C.

CHAPTER II.

CHILDHOOD.

EDGAR ALLAN POE was born at Boston, on the 19th
of January 1809. His parents' professional engagements and restricted means could not have permitted
them to give any very cordial welcome to this addition
to their limited *ménage*. When the child was only
five weeks old it was taken by its parents to Baltimore, and left in the charge of its grandfather's household, where the beauty and talent of its mother appear
to have effected a reconciliation between the General
and his prodigal son. After staying some months
with his relatives in Maryland, Edgar was reclaimed
by his parents, and apparently stayed with his mother
until her death in 1811.

The poor little orphan is recorded to have already
manifested promise of great beauty. At the solicita-
tions of his wife, Mr. John Allan agreed to adopt
the boy, who, for several subsequent years, was to
be known as Edgar Allan. Mr. Allan, a native
of Ayrshire, Scotland, had emigrated to the United
States, and settled in Virginia, where he made a considerable fortune by the purchase and export of tobacco:
at the time when he adopted this child he was only
thirty-one, although, apparently, he had been already
long married. Not only was Edgar a handsome and
precocious boy, but he was in some way related to
his godfather, who had, therefore, every cause to com-

POE'S SCHOOL AT STOKE NEWINGTON.

passionate the little orphan's condition. In the home of his adoptive parents the boy found much of the luxury wealth could provide, and in the person of Mrs. Allan as much affection as a childless wife could bestow. Edgar won the admiration, even if he did not gain the affection, of Mr. Allan, who became extremely proud of his youthful *protégé*, and treated him in many respects as his own son. Although little that is trustworthy can now be learned of the poet's early days, it is worth record that a tenacious memory and a musical ear are said to have enabled him to learn by rote, and declaim with effect, the finest passages of English poetry, to the evening visitors at his godfather's house. "The justness of his emphasis, and his evident appreciation of the poems he recited, made a striking impression upon his audience, while every heart was won by the ingenuous simplicity and agreeable manners of the pretty little elocutionist." Gratifying as these exhibitions may have been to Mr. Allan's vanity, the probable consequence of such a system of recurring excitements upon the boy's morbidly nervous organisation could scarcely fail to prove injurious. Indeed, in after years, the poet bitterly bewailed the pernicious effects of his childhood's misdirected aims. "I am," he declared, "the descendant of a race whose imaginative and easily excitable temperament has at all times rendered them remarkable ; and in my earliest infancy I gave evidence of having fully inherited the family character. As I advanced in years it was more strongly developed, becoming, for many reasons, a cause of serious disquietude to my friends, and of positive injury to myself. . . . My voice was a household law, and at an age when few children have abandoned their leading-strings, I was left to the guidance of my own will, and became, in all but name, the master of my own actions."

After receiving the rudiments of his education in an academy at Richmond, Poe accompanied the Allans to Europe, whither they were called on matters connected with the disposal of some property left to Mr. Allan by a relative. Edgar is supposed to have visited several portions of Great Britain in the company of his adoptive parents, and a sister of Mrs. Allan's. Upon their arrival in London, in 1816, the boy was placed at a school in Stoke Newington, then a distinct town, but now a suburb of the metropolis. Part of the time Edgar was under the charge of the Rev. Dr. Bransby, the Allans resided in the vicinity of Russell Square, whither every recurring Friday he returned, remaining with them until the following Monday.*

The Rev. Dr. Bransby, afterwards so quaintly portrayed by Poe in his story of *William Wilson,* "is remembered as having had the reputation of being a thorough scholar, very apt at quotation, especially from Shakespeare and Horace," and also as "a strict disciplinarian." When young "Allan," as Edgar was styled, was placed under Dr. Bransby's care, he was found to be "very backward with his studies, not having had any regular instruction;" but when he left the Stoke Newington Manor House School, "he was able to speak French, construe any easy Latin author, and was far better acquainted with history and literature than many boys of a more advanced age, who had had greater advantages than he had."† "Edgar Allan" was described by Dr. Bransby as "a quick

* Mrs. Clemm's Letters to Judge Neilson Poe.
† *Athenæum,* No. 2660, pp. 496 97, October 19, 1878.

and clever boy," who " would have been a very good
boy had he not been spoilt by his parents," as he
termed the Allans; " but they spoilt him, and allowed
him an extravagant amount of pocket-money, which
enabled him to get into all manner of mischief. Still,
I liked the boy," added the schoolmaster; " poor
fellow, his parents spoilt him."

To his sojourn in England Poe looked back with
anything but ungrateful reminiscences, as a reference
to his tale of *William Wilson* proves. His description of Stoke Newington, as it was when he resided
there, is unusually accurate in its suggestive details.
Many of the features of his school and school-life are
reproduced with a graphicality unequalled anywhere,
save in the parallel records of Balzac's " *Louis Lambert.*"
It is not presuming too much upon the probabilities
to suggest, that much of the gloom and glamour which
pervade Poe's writings originated in the strangeness
and isolation of the lad's position in that foreign and
" excessively ancient house," of that " misty-looking
village of England." The dreamy walks, even now
overshadowed by immemorial elms, and the mouldering
dwellings that then abounded—some few remain—in
the vicinity of his English schoolhouse, could not
fail to exercise a marked influence upon a mind so
morbidly sensitive to impressions as was Poe's; nor
can it be doubted that in the *lustrum* of his life there
spent he acquired some portion at least of that curious
and *outré* classic lore which, in after years, became one
of the chief ornaments of his weird works.

When Poe resided at Stoke Newington the Manor
House school-grounds occupied a very large area; but
of late years, owing to the continuous encroachments

of enterprising builders, they have been much circumscribed in extent, and the house greatly altered in appearance. The description of the place, as well as the representation of his school-life there, had, the poet declared, been faithfully given in *William Wilson*, but in order to trace out this *vraisemblance*—at least, as regards the building and some minor *data*—the earliest known version of the story must be referred to, subsequent revisions which it afterwards underwent at its author's hands having somewhat detracted from its fidelity to fact. "The large, rambling, Elizabethan house," into which Poe ultimately, and evidently for the purpose of heightening the picturesque effect, metamorphosed the "old, irregular, and cottage-built" dwelling, portrayed more correctly the appearance of a fine old manorial residence that formerly faced the school, but which quite recently has been ruthlessly razed for "improvements."

"In truth," remarks the *soi-disant* "William Wilson," "it was a dream-like and spirit-soothing place, that venerable old town," and it is not strange the boy's plastic mind should have retained, indelibly imprinted upon it, a vivid impression of "the refreshing chilliness of its deeply-shadowed avenues," and, in fancy, "inhale the fragrance of its thousand shrubberies, and thrill anew with indefinable delight at the deep hollow note of the church-bell, breaking each hour, with sullen and sudden roar, upon the stillness of the dusky atmosphere in which the old fretted Gothic steeple lay imbedded and asleep."

Within this dream-engendering place the quondam Edgar Allan spent about five years of his brief existence; and, notwithstanding the apparent monotony of school-life, was doubtless fully justified in looking back upon the days passed in that venerable academy with pleasurable feelings. "The teeming brain of childhood," to repeat Poe's own words, "requires no external world of incident to occupy or amuse it. The morning's awakening, the nightly summons to bed; the connings, the recitations, the periodical half holidays and perambulations; the playground, with its broils, its pastimes, its intrigues—these, by a mental sorcery long forgotten, were made to involve a wilderness of sensation, a world of rich incident, a universe of varied emotion, of excitement the most passionate and spirit-stirring. *' Oh, le bon temps, que ce siècle de fer !'*"

"Old and irregular," as the poet described it, the house still is. "The grounds," he remarks further, " were extensive, and a high and solid brick wall, topped with a bed of mortar and broken glass, encompassed the whole. This prison-like rampart formed the limit of our domain ; beyond it we saw but thrice a week—once every Saturday afternoon, when, attended by two ushers, we were permitted to take brief walks in a body through some of the neighbouring fields— and twice during Sunday, when we were paraded in the same formal manner to the morning and evening service in the one church of the village. Of this church the principal of our school was pastor. With how deep a spirit of wonder and perplexity was I wont to regard him from our remote pew in the gallery, as, with step solemn and slow, he ascended the pulpit ! This reverend man, with countenance so demurely benign, with robes so glossy and so clerically flowing, with wig so minutely powdered, so rigid and so vast,—could this be he who, of late, with sour visage, and in snuffy habiliments, administered, ferule in hand, the Draconian laws of the academy ? Oh, gigantic paradox, too utterly monstrous for solution !

"At an angle of the ponderous wall frowned a more ponderous gate. It was riveted and studded with iron bolts, and surmounted with jagged iron spikes. What impressions of deep awe did it inspire ! It was never opened save for the three periodical egressions and ingressions already mentioned ; then, in every creak of its mighty hinges, we found a plenitude of mystery—a world of matter for solemn remark, or for more solemn meditation.

" The extensive enclosure was irregular in form, having many capacious recesses. Of these, three or four of the largest constituted the playground. It was level, and covered with fine hard gravel. I well remember it had no trees, nor benches, nor anything similar within it. Of course it was in the rear of the house. In front lay a small parterre, planted with box and other shrubs ; but through this sacred division we passed only upon rare occasions indeed—such as a first advent to school or final departure thence ; or perhaps, when a parent or friend having called for us, we joyfully took our way home for the Christmas or Midsummer holidays.

" But the house !—how quaint an old building was this !— to me how veritably a palace of enchantment ! There was really no end to its windings—to its incomprehensible subdivisions. It was difficult, at any given time, to say with certainty upon which of its two stories one happened to be. From each room to every other there were sure to be found three or four steps either in ascent or descent. Then the lateral branches were innumerable—inconceivable—and so returning in upon themselves, that our most exact ideas in regard to the whole mansion were not very far different from those with which we pondered upon infinity. During the five years of my residence here, I was never able to ascertain, with precision, in what remote locality lay the little sleeping apartment assigned to myself and some eighteen or twenty other scholars.

" The schoolroom was the largest in the house—I could not help thinking, in the world. It was very long, narrow, and dismally low, with pointed Gothic windows and a ceiling of oak. In a remote and terror-inspiring angle was a square enclosure of eight or ten feet, comprising the *sanctum*, ' during hours,' of our principal, the Reverend Dr. Bransby. It was a solid structure, with massy door, sooner than open which, in the absence of the ' Dominie,' we would all have willingly perished by the *peine forte et dure*. In other angles were two other similar boxes, far less reverenced, indeed, but still greatly matters of awe. One of these was the pulpit of the 'classical' usher, one of the 'English and mathematical.' Interspersed about the room, crossing and recrossing in endless irregularity, were innumerable benches and desks, black, ancient, and time - worn, piled desperately with much-be-thumbed books, and so beseamed with initial letters, names at full length, grotesque figures, and other multiplied efforts of the knife, as to have entirely lost what little of original form might have been their portion in days long departed. A huge bucket with water stood at one extremity of the room, and a clock of stupendous dimensions at the other."

"The ardour, the enthusiasm, and the imperiousness" which are declared to have rendered the "William Wilson" of the story a marked character among his schoolmates, so that by slow but natural gradations he obtained an ascendancy over all not greatly older than himself, may safely be assumed to represent Poe's own idiosyncrasies, even at this early epoch of his life. A consistency of passion and thought, however diverted or thwarted by occasional circumstance, runs through Poe's whole career, and what was truly representative of him at the first is found a faithful portraiture at the last. "In childhood," he exclaims, "I must have felt with the energy of a man what I now find stamped upon memory in lines as vivid, as deep, and as durable, as the exergues of the Carthaginian medals."

The lad was recalled to America in 1821, and for some months spent his time in what he termed "mere idleness," but which really consisted in composing verses, and in thinking out future poems. Indeed, as he subsequently states, in the interesting *Preface* to his first printed book, its contents were written during the years 1821-22, and before the author had completed his fourteenth year.

CHAPTER III.

BOYHOOD.

IN 1822 Mr. Allan placed his adopted son, who now reassumed his own surname of Poe, in an academy in Richmond, Virginia, in which city the Allans continued to reside. Many most interesting reminiscences of the embryo poet during his attendance at this preparatory school, then kept by Mr. John Clarke, have been placed at our disposal by fellow-pupils of Poe; and the following, from the pen of Colonel John T. L. Preston, husband of Mrs. Margaret J. Preston, the poetess, cannot fail to charm:—

"Although I was several years Poe's junior, we sat together at the same form for a year or more at a classical school in Richmond, Virginia. Our master was John Clarke, of Trinity College, Dublin. At that time his school was the one of highest repute in the metropolis. Master Clarke was a hot-tempered, pedantic, bachelor Irishman; but a Latinist of the first order, according to the style of scholarship of that date, he unquestionably was. I have often heard my mother amuse herself by repeating his pompous assurance that in his school her boy should be taught 'only the pure Latinity of the Augustan age.' It is due to his memory * to say, that if her boy was not properly grounded in his rudiments, it was not the fault of his teacher. What else we were taught I have forgotten; but my drilling in Latin, even to its minutiæ, is clear to my view as if lying on the surface of yesterday.

"Edgar Poe might have been at this time fifteen or sixteen, he being one of the oldest boys in the school, and I one of

---

* Professor John Clarke is still alive.—J. H. I.

the youngest. His power and accomplishments captivated me, and something in me, or in him, made him take a fancy to me. In the simple school athletics of those days, when a gymnasium had not been heard of, he was *facile princeps.* He was a swift runner, a wonderful leaper, and what was more rare, a boxer, with some slight training. I remember, too, that he would allow the strongest boy in the school to strike him with full force in the chest. He taught me the secret, and I imitated him, after my measure. It was to inflate the lungs to the uttermost, and at the moment of receiving the blow to exhale the air. It looked surprising, and was, indeed, a little rough ; but with a good breast- bone, and some resolution, it was not difficult to stand it. For swimming he was noted, being in many of his athletic proclivities surprisingly like Byron in his youth. There was no one among the schoolboys who would so dare in the midst of the rapids of the James River. I recall one of his races. A challenge to a foot-race had been passed between the two classical schools of the city ; we selected Poe as our champion. The race came off one bright May morning at sunrise, in the Capitol Square. Historical truth compels me to add that on this occasion our school was beaten, and we had to pay up our small bets. Poe ran well, but his competitor was a long-legged, Indian-looking fellow, who would have outstripped Atalanta without the help of the golden apples. Ah, how many of those young racers on Capitol Square that fair May morning, and how many of the crowd that so eagerly looked on, are very still now !

"In our Latin exercises in school Poe was among the first —not first without dispute. We had competitors who fairly disputed the palm. Especially one—Nat Howard—afterwards known as one of the ripest scholars in Virginia, and distinguished also as a profound lawyer. If Howard was less brilliant than Poe, he was far more studious ; for even then the germs of waywardness were developing in the nascent poet, and even then no inconsiderable portion of his time was given to versifying. But if I put Howard as a Latinist on a level with Poe, I do him full justice. One exercise of the school was a favourite with Poe : it was what was called ' capping verses.' The practice is so absolutely obsolete now, at least in our country, that the term may require explanation.

" Before the close of the school, all the Latinists, without

B

regard to age or respective advancement in the language, were drawn up in a line for 'capping verses;' just as, in old-fashioned schools, all scholars had to take their place in the spelling-line before dismission.   At the head of the line stood the best scholar, who gave from memory some verse of Latin poetry to be 'capped:' that is, he challenged all the line to give from memory another verse beginning with the same letter.   Whoever was able to do this, took the place of the leader ; and in his turn propounded another verse to be capped in like manner.   This we called 'simple capping.' 'Double capping' was more difficult, inasmuch as the respond-ing verse must both begin and end with the same letters as the propounded verse.   To give an example, and at the same time to illustrate how a memory, like a sieve, may let through what is valuable, and yet retain in its reticulations a worthless speck, I recall a 'capping' which, while I have forgotten ten thousand things that would have been serviceable if remem-bered, comes back to me with distinctness after the lapse of so many years.

"Nat Howard stood at the head of the line, and gave out for double capping a verse beginning with *d*, and ending with *m*.   It passed Edgar Poe, it passed other good scholars, as well it might, until it reached me, a tyro, away down the line. To the surprise of everybody, and not less to my own, there popped into my mind the line of Virgil :—

       ' Ducite ab urbe domum, mea carmina, ducite Daphnim.'

And with pride and amazement I saw myself where I never was before and never was afterwards,—above Nat Howard and Edgar Poe.

"The practice looks absurd, and so it would be now.   True, it stored the memory with many good quotations for ready use.   But after the fashion of Master Clarke—a fashion brought from Trinity—this 'capping verses' was much in vogue, and Edgar Poe was an expert at it.

"He was very fond of the Odes of Horace, and repeated them so often in my hearing that I learned by sound the words of many, before I understood their meaning.   In the lilting rhythm of the Sapphics and Iambics, his ear, as yet untutored in more complicated harmonies, took special delight.

Two odes, in particular, have been humming in my ear all my life since, set to the tune of his recitation :—

> 'Jam satis terris nivis atque diræ
> Grandinis misit Pater, et rubente '—

and,

> ' Non ebur neque aureum
> Mea renidet in domo lacunar,' &c.

" When I think of his boyhood, his career, and his fate, the poet, whose lines I first learned from his musical lips, supplies me with his epitaph :

> ' Ille, mordaci velut icta ferro
> Pinus, aut impulsa cupressus Euro,
> Procidit late, posuitque collum in
> Pulvere Teucro.'

"I remember that Poe was also a very fine French scholar. Yet, with all his superiorities, he was not the master-spirit, nor even the favourite, of the school. I assign, from my recollection, this place to Howard. Poe, as I recall my impressions now, was self-willed, capricious, inclined to be imperious, and though of generous impulses, not steadily kind, or even amiable ; and so what he would exact was refused to him. I add another thing which had its influence, I am sure.

" At the time of which I speak, Richmond was one of the most aristocratic cities on this side the Atlantic. I hasten to say that this is not so now. Aristocracy, like capping verses, has fallen into desuetude — perhaps for the same reason : times having changed, other things pay better. Richmond was certainly then very English, and very aristocratic. A school is, of its nature, democratic ; but still boys will unconsciously bear about the odour of their fathers' notions, good or bad. Of Edgar Poe it was known that his parents had been players, and that he was dependent upon the bounty that is bestowed upon an adopted son. All this had the effect of making the boys decline his leadership ; and on looking back on it since, I fancy it gave him a fierceness he would otherwise not have had. . . .

"Not a little of Poe's time in school, and out of it, was occupied with writing verses. As we sat together, he would show them to me, and even sometimes ask my opinion, and now and then my assistance. I recall at this moment his consulting me about one particular line, as to whether the word 'groat' would properly rhyme with 'not.' It would not surprise me now if I should be able, by looking over his juvenile poems, to identify that very line. As it is my only chance for poetic fame, I must, I think, undertake the search.

"My boyish admiration was so great for my schoolfellow's genius, that I requested his permission to carry his portfolio home for the inspection of my mother. If her enthusiasm was less than mine, her judgment did not hesitate to praise the verses very highly ; and her criticism might well gratify the boyish poet, for she was a lady who, to a natural love for literature, inherited from her father, Edmund Randolph,* had added the most thorough and careful culture obtained by the most extensive reading of the English classics,—the established mode of female education in those days. Here, then, you have the first critic to whom were submitted the verses of our world-famed poet. Her warm appreciation of the boy's genius and work was proof of her own critical taste."

One paragraph of Colonel Preston's recollections throws a lurid and most suggestive light upon the causes which rendered the boy's early life unhappy, and tended to blight his budding hopes. Although, as seen, mixing with scions of the best families, and endowed with the innate pride derivable from gentle birth—fostered by all the indulgences of wealth and the consciousness of intellect—Edgar Poe was made to feel that his parentage was obscure, and his position in society dependent upon the charitable caprice of a benefactor. Many boys might have endured such a condition of life with equanimity, but to one of this

* The well-known statesman.—J. H. I.

lad's temperament it must have been a source of continual torment, and all allusions to it gall and wormwood for his haughty spirit. Generally, Mr. Allan appears to have been proud of his handsome and precocious godson, and willing enough to provide him with the advantages proffered by educational institutions; but of parental affection, and of that family sympathy for which the poor orphan boy yearned—as his words and works prove—he seems to have been utterly devoid. Not but what the imperious youth was frequently indulged in all money could purchase, yet the pettings and rebuffs which he was alternately subjected to were scarcely calculated to conciliate *his* disposition. Throughout life a morbid sensitiveness to affection was one of Poe's most distinguishing traits, and it was the want of this which drove him frequently to seek in the society of dumb creatures the love denied him, or which he sometimes *believed* denied him, by human beings. In his terrible tale of *The Black Cat* there is a paragraph which those who were intimately acquainted with its author will at once recognise the autobiographical fidelity of. " From my infancy," remarks Poe, " I was noted for the docility and humanity of my disposition. My tenderness of heart was even so conspicuous as to make me the jest of my companions. I was especially fond of animals, and was indulged by my parents with a great variety of pets. With these I spent most of my time, and never was so happy as when feeding and caressing them. This peculiarity of character grew with my growth, and in my manhood I derived from it one of my principal sources of pleasure. To those who have cherished an affection for a faithful and sagacious dog, I need hardly be at the trouble of explaining the nature or the intensity of the gratification thus derivable. There is something in the unselfish and self-sacrificing love of a brute, which goes directly to the heart of him who has had frequent occasion to test the paltry friendship and gossamer fidelity of mere *man.*"

Many of Poe's schoolfellows at the Richmond Academy corroborate and supplement Colonel Preston's reminiscences. Dr. R. C. Ambler writes : " I recollect my old playmate Edgar Allan Poe. I passed my early life in the city of Richmond, and in the years 1823–24 I was in the habit of constant intercourse with the boy. No one now living, I daresay, had better opportunities of becoming acquainted with his physique, as for two summers we stripped together for a bath daily, and learned to swim in the same pool in Shockoe Creek. . . . Poe was not apt at learning to swim, though at a subsequent period he became famous for swimming from Mayo's Bridge to Warwick." In allusion to this long-remembered boyish feat, the poet himself remarked, " Any ' swimmer in the falls ' in my days would have swum the Hellespont, and thought nothing of the matter. I swam from Ludlam's Wharf to Warwick (six miles) in a hot June sun, against one of the strongest tides ever known in the river. It would have been a feat comparatively easy to swim twenty miles in still water. I would not think much," concluded Poe, in his strain of not infrequent exaggeration, " of attempting to swim the British Channel from Dover to Calais." Whatever he might not think much of " attempting," the lad did not, certainly, shrink from doing a deed of no little daring in his famous swim, an account of which is thus furnished by Colonel

Robert Mayo, junior, at that time a companion and schoolmate of the poet:—" I started with Poe in his celebrated swim from Richmond to Warwick Bar, six miles down James River. The day was oppressively hot, and I concluded rather than endure the infliction to stop at Tree Hill, three miles from town. Poe, however, braved the sun and kept on, reaching the goal, but emerging from the water with neck, face, and back blistered."

The truth of this feat having been publicly questioned, Poe, who was intolerant of contradiction, obtained from Dr. Cabell and published the following certification of his prowess:—

" I was one of several who witnessed this swimming feat. We accompanied Mr. Poe in boats. Messrs. Robert Stannard, John Lyle (since dead), Robert Saunders, John Munford, I think, and one or two others, were also of the party. Mr. Poe did not seem at all fatigued, and *walked* back to Richmond immediately after the feat—which was undertaken for a wager.   ROBERT G. CABELL."

A yet more dangerous exploit in natation is recorded of the daring boy by Colonel Mayo. One day in midwinter, when standing on the banks of the James River, Poe bantered his companion into jumping in, in order to swim to a certain point with him. After floundering about in the nearly frozen stream for some time they reached the piles upon which Mayo's Bridge then rested, and were glad enough to stop and try to gain the shore by climbing up the log abutment to the bridge. To their dismay, upon reaching the bridge, they discovered that its flooring overlapped the abutment by several feet, and that ascent by such means was impossible. Nothing remained for them but to

descend and retrace their steps, which, weary and partly
frozen, they did: Poe reached the land in an exhausted
state, whilst Mayo was fished out by a friendly boat,
just as he was about to succumb. On getting ashore,
Poe was seized with a violent attack of vomiting, and
both the lads were ill for several weeks. Colonel Mayo
recalls Poe to mind as a haughty, handsome, impetuous
boy, self-willed, defiant, and not indisposed for fight,
but with great mental power and an ever-present
anxiety to grapple with and solve difficult mental
problems.

Dr. Ambler, recurring to this period of Poe's career,
remarks, " Of course I was too young at that date to
appreciate the poet's mental capabilities; but I remember to have heard some verses of his, in the shape of a
satire upon the members of a debating society to which
he belonged. . . I cannot recall a line of these verses,
but do remember that I envied him his ability to write
them. These lines, as far as I know, were never published, but were circulated in manuscript among the
boys, and were, probably, the first known out of his
family."

Mr. John Clarke, having relinquished the guidance
of the Richmond school, was succeeded, in the autumn
of 1823, by a Mr. William Burke, and amongst the
pupils who remained in his charge was Edgar Allan
Poe. Mr. Andrew Johnston, another of his schoolfellows at Richmond, states that when he went to
Mr. Burke's on the 1st of October 1823, he found
Poe there. "I knew him before," he writes, "but not
well, there being two, if not three, years difference in
our ages. We went to school together all through
1824, and the early part of 1825. Some time in the

latter year (I cannot recollect at what time exactly) he left the school. . . Poe was a much more advanced scholar than any of us; but there was no other class for him—that being the highest—and he had nothing to do, or but little, to keep his headship of the class. I daresay he liked it well, for he was fond of desultory reading, and even then wrote verses. . . We all recognised and admired his great and varied talents, and were proud of him as the most distinguished schoolboy of the town. At that time Poe was slight in person and figure, but well made, active, sinewy, and graceful. In athletic exercises he was foremost. Especially, he was the best, the most daring, and most enduring swimmer that I ever saw in the water. . . . His disposition was amiable, and his manners pleasant and courteous." *

These somewhat similarly-minded reminiscences by the poet's playmates—doubtless slightly, albeit unconsciously, biassed in tone by the after celebrity of Poe —serve to illustrate and prove that even at that early age the lad had strongly impressed his comrades with a belief in his intellectual superiority, and that he had already begun to entertain a proud and somewhat pugnacious contempt for those less richly endowed by nature. Other equally marked idiosyncrasies of his character—extraordinary fidelity of friendship, and intense sensitiveness to kindness—are strikingly portrayed by some well-authenticated incidents in this period of his life, and to which the late Mrs. Whitman was the first to draw attention.† The correctness of her remarks in connection with these episodes has

* Didier, *Life of Edgar A. Poe*, pp. 33, 34.
† *Edgar Poe and his Critics*, pp. 48–55.

been amply confirmed by the correspondence of Mrs. Clemm and Poe himself. Referring to the passionate, almost fanatical, devotion of the poet for those who became the objects of his affection, Mrs. Whitman relates this characteristic anecdote of his boy-hood :—

"While at the academy in Richmond, he one day accompanied a schoolmate to his home, where he saw for the first time Mrs. H[elen] S[tannard], the mother of his young friend. This lady, on entering the room, took his hand and spoke some gentle and gracious words of welcome, which so penetrated the sensitive heart of the orphan boy as to deprive him of the power of speech, and for a time almost of conscious-ness itself. He returned home in a dream, with but one thought, one hope in life—to hear again the sweet and gracious words that had made the desolate world so beautiful to him, and filled his lonely heart with the oppression of a new joy. This lady afterwards became the confidant of all his boyish sorrows, and hers was the one redeeming influence that saved and guided him in the earlier days of his turbulent and passionate youth."

Writing on the same subject, Mrs. Clemm records that he entertained a most profound devotion for this lady, and that, "when he was unhappy at home (which was very often the case) he went to her for sympathy, for consolation, and for advice." But, alas! the sad destiny which appeared to haunt the poor lad, and all dear to him, overtook his beloved friend! This lady herself was overwhelmed by fearful and peculiar sorrows, and at the very moment when her guiding voice was most needed, fell a prey to mental alienation; and when she died and was entombed in a neighbouring cemetery, her poor boyish admirer could not endure the thought of her lying there lonely and forsaken in her vaulted home. For months after her decease, Poe—like his great Hungarian contemporary Petöfi, at the grave of his girl-love Etelka—would go nightly to visit the tomb of his revered friend, and when the nights were very drear and cold, "when the autumnal rains fell, and the winds wailed mournfully over the graves, he lingered longest, and came away most regretfully."

For years, if not for life, the memory of this unfortunate lady tinged all Poe's fancies, and filled his mind with saddening things. In a letter, written within a twelvemonth of his own death, to Mrs. Whitman, the poet broke through his usual reticence as to the facts of his early life, and confessed that his exquisitely beautiful stanzas "To Helen," * were inspired by the memory of this lady—by "the one idolatrous and purely ideal love" of his tempest-tossed boyhood. In the early versions of his youthful verses, the name of "Helen" continually recurs, and it was undoubtedly to her that he devoted "The Pæan," a juvenile poem which subsequently he greatly improved in both rhythm and form, and republished under the musical name of "Lenore." The weird thoughts which he experienced when he beheld this lady robed in her grave garments are hinted at in "Irene," † and the description which he gave to a friend of the fantasies that haunted his brain during

---

* Beginning, "Helen, thy beauty is to me."
† Published in 1831.

his desolate vigils in the cemetery,—the nameless
fears and indescribable phantasmata—

> " Flapping from out their Condor wings
> Invisible Woe ! "—

she compares to those which overwhelmed De
Quincey at the burial of his sweet sister-playmate.

Those willing to study Poe's idiosyncrasies should
not object to linger over this little-known epoch of
his story, because we are indeed convinced that in
" those solitary churchyard vigils, with all their
associated memories," Mrs. Whitman has found " a
key to much that seems strange and abnormal in the
poet's after life."   There can be no doubt that those
who would seek the clue to the psychological phenomena of his strange existence—" that intellect," as
Poe himself remarked, which would try to reduce
his " phantasm to the commonplace "—must know,
and even analyse, this phase of his being.   The mind
which could so steadfastly trace, step by step, the
gruesome gradations of *sentience after death,* as does
Edgar Poe in his weird " Colloquy of Monos and
Una," must indeed have been one that had frequently
sought to wrest its earthy secrets from the charnel-
house.

Throughout life Poe was haunted by the idea that
the dead are not wholly dead to consciousness—was
haunted, as Mrs. Whitman says, by " ideas of terror and
indescribable awe at the thought of that mysterious
waking sleep, that powerless and dim vitality, in
which ' the dead ' are presumed, according to our
popular theology, to await ' the general resurrection

at the last day ' "—and it was this feeling, those who knew him believe, that restrained him more than once from contracting another marriage after his beloved wife's death. The feeling, so powerfully expounded in some of his tales and his poems *—

> " *Lest the dead, who is forsaken,*
> *May not be happy now,*"—

overclouded his mind until the very last days of his " lonesome latter years."

* Compare "Eleonora;" " The Bridal Ballad;" and article, "Undine," in *Marginalia.*

CHAPTER IV.

FIRST LOVE.

BETWEEN the date of Poe's leaving Mr. Burke's school and his departure for the University of Virginia, early in the following year, 1826, little or nothing authentic is known of the youthful poet's deeds or adventures. During this interregnum of six months or so, there is good reason for believing, however, that he was pleasantly engaged in both making verses and making love, a combination of occupations, it need scarcely be pointed out, by no means unfrequent.

Quoting the assertion of " George Sand " that " *les anges ne sont plus pures que le cœur d'un jeune homme qui aime en vérité,*" Poe remarks that "the hyperbole is scarcely less than true," but that " it would be truth itself were it averred of the love of him who is at the same time young and a poet. The boyish poet-love," he emphatically declares, "is indisputably that one of the human sentiments which most nearly realises our dreams of the chastened voluptuousness of heaven." Thinking and speaking thus, and having in memory a similar influence exercised over a short period of his earlier life, he refers to the boyish poet-love of Byron for Mary Chaworth, as an earnest and long-abiding attachment that sublimated and purified from earthliness all his works alluding to it. And yet, he adds, this passion, " if passion it can properly be termed, was of the most thoroughly romantic, shadowy, and

imaginative character. It was born of the hour, and
of the youthful necessity to love. . . . It had no
peculiar regard to the person, or to the character, or to
the reciprocating affection of Mary Chaworth. Any
maiden, not immediately and positively repulsive,"
he deems Byron would have loved in similar circumstances of frequent and unrestricted intercourse, such
as the children are represented as having enjoyed.
" The result," opines Poe, " was not merely natural,
or merely probable, it was as inevitable as destiny
itself."

Any ordinary maiden would have served " sufficiently well as the incarnation of the ideal that haunted
the fancy of the poet," continues the young critic, notwithstanding the fact that the affection may not have
been reciprocated; or, " if *she* felt at all, it was only
while the magnetism of *his* actual presence compelled
her to feel." With evident remembrance of the ideal
of his own boyhood before him, he believes that to
Mary Chaworth Byron was merely " a not unhandsome and not ignoble, but somewhat portionless, somewhat eccentric young man," whilst " she to him was
the Egeria of his dreams—the Venus Aphrodite that
sprang, in full and supernal loveliness, from the bright
foam upon the storm-tormented ocean of his thoughts."
Reading his own story by these words, it is suggestive
to find how closely the loves of the two contemporary
poets were paralleled.

Between the years 1822–25, as has been told,
Edgar Poe was a scholar in a well-known academy at
Richmond. The adopted son and reputed heir of Mr.
Allan, and " a not unhandsome," if " somewhat eccen-
tric young man," the youthful poet made no mean

figure among his Virginian companions, notwithstanding any drawbacks incidental to his obscure parentage. Admired by his fellow-students for his superior educational attainments, his daring athletic feats, and for a certain magnetic rather than sympathetic influence which he exercised over them, it is not surprising to learn that he was introduced into, and mingled with, the best society of the Old Dominion. In the coteries into which he was received was a little maiden but a year or two younger than himself, who speedily became fascinated by the charms of his presence.

S. Elmira Royster lived with her father opposite to the Allans in Richmond, and in the usual course of events she made the acquaintance of their adopted son. She remembers Edgar Poe as "a beautiful boy," as not very talkative, and whose "general manner was sad," but whose conversation, when he did talk, was truly pleasant. "Of his own parents he never spoke," but "he was devoted to the first Mrs. Allan, and she to him. He had very few associates, but he was very intimate with Ebenezer Berling, a widow's son of about the same age as himself. Berling was an interesting, intelligent young man, but somewhat inclined to dissipation. They used to visit our house together very frequently. Edgar," continues the lady, "was very generous," and "warm and zealous in any cause he was interested in, being enthusiastic and impulsive." Dowered with "the hate of hate, the scorn of scorn," the youthful lover is remembered to have had strong prejudices, and, with his adoration for beauty already fully developed, to have detested everything coarse or wanting in refinement. It is also within the memory

of the lady that her young admirer drew beautifully:
"he drew a pencil likeness of me," she relates, "in a
few minutes." He was even then passionately fond
of music, "an art which in after life he loved so
well."

The love passages were kept up between the youthful
pair until Poe left for the University; he had, indeed,
engaged to marry Miss Royster, and wrote to her
frequently after his departure. Her father intercepted
the letters, deeming his daughter "o'er young to
marry," and it was not until a year or so later, and
when, having attained the mature age of seventeen,
she became Mrs. Shelton, that the young poet learned
how it was that his passionate appeals had failed to
elicit any response from the object of his affections.
The influence and memory of this attachment tinged
much of Poe's juvenile verse, threading like a misty
autobiographic reminiscence through the initial version
of his "Tamerlane," and pervading with unpassionate
melancholy many of his earliest stanzas. Recurring
once more to his remarks on Byron's boy-love, how
naturally do these words appear to shadow forth the
thoughts appertaining to the result of his own youthful amours. "It is perhaps better," he thinks, "for
the mere romance of the love passages between the
two, that their intercourse was broken up in early life,
and never uninterruptedly resumed in after years.
Whatever of warmth, whatever of soul passion, whatever of the truer share and essentiality of romance
was elicited during the youthful association, is to be
attributed altogether to the poet. If *she* felt at all,
it was only while the magnetism of *his* actual presence
compelled her to feel. If *she* responded at all, it was

c

merely because the necromancy of *his* words of fire
could not do otherwise than extort a response. In
absence, the bard bore easily with him all the fancies
which were the basis of his flame—a flame which
absence itself but served to keep in vigour—while the
less ideal but at the same time the less really substantial affection of his lady-love, perished utterly and
forthwith, through simple lack of the element which
had fanned it into being."

CHAPTER V.

ALMA MATER.

THE University of Virginia, or " Jefferson's University," as it has been frequently called in honour of President Jefferson, by whom it was founded, is beautifully situated upon an extensive plateau in the centre of the Old Dominion. It is surrounded by some of the most picturesque scenery in the United States, and in every respect reflects credit upon its worthy and disinterested founder. The establishment of this University was a darling, and indeed a daring, scheme of President Jefferson ; and had occupied a very large portion of his time from the first inception of the plan in 1779, until the opening of the institution on March 7th, 1825. The founder's labours in connection with the University were immense, and even after all opposition, latent and declared, had been overcome by the successful completion of the various buildings connected with it ; and by the engagement of such men for the professorships as Charles Bonnycastle, the late Thomas Hewitt Key, George Long, Dunglison, Blättermann, and other well-known men, his difficulties were by no means ended. His idea had been to make the students their own governors, and in lieu of punishments, to rely upon appeals to their honour and patriotism. A code of laws was framed in accordance with these views, but unfortunately proved useless ; and the appeals to " their reason, their hopes, and their generous feelings," which the illustrious patriot had so firmly relied upon for swaying the youthful multitude, ended in confusion. This disaster arose, apparently, from a mistaken view the students took of the duties required of them. The librarian, Mr. William Wertenbaker, the only surviving officer of the earliest *régime*, informs us :—

"The session of 1825 was commenced without any discipline at all, and without an effort on the part of the Faculty to enforce obedience to the laws. They were expecting and waiting for the students to inaugurate Mr. Jefferson's system of self-government, but this they resolutely refused to do. Neither the entreaties of Mr. Jefferson, nor the persuasion of the professors, could induce a single student to accept the office of Censor. The plan was that a Board of Censors, consisting of six of the most discreet students, should inquire into the facts in all cases of minor offences, and name the punishment which they thought proportioned to the offence.

"In this state of affairs, and for several months, insubordination, lawlessness, and riot ruled the institution, and became so intolerable to the professors that they suspended operations, and tendered their resignations to the Board of Visitors. The Board met immediately ; abandoned the plan of self-government ; enacted new laws ; ordered a course of rigid discipline to be pursued, and invested the Faculty with full authority to rule and govern the institution.

"In exercising the power now granted them, the Faculty (as in the circumstances it was quite natural for them to do) perhaps erred in going to the opposite extreme of punishing offenders with too great severity. . . At no period during the past history of the University were the Faculty more diligent in ferreting out offenders, and more severe in punishing them, than during the session of 1826. . . .

"Mr. Poe was a student during the second session, which commenced February 1st, and terminated December 15th, 1826. He signed the matriculation book on the 14th of February, and remained in good standing until the session closed. . . . He entered the schools of Ancient and Modern Languages, attending the lectures on Latin, Greek, French, Spanish, and Italian. I was a member of the last three classes, and can testify that he was tolerably regular in his attendance, and a successful student, having obtained distinction at the final examination in Latin and French, and this was at that time the highest honour a student could obtain. The present regulations in regard to degrees had not then been adopted. Under existing regulations, he would have graduated in the two languages above named, and have been entitled to diplomas."

Dr. Harrison, Chairman of the Faculty, fully confirms this statement of Poe's classmate, stating that the poet was a great favourite among his fellow-students at Charlottesville, and that he is remembered for the remarkable rapidity with which he prepared his recitations, and their general accuracy; his translations from the living languages being especially noteworthy.

Many of his classmates still retain a vivid recollection of their gifted companion, not from the fact of any particular geniality or *bonhomie* on his part, for he was always of a wayward and exclusive disposition, but from his self-reliant pride, and from the indisputable fact that he was *facile princeps* in nearly all their pursuits, mental and physical. Mr. John Willis, a fellow-student at the University,* recalls Poe as one who "had many noble qualities," and whom nature had endowed "with more of genius, and a far greater diversity of talent, than any other whom it had been my lot to have known;" but, adds this gentleman, "his disposition was rather *retiring*, and he had few intimate associates."

This reserve of Poe is noticed and confirmed by

---

* In a letter to the late Mrs. Whitman.

many others who came in general contact with him.
Mr. Thomas Bolling, another of his fellow-students,
says, " I was *acquainted* with him in his youthful days,
but that was about all. My impression was, and is,
that no one could say that he *knew* him. He wore a
melancholy face always, and even his smile—for I do
not ever remember to have seen him laugh—seemed
to be forced. When he engaged sometimes with others
in athletic exercises, in which, so far as high or long
jumping, I believe he excelled all the rest, Poe, with
the same ever-sad face, appeared to participate in what
was amusement to the others more as a task than
sport. Upon one occasion, upon a slight declivity, he
ran and jumped twenty feet, which was more than the
others could do, although some attained nineteen feet.
His chief competitor in these exercises was Labranche,
an especial friend of mine from Louisiana, who, although
of lower stature by several inches, had had the advantage, previous to entering the University, of being educated in France, where gymnastics are taught and practised as part of the course." Powell, in his *Authors of
America*, alludes to Poe having had the habit of covering the walls of his dormitory with charcoal sketches ;
Mr. John Willis states that he had a talent for drawing,
and that the walls of his room at college were completely covered with his crayon sketches, whilst Mr.
Bolling mentions in connection with his artistic facility
the following suggestive incidents. The two young
men invested in Byron's Poems, purchasing copies of
an English edition that contained several handsome
steel engravings. Poe appeared much interested in
these plates, and upon visiting him a few days later,
Mr. Bolling found him engaged in copying one with

crayon on the ceiling of his dormitory. He continued
to amuse himself in this way from time to time, says
our authority, until he had filled all the space in his
room. These life-size figures were, in the memory of
those who saw them, extremely ornamental and attractive, but all such vestiges of his boyish aspirations
have long since disappeared. Mr. Bolling remarks
that he never saw Poe attempt to sketch anything on
paper; as if, indeed, such material afforded too limited
a space for the boundless fancies of his youthful
ambition.

Mr. Bolling remembers that when he was talking
to his eccentric associate, Poe continued to scratch
away with his pencil as if writing, and when his visitor
jestingly remarked on his want of politeness, he
answered that he had been all attention, and proved
that he had by suitable comment, giving as a reason
for his apparent want of courtesy that he was trying
to *divide his mind*—carry on a conversation, and at
the same time write sense on a totally different subject! Several times did Mr. Bolling detect him
engaged in these attempts at mental division; and he
says the verses handed to him as the part results of
the dual labours certainly rhymed pretty well.
Whether this reminiscence only affords an early
instance of Poe's inveterate love of quizzical mystification, or, as is more probable, of his attempts at mental
analysis, it is wonderfully suggestive of the later
man.

Powell records that the poet's time at the University
was divided between lectures, debating societies, and
rambles in the Blue Ridge mountains, and of this last-
named occupation—so congenial to one who shrank

from contact with unsympathising or uncomprehend-
ing companions — Poe has left some vivid reminiscences in various parts of his works. Alone, or
accompanied only by a dog, he was in the habit of
making long expeditions into what he deemed the
"wild and dreary hills that lie westward and south-
ward of Charlottesville, and are there dignified by the
title of the Ragged Mountains." Alluding to a solitary ramble through the unfrequented fastnesses of
this chain of lofty hills, he indulges in the following
train of ideas, so accordant with his theories of thought:
—"The scenery which presented itself on all sides,
although scarcely entitled to be called grand, had about
it an indescribable and, to me, a delicious aspect of
dreary desolation. The solitude seemed absolutely
virgin. I could not help believing that the green sods
and the grey rocks upon which I trod had been trodden
never before by the foot of a human being. So entirely
secluded, and in fact inaccessible, except through a
series of accidents, is the entrance of the ravine, that
it is by no means impossible that I was indeed the
first adventurer—the very first and sole adventurer
who had ever penetrated its recesses."

But these lonely rambles and their attendant day-
dreams were the occasional relaxations of a hard-
working student; among the professors he had the
reputation of being a sober, quiet, orderly young man,
and the officials of the University bear witness to the
fact that his behaviour was uniformly that of an
intelligent and polished gentleman. In evidence of
his generally studious conduct Mr. Wertenbaker
records that, "on one occasion Professor Blättermann
requested his Italian class to render into English verse

a portion of the lesson in Tasso, which he had assigned them for the next lecture. He did not require this of them as a regular class exercise, but recommended it as one from which he thought the student would derive benefit. At the next lecture on Italian, the professor stated from his chair that ' Mr Poe was the only member of the class who had responded to his suggestion,' and paid a very high compliment to his performance."

Referring to his own personal experience of the youthful poet, Mr. Wertenbaker says, " As librarian I had frequent official intercourse with Mr. Poe, but it was at or near the close of the session before I met him in the social circle. After spending an evening together at a private house, he invited me, on our return, into his room. It was a cold night in December, and his fire having gone pretty nearly out, by the aid of some tallow candles, and the fragments of a small table which he broke up for the purpose, he soon rekindled it, and by its comfortable blaze I spent a very pleasant hour with him. On this occasion he spoke with regret of the large amount of money he had wasted, and of the debts he had contracted, during the session. If my memory be not at fault, he estimated his indebtedness at $2000, and though they were gaming debts, he was earnest and emphatic in the declaration that he was bound by honour to pay them at the earliest opportunity." Whilst at the University, Poe appears to have been much addicted to gambling, seeking, in the temporary excitement and absorbing nature of cards, that refuge from sorrowful thought which he subsequently sought for in other sources. Although his practice of gaming did escape detection, Mr. Wertenbaker assures us that "the hardihood, intemperance, and reckless wildness imputed to him by biographers—had he been guilty of them—must inevitably have come to the knowledge of the Faculty, and met with merited punishment. The records," he continues, "of which I was then, and am still, the custodian, attest that at no time during the session did he fall under the censure of the Faculty." Although Poe may, and doubtless did, occasionally take his share in a college frolic, Mr. Wertenbaker most emphatically repudiates the assertion that he was habitually intemperate, adding, "I often saw him in the lecture-room and in the library, but never in the slightest degree under the influence of intoxicating liquors."

"Poe's connection with the University was dissolved by the termination of the session on the 15th of December 1826, when he wanted little more than a month to attain the age of eighteen. The date of his birth was plainly entered in his own handwriting on the matriculation book. . . . He never returned to the University, and I think it probable that the night I visited him was the last he spent here," says our informant, drawing this inference from the fact that, having no further need of his candles and table, the poet used them for fuel.

As an interesting and suggestive memento of Poe's residence at Charlottesville, Mr. Wertenbaker has furnished us with a copy, from the register, of a list of books the poet borrowed from the library whilst a student; and those who have studied his works will recognise the good use made, in after life, of the young collegian's selection. Rollin's "Histoire Ancienne,"

" Histoire Romaine," Robertson's " America," Marshall's " Washington," Voltaire's " Histoire Particulière," and Dufief's " Nature Displayed," are the works he made use of.

Short as was Edgar Poe's University career, he left such honourable memories behind him that his *alma mater* has been only too proud to enrol his name among her sons. His adopted father, however, does not appear to have regarded his godson's collegiate proceedings with equal favour ; whatever view he may have taken of the lad's scholastic successes, he resolutely refused to liquidate his gambling debts—his debts of *honour*—and the consequence was a violent altercation, terminating in the young student hastily quitting his home, with the determination of trusting to his own resources to make his way in the world. For a time he appears to have thought of supporting himself by literature, and, like most neophytes in that career, commenced with a volume of verse. Additional motive for his hasty departure from Richmond may be found in the fact of Miss Royster's marriage to Mr. Shelton, an event doubtless commemorated in some lines "To ——," included in his first—the 1827 —volume, beginning

> " I saw thee on the bridal day,
>   When a burning blush came o'er thee ;
> Though happiness around thee lay,
>   The world all love before thee."

It may well be conjectured that a youth of Poe's proud and impetuous disposition would scarcely remain plodding quietly at home, constantly in sight of another enjoying happiness which he had, presumedly, lost.

CHAPTER VI.

DAWNINGS OF GENIUS.

EDGAR POE'S first literary venture was printed in its author's natal city of Boston, in 1827. What caused him to visit his birthplace is a mystery. Whether a longing to learn something further of his mother and her family—and neglected honours to her memory caused him frequent qualms of conscience in after years—or whether he merely pilgrimaged to the capital of Massachusetts in hopes of there finding a good market for his poetic labours, has not been, and probably never will be, discovered. At all events, the remembrances which he brought away with him of the "American Athens" were anything but pleasing, although then and there it was, apparently, that he made the acquaintance of his mother's friends, the Ushers and the Wilsons, people whose names, at least, he made literary use of a few years later on.

His first known literary venture, a tiny tome consisting of only forty pages, inclusive of *Preface* and *Notes*, although printed for publication, was "suppressed through circumstances of a private nature." The title of the little book runs thus:—

TAMERLANE,

AND

OTHER POEMS.

BY A BOSTONIAN.

" Young heads are giddy, and young hearts are warm,
And make mistakes for manhood to reform."—*Cowper*.

BOSTON : CALVIN S. THOMAS.

1827.

What the private reasons were which caused the suppression of this most interesting memento of the poet's early life can only be conjectured. It is not improbable that the too palpable nature of the autobiographical allusions, the doubtless obnoxious family researches which might be instituted by some, when the " Bostonian " of the title-page became identified with Edgar Allan Poe, and perchance the appeal for forgiveness foreshadowed in the motto from Cowper, all combined, or any one separately, may have led to the withdrawal of the book from circulation.

In the *Preface* to this volume the youthful poet informs his anticipated readers, that the greater part of its contents " were written in the year 1821–22, when the author had not completed his fourteenth year. They were, of course, not intended for publication," he remarks, and " why they are now published concerns no one but himself. Of the smaller pieces," he deems " very little need be said : they, perhaps, savour too much of egotism, but they were written by one too young to have any knowledge of the world but from his own breast. In 'Tamerlane,'" says the boy-poet, " he has endeavoured to expose the folly of even *risking*

the best feelings of the heart at the shrine of Ambition.
He is conscious that in this there are many faults
(besides that of the general character of the poem)
which, he flatters himself, he could with little trouble
have corrected, but, unlike many of his predecessors,
has been too fond of his early productions to amend
them in his *old age.*   He will not," he confesses, " say
that he is indifferent as to the success of these poems
—it might stimulate him to other attempts—but he
can safely assert that failure will not at all influence
him in a resolution already adopted.   This is challenging criticism—let it be so.   *Nos hœc novimus esse nihil,"*
which concluding assertion, it may be remarked, he
lived to prove the falsity of.

Following the preface is " Tamerlane," which occupies
about seventeen pages of the booklet; it is a very
different poem from that of Poe's later years, known
by the same title, and is replete with the Byronian
influence.   A more connected story is afforded by this
version than by the later editions; the heroine is
named as Ada, and the hero as Alexis, " Tamerlane "
being deemed to have been only a *nom-de-guerre* of
the famous warrior.   Very many lines, indeed many
whole stanzas, are filled with personal allusions to
their author, as those alluding to his innate pride
and habitual day-dreaming, and when referring to one
loved and lost even before what *passion* was could be
known.   A belief in his own budding powers is certainly portrayed in such lines as—

> " The soul which feels its innate right—
> The mystic empire and high power
> Given by the energetic might
> Of genius, at its natal hour "—

and

> "There is a power in the high spirit
> To *know* the fate it will inherit :
> The soul, which knows such power, will still
> Find *pride* the ruler of its will"—

and allusion to those around him may readily be dis-covered in those sceptics

> "Who hardly will conceive
> That any should become 'great,' born
> In their own sphere—will not believe
> That they shall stoop in life to one
> Whom daily they are wont to see
> Familiarly—whom Fortune's sun
> Hath ne'er shone dazzlingly upon,
> Lowly—and of their own degree."

The idea which the young aspirant for fame enun-ciated in verse, he also devoted a note to, to demon-strate that it is very difficult "to make the generality of mankind believe that one with whom they are upon terms of intimacy shall be called in the world a 'great man,'" and he deems the evident reason to be that "there are few great men, and that their actions are constantly viewed by the mass of people through the medium of distance. The prominent parts of their char-acters are alone noted ; and those properties which are minute and common to every one, not being observed, seem to have no connection with a great character."

The "Fugitive Pieces" which follow "Tamerlane" are all more or less tinged with the same cast of thought which from first to last characterised their author, although perhaps more indicative of the influ-ence of contemporary poets than any of his later pro-ductions. Haunting sorrow, strong ambition, and mental rambles into the shadowy realms of dreamland, permeate these earliest verses of his boyhood as profusely as they do the musical refrains of his " lonesome latter years." In one of these mental adumbrations he cries—

> " Oh ! that my young life were a lasting dream !
> My spirit not awaking till the beam
> Of an eternity should bring the morrow.
> Yes ! though that long dream were of hopeless sorrow,
> 'Twere better than the cold reality
> Of waking life, to him whose heart must be,
> And hath been, still upon the lovely earth,
> A chaos of deep passion from his birth."

The " Visit of the Dead," which follows the piece quoted from, is evidently inspired by Byron's " Dream," whilst a succeeding lyric from the same source is confessedly entitled " Imitation ;" some lines in it, however, are very characteristic, such as—

> " A dark unfathomed tide
> Of interminable pride—
> A mystery and a dream
> Should my early life seem."

The well-known little lyric, " A Dream," which appeared in this edition, also contained this initial stanza —afterwards omitted—of significant self-allusion :—

> " A wildered being from my birth,
> My spirit spurned control ;
> But now, abroad on the wide earth,
> Where wanderest thou, my soul ? "

whilst the following penultimate piece, entitled " The Happiest Day," to those who have thus far followed

his story, cannot fail to be replete with autobiographical implication :—

" The happiest day—the happiest hour—
   My seared and blighted heart hath known ;
The highest hope of pride and power,
   I feel hath flown.

" Of power ! said I ? Yes ! such I ween ;
   But they have vanished long, alas !
The visions of my youth have been—
   But let them pass.

" And pride, what have I now with thee ?
   Another brow may ev'n inherit
The venom thou hast poured on me—
   Be still, my spirit.

" The happiest day—the happiest hour—
   Mine eyes shall see—have ever seen ;
The brightest glance of pride and power,
   I feel—have been.

" But were that hope of pride and power
   Now offered with the pain
Ev'n *then* I felt—that brightest hour
   I would not live again :

" For on its wing was dark alloy,
   And as it fluttered, fell
An essence, powerful to destroy
   A soul that knew it well."

With the lines entitled " The Lake "—the best
poem in the collection—Edgar Poe's earliest literary
venture closes.

Taken altogether, and due allowance being made for
some exceptional beauties and occasional originalities,
there was not much in this 1827 volume to show
the world that a new poetic power was about to
arise; its author's incomparable melody of rhythm

D

and haunting power of words were not, as yet, fore-shadowed.

But this little book was suppressed, and its author, in all probability, recalled to Richmond. Whatever arrangements were made as to the future can only be speculated upon—the result was, however, unless the poet's most solemn word is to be doubted, that he departed for Europe; and it is generally supposed, and by Poe was never contradicted, in order to offer his services to the Greeks against their Turkish tyrants.

CHAPTER VII.

*EASTWARD HO!**

TOWARDS the end of June 1827, Edgar Poe would appear to have left the United States for Europe. It is very problematical whether he ever reached his presumed destination, the scene of the Greco-Turkish warfare, or ever saw aught, save in his "mind's eye," of

> " The glory that *was* Greece,
> And the grandeur that *was* Rome."

The poems which he wrote either during his absence abroad or directly after his return home (such as "Al Aaraaf" and the "Sonnet to Zante"), contain allusions to Greece and its scenery that, in some instances, appear to be the result of personal reminiscence or impression; but with a mind of such identificative power as was Poe's, these coincidences cannot be allowed to count for much. Hannay says—and how many will agree with him?— "I like to think of Poe in the Mediterranean, with his passionate love of the beautiful,—in ' the years of April blood,'—in a climate which has the perpetual luxury of a bath—he must have had all his perceptions of the lovely intensified wonderfully. What he did there we have now no means of discovering."† Poe had, undoubtedly, been excited by the heroic efforts the

* This account of Poe's adventures in Europe is derived from *memoranda* made at his own request—during a dangerous illness which it was deemed might end fatally—shortly after his wife's decease. There does not appear to be any reason for doubting the accuracy of this any more than of any other of the poet's statements.—J. H. I.

† J. Hannay, *The Life and Genius of Edgar Allan Poe*, 1852.

insurgent Greeks were making to throw off the yoke of their Turkish oppressors, and was, probably, emulous of Byron, whose example and Philhellenic poesy had aroused the chivalric aspirations of the boys of both continents, and whose writings, certainly, strongly influenced our hero's own muse at this epoch of his life.

Powell states that it was in conjunction with an acquaintance, Ebenezer Berling, that the youthful poet formed the design of participating in the Hellenic revolution, and conjectures that Poe went alone in consequence of his companion's heart failing him.[*] Whatever may have been the truth with regard to Berling, at that time the lad's most intimate and most trusted acquaintance, it must be remembered that *he* —unlike Poe the orphan—was a widow's only son, and, doubtless, in delicate health, as he died not long after his friend's departure.

A most interesting and suggestive memento of the youthful crusader's enthusiasm is to be found in an unknown translation by him of the famous " Hymn in honour of Harmodius and Aristogeiton." As an excuse for the omission of the latter hero's name, Poe pleads the impossibility of making it scan in English verse. If this juvenile version of these oft-translated verses does not display any very great poetic merit, it is at least as good, and, indeed, much better than many other renderings of the " Hymn " by well-known bards :—

" Wreathed in myrtle, my sword I'll conceal,
   Like those champions, devoted and brave,
When they plunged in the tyrant their steel,
   And to Athens deliverance gave.

---

* Powell, *Living Poets of America*, 1850.

" Beloved heroes ! your deathless souls roam
 In the joy-breathing isles of the blest ;
Where the mighty of old have their home—
 Where Achilles and Diomed rest.

" In fresh myrtle my blade I'll entwine,
 Like Harmodius, the gallant and good,
When he made at the tutelar shrine
 A libation of Tyranny's blood.

" Ye deliverers of Athens from shame—
 Ye avengers of Liberty's wrongs !
Endless ages shall cherish your fame,
 Embalmed in their echoing songs."

Edgar Poe was absent from America on his Hellenic journey about eighteen months. The real adventures of his expedition have never, it is believed, been published. That he reached England is probable, although in the account of his travels, derived from his own dictation, that country was not alluded to any more than was the story of his having reached St. Petersburg, and there having been involved in difficulties that necessitated ministerial aid to extricate him. The latter incident is now stated to have occurred to his brother, William Henry Leonard,* whilst Edgar himself, it has been suggested by a writer claiming personal knowledge of him, resided for some time in London, formed the acquaintance of Leigh Hunt and Theodore Hook, and, like them, lived by literary labour.

According to Poe's own story—which apparently accounts only for a portion of his time—he arrived, eventually, at a certain seaport in France. Here he was drawn into a quarrel about a lady, and in a fight which ensued was wounded by his antagonist, a

* *Vide* Appendix B.

much more skilful swordsman than he was. Taken
to his lodgings, and, possibly, ill tended, he fell into a
fever. A poor woman, who attended to his needs and
pitied him, made his case known to a Scotch lady of
position, who was visiting the town in the hope of
persuading a prodigal brother to relinquish his evil
ways and return home with her. This lady came to
see the wounded stranger, and for thirteen weeks had
him cared for, providing for all his wants, including
the attendance of a skilled nurse, whose place, indeed,
she often took herself. Whilst Poe was in a precarious condition she visited him daily, and even
persuaded her brother to come and see the young
Englishman, as his language led them to believe he
was. When the patient became convalescent, he was,
naturally, intensely grateful to his generous benefactor.
As the only means he possessed at that time of
showing his gratitude, he wrote a poem to her, which
he entitled "Holy Eyes," with reference to the trust,
sympathy, and faith which he deemed her blue eyes
typical of. Indeed, according to Poe's description,
this lady's eyes were her chief personal attraction, she
being otherwise plain, large-featured, and old-maidish.
Owing to the peculiarity of her position in this foreign
seaport, she did not wish her name made public, and
impressed this upon the youthful poet. She made
him promise to return to America—and perhaps supplied the means for him to do so—and adopt a profession, in which she expressed a hope of some day
hearing that he had become famous.

During his stay in France, so runs Poe's narration,
he wrote a novel, in which his own adventures were
described under the garb of fiction. The manuscript

of this story he carried back with him to America, and retained it in his possession until, at least, some few years before his death. When asked why he had not published it, he replied that a French version of it had been published, and had been accredited to Eugene Sue, but that he would not sanction its publication in English, because it was too sensational; that it was not to his taste; that it had too much of the " yellow cover novel style " for him to be proud of it, and, moreover, that it contained " Scenes and pictures so personal, that it would have made him many enemies among his kindred, who hated him for his vanity and pride already, and in some respects very justly—the faults of his early education." The truth in his story, he asserted, was yet more terrible than the fiction. " The Life of an Artist at Home and Abroad " was the title by which Poe at one time designated this youthful novel; it was written entirely in the third person, and was pronounced by its author to be " commonplace."

Such is the story dictated by Poe from what, it was deemed at the time, might be his deathbed. Whether it was fact, or fact and fiction deliriously interwoven, or mere fiction, invented in such a spirit of mischief as, like Byron, he frequently indulged in at the expense of his too-inquisitive questioners, is, at this late date, difficult to decide. As he told the tale to one whom he trusted, so it is here recounted.

After his long absence from home, if Mr. Allan's residence may so be termed, Poe reached Richmond safely in the beginning of March 1829, with little besides a trunk-load of books and manuscripts. His adopted mother had died during his absence: unfor-

tunately he arrived too late to take a last farewell of
her, she having been interred the day before his arrival.
Mrs. Allan was buried in the family grave at Shockoe
Hill Cemetery, and a stone bearing the following in-
scription was erected over her remains :—

Sacred
to the Memory of
FRANCES KEELING ALLAN,
who departed
this transitory life
on the Morning of the 28th of
February 1829.
This Monument is erected by
JOHN ALLAN, her Husband,
in testimony of his gratitude for her
unabated affection to him,
her zeal to discharge her domestic duties,
and the fervour she manifested, both by
precept and example,
in persuading all to trust in the
promises of the Gospel.

Apparently, the deceased lady had exercised a con-
ciliatory influence in the Allan household, where,
indeed, it is stated, it was not unfrequently needed,
and the poor tempest-tossed youth—who in after life
always referred to her with affection—soon had to
experience the effects of her loss. Mr. Allan does not
appear to have manifested much pleasure at the
prodigal's return, and it was not long before Poe
again departed. He visited some of his paternal
relatives, and is believed to have inspired one of his
uncles, probably Mr. George Poe, with a belief in his
genius. This relative seems to have taken some interest in his nephew's welfare, and at this time wrote
to the late John Neal to solicit his confidential opinion

as to the youth's poetic abilities. The reply was not altogether unfavourable, and the consequence of it was that Poe wrote to Neal, and proposed to publish a volume of poems dedicated to him. This proposition Neal sought to discourage, so far as regarded the intended dedication, contending that his unpopularity in the United States might injure the sale of the book. This remonstrance was not calculated to have much effect upon one of Poe's disposition—in fact, when shortly after this he published a new version of "Tamerlane," he dedicated it to his first literary correspondent.

After a short absence, the poet returned once more to Richmond, and it is within the recollection of Mr. Bolling, his fellow-student at the University, that he accidentally met Poe the second night after he got back. The wanderer gave him a long account of the hardships he had had to endure, and what shifts he had been put to for a living, remarking that he had, as the only alternative for relief, betaken himself to authorship. The publication of "Al Aaraaf" was one result of this exertion. The poem, he informed his old friend, was then on sale at Sanxy's, a bookseller of Richmond, and he desired him to call there and obtain as many copies as he wished, adding, that should Bolling meet with any of their old college mates who would care to see the volume, he would like them presented with a copy, only it was to be presented as coming from Bolling, and not as from the author. The following day Poe accompanied his friend to Sanxy's store, gave him a copy of the book in question, and left the requisite instructions with the bookseller for Mr. Bolling to have as many more copies as he might require.

Previous to the publication of this, his first acknowledged collection of poems, Edgar Poe, as already remarked, wrote from Baltimore to John Neal, who was then editing *The Yankee*, in order to obtain his candid opinion of the forthcoming volume, sending him specimens of the contents. Through the columns of his paper, the editor replied, " If E. A. P. of Baltimore, whose lines about Heaven—though he professes to regard them as altogether superior to any in the whole range of American poetry, save two or three trifles referred to—are, though nonsense, rather exquisite nonsense, would but do himself justice, he might make a beautiful, and perhaps a magnificent poem. There is a good deal to justify such a hope in—

> " ' Dim vales and shadowy floods—
>   And cloudy-looking woods ;
>   Whose forms we can't discover,
>   For the tears that drip all over.
>
> .   .   .   .   .
>
>   The moonlight . . . . falls
>   Over hamlets, over halls,
>   Wherever they may be,
>   O'er the strange woods, o'er the sea,
>   O'er spirits on the wing,
>   O'er every drowsy thing,
>   And buries them up quite
>   In a labyrinth of light.
>   And then, how deep !   *Oh deep*,
>   Is the passion of their sleep.'

We have no room for others."

In response to this praise—this faint first recognition of his ability *to do* something meritorious—Poe's gratitude and craving for sympathy prompted him to send the following letter :—

"I am young—not yet twenty—*am* a poet, if deep worship of all beauty can make me one—and wish to be so in the common meaning of the word. I would give the world to embody one-half the ideas afloat in my imagination. (By the way, do you remember, or did you ever read, the exclamation of Shelley about Shakespeare, 'What a number of ideas must have been afloat before such an author could arise !') I appeal to you as a man that loves the same beauty which I adore—the beauty of the natural blue sky and the sunshiny earth—there can be no tie more strong than that of brother for brother. It is not so much that they love one another, as that they both love the same parent—their affections are always running in the same direction—the same channel, and cannot help mingling. I am, and have been from my childhood, an idler. It cannot therefore be said that—

> " 'I left a calling for this idle trade,
>   A duty broke—a father disobeyed'—

for I have no father—nor mother.

"I am about to publish a volume of 'Poems'—the greater part written before I was fifteen. Speaking about 'Heaven,' the editor of *The Yankee* says, ' He might write a beautiful, if not a magnificent poem '—(the very first words of encouragement I ever remember to have heard). I am very certain that as yet I have not written *either*—but that I *can*, I will take my oath—if they will give me time.

"The poems to be published are 'Al Aaraaf,' 'Tamerlane,' one about four, the other about three hundred lines, with smaller pieces. ' Al Aaraaf ' has some good poetry and much extravagance, which I have not had time to throw away.

"'Al Aaraaf' is a tale of another world—the star discovered by Tycho Brahe, which appeared and disappeared so suddenly —or rather it is not a tale at all. I will insert an extract about the palace of its presiding deity, in which you will see that I have supposed many of the lost sculptures of our world to have flown (in spirit) to the star ' Al Aaraaf '—a delicate place more suited to their divinity :—

> " ' Upreared upon such height arose a pile,' &c." *

---

* Here follow 32 lines from the poem of " Al Aaraaf."—J. H. I.

After this the youthful poet quotes another passage of eight lines, beginning " Silence is the voice of God," and ending with " And the red woods are withering in the sky," and then two lengthy passages from " Tamerlane," and the following fourteen lines from an untitled poem :—

> " If my peace hath flown away
> In a night—or in a day—
> In a vision—or in none—
> Is it therefore the less gone ?
> I am standing 'mid the roar
> Of a weather-beaten shore,
> And I hold within my hand
> Some particles of sand—
> How few ! and how they creep
> Through my fingers to the deep !
> My early hopes ? No—they
> Went gloriously away,
> Like lightning from the sky
> At once—and so will I."

In acknowledgment of this communication, John Neal gave Poe generous notice, at the same time letting him know that, in his opinion, if the remainder of " Al Aaraaf " and " Tamerlane " was as good as the extracts given, with all their faults, to say nothing of the more valuable portions, their author " deserved to stand high, very high, in the estimation of the shining brotherhood." Whether Poe would do so, however, he opined must depend not so much upon his present as upon his future worth, and he exhorted him to attempts yet loftier and more generous, alluding,—these, of course, being Neal's own words,—" to the stronger properties of the mind—to the magnanimous deter- mination that enables a youth to endure the present, whatever the present may be, in the hope or rather in the belief—the fixed, unwavering belief—that in the future he will find his reward."

It is, of course, quite impossible to imagine what view the young poet took of Neal's friendly criticism, but one thing is certain, and that is, that the literary correspondence thus cordially commenced continued in a similar sympathetic strain until Poe's death. The second printed but first published volume of Poe, to which the above correspondence refers, bears the following title-page :—

AL AARAAF,
Tamerlane,
AND
Minor Poems.
By Edgar A. Poe.
Baltimore: Hatch and Dunning.
1829.

This volume—published, apparently, at the close of the year—is stated to have been for private circulation. It contains only sixty-six pages, and many of these are merely extra leaves and bastard titles. The real contents include " Al Aaraaf," substantially as now printed, and prefixed to it, but unnamed, the sonnet now styled " To Science." The present version of " Tamerlane " —then dedicated to John Neal—follows, and thereafter succeed ten " Miscellaneous Poems." These included the lines now known as " Romance," but then called " Preface ; " the song, " I saw thee on the bridal day ; " " The Lake," from the suppressed volume of 1827, and seven other pieces. Six of these latter are, save some slight variations, as still published, but in the following lines, " To M——,"

appear three stanzas subsequently omitted, as well as a
few trifling alterations.   The whole poem, as it stands
in the 1829 edition, reads thus :—

> " Oh ! I care not that my earthly lot
>   Hath little of earth in it—
>   That years of love have been forgot
>   In the fever of a minute.
>
> " I heed not that the desolate
>   Are happier, sweet, than I—
>   But that *you* meddle with *my* fate
>   Who am a passer-by.
>
> " It *is* not that my founts of bliss
>   Are gushing—strange ! with tears—
>   Or that the thrill of a single kiss
>   Hath palsied many years—
>
> " 'Tis not that the flowers of twenty springs,
>   Which have withered as they rose,
>   Lie dead on my heart-strings
>   With the weight of an age of snows.
>
> " Nor that the grass —oh ! may it thrive !—
>   On my grave is growing or grown,
>   But that, while I am dead, yet alive,"
>   I cannot be, lady, alone."

These somewhat indefinite stanzas are typical of
the whole of the fugitive pieces in the little book, and
are, as usual, characteristic of his life and idiosyncrasies ;
—morbid sensibility to kindness, haunting regrets for
an unprofited past, and a hopeless, utterly despairing
dread of the future.   These " Miscellanous Poems,"
labelled—

> " My nothingness—my wants—
>   My sins—and my contritions " —

are hinted at, in " Romance," as "*forbidden things*" in

ordinary hours, and were, but too probably, occupations
interdicted by his godfather. But from some suppressed lines in another piece, inscribed to an unknown
person, it is clear that no amount of authority would
have constrained him from pursuing his own subjects.
He exclaims, after bewailing his early hopes, and alluding to an intention of *disappearing altogether :*—

> "So young ! ah no—not now—
> Thou hast not seen my brow,
> But they tell thee I am proud—
> They lie—they lie aloud—
> My bosom beats with shame
> At the paltriness of name
> With which they dare combine
> A feeling such as mine—
> Nor Stoic ? I am not :
> In the tenor of my lot
> I laugh to think how poor
> That pleasure " to endure ! "
> What ! shade of Zeno !—I !
> Endure !—no—no—defy."

And that he did *defy* all parental, or assumed parental,
power to suppress his poetic aspirations, it is easy to
comprehend. But in " Spirits of the Dead " a more
faithful representation of his self-styled " funereal
mind " is to be found—a very portrayal in one stanza,
wherein he alludes to the living being overshadowed
by the *will* of the dead. It was, indeed, a never-ending phantasy with him, that death was not absolute
separation from life—that the dead were not wholly
heedless of the deeds of the living.

But the two long poems constituted the chief value
of the 1829 edition. " Al Aráf," or " Al Aaraaf," as
the poet preferred styling it, is designed by the

Mohammedan imagination as an abode wherein a gentle system of purgatory is instituted for the benefit of those who, though too good for hell, are not fitted for heaven—

"Apart from heaven's eternity—and yet how far from hell!"

Poe chose to locate this intermediate region in a star discovered, or rather examined, by Tycho Brahe (and which it is now conjectured must have been a sun in course of conflagration), that appeared suddenly in the heavens, and after having rapidly attained a brilliancy surpassing that of Jupiter, gradually disappeared and has never since been seen.[*] This poem of "Al Aaraaf" abounds in happy and melodious passages, and has never yet received its due meed of praise: some portions of the lyrical intermedial chant are exquisitely and musically onomatopœial in construction. The revised version of "Tamerlane," too, given in this volume, is in every respect a great advance upon the previous printed draft: besides its enhanced poetic value, it is also far superior as a work of art, improved punctuation and indented lines affording evidence of more skilled handicraft than that employed upon the former copy.

[*] *Vide* Mr. R. Proctor's *Myths and Marvels of Astronomy.*

CHAPTER VIII.

WEST POINT.

IN 1802, the founders of the young Republic saw the necessity of officering their troops with skilled soldiers, and, with a foresight their children have not always shown, instituted the West Point Military Academy— a military school in many respects equal to the best of Europe. Education and subsistence are gratuitous, and a monthly allowance of twenty-eight dollars is made to each of the cadets, so as to place them, as it were, beyond the *necessity* of appealing to relatives for anything. The course of study covers a period of four years, during which the student is placed under a discipline little less rigid than that of a soldier on active duty. The number of cadets is limited, and very great interest is required, as will be readily comprehended, in order to obtain a nomination.

It was, doubtless, the prospect or promise of receiving a nomination to this institution that induced Poe to return to Mr. Allan's. General Scott, and other influential friends, interested themselves on the youth's behalf, and eventually obtained him an appointment. According to the rules of the Military Academy, nominations are not given to candidates after they have attained their twenty-first birthday, consequently Poe was only just in time to receive his appointment. The West Point records show that he was admitted into the institution as a cadet on the 1st of July 1830.

E

At the time Poe was admitted, the Military Academy was anything but a suitable place for the residence of a high-spirited and sensitive youth. The discipline was not only of the most severe description, but the place itself was utterly unfit for the habits of growing lads. An inquiry having been made into the rules and regulations of the institution, in consequence of an excitement caused by the death of some of the cadets, the Board sent in a report to the Secretary of War, about a year previous to the poet's admission, in which, after the examination of special cases, they said, " With regard to all the cadets, however, it may be averred, that they are constantly tasked to the utmost in the way of mental exertion, while from the nature of the climate, for very nearly an entire moiety of the year, they are, for all the purposes of recreation, debarred from the use of their limbs," and, to obviate this latter objection, a building for exercise was recommended.

Poe is declared to have entered upon his new mode of living with customary energy—for the idleness which he vaunted to Neal was more in theory than in practice—but he speedily discovered how totally unsuited for him was the strict discipline and monotonous training of such a place as West Point. The wayward and erratic course of existence to which he had been so long accustomed, as well as the fact that he had for so long a time been sole master of his own actions, rendered the restraints of the Academy most galling ; nevertheless, that docility and amiability which he generally manifested towards those with whom he came in personal contact, caused him to become a general favourite and a not altogether unhopeful cadet. One of his fellow-cadets, speaking of Poe's inability to follow the mathematical requirements of the place, says, "His mind was off from the matter-of-fact routine of the drill, which, in such a case as his, seemed practical joking, on some ethereal visionary expedition." "His utter inefficiency and state of abstractness at that place" were, doubtless, the reasons that caused this authority to deem him "marked for an early death." *

Complaints of the severity of the rules frequently crop up in the press of the period: *Niles' Register* for September 19th, 1829, after remarking that "each cadet is to remain four years at the institution, and then serve one year in the military establishment of the United States," goes on to state, "But the service is so strict, and the punishment so uniformly inflicted, that many are suspended or expelled before the expiration of the four years—and it is generally rather a small minority of the whole number that is seen to pass through the whole tour of service;" finally, the report declares that out of a total of 204 cadets only 26 are without black marks attached to their names. Whether Poe would have been one of the "small minority" had not events occurred to render, in his own opinion, his withdrawal requisite, is a debatable subject. According to the most circumstantial account furnished of his residence at West Point,† the poet's career in the Military Academy was one scarcely calculated to cover him with institutional honours; but Mr. Thomas W. Gibson, its author—a

* Duyckinck's *Cyclopedia of American Literature,* vol. ii., Article "Poe, E. A."

† *Harper's New Monthly Magazine,* November 1867, pp. 754–756.

fellow-cadet, and a fellow-prisoner at a subsequent Court-Martial—is occasionally so inaccurate in his memory of the facts, that the whole of his narrative must be received *cum granô salis.*

"Number 28 South Barracks," says Mr. Gibson, "in the last months of the year of our Lord 1830, was pretty generally regarded as a hard room. Cadets who aspired to high standing on the Merit Roll were not much given to visiting it, at least in daytime. To compensate in some measure for this neglect, however, the inspecting officer was uncommonly punctual in his visits, and rarely failed to find some subject for his daily report of demerit. The old barracks have passed away, and are now only a dream of stone and mortar; but the records of the sins of omission and commission of Number 28 and its occupants remain, and are piled carefully away among the dusty archives of the Academy.

"Edgar A. Poe was one of the occupants of the room. 'Old P——' [Henderson?] and the writer of this sketch completed the household. . . . Poe at that time, though only about twenty years of age, had the appearance of being much older. He had a worn, weary, discontented look, not easily forgotten by those who were intimate with him. Poe was easily fretted by any jest at his expense, and was not a little annoyed by a story that some of the class got up, to the effect that he had procured a cadet's appointment for his son, and the boy having died, the father had substituted himself in his place. Another report current in the corps was that he was a grandson of Benedict Arnold.* Some good-natured friend told him of it, and Poe did not contradict it, but seemed rather pleased than otherwise at the mistake.

"Very early in his brief career at the Point he established a high reputation for genius, and poems and squibs of local interest were daily issued from Number 28, and went the round of the classes. One of the first things of the kind that he perpetrated was a diatribe in which all of the officers of the

---

* Arnold was Governor of West Point at the time when his treachery to the Americans was discovered through the apprehension of Major Andrè.—J. H. I.

Academy, from Colonel Thayer down, were duly if not favourably noticed. I can recall but one stanza. It ran thus :—

> ' John Locke was a very great name ;
> Joe Locke was a greater ; in short,
> The former was well known to Fame,
> The latter well known to Report.'

"Joe Locke, it may be remarked by way of explanation, was
one of the instructors of tactics, and *ex officio* Inspector of
Barracks, and supervisor of the morals and deportment of
cadets generally. In this capacity it was his duty to report to
head-quarters every violation of the regulations falling under
his observation : a duty in which he was in nowise remiss, as
the occupants of Number 28 could severally testify.

"The studies of the Academy Poe utterly ignored. I doubt
if he ever studied a page of Lacroix, unless it was to glance
hastily over it in the lecture-room while others of his section
were reciting. . . .

"The result of one of these foraging-parties after supplies
created for a time no little excitement in the South Barracks.
People had been burned and hung in effigy from time immemorial, but it was reserved for Number 28 to witness the
eating of a Professor in effigy. It was a dark, cold, drizzling
night, in the last days of November, when this event came off.
The brandy bottle had been empty for two days, and just at
dusk Poe proposed that we should draw straws—the one who
drew the shortest to go down to old Benny's and replenish our
stock. The straws were drawn, and the lot fell on me.

"Provided with four pounds of candles and Poe's last blanket
for traffic (silver and gold we had not, but such as we had we
gave unto Benny), I started just as the bugle sounded to
quarters. It was a rough road to travel, but I knew every foot
of it by night or day, and reached my place of destination in
safety, but drenched to the skin. Old Benny was not in the
best of humours that evening. Candles and blankets and
regulation shoes, and similar articles of traffic, had accumulated largely on his hands, and the market for them was dull
in that neighbourhood. His chicken-suppers and bottles of
brandy had disappeared very rapidly of late, and he had received
little or no money in return.

"At last, however, I succeeded in exchanging the candles

and blanket for a bottle of brandy and the hardest-featured, loudest-voiced old gander that it has ever been my lot to encounter. To chop the bird's head off before venturing into barracks with him was a matter of pure necessity; and thus, in fact, old Benny rendered him before delivery. I reached the suburbs of the barracks about nine o'clock. The bottle had not as much brandy in it as when I left old Benny's; but I was very confident I had not spilled any. I had carried the gander first over one shoulder and then over the other, and the consequence was, that not only my shirt-front but my face and hands were as bloody as the entire contents of the old gander's veins and arteries could well make them.

"Poe was on the look-out, and met me some distance from the barracks, and my appearance at once inspired him with the idea of a grand hoax. Our plans were perfected in an instant. The gander was tied, neck and feet and wings together, and the bloody feathers bristling in every direction gave it a nondescript appearance that would have defied recognition as a gander by the most astute naturalist on the Continent. Poe took charge of the bottle and preceded me to the room 'Old P——' was puzzling his brains over the binomial theorem, and a visitor from the North Barracks was in the room awaiting the result of my expedition.

"Poe had taken his seat, and pretended to be absorbed in the mysteries of 'Leçons Françaises.' Laying the gander down at the outside of the door, I walked or rather staggered into the room, pretending to be very drunk, and exhibiting in clothes and face a spectacle not often seen off the stage.

"'My God! what has happened?' exclaimed Poe, with well-acted horror.

"'Old K——! Old K——!' I repeated several times, and with gestures intended to be particularly savage.

"'Well, what of him?' asked Poe.

"'He won't stop me on the road any more!' and I produced a large knife that we had stained with the few drops of blood that remained in the old gander. 'I have killed him!'

"'Nonsense!' said Poe. 'You are only trying one of your tricks on us.'

"'I didn't suppose you would believe me,' I replied, 'so I cut off his head and brought it into barracks. Here it is!' And reaching out of the door, I caught the gander by the legs, and giving it one fearful swing around my head, dashed it at the only candle in the room, and left them all in darkness, with what two of them believed to be the head of one of the Professors. The visitor leaped through the window and alighted in the slop-tub, and made fast time for his own room in the North Barracks—spreading, as he went, the report that I had killed Old K——, and that his head was then in Number 28. The story gained ready credence, and for a time the excitement in barracks ran high. When we lit the candle again 'Old P——' was sitting in one corner a blank picture of horror, and it was some time before we could restore him to reason.

"The gander was skinned—picking the feathers off was out of the question—and after taps we cut him up in small pieces and cooked him in a tin wash-basin, over an anthracite fire, without seasoning of any kind. It was perhaps the hardest supper on record, but we went through with it without flinching. We had set out to eat old K—— in effigy, and we did it; whether he ever learned of the honours we paid him that night I never learned."

Comment on this melodramatic and journalistically wrought-out story is needless, unless it be to remark, that it presents a picture of life in the Military Academy of those days which, even if highly coloured, is, doubtless, to some extent representative. Mr. Gibson notes that "the impression left by Poe in his short career at West Point was highly favourable to him. If he made no fast friends, he left no enemies behind him. But up to that time he had given," in the opinion of his fellow-cadet, "no indication of the genius which has since secured for him a world-wide fame. His acquaintance with English literature," says Mr. Gibson, "was extensive and accurate, and his verbal memory wonderful. He would repeat both prose and poetry by the hour, and seldom or never repeated the same passage twice to the same audience."

Until the close of 1830, Poe would appear to have maintained, if not a very high, at all events, a respect-

able position in the institution.   In November of that
year the Inspector issued a warning to the cadets of
the approaching semi-annual examination, and pointed
out that " if dismissed, strong and satisfactory reasons
will be required to obtain a restoration," showing
thereby that dismissal from the Academy was considered no unusual occurrence, nor an unpardonable
offence.   The young poet would appear to have passed
through the old year without committing any crime
sufficiently heinous to bring down upon his head the
threatened terrors.   On the 31st of December a Court-
Martial was ordered to meet on the following 7th of
January, and was subsequently adjourned until the
28th instant.   Up to the 7th of January Poe would
appear to have maintained his position in the Academy,
but by that date events appear to have occurred to
render him determined to leave the service.   He
wished to resign, but without the consent of parent or
guardian his resignation could not be accepted, and
Mr. Allan, it is declared, withheld the required permission.*   The second marriage of Mr. Allan to the
young and " beautiful Miss Patterson," soon after the
death of his first wife, and the birth of a son and
heir, it is presumed, influenced the poet's godfather in
withholding his consent.   A young wife, and the prospect of a young family, were undoubtedly sufficient
inducements for a man of Mr. Allan's temperament to
make him endeavour to retain his godson in a place
where his claims upon the home purse need be little
or nothing, and whence he could at once proceed to a
profession without calling upon his guardian for any
pecuniary or other aid.   As usual, Poe had his own
views upon the subject, and, with his customary

* Didier, *Life of E. A. Poe*, p. 44.

impetuosity, took the decision into his own hands. His plan of proceeding and its result—evidently foreseen and desired by him—will be best comprehended by a recapitulation of the "orders" issued in his case pursuant to the General Court-Martial. It should, however, be pointed out, that had the prisoner pleaded "guilty" to all the charges made against him, some leniency might have been shown, and his dismission not have been ordered; but, in order to render his offence unpardonable, he entered a plea of "not guilty" to an easily-provable charge, and then, to render his case utterly hopeless, declined to plead.

"MILITARY ACADEMY   "ENGINEER DEPARTMENT,
    ORDER NO. 7.   WASHINGTON, *February* 8, 1831.

"At the General Court-Martial, of which Lieutenant Thomas J. Leslie, of the Corps of Engineers, is President, convened at West Point, New York, on the 5th ult., in virtue of Military Academy Order No. 46 dated the 31st December 1830, was arraigned and tried. . . .

"Cadet E. A. Poe.

"The Court next proceeded to the trial of Cadet E. A. Poe of the U. S. Military Academy on the following charges and specifications :—

"CHARGE 1st.—Gross neglect of duty.

"Specification 1st.—In this, that he, the said Cadet Poe, did absent himself from the following parades and roll-calls between the 7th January and 27th January 1831, viz., absent from evening parade on the 8th, 9th, 15th, 20th, 24th, and 25th January 1831 ; absent from *reveillé* call on the 8th, 16th, 17th, 19th, 21st, 25th, and 26th January 1831 ; absent from class parade on the 17th, 18th, 19th, 20th, 24th, and 25th January 1831 ; absent from guard-mounting on the 16th January 1831, and absent from church parade on the 23rd January 1831 ; all of which at West Point, New York.

"Specification 2nd.—In this, that he, the said Cadet E. A. Poe, did absent himself from all his Academical duties between the 15th and 27th January 1831. . . .

"CHARGE 2nd.—Disobedience of orders.

"Specification 1st.—In this, that he, the said Cadet Poe, after having been directed by the officer of the day to attend church on the 23rd January 1831, did fail to obey such order; this at West Point, New York.

"Specification 2nd.—In this, that he, the said Cadet Poe, did fail to attend the Academy on the 25th January 1831, after having been directed so to do by the officer of the day; this at West Point, New York.

"To which charges and specifications the prisoner pleaded as follows :—To the 1st specification of the 1st charge, 'Not Guilty;' to the 2nd specification of the 1st charge, 'Guilty;' and 'Guilty' to the 2nd charge and its specifications. . . .

"The Court, after mature deliberation on the testimony adduced, find the prisoner 'Guilty' of the 1st specification, 1st charge, and confirm his plea to the remainder of the charges and specifications, and adjudge that he, Cadet E. A. Poe, be *dismissed* the service of the United States. . . .

"The proceedings of the General Court-Martial. . . . in the cases of Cadets ——, ——, E. A. Poe, ——, ——, have been laid before the Secretary of War and are approved. . .

"Cadet Edgar A. Poe will be *dismissed* the service of the United States, and cease to be considered a member of the Military Academy after the 6th March 1831."

During the trial ample evidence was adduced for the prosecution, and only one witness, Cadet Henderson, who " roomed " with the prisoner, and whose evidence amounted to nothing, appeared for the defence; Poe himself, indeed, declined to plead, and evidently had, deliberately, determined to leave the service. Upon the 7th of January the Court-Martial met to try various offenders; and upon the very next day, and every day up to the date of the adjourned sitting, he purposely absented himself from all duties ! The fact most certainly was that, apart from his dislike to the military profession, he saw that his prospects of a wealthy inheritance were shattered, and he determined at once to seek a livelihood in a profession more in accordance with his natural tastes.

CHAPTER IX.

LITERATURE.

FOR some time after leaving West Point, Poe appears to have lived in New York. A few months after he left the Military Academy, it was announced that a volume of his poems would be published by subscription at the price of two and a half dollars per copy. " Permission was granted," says Mr. Gibson, " by Colonel Thayer to the corps to subscribe for the book, and as no cadet was ever known to neglect any opportunity of spending his pay, the subscription was pretty nearly universal. The book was received with a general expression of disgust; . . . . it contained not one of the squibs and satires upon which his reputation at the Academy had been built up. Few of the poems contained in that collection now appear in any of the editions of his works, and such as have been preserved have been very much altered for the better. For months afterwards quotations from Poe formed the standing material for jest in the corps, and his reputation for genius went down at once to zero." As Mr. Gibson seems to have had to leave West Point at the same time as Poe, his reminiscences of the effects produced by the little volume are, doubtless, derived from hearsay ; but, unlike his inaccurate account of the book itself, they are confirmed by other evidence. General George W. Cullum states,* " As Poe was of

* *Harper's New Monthly Magazine*, vol. xlv. p. 561.

the succeeding class to mine at West Point, I remember him very well as a cadet. . . . While at the
Academy he published a small volume of poems. . . .
These verses were the source of great merriment with
us boys, who considered the author cracked, and the
verses ridiculous doggerel."

This 1831 collection does not contain any poem
not included in the existing editions, but includes
many variations from, and lines extra to, the pieces
as now published; the title-page reads thus :—

POEMS.

BY

EDGAR A. POE.

" *Tout le monde a raison.*"—ROCHEFOUCAULD.

Second Edition.

New York : Elam Bliss.

1831.

The little book contained 124 pages, and was dedicated to the United States Corps of Cadets. Prefixed
to the poems was a lengthy letter to a "Mr. B——,"
apparently a mythical personage, dated "West Point,
1831." The poet begins—

"DEAR B——,—Believing only a portion of my former volume
to be worthy a second edition—that small portion I thought it
as well to include in the present book as to republish by itself.
Nor have I hesitated to insert from the 'Minor Poems,' now
omitted, whole lines, and even passages, to the end that being
placed in a fairer light, and the trash shaken from them in
which they were embedded, they may have some chance of being
seen by posterity.

"It has been said, that a good critique on a poem may be
written by one who is no poet himself. This, according to *your*
idea and *mine* of poetry, I feel to be false—the less poetical the
critic, the less just the critique; and the converse. On that

account, and because there are but few B——s in the world, I
would be as much ashamed of the world's good opinion as proud
of your own. Another than yourself might here observe,
'Shakespeare is in possession of the world's good opinion, and
yet Shakespeare is the greatest of poets. It appears then that
the world judge correctly ; why should you be ashamed of their
favourable judgment ?' The difficulty lies in the interpretation
of the word 'judgment' or 'opinion.' The opinion is the world's,
truly, but it may be called theirs as a man would call a book
his ; they did not originate the opinion, but it is theirs. A
fool, for example, thinks Shakespeare a great poet—yet the fool
has never read Shakespeare. But the fool's neighbour, who is
a step higher on the Andes of the mind, whose head [that is to
say, his more exalted thought] is too far above the fool to be
seen or understood, but whose feet [by which I mean his everyday actions] are sufficiently near to be discerned, and by means
of which that superiority is ascertained, which *but* for them
would never have been discovered—this neighbour asserts that
Shakespeare is a great poet—the fool believes him, and that is
henceforward his *opinion.* This neighbour's own opinion has,
in like manner, been adopted from one above *him,* and so,
ascendingly, to a few gifted individuals, who kneel around the
summit, beholding face to face the master spirit who stands
upon the pinnacle. . . .

" You are aware of the great barrier in the path of an American writer. He is read, if at all, in preference to the combined
and established wit of the world. I say established ; for it is
with literature as with law or empire—an established name
is an estate in tenure, or a throne in possession. Besides, one
might suppose that books, like their authors, improve by travel
—their having crossed the sea is, with us, so great a distinction.
Our antiquaries abandon time for distance ; our very fops
glance from the binding to the bottom of the title-page, where
the mystic characters which spell London, Paris, or Genoa, are
precisely so many letters of recommendation.

" I mentioned just now a vulgar error as regards criticism. I
think the notion that no poet can form a correct estimate of his
own writings is another. I remarked before that in proportion
to the poetical talent would be the justice of a critique upon
poetry. Therefore a bad poet would, I grant, make a false
critique, and his self-love would infallibly bias his little judg-

ment in his favour ; but a poet, who is indeed a poet, could not, I think, fail of making a just critique ; whatever should be deducted on the score of self-love might be replaced on account of his intimate acquaintance with the subject ; in short, we have more instances of false criticism than of just where one's own writings are the test, simply because we have more bad poets than good. There are, of course, many objections to what I say : Milton is a great example of the contrary ; but his opinion with respect to the ' Paradise Regained ' is by no means fairly ascertained. By what trivial circumstances men are often led to assert what they do not really believe ! Perhaps an inadvertent word has descended to posterity. But, in fact, the ' Paradise Regained ' is little, if at all, inferior to the ' Paradise Lost,' and is only supposed so to be because men do not like epics, whatever they may say to the contrary ; and reading those of Milton in their natural order, are too much wearied with the first to derive any pleasure from the second.

"I dare say Milton preferred Comus to either—if so— justly.

"As I am speaking of poetry, it will not be amiss to touch slightly upon the most singular heresy in its modern history— the heresy of what is called, very foolishly, the Lake School. Some years ago I might have been induced, by an occasion like the present, to attempt a formal refutation of their doctrine ; at present it would be a work of supererogation. The wise must bow to the wisdom of such men as Coleridge and Southey, but being wise, have laughed at poetical theories so prosaically exemplified.

"Aristotle, with singular assurance, has declared poetry the most philosophical of all writings *—but it required a Wordsworth to pronounce it the most metaphysical. He seems to think that the end of poetry is, or should be, instruction—yet it is a truism that the end of our existence is happiness ; if so, the end of every separate part of our existence—everything connected with our existence — should be still happiness. Therefore the end of instruction should be happiness ; and happiness is another name for pleasure ;—therefore the end of instruction should be pleasure ; yet we see the above-mentioned opinion implies precisely the reverse.

"To proceed : *cæteris paribus,* he who pleases is of more

* Σπουδιοτάτων και φιλοσοφικοτατον γενος.

importance to his fellow-men than he who instructs, since utility is happiness, and pleasure is the end already obtained which instruction is merely the means of obtaining.

"I see no reason, then, why our metaphysical poets should plume themselves so much on the utility of their works, unless indeed they refer to instruction with eternity in view; in which case, sincere respect for their piety would not allow me to express my contempt for their judgment; contempt which it would be difficult to conceal, since their writings are professedly to be understood by the few, and it is the many who stand in need of salvation. In such case I should no doubt be tempted to think of the devil in Melmoth, who labours indefatigably, through three octavo volumes, to accomplish the destruction of one or two souls, while any common devil would have demolished one or two thousand.

"Against the subtleties which would make poetry a study— not a passion—it becomes the metaphysician to reason—but the poet to protest. Yet Wordsworth and Coleridge are men in years ; the one imbued in contemplation from his childhood, the other a giant in intellect and learning. The diffidence, then, with which I venture to dispute their authority would be overwhelming did I not feel, from the bottom of my heart, that learning has little to do with the imagination—intellect with the passions—or age with poetry.

" 'Trifles, like straws, upon the surface flow,
   He who would search for pearls must dive below,'

are lines which have done much mischief. As regards the greater truths, men oftener err by seeking them at the bottom than at the top ; the truth lies in the huge abysses where wisdom is sought—not in the palpable palaces where she is found. The ancients were not always right in hiding the goddess in a well ; witness the light which Bacon has thrown upon philosophy ; witness the principles of our divine faith—that moral mechanism by which the simplicity of a child may overbalance the wisdom of a man.

"We see an instance of Coleridge's liability to err, in his ' Biographia Literaria '—professedly his literary life and opinions, but, in fact, a treatise *de omni scibili et quibusdam aliis.* He goes wrong by reason of his very profundity, and of his error we have a natural type in the contemplation of a star.

He who regards it directly and intensely sees, it is true, the star, but it is the star without a ray—while he who surveys it less inquisitively is conscious of all for which the star is useful to us below—its brilliancy and its beauty.

"As to Wordsworth, I have no faith in him. That he had in youth the feelings of a poet I believe—for there are glimpses of extreme delicacy in his writings—(and delicacy is the poet's own kingdom—his *El Dorado*)—but they have the appearance of a better day recollected ; and glimpses, at best, are little evidence of present poetic fire —we know that a few straggling flowers spring up daily in the crevices of the glacier.

"He was to blame in wearing away his youth in contemplation with the end of poetising in his manhood. With the increase of his judgment the light which should make it apparent has faded away. His judgment consequently is too correct. This may not be understood,—but the old Goths of Germany would have understood it, who used to debate matters of importance to their State twice, once when drunk, and once when sober—sober that they might not be deficient in formality—drunk lest they should be destitute of vigour.

"The long wordy discussions by which he tries to reason us into admiration of his poetry speak very little in his favour : they are full of such assertions as this (I have opened one of his volumes at random)—'Of genius the only proof is the act of doing well what is worthy to be done, and what was never done before '—indeed ? then it follows that in doing what is *un*worthy to be done, or what *has* been done before, no genius can be evinced ; yet the picking of pockets is an unworthy act, pockets have been picked time immemorial, and Barrington, the pickpocket, in point of genius, would have thought hard of a comparison with William Wordsworth, the poet.

"Again—in estimating the merit of certain poems, whether they be Ossian's or Macpherson's can surely be of little consequence, yet, in order to prove their worthlessness, Mr. W. has expended many pages in the controversy. *Tantæne animis ?* Can great minds descend to such absurdity ? But worse still : that he may bear down every argument in favour of these poems, he triumphantly drags forward a passage, in his abomination of which he expects the reader to sympathise. It is the beginning of the epic poem ' *Temora.*' ' The blue waves of Erin roll in light. The mountains are covered with day. Trees shake their dusky heads in the breeze.' And this—this gorgeous, yet simple imagery, where all is alive and panting with immortality—this, William Wordsworth, the author of 'Peter Bell,' has *selected* for his contempt. We shall see what better he, in his own person, has to offer. Imprimis :

> ' ' And now she's at the pony's tail,
> And now she's at the pony's head—
> On that side now, and now on this ;
> And, almost stifled with her bliss,
> A few sad tears does Betty shed. . . .
> She pats the pony, where or when
> She knows not, happy Betty Foy !
> Oh, Johnny, never mind the doctor !'

" Secondly :

> " ' The dew was falling fast, the—stars began to blink ;
> I heard a voice : it said, drink, pretty creature, drink !
> And, looking o'er the hedge, be—fore me I espied
> A snow-white mountain lamb, with a—maiden at its side.
> No other sheep were near—the lamb was all alone,
> And by a slender cord was—tether'd to a stone.'

" Now, we have no doubt this is all true : we *will* believe it, indeed, we will, Mr. W. Is it sympathy for the sheep you wish to excite? I love a sheep from the bottom of my heart.

" But there are occasions, dear B——, there are occasions when even Wordsworth is reasonable. Even Stamboul, it is said, shall have an end, and the most unlucky blunders must come to a conclusion. Here is an extract from his preface—

" ' Those who have been accustomed to the phraseology of modern writers, if they persist in reading this book to a conclusion (*impossible !*) will, no doubt, have to struggle with feelings of awkwardness (ha ! ha ! ha !) ; they will look round for poetry (ha ! ha ! ha ! ha !), and will be induced to inquire by what species of courtesy these attempts have been permitted to assume that title.' Ha ! ha ! ha ! ha ! ha !

" Yet, let not Mr. W. despair ; he has given immortality to a waggon, and the bee Sophocles has transmitted to eternity a sore toe, and dignified a tragedy with a chorus of turkeys.*

" Of Coleridge I cannot speak but with reverence. His

---

* This is a mistake, as turkeys were unknown in Europe before the discovery of America, whence they were imported.—J. H. I.

towering intellect ! his gigantic power ! To use an author quoted by himself, '*J'ai trouvé souvent que la plupart des sectes ont raison dans une bonne partie de ce qu'elles avancent, mais non pas en ce qu'elles nient.*' And to employ his own language, he has imprisoned his own conceptions by the barrier he has erected against those of others. It is lamentable to think that such a mind should be buried in metaphysics, and, like the Nyctanthes, waste its perfume upon the night alone. In reading that man's poetry, I tremble like one who stands upon a volcano, conscious, from the very darkness bursting from the crater, of the fire and the light that are weltering below.

"What is poetry?—Poetry ! that Proteus-like idea, with as many appellations as the nine-titled Corcyra ! 'Give me,' I demanded of a scholar some time ago, 'give me a definition of poetry.' '*Très-volontiers ;*' and he proceeded to his library, brought me a Dr. Johnson, and overwhelmed me with a definition. Shade of the immortal Shakespeare ! I imagine to myself the scowl of your spiritual eye upon the profanity of that scurrilous Ursa Major. Think of poetry, dear B——, think of poetry, and then think of Dr. Samuel Johnson ! Think of all that is airy and fairy-like, and then of all that is hideous and unwieldy ; think of his huge bulk, the Elephant ! and then—and then think of the Tempest—the Midsummer Night's Dream—Prospero—Oberon—and Titania !

" A poem, in my opinion, is opposed to a work of science by having, for its *immediate* object, pleasure, not truth ; to romance, by having, for its object, an *indefinite* instead of a *definite* pleasure, being a poem only so far as this object is attained ; romance presenting perceptible images with definite, poetry with *in*definite sensations, to which end music is an *essential*, since the comprehension of sweet sound is our most indefinite conception. Music, when combined with a pleasurable idea, is poetry ; music, without the idea, is simply music ; the idea, without the music, is prose, from its very definitiveness.

"What was meant by the invective against him who had no music in his soul ?

"To sum up this long rigmarole, I have, dear B——, what you, no doubt, perceive, for the metaphysical poets as poets, the most sovereign contempt. That they have followers proves nothing—

      " ' No Indian prince has to his palace
      More followers than a thief to the gallows.' "

Apart from the fact that the theory herein enunciated as to the object and aim of poetry is one which its author never through life deviated from, this letter is valuable and most interesting as the earliest known specimen of Poe's prose work. In the 1831 volume it is followed by a poetical " Introduction " of sixty-six lines, an expansion of the twenty-one lines of the 1829 " Preface." These additional verses were subsequently suppressed, but a portion of them is well worthy preservation here, not only as a fair sample of their youthful inditer's poetic powers, but also for their autobiographical allusions :—

" Succeeding years, too wild for song,
    Then rolled like tropic storms along,
    Where, though the garish lights that fly
    Dying along the troubled sky,
    Lay bare, through vistas thunder-riven,
    The blackness of the general heaven ;
    That very blackness yet doth fling
    Light on the lightning's silver wing.

" For, being an idle boy lang syne,
    Who read Anacreon and drank wine,
    I early found Anacreon-rhymes
    Were almost passionate sometimes—
    And by strange alchemy of brain
    His pleasures always turned to pain—
    His naïveté to wild desire—
    His wit to love—his wine to fire ;
    And so, being young and dipt in folly,
    I fell in love with melancholy,
    And used to throw my earthly rest
    And quiet all away in jest.
    I could not love except where Death
    Was mingling his with Beauty's breath—
    Or Hymen, Time, and Destiny
    Were stalking between her and me. . . .

" But *now* my soul hath too much room—
Gone are the glory and the gloom ;
The black hath mellowed into grey,
And all the fires are fading away.

" My draught of passion hath been deep—
I revelled, and I now would sleep—
And after drunkenness of soul
Succeeds the glories of the bowl—
An idle longing night and day
To dream my very life away. . . . "

To those acquainted with Poe's history thus far,
the pathos of the four final lines of the second stanza
will not be overlooked.   These idiosyncratic verses
are followed by the exquisite lyric "To Helen," * a poem
written in commemoration of Mrs. Stannard, as Poe
himself afterwards acknowledged ; then comes the
earliest known version of "Israfel ;" which is succeeded by " The Doomed City "—a poem afterwards
improved and re-christened " The City in the Sea " ;
expanded and weakened versions of " Fairyland," and
" The Sleeper," follow ; next comes " A Pæan," chiefly
remarkable as being the germ of that melodious, exultant defiance of death—" Lenore "—and then, finally,
so far as the " Miscellaneous Poems " are concerned,
some lines entitled " The Valley Nis "—ultimately
revised and published as " The Valley of Unrest."

The collection concludes with expanded reprints of
" Al Aaraaf " and " Tamerlane," but the additions and
variations are, generally, inferior in poetic value to the
earlier versions.   Ultimately, upon their next republication, the poet's more matured judgment caused
him to curtail the proportions of most of the pieces
in this " second edition," by discarding the so strangely

* Beginning, " Helen, thy beauty is to me."

added new lines. It should also be noted, in connection with this 1831 volume, that the punctuation is not so good nor so characteristic as in its immediate predecessor, and that the whole book has the appearance of having been very hastily prepared for the press.

The profits, if any, on his " Poems," could not have sufficed long for Poe's maintenance, and, indeed, in a very short space of time he appears to have retraced his journey to Richmond. Upon his arrival at Mr. Allan's he did not receive a very gracious reception, as may be readily imagined, from his godfather's second wife. Mr. Allan, he was told, was confined to his bed by severe illness, and his request to be admitted to the sick man's chamber was refused. Excited by the refusal, he quarrelled with Mrs. Allan and left the house—the only home he had ever known—for ever, and in wrath. Mr. Allan was informed of the visit, and his godson's conduct was, apparently, represented to him in anything but favourable colours, for he wrote an angry letter forbidding him the house. The poet answered in a similar spirit, and never again, it is believed, held any further communication with his adopted father—with the man whom he had been taught to look to for aid and support, and whose property he had been led to believe was destined to be his own inheritance. All was over now, and he who a short time before had been regarded as the spoilt child of Fortune, was now homeless and penniless!

All attempts hitherto made to explain what Poe did, and whither he wandered, during the next two years succeeding his expulsion from his godfather's home, have signally failed. The assertion that he was residing at Baltimore with his aunt, Mrs. Clemm, is

not in accordance with fact, her correspondence proving *that she never did know* where her nephew was
during this interregnum in his history, and the poet
himself does not appear to have ever afforded any
reliable clue to the truth.   Powell, in his well-mean-
ing, but somewhat imaginative, sketch of Poe, asserts
that the chivalrous youth left Richmond with the
intention of offering his services to the Poles in their
heroic struggle against Russia.   Another biographer,
of proven unreliability, suggests that Poe enlisted in
the army, but after a short service deserted, although,
in a previous sketch of the poet, this same writer
stated that during the period referred to the youth
endeavoured to subsist by authorcraft, only " his contributions to the journals attracted little attention,
and his hopes of gaining a livelihood by the profession of literature were nearly ended at length in
sickness, poverty, and despair."   Other attempts, all
more or less romantic, have been made to bridge over
this chasm in Poe's life, but none possess such probability as that last cited.   In no portion of his career
did the poet prove the waters of Helicon Pactolian, and
in his earliest efforts to obtain a subsistence by literary labour it almost necessarily follows—considering
the then position of American letters—that his exertions were fruitless.

Poe's place of abode has not been discovered from
the time he left Richmond in 1831 until the autumn
of 1833, when he is again heard of as in Baltimore,
and in apparently very straitened circumstances.
It has been stated * that Poe was at this time residing with Mrs. Clemm in Cove Street, but, according

* E. L. Didier, *Life of E. A. Poe*, p. 50.

to the Baltimore Directories—which are far better
evidence than any personal memory—that lady resided
in Wilks Street in 1831-2, and thence removed to
No. 3 Amity Street, whilst extant correspondence
proves that her nephew did *not* reside with her then,
and, apparently, that he never lived with her until
after his marriage. During this mysterious interval
in the poet's life, it is claimed that he wrote the
earlier versions of some of his finest stories, and even
had some of them accepted and published, but not
paid for, by contemporary editors. He himself stated
in a note to the "MS. Found in a Bottle," that
that tale was originally published in 1831, but the
last figure is probably a misprint for 3.

In the autumn of 1833, the proprietors of the
Saturday Visitor, a weekly literary journal, started
in Baltimore the previous year, and then under the
editorial charge of Mr. L. A. Wilmer, offered prizes of
one hundred dollars and fifty dollars respectively, for
the best story and the best poem. This offer coming
to the knowledge of Poe, he selected six of his tales,
and some lines—which he christened "The Coliseum "
—out of a drama he was writing, and sent them
to the committee appointed to inspect the manuscripts. After a careful consideration of the various
contributions received, the adjudicators, three well-
known gentlemen, unanimously decided that those
by Edgar Poe—a stranger to them all—were entitled
to both premiums, but subsequently were induced, it is
stated, to award the lesser prize to another competitor,
in consideration of Poe having gained the larger
amount.

Not content with this award, the adjudicators even

went out of their way to draw up and publish the
following flattering critique on the merits of the writings submitted by Poe, and published it in the *Saturday Visitor*, on the 12th of October 1833 :—

"Amongst the prose articles were many of various and distinguished merit, but the singular force and beauty of those
sent by the author of 'The Tales of the Folio Club' leave us
no room for hesitation in that department. We have accordingly awarded the premium to a tale entitled the 'MS. Found
in a Bottle.' It would hardly be doing justice to the writer
of this collection to say that the tale we have chosen is the
best of the six offered by him. We cannot refrain from saying
that the author owes it to his own reputation, as well as to
the gratification of the community, to publish the entire
volume ('Tales of the Folio Club'). These tales are eminently
distinguished by a wild, vigorous, and poetical imagination, a
rich style, a fertile invention, and varied and curious learning.
                    (Signed)   JOHN P. KENNEDY.
                                 J. H. B. LATROBE.
                                 JAMES H. MILLAR."

From Mr. Latrobe's reminiscences of the award and
its result, written to a correspondent soon after the
poet's decease, it is learned that he, Mr. Latrobe, was
the reader of the manuscripts adjudicated upon, and
that the little volume of tales submitted by Poe
proved to be so enthralling, and so very far superior to
anything else before the committee, that they read it
through from beginning to end, and had no hesitation
whatever in awarding the first prize to the author.
"Our only difficulty," says Mr. Latrobe, "was in
selecting from the rich contents of the volume."

Mr. Kennedy, the author of "Horse-Shoe Robinson," and other popular works, was so interested in the
successful but unknown competitor, that he invited
him to his house. Poe's response, written in his usual

beautiful, clear caligraphy, proves into what a depth of misery he had sunk. How his heart bled to pen these words, few probably can imagine :—

" Your invitation to dinner has wounded me to the quick. I cannot come for reasons of the most humiliating nature — my personal appearance. You may imagine my mortification in making this disclosure to you, but it is necessary."

Impelled by the noblest feelings, Mr. Kennedy at once sought out the unfortunate youth, and found him, as he records in his diary, friendless and almost starving. Poe's wretched condition inspired the kind-hearted author with pity, as did his palpable genius with admiration, and henceforward he became a sincere and disinterested friend. So far from contenting himself with mere courtesies, Mr. Kennedy assisted his new *protégé* to re-establish himself in the world, and in many respects treated him more like an esteemed relative than a chance acquaintance. In his diary he records, " I gave him .... free access to my table, and the use of a horse for exercise whenever he chose ; in fact, brought him up from the very verge of despair." Aided by such a friend, Poe's affairs could not but begin to improve.

On the 27th March 1834, Mr. Allan died, in the 54th year of his age, and was interred beside his first wife in Shockoe Hill Cemetery. If Poe retained any lingering hope of inheriting any portion of his godfather's wealth, he was at last undeceived, as his name was not even mentioned in the will. Aided, however, by his new-made literary friends, and the reputation of his recent success, the young poet now began to earn his own livelihood. Mr. Kennedy relates that he set him " drudging upon whatever may make money," but Poe, as the moth to the candle, could not altogether refrain from the still " forbidden things " of poesy, and "when an hour with calmer wings" intervened, returned to work upon his long commenced tragedy of " Politian."

The incidents of this drama were suggested by real events connected with Beauchampe's murder of Sharp, the Solicitor-General of Kentucky, the facts of which celebrated case are fully as romantic as the poet's fiction. Poe appears to have written a portion of " Politian " as early at least as 1831, and to have first published some fragments of it in the *Southern Literary Messenger* of 1835–36 as " Scenes from an Unpublished Drama." From the poet's manuscript copy* is seen the fact that this tragedy had been nearly, if not quite, completed, and although youthful *niaiseries* in some parts of this—the first draft, apparently—might have been justifiably excised, it cannot but be a subject for deep regret that the entire drama was not eventually published. As a rule, it must be conceded that the scenes selected and published by Poe were decidedly the most poetical, yet there are several very interesting and even meritorious passages in the manuscript that need not have been discarded. The omission of the humorous characters was no great loss, but the transformation of Politian from " a young and noble Roman," and " his friend," Baldazzar, into English noblemen, was in no way necessary to, and certainly did not increase the *vraisemblance* of, the play.

That " Politian " has attracted less attention than its author's other poetical works is not strange; unequal in execution, a fragment, and a mystery, the

---

* Now my property.—J. H. I.

public naturally passed it by. Monsieur Hughes, it is true, when he translated it into French, spoke of it as a tragedy "*où vivent des caractères vraiment humains,*" but he appears to have been the only person who has had a good word to say for it. This same author, moreover, draws attention to the noteworthy fact that the hero of the drama is, to some extent, and in some of his idiosyncrasies, a reflex of the author himself; "*comme tous les grands ecrivains,*" he remarks, "*Edgar Poe prête aux personnages qu'il met en scène ses sensations et ses sentiments personnel.*" In the third (of the published) scenes occur the following words of Politian's, which M. Hughes draws attention to as words that might well stand for Poe's own response to advising friends :—

> "What would'st thou have me do?
> At thy behest I will shake off that nature
> Which from my forefathers I did inherit ;
> Which with my mother's milk I did imbibe,
> And be no more Politian, but some other."

" Give not thy soul to dreams," is the counsel of Baldazzar, and he bids him seek befitting occupation in the court or camp. " Speak no more to me," responds Politian, " of thy camps and courts. I am sick, sick, sick, even unto death ! " he exclaims, " of the hollow and high-sounding vanities of the populous earth ! " And further, when intimating that he is about to engage in a hostile encounter, Poe himself is seen clearly through his hero's words when he cries—

> " I *cannot* die, having within my heart
> So keen a relish for the beautiful,"

And in a later scene are words so intensely Poësque that it needs no stretch of fancy to deem the poet speaking on his own behalf :—

> "Speak not to me of glory !
> I hate—I loathe the name ; I do abhor
> The unsatisfactory and ideal thing. . . .
> Do I not love—art thou not beautiful—
> What need we more ? Ha ! glory ! now speak not of it :
> By all I hold most sacred and most solemn—
> By all my wishes now—my fears hereafter—
> By all I scorn on earth and hope in heaven—
> There is no deed I would more glory in,
> Than in thy cause to scoff at this.same glory
> And trample it under foot."

One of the most interesting facts connected with this early draft—almost as fine a specimen of Poe's exquisite calligraphy as is his latest manuscript—is that it contains, in the form of a soliloquy uttered by Politian, the lines published as "The Coliseum."

In August of 1834, the *Southern Literary Messenger*, a publication soon to be connected with Poe's fortunes, was started at Richmond, Virginia, by Mr. Thomas W. White, an energetic and worthy man. Such a magazine was a very hazardous speculation for that time ; it was started in opposition to the advice of its promoter's friends, and, but for a fortunate accident, might have caused his ruin.

After the magazine had passed through an erratic existence of some few months, its proprietor appealed to various well-known writers for literary aid, and amongst others, Mr. Kennedy was solicited ; but he, being otherwise engaged, recommended Poe to send something. Acting upon this suggestion, our poet sent his manuscript "Tales of the Folio Club," and Mr.

White's editor, Mr. James E. Heath, it is believed, greatly pleased with their style, alluded to them in very flattering terms in the *Messenger*.

In March 1835, " Berenice," Poe's first contribution, appeared in the new periodical, and the editor called marked attention to it and its author in these words : " Whilst we confess that we think there is too much German horror in his subject, there can be but one opinion as to the force and elegance of his style." This editorial idea of " Berenice " was not far from the truth, as regards the mere literary value of the work ; but although its horrible *dénouement* is too disgusting for even the genius of Poe to render palatable, for those who have obtained an insight into its author's mental history it is one of the most remarkable, as it is also one of the earliest, of his tales. No writer of repute has more thoroughly unbosomed the secrets of his imagination, and more clearly disclosed the workings of his brain, than has Edgar Poe, and in none of his writings have these autobiographic glimpses been more abundantly vouchsafed than in this story of " Berenice ; " indeed, it may be better described as an essay on its author's idiosyncrasies than as a tale.

Among the various peculiarities of the early draft of this work—some of which disappeared in the later versions—it will be noted by his readers, is the first development of Poe's assumed belief in metempsychosis, a doctrine that, in subsequent writings, he recurred to again and again, and which, it is scarcely assuming too much to say, at times he evidently partially believed in. One of the suppressed passages alludes to its hero's " immoderate use of opium," a drug which

Poe occasionally resorted to, at least in after years, even if he had not then already essayed its powers. It is noteworthy to find him declaring, in 1845, in connection with De Quincey's "Confessions of an English Opium-Eater," "there is yet room for a book on opium-eating, which shall be the most profoundly interesting volume ever penned." Returning to an analysis of "Berenice"—that "Berenice" who is depicted as the hero's *cousin*—we find, as in so many of his youthful works, constant allusions to hereditary traits and visions of ancestral glories; but these boyish dreams are not, as generally supposed, referable to paternal but to maternal bygone splendours: to Arnheim—to the *hold* or *home* of the Arns (*i.e.,* the Arnolds)—to the Arnheim of the first and of the last of his stories. But perhaps the most representative —the almost prophetic—record of its author's idiosyncrasies, the trait which through after-life would have most faithfully portrayed him, is contained in these words of the tale : "In the strange anomaly of my existence, feelings with me had never *been* of the heart, and my passions *always* were of the mind."

In the next month, April, appeared "Morella," one of Poe's favourite stories, and one which elicited from the Editor of the *Messenger* the comment that, whilst it would unquestionably prove its author's "great powers of imagination, and a command of language seldom surpassed," yet called forth the "lament that he has drunk so deep at some enchanted fountain, which seems to blend in his fancy the shadows of the tomb with the clouds and sunshine of life." "Morella," amid much that is typical, alludes to that all overpowering and overshadowing horror of Poe's life, to the notion that the consciousness of our identity is not lost at death, and that sentience survives the entombment. The early version of this tale contained " a Catholic hymn," which subsequently, much revised, appeared as a separate poem.

Mr. Kennedy had now had eighteen months' experience of Poe without discovering anything to alter the favourable opinion he originally formed of him, and he thus expressed himself to Mr. White on the subject :—

"BALTIMORE, *April* 13, 1835.

" DEAR SIR,—Poe did right in referring to me. He is very clever with his pen—classical and scholar-like. He wants experience and direction, but I have no doubt he can be made very useful to you. And, poor fellow ! he is *very* poor. I told him to write something for every number of your magazine, and that you might find it to your advantage to give him some permanent employ. He has a volume of very bizarre tales in the hands of ——, in Philadelphia, who for a year past has been promising to publish them. This young fellow is highly imaginative, and a little given to the terrific. He is at work upon a tragedy, but I have turned him to drudging upon whatever may make money, and I have no doubt you and he will find your account in each other."

In the May number of the *Messenger* appeared " Lionizing," one of the " Folio Club Tales," and on the 30th of the same month its author is stated to have said in a letter to Mr. White :—

" In regard to my critique of Mr. Kennedy's novel I seriously feel ashamed of what I have written. I fully intended to give the work a thorough review and examine it in detail. Ill health alone prevented me from so doing. At the time I made the hasty sketch I sent you, I was so ill as to be hardly able to see the paper on which I wrote, and I finished it in a state of complete exhaustion. I have not, therefore, done anything like justice to the book, and I am vexed about the matter ; for Mr.

Kennedy has proved himself a kind friend to me in every respect, and I am sincerely grateful to him for many acts of generosity and attention. You ask me if I am perfectly satisfied with your course. I reply that I am entirely. My poor services are not worth what you give me for them."

Besides his intercourse with Mr. Kennedy, Poe, says Mr. Latrobe (who will be recollected as another of the *Saturday Visitor's* Committee), "at my instance called upon me sometimes, and entered at length into the discussion of subjects on which he proposed to employ his pen. When he warmed up he was most eloquent. . . . He seemed to forget the world around him, as wild fancy, logical truth, mathematical analysis, and wonderful combination of facts, flowed in strange commingling from his lips, in words choice and appropriate, as though the result of the closest study. I remember being particularly struck with the power that he seemed to possess of identifying himself with whatever he was describing. He related to me all the facts of a voyage to the moon, I think (which he proposed to put upon paper), with an accuracy of minute detail, and a truthfulness as regarded philosophical phenomena, that impressed you with the idea that he had just returned from the journey."

The voyage to the moon referred to by Mr. Latrobe is the famous "Hans Pfaall," or "Phaall," as it was originally spelt, which appeared in the June number of the *Messenger*, and created quite a *furor* at the time. Three weeks after the appearance of Poe's story, the notorious "Moon Hoax" of Richard Adams Locke was published by the *New York Sun ;* and both *jeux d'esprit* were presumed, by some journalists, to have been the work of one author. As even now some confusion exists between the respective dates of publication of the ephemeral hoax and the immortal story, Poe's own version, corroborated by independent evidence, shall be given:—

"About six months before this occurrence,* the Harpers had issued an American edition of Sir John Herschel's 'Treatise on Astronomy,' and I had been much interested in what is there said respecting the possibility of future lunar investigations. The theme excited my fancy, and I longed to give free rein to it in depicting my day-dreams about the scenery of the moon —in short, I longed to write a story embodying these dreams. The obvious difficulty, of course, was that of accounting for the narrator's acquaintance with the satellite; and the equally obvious mode of surmounting the difficulty was the supposition of an extraordinary telescope. I saw at once that the chief interest of such a narrative must depend upon the reader's yielding his credence in some measure as to details of actual fact. At this stage of my deliberations, I spoke of the design to one or two friends—to Mr. John P. Kennedy, the author of 'Swallow Barn,' among others—and the result of my conversations with them was, that the optical difficulties of constructing such a telescope as I conceived were so rigid and so commonly understood, that it would be in vain to attempt giving due verisimilitude to any fiction having the telescope as a basis. Reluctantly, therefore, and only half convinced (believing the public, in fact, more readily gullible than did my friends), I gave up the idea of imparting very close verisimilitude to what I should write—that is to say, so close as really to deceive. I fell back upon a style half plausible, half bantering, and resolved to give what interest I could to an actual passage from the earth to the moon, describing the lunar scenery as if surveyed and personally examined by the narrator. In this view I wrote a story which I called 'Hans Pfaall,' publishing it about six months afterwards in *The Southern Literary Messenger*.

"It was three weeks after the issue of the *Messenger* containing 'Hans Pfaall,' that the first of the 'Moon Hoax' editorials made its appearance in the *Sun*, and no sooner had I seen the

---

* *I.e.*, the publication of Mr. Locke's *Moon Hoax*.

paper than I understood the jest, which not for a moment could I doubt had been suggested by my own *jeu d'esprit.* Some of the New York journals (the *Transcript* among others) saw the matter in the same light, and published the 'Moon Story' side by side with 'Hans Pfaall,' thinking that the author of the one had been detected in the author of the other. Although the details are, with some exception, very dissimilar, still I maintain that the general features of the two compositions are nearly identical. Both are *hoaxes* (although one is in a *tone* of mere banter, the other of downright earnest) ; both hoaxes are on one subject, astronomy ; both on the same point of that subject, the moon ; both professed to have derived exclusive information from a foreign country ; and both attempt to give plausibility by minuteness of scientific detail. Add to all this, that nothing of a similar nature had ever been attempted before these two hoaxes, the one of which followed immediately upon the heels of the other.

" Having stated the case, however, in this form, I am bound to do Mr. Locke the justice to say, that he denies having seen my article prior to the publication of his own : I am bound to add, also, that I believe him.

" Immediately on the completion of the 'Moon Story' (it was three or four days in getting finished), I wrote an examination of its claims to credit, showing distinctly its fictitious character, but was astonished at finding that I could obtain few listeners, so really eager were all to be deceived, so magical were the charms of a style that served as the vehicle of an exceedingly clumsy invention.

" It may afford even now some amusement to see pointed out those particulars of the hoax which should have sufficed to establish its real character. Indeed, however rich the imagination displayed in this fiction, it wanted much of the force which might have been given it by a more scrupulous attention to general analogy and to fact. That the public were misled, even for an instant, merely proves the gross ignorance which is so generally prevalent upon subjects of an astronomical nature."

The singular blunders to which he referred included a literal reproduction, in a winged man-bat, of Peter Wilkins' flying islanders, and it is impossible to refrain from expressing, with Poe, our wonder at the prodigious *success* of the hoax.

"Not one person in ten discredited it," he says, "and, (strangest point of all!) the doubters were chiefly those who doubted without being able to say why—the ignorant, those uninformed in astronomy—people who *would not* believe because the thing was so novel, so entirely 'out of the usual way.' A grave professor of mathematics in a Virginian college told me seriously that he had *no doubt* of the truth of the whole affair! The great effect wrought upon the public mind is referable, first, to *the novelty of the idea;* secondly, to the fancy-exciting and reason-repressing character of the alleged discoveries; thirdly, to the consummate tact with which the deception was brought forth; fourthly, to the exquisite *vraisemblance* of the narration. The hoax was circulated to an immense extent, was translated into various languages—was even made the subject of (quizzical) discussion in astronomical societies; drew down upon itself the grave denunciations of Dick,* and was, upon the whole, decidedly the greatest *hit* in the way of *sensation* — of merely popular sensation — ever made by any similar fiction either in America or in Europe.

"Having read the 'Moon Story' to an end," continues Poe, "and found it anticipative of all the main points of my 'Hans Pfaall,' I suffered the latter to remain unfinished. The chief design in carrying my hero to the moon was to afford him an opportunity of describing the lunar scenery, but I found that he could add very little to the minute and authentic account *of Sir John Herschel.* The first part of 'Hans Pfaall,' occupying about eighteen pages of the *Messenger,* embraced merely a journal of the passage between the two orbs, and a few words of general observation on the most obvious features of the satellite; the second part will most probably never appear. I did not think it advisable even to bring my voyager back to his parent earth. He remains where I left him, and is still, I believe, 'the man in the moon.'"

Had Poe carried out his design of describing lunar scenery, what a rich feast of fantasy would have been

---

* Dr. Thomas Dick, the well-known astronomical writer.—J. H. I.

provided for his admirers! A slight glimmering of the gloomy glories he intended to portray is afforded by some passages in what he did complete. "Fancy," says he,* "revelled in the wild and dreamy regions of the moon. Imagination, feeling herself for once unshackled, roamed at will among the ever-changing wonders of a shadowy and unstable land. Now there were hoary and time-honoured forests, and craggy precipices, and waterfalls tumbling with a loud noise into abysses without bottom. Then I came suddenly into still noonday solitudes where no wind of heaven ever intruded, and where vast meadows of poppies, and slender, lily-looking flowers, spread themselves out a weary distance, all silent and motionless for ever. Then again I journeyed far down, away into another country, where it was all one dim and vague lake, with a boundary line of clouds. And out of this melancholy water arose a forest of tall eastern trees like a wilderness of dreams. And I bore in mind that the shadows of the trees which fell upon the lake remained not on the surface where they fell—but sunk slowly and steadily down, and commingled with the waves, while from the trunks of the trees other shadows were continually coming out, and taking the place of their brothers thus entombed. 'This then,' I said thoughtfully, 'is the very reason why the waters of this lake grow blacker with age, and more melancholy as the hours run on.' But fancies such as these were not the sole possessors of my brain. Horrors of a nature most stern and most appalling would frequently obtrude themselves upon my mind, and shake the innermost depths of my soul with the bare supposition of their

* *Tales of the Grotesque and Arabesque*, vol. ii. pp. 68, 69, 1840 edit.

possibility. Yet I would not suffer my thoughts for any length of time to dwell upon these latter speculations."

After the publication of "Hans Pfaall," Mr. White seems to have determined to obtain, if possible, the exclusive services of his talented contributor. Editor after editor had assisted in managing the *Messenger* for a few months, and had then relinquished the onerous but not very remunerative task: Messrs. Heath, Tucker, Sparhawk, and others had followed in rapid succession, until, in June, Mr. White, again editorless, bethought him of Poe, and in answer to his inquiries, received these words:—" You ask me if I would be willing to come on to Richmond if you should have occasion for my services during the coming winter. I reply that nothing would give me greater pleasure. I have been desirous for some time past of paying a visit to Richmond, and would be glad of any reasonable excuse for so doing. Indeed, I am anxious to settle myself in that city, and if, by any chance, you hear of a situation likely to suit me, I would gladly accept it, were the salary even the merest trifle. I should, indeed, feel myself greatly indebted to you, if through your means I could accomplish this object. What you say in the conclusion of your letter, in relation to the supervision of proof-sheets, gives me reason to hope that possibly you might find something for me to do in your office. If so, I should be very glad—for at present only a very small portion of my time is employed."

Meanwhile, Mr. White having succeeded in obtaining the aid of another *littérateur*, who promised " to devote his exclusive attention" to the editorial work of the *Messenger*, was in no hurry to complete an arrangement with Poe, who, however, contributed to the

July number "The Visionary"—a tale afterwards retitled "The Assignation"—and these lines "To Mary":—

> " Mary, amid the cares—the woes
>   Crowding around my earthly path
> (Sad path, alas ! where grows
> Not ev'n one lonely rose),
>   My soul at least a solace hath
> In dreams of thee, and therein knows
> An Eden of sweet repose.
>
> " And thus thy memory is to me
>   Like some enchanted, far-off isle,
> In some tumultuous sea—
> Some lake beset as lake can be
>   With storms—but where, meanwhile,
> Serenest skies continually
> Just o'er that one bright island smile."

To the August *Messenger* Poe contributed the sarcastic sketch of "Bon-Bon," and "The Coliseum: Prize Poem from the *Baltimore Visitor*." By this time the new editor, who had assisted at the gestation of two numbers of Mr. White's magazine, followed the example of his numerous predecessors and retired, whereupon our poet was invited to Richmond to assist in the editorial duties, at a salary of five hundred and twenty dollars per annum.

At the very moment when Poe received this offer, he was arranging with Mr. L. A. Wilmer for the publication, in co-operation with that gentleman, of a literary magazine or newspaper in Baltimore. Some correspondence had already passed between the two young *literati*, and Poe, says Mr. Wilmer, "proposed to join with me in the publication of a monthly magazine of a superior, intellectual character, and had written a prospectus, which he transmitted to me for examination." Mr. White's proposition completely demolished the project, for, as both the promoters of it were devoid of pecuniary means, Poe immediately accepted the proffered post, and thus, as his intended partner remarks, " the grand intellectual illumination we had proposed to make in Baltimore was necessarily postponed." *

Upon revisiting the abode of his earlier days, and in circumstances so altered from those of yore, the unfortunate poet was afflicted with a terrible melancholia—an affliction which frequently beset him on his journey through life, and which was, apparently, not merely the natural outcome of privation and grief, but also to some extent hereditary. Writing to his friend Kennedy to acquaint him with the fact of his appointment on the *Messenger*, he says :—

"RICHMOND, *September* 11, 1835.

"DEAR SIR,—I received a letter from Dr. Miller, in which he tells me you are in town. I hasten, therefore, to write you, and express by letter what I have always found it impossible to express orally—my deep sense of gratitude for your frequent and ineffectual assistance and kindness. Through your influence Mr. White has been induced to employ me in assisting him with the editorial duties of his magazine at a salary of five hundred and twenty dollars per annum. The situation is agreeable to me for many reasons, but, alas ! it appears to me that nothing can give me pleasure, or the slightest gratification. Excuse me, my dear sir, if in this letter you find much incoherency. My feelings at this moment are pitiable, indeed. I am suffering under a depression of spirits such as I never felt before. I have struggled in vain against the influence of this melancholy ; *you will believe me* when I say that I am still miserable in spite of the great improvement in my circumstances. I say you will believe me, and for this simple reason, that a man who is writing for *effect* does not write thus. My heart is open before

---

* L. A. Wilmer, *Our Press Gang*, p. 35.

you ; if it be worth reading, read it. I am wretched, and know not why. Console me, for you can. But let it be quickly, or it will be too late. Write me immediately ; convince me that it is worth one's while—that it is at all necessary to live, and you will prove yourself indeed my friend. Persuade me to do what is right. I do mean this. I do not mean that you should consider what I now write you a jest. Oh, pity me ! for I feel that my words are incoherent ; but I will recover myself. You will not fail to see that I am suffering under a depression of spirits which will ruin me should it be long continued. Write me then and quickly; urge me to do what is right. Your words will have more weight with me than the words of others, for you were my friend when no one else was. Fail not, as you value your peace of mind hereafter.   E. A. POE."

To this saddening wail of despair Kennedy responded :—

" I am sorry to see you in such plight as your letter shows you in. It is strange that just at this time, when everybody is praising you, and when fortune is beginning to smile upon your hitherto wretched circumstances, you should be invaded by these blue devils. It belongs, however, to your age and temper to be thus buffeted—but be assured, it only wants a little resolution to master the adversary for ever. You will doubtless do well henceforth in literature, and add to your *comforts*, as well as to your reputation, which it gives me great pleasure to assure you is everywhere rising in popular esteem."

Notwithstanding his " blue devils," as his friend phrased it, the new editor worked wonders with the *Messenger*. "His talents," records Kennedy, "made that periodical quite brilliant while he was connected with it," and indeed, within little more than a twelvemonth from Poe's appointment in the following December, as sole editor, the circulation increased from seven hundred to nearly five thousand—an increase quite unparalleled at that time in the history of this class of magazines. The success was, of course, due to the originality and fascination of Poe's stories, and the fearlessness of his trenchant critiques.

The *Messenger* for September contained the "Loss of Breath" and "King Pest," two of Poe's poorest stories : the latter is one of those quizzical hoaxes upon which he sometimes squandered his genius, and upon which his readers have frequently wasted their time in vain attempts to discover meanings not discoverable because not existent. The same number which completed the first volume also contained "Shadow," one of its author's phenomenal prose poems, and these "Lines written in an Album : "—

> "Eliza ! let thy generous heart
> From its present pathway part not ;
> Being everything which now thou art,
> Be nothing which thou art not.
>
> So with the world thy gentle ways—
> Thy unassuming beauty—
> And truth—shall be a theme of praise
> For ever—and love a duty."

The "Eliza," in whose album these lines were written, was the daughter of Mr. White ; after her father's death in 1842 she was an occasional and esteemed visitor at the house of the poet, spending many months with his wife and aunt at their Fordham home.

In the December number of the *Messenger*, at Mr. White's instance apparently, he commenced that system of literary scarification——that crucial dissection of bookmaking mediocrities—which, whilst it created throughout the length and breadth of the States terror of his powerful pen, at the same time raised up against him a host of implacable, although unknown,

enemies, who henceforth never hesitated to accept and
repeat any story, howsoever improbable, to his discredit.   It would have been far better for his future
welfare and fame if, instead of affording contemporary nonentities a chance of literary immortality
by impaling them upon his pen's sharp point, he had
devoted the whole of his time to the production of
his wonderful tales and still more wondrous poems.

The second volume of the *Messenger* began in
December, and, among other contributions by the new
editor, contained a crushing critique on a work styled
" Norman Leslie."   This was the first of those reviews
already alluded to that did their author so much injury
—personal and posthumous.   In the initial number
of 1836 appeared various critical articles, and the
singular tale of metempsychosis, " Metzengerstein."   In
the early version of this fiction the poet introduced
some of those family reminiscences he was wont to
intersect his writings with : after stating that the death
of the hero's father was quickly followed by that of his
mother, he exclaims, with as much prophetic as retro-
spective truth, " How *could* she die ?—and of consumption !   But it is a path I have prayed to follow.
I would wish all I love to perish of that gentle
disease.   How glorious ! to depart in the heyday of
the young blood—the heart all passion—the imagination all fire—amid the remembrances of happier
days !"

The next issue of the *Messenger* contained various
critiques—including an eulogistic one of Bulwer—the
story of the " Duke de l'Omelette," and the first part
of Poe's papers on " Autography," the second appearing in a subsequent number.   The amusement, excite-

ment, and ill-temper these articles aroused will be best gathered from the author's own subsequent account of the *jeu d'esprit :*—

" Some years ago there appeared, in the *Southern Literary Messenger*, an article which attracted very general attention, not less from the nature of its subject, than from the peculiar manner in which it was handled. The editor introduces his readers to a certain Mr. Joseph Miller, who, it is hinted, is not merely a descendant of the illustrious Joe of jest-book notoriety, but is that identical individual in proper person :—

" The object of his visit to the editor is to place in his hands the autographs of certain distinguished American *literati*. To these persons he had written rigmarole letters on various topics, and in all cases had been successful in eliciting a reply. The replies only (which it is scarcely necessary to say are all fictitious) are given in the Magazine with a genuine autograph facsimile appended, and are either burlesques of the supposed writer's usual style, or rendered otherwise absurd by reference to the nonsensical questions imagined to have been propounded by Mr. Miller.

" With the public this article took amazingly well, and many of our principal papers were at the expense of reprinting it with the woodcut autographs. Even those whose names had been introduced, and whose style had been burlesqued, took the joke, generally speaking, in good part. Some of them were at a loss what to make of the matter. Dr. W. E. Channing of Boston was at some trouble, it is said, in calling to mind whether he had or had not actually written to some Mr. Joseph Miller the letter attributed to him in the article. This letter was nothing more than what follows :—

" ' BOSTON, ——.

" ' DEAR SIR,—No such person as Philip Philpot has ever been in my employ as a coachman or otherwise. The name is an odd one, and not likely to be forgotten. The man must have reference to some other Doctor Channing. It would be as well to question him closely.—Respectfully yours,

" ' W. E. CHANNING.

" ' To JOSEPH X. MILLER, Esq.'

"The precise and brief sententiousness of the divine is here, it will be seen, very truly adopted or 'hit off.'

"In one instance only was the *jeu d'esprit* taken in serious dudgeon. Colonel Stone and the *Messenger* had not been upon the best of terms. Some one of the Colonel's little brochures had been severely treated by that journal, which declared that the work would have been far more properly published among the quack advertisements in a square corner of the *Commercial.* The Colonel had retaliated by whole-sale vituperation of the *Messenger.* This being the state of affairs, it was not to be wondered at that the following epistle was not quietly received on the part of him to whom it was attributed :—

"'NEW YORK, ——.

"'DEAR SIR,—I am exceedingly and excessively sorry that it is out of my power to comply with your rational and reasonable request. The subject you mention is one with which I am utterly unacquainted. Moreover, it is one about which I know very little—Respectfully,

"'W. L. STONE.

"'JOSEPH V. MILLER, Esq.'

"These tautologies and anti-climaxes were too much for the Colonel, and we are ashamed to say that he committed himself by publishing in the *Commercial* an indignant denial of ever having indited such an epistle.

"The principal feature of this autograph article, although perhaps the least interesting, was that of the editorial comment upon the supposed MSS., regarding them as indicative of character. In these comments the design was never more than semi-serious. At times, too, the writer was evidently led into error or injustice through the desire of being pungent—not unfrequently sacrificing truth for the sake of a *bon mot.* In this manner qualities were often attributed to individuals, which were not so much indicated by their handwriting, as suggested by the spleen of the commentator. But that a strong analogy *does* generally and naturally exist between every man's chirography and character, will be denied by none but the unreflecting."

Poe's contributions to the remaining numbers of the

Messenger for 1836 included, besides reprints of his poems, the "Pinakidia," or commonplace book notes, several critiques on contemporary books and authors, the story of "Epimanes"—now styled "Four Beasts in One"—a "Tale of Jerusalem," and a masterly analysis of Maelzel's *soi-disant* "Automaton Chess-player." In this last-named paper, the poet demonstrated by clear, concise, and irrefutable arguments, that the machine then being exhibited before the citizens of Richmond must be regulated in its operations by *mind*—that, in fact, it was no automaton at all, but simply a piece of mechanism guided by human agency.

CHAPTER X.

MARRIAGE.

EARLY in 1836, a gleam of hope broke in upon Poe's overclouded career. Amongst those of his father's kindred whom the poet had sought out at Baltimore was his aunt Maria, widow of Mr. William Clemm, a man who, it is stated, had expended his property on behalf of a not over-grateful country. Mrs. Clemm was in greatly reduced circumstances, but she proffered her brother's son such welcome as was in her power, and a strong mutual affection sprang up between the two relatives. Mrs. Clemm had an only child, her daughter Virginia, described by all parties as an exquisitely lovely and amiable girl. Virginia Clemm, born on the 13th of August 1822, was still a child when her handsome cousin Edgar revisited Baltimore after his escapade at West Point. A more than cousinly affection, which gradually grew in intensity, resulted from their frequent communion, and ultimately, whilst one, at least, of the two cousins was but a child, they were married.

In that beautiful allegory of his life — in his unrhymed rhapsody of "Eleonora" *—Poe tells in thrilling words how, ere the knowledge of his love had dawned upon him, he dwelt in a world of his own creative imagination, in the symbolic "Valley of the Many-Coloured Grass," apart from the outer and,

* Published in *The Gift* in 1842.

MRS. CLEMM.

to him, less real world. There they dwelt—he and
his cousin and her mother—and there they, he and
she, who was but a child, had dwelt for many years
before consciousness of love had entered into their
hearts, until one evening when their secret was unveiled
to them, and so, murmurs the poet, "we spoke no
words during the rest of that sweet day, and our
words even upon the morrow were tremulous and
few. . . . And now we felt enkindled within us the
fiery souls of our forefathers. The passions which
had for centuries distinguished our race came throng-
ing with the fancies for which they had been equally
noted, and together breathed a delirious bliss over the
'Valley of the Many-Coloured Grass.'" And then,
in magic words, he tells of the revolution, wrought
beneath the wizard spells of Love, of how "a change
came o'er the spirit of *his* dream," and of how all
things beautiful became more beauteous; how "strange,
brilliant flowers burst out upon the trees where no
flowers had been known before;" how the "tints of
the green grass deepened," and how a myriad things
of nature, before unnoted, bloomed and blossomed into
being.

Then is the delicate loveliness of his child-bride
compared by the poet to "that of the Seraphim," and
she was, he reminds himself, "a maiden artless and
innocent as the brief life she had led among the
flowers. No guile disguised the fervour of love which
animated her heart, and she examined with me its
inmost recesses as we walked together." Rarely, if
ever before, was poet blessed with so sweet a bride,
or with more artless affection than was Poe when he

acquired the heart and hand of her of whom he sang—

> " And this maiden, she lived with no other thought
> Than to love and be loved by me."

It has been stated, but with palpable incorrectness, that the young cousins were married in Baltimore on the 2nd of September 1835, previous to Poe's departure for Richmond, but that the youthful pair did not live together for more than a year, and that they were again married in Richmond, where they were to reside, this second marriage ceremony taking place to save comment, as the previous one had been so private. This circumstantial romance must be consigned to the limbo whence so many of the legends accumulated round the poet's memory have been dismissed. The facts are :—When it was learned that the young *littérateur* purposed marrying his cousin, who was still under fourteen, her half-sister's husband—Edgar Poe's first cousin—Mr. Neilson Poe, to hinder so premature a marriage, offered her mother to receive Virginia into his own family, and provide for her education, with the understanding, that if after a few years the cousins still entertained the same affection for each other, they should be married. When Poe heard of this he indited an earnest, passionate protest against the arrangement to Mrs. Clemm, who, consequently, declined the offer, and the marriage soon afterwards took place.

Edgar Poe was married to Virginia Clemm, in Richmond, on the 6th of May 1836, and, says Mrs. Clemm, Judge Stannard and his son Robert, Edgar's old schoolfellow, were among the first callers. Mrs.

Clemm took up her residence with the young couple, both so doubly related to her, and became as it were their guardian and protector. But few weeks, however, had passed over the heads of the wedded pair before darksome troubles began to hover over them: "the fair and gentle Eulalie" had indeed become the poet's "blushing bride," but it was a "dream too bright to last" to deem the fatality which dogged his footsteps had forsaken him. Some inkling of his troubles may be gleaned from this letter to his friend Kennedy:—

"RICHMOND, VA., *June 7,* 1836.

"DEAR SIR,—Having got into a little temporary difficulty, I venture to ask you, once more, for aid, rather than apply to any of my new friends in Richmond.

"Mr. White, having purchased a new house, at $10,000, made propositions to my aunt to rent it to her, and to board himself and family with her. This plan was highly advantageous to us, and, having accepted it, all arrangements were made, and I obtained credit for some furniture, &c., to the amount of $200, above what little money I had. But upon examination of the premises purchased, it appears that the house will barely be large enough for one family, and the scheme is laid aside—leaving me now in debt (to a small amount) without those means of discharging it upon which I had depended.

"In this dilemma I would be greatly indebted to you for the loan of $100 for six months. This will enable me to meet a note for $100 due in three months—and allow me three months to return your money. I shall have no difficulty in doing this, as, beyond this $100, I owe nothing, and I am now receiving $15 per week, and am to receive $20 after November. All Mr. White's disposable money has been required to make his first payment.

"Have you heard anything further in relation to Mrs. Clemm's estate?

"Our *Messenger* is thriving beyond all expectation, and I myself have every prospect of success.

H

"It is our design to issue, as soon as possible, a number of the Magazine consisting entirely of articles from our most distinguished *literati*. To this end we have received, and have been promised, a variety of aid from the highest sources —Mrs. Sigourney, Miss Sedgwick, Paulding, Flint, Halleck, Cooper, Judge Hopkinson, Dew, Governor Cass, J. Q. Adams, and many others. Could you not do me so great a favour as to send a scrap, however small, from your portfolio? Your name is of the greatest influence in that region where we direct our greatest efforts—in the South. Any little reminiscence, tale, *jeu d'esprit*, historical anecdote—anything, in short, *with your name*, will answer all our purposes.

"I presume you have heard of my marriage.—With sincere respect and esteem, yours truly,

"EDGAR A. POE.

"J. P. KENNEDY."

The pecuniary embarrassment to which this communication alludes, even if temporarily relieved by his friend, was doubtless of a chronic character, and probably the chief cause of Poe quitting Richmond, and resigning his connection with the *Literary Messenger*. Although he parted on friendly terms from Mr. White, and in after years wrote and spoke of him with kindliness, there is little doubt but that the poet relinquished his post on the magazine in consequence of the rate of remuneration he received being not only much less than he deemed his name and *entire* services entitled him to, but even less than he could decently maintain his household upon. The number of the magazine for January 1837 was the last *Messenger* under Poe's editorship, and it contained, in addition to certain reviews and reprinted poems of his, the first part of "Arthur Gordon Pym;" a second instalment of the romance appearing in the following number, after its author's severance from the periodical.

Previous to giving up charge of the *Messenger*, Poe, with that thoughtfulness of friends which he often manifested, wrote to Mr. Wilmer, to tell him of his intention of leaving Richmond, and suggesting that he, Wilmer, should come thither without delay, as he was certain he could obtain the post he was about to vacate. Mr. Wilmer, however, could not avail himself of the offer, as he was preparing to leave for Philadelphia.*

Apparently, Mr. White parted with his clever editor with much reluctance, yet he could not, or he would not, comply with his requirements — requirements, indeed, it has been suggested, that included partnership in the publication. In the number of the magazine containing Poe's resignation of the editorship, announced in the words, " Mr. Poe's attention being called in another direction, he will decline, with the present number, the editorial duties of the *Messenger,*" the proprietor issued a notice to the effect, that " Mr. Poe, who has filled the editorial department for the last twelve months with so much ability, retired from that station on the 3rd instant," but will, so it was promised, " continue to furnish its columns from time to time with the effusions of his vigorous and popular pen."

How soon after this Poe left Richmond, and what he was doing for the next few months, are still unanswered questions. After the expiration of a short interregnum, he is discovered as settled in New York once more, and this time accompanied by his

* L. A. Wilmer, *Our Press Gang.*

wife and her mother. During one portion, at least, of this residence in New York, the Poes lived at 113½ Carmine Street, where Mrs. Clemm attempted, as one method of lessening the household expenses, to keep a boarding-house, but the experiment does not appear to have met with any success, and the family fell into very poor circumstances. An interesting account of the poet's limited *mènage* at this epoch of the story has been given by the late William Gowans, the wealthy and eccentric bibliopolist, who boarded with Mrs. Clemm.*

Alluding to the untruthfulness of the prevalent idea of Poe's character, the shrewd old man remarks—

"The characters drawn of Poe by his various biographers and critics may with safety be pronounced an excess of exaggeration ; but this is not to be much wondered at, when it is taken into consideration that these men were rivals either as poets or prose writers, and it is well known that such are generally as jealous of each other as are the ladies who are handsome, or those who desire to be considered to be possessed of the coveted quality. It is an old truism, and as true as it is old, 'that in the midst of counsel there is safety.'

"I, therefore, will also show you my opinion of this gifted but unfortunate genius. It may be estimated as worth little, but it has this merit—it comes from an eye and ear witness ; and this, it must be remembered, is the very highest of legal evidence. For eight months or more, 'one house contained us, us one table fed !' During that time I saw much of him, and had an opportunity of conversing with him often ; and I must say, that I never saw him the least affected with liquor, nor even descend to any known vice, while he was one of the most courteous, gentlemanly, and intelligent companions I have met with during my journeyings and haltings through divers divisions of the globe ; besides, he had an

* In the *New York Evening Mail*, December 1870.

extra inducement to be a good man as well as a good husband, for he had a wife of matchless beauty and loveliness ; her eyes could match that of any houri, and her face defy the genius of a Canova to imitate ; a temper and disposition of surpassing sweetness ; besides, she seemed as much devoted to him and his every interest as a young mother is to her first-born. . . . Poe had a remarkably pleasing and prepossessing countenance, what the ladies would call decidedly handsome."

Mr. Gowans—who is remembered as "one of the most truthful and uncompromising of men"—in conversing with Mr. Thomas C. Latto with reference to Poe and his young wife, whom he described as fragile in constitution, but of remarkable beauty, testified that the poet "was uniformly quiet, reticent, gentlemanly in demeanour, and during the whole period he lived there, not the slightest trace of intoxication or dissipation was discernible in the illustrious inmate, who was at that time engaged in the composition of 'Arthur Gordon Pym.' Poe "kept good hours," he said, "and all his little wants were seen to by Mrs. Clemm and her daughter, who watched him as sedulously as if he had been a child." Mr. Gowans was a man of known intelligence, and, writes Mr. Latto, "being a Scotchman, is by no means averse to '*a twa-handed crack*,' but he felt himself kept at a distance somewhat by Poe's aristocratic reserve." * Mr. Gowans only left when the household was broken up, and the close connection which he was daily brought into with members of it, and the opportunity which he had of seeing what kind of life the poet was then leading, render his testimony valuable.

Res angustæ domi notwithstanding, the domestic

* In a letter to the late Mrs. Whitman, dated July 8th, 1870.

life of the poet, at this period at least, was not altogether unhappy. As yet, the fact had not manifested
itself to him that his girlish bride's beauty was but
the signal of the fatal disease that she was destined
to fall an early victim to; nor could he forebode,
that she was to succumb to that fell complaint he
had erstwhile so rashly wished all he loved to perish
of. A little while later and the devoted husband
learnt, as he bemoaned, that " the finger of death was
upon her bosom—that, like the ephemeron, she had
been made perfect in loveliness only to die." Ever
since his marriage Poe had spent his leisure hours in
continuing his young wife's education, and under his
careful tuition she became highly accomplished. " She
was an excellent linguist and a perfect musician, and
she was *so very beautiful*," records her bereaved
mother. " How often has Eddie* said, ' I see no one
so beautiful as my sweet little wife.' "

" Eddie," declares his " more than mother," " was
domestic in all his habits, seldom leaving home for an
hour unless his darling Virginia, or myself, were with
him. He was truly an affectionate, kind husband,
and a devoted son to me. He was impulsive, generous, affectionate, and *noble*. His tastes were very
simple, and his admiration for all that was good and
beautiful very great. . . . We three lived only for
each other." †

This epoch of quiet domestic happiness does not
appear to have been one very fruitful of literary produce, or, if it were, the result has been lost sight of.
During 1837 Poe contributed a critique of Stephens's

---

* The poet's pet name at home.
† Letter to Judge Neilson Poe, August 19th, 1860.

" Incidents of Travel in Egypt, Arabia Petræa, and the Holy Land," to the October number of the *New York Review.* This Quarterly was a theological publication, and required a class of writing utterly unsuited to Poe's range of thought, he therefore wisely forbore from attempting anything of a similar kind again. His next literary essay was the completion of " The Narrative of Arthur Gordon Pym," the first and second instalments of which romance, as already pointed out, had appeared in the *Southern Literary Messenger.* The interest the work had aroused during its issue in the magazine determined Poe to complete it, that is to say, as far as he ever intended to complete it, the abrupt and unfinished state of its closing paragraph having, evidently, been intentional. The story was not issued in book form until July 1838. It is said that it did not excite much notice in America, but it was very successful in England, where, besides the authorised reprints of Messrs. Wiley and Putnam, several other editions were speedily disposed of. The truthful air of " The Narrative," and the circumstantiality of the title-page and preface, doubtless attracted attention, but indeed the whole romance is detailed with such Defoe-like minuteness—with such an apparent want of art—especially in lengthy, almost tedious, citations from presumable kindred works—that the reading public was bound to submit to the temporary fascination, and accept the *vraisemblance* for truth itself. The abrupt termination of " The Narrative," and the pretext alleged for it, both contributed greatly to the apparent fidelity to fact. The chief defect in the tale is the supernatural final paragraph—wisely omitted in the London reprint—which neither adds to the interest nor increases the life-like truthfulness. The original title-page of Poe's longest tale deserves reproduction here; it reads thus:—

"THE NARRATIVE

of

ARTHUR GORDON PYM,

of Nantucket;

Comprising the Details of a Mutiny and Atrocious Butchery on Board the American Brig Grampus, on her way to the South Seas—with an Account of the Recapture of the Vessel by the Survivors; their Shipwreck, and subsequent Horrible Sufferings from Famine, their Deliverance by means of the British Schooner Jane Guy; the brief Cruise of this latter Vessel in the Antarctic Ocean: her Capture, and the Massacre of her Crew among a Group of Islands in the 84th parallel of Southern Latitude, together with the incredible Adventures and Discoveries still further South, to which that distressing Calamity gave rise.

New York: Harper & Brothers.
1838."

Students of Poe's works who have learned to recognise his method of thought, know how frequently he discloses his mental history in those parenthetical passages he so much affected. In the above narrative these disclosures, interwoven with autobiographical *data,* occur both oft and o'er. In the "preliminary notice," and in the first chapter of the romance, fact and fiction are ingeniously blended, and real and ideal personages are mingled somewhat confusingly together. His readers are well aware how clearly Poe's idiosyncrasies, both in his prose and in his verse, show through the transparent masks behind which his heroes are supposed to be hidden, and in this "Narrative" it is rarely that the imaginary hero is thought of otherwise than as identical with Poe himself. The adventurous lad Pym is certainly not the person to whom our thoughts tend when the second chapter of this tale begins, "In no affairs of mere prejudice, *pro* or *con*, do we deduce inferences with entire certainty, even from the most simple *data*," and we are at no loss to comprehend the autobiographic fidelity of the author when he says, under the pseudonym of Pym, "One of my enthusiastic temperament, and somewhat gloomy, although glowing imagination;" and, "It is strange, too, that he most strongly enlisted my feelings in behalf of the life of a seaman, when he depicted his more terrible moments of suffering and despair. For the bright side of the painting I had a limited sympathy."

Dreams of the day and of the night are plentiful in Pym's narrative, and are rather more typical of the psychological introspection of the poet than of the healthy animalism and muscular energy of the sailor. And yet they are not out of harmony with the tone of this work, nor discordant with the overwrought imagination of a sensitive youth. A dreaming fit is described in the second chapter—that whence Pym is aroused by the dog "Tiger"—which fully equals in descriptive terror and power of language any of the English Opium-Eater's "Confessions;" whilst the analysis of the various mental phases through which the hero passes—as told in Chapter xxiv.—from the time he commences his descent of the soapstone cliff and *must not think*, until the *longing to fall* is finally finished by the fall, quite equals in psychological subtlety anything that De Quincey ever did. Another noteworthy passage is that in Chapter xxi., wherein is described the horrible dread, ever recurring with such ghastly effect in Poe's tales, of entombment alive: "The supremeness of mental and bodily distress of living inhumation" continually overshrouds his imagination, and his readers are goaded into believing that the narrator himself must have experienced the so-graphically-portrayed horrors of "the blackness of darkness which envelops the victim, the terrific oppression of lungs, the stifling fumes from the damp earth," and all the appalling paraphernalia of a death-scene, which he shudderingly declares, even as he describes, are "not to be tolerated—never to be conceived."

The originality of Poe's genius, as shown in this "Narrative," will doubtless be the more generally admired, although less real, in such things as where he explains the singular character of the many-hued waters—which never seemed limpid—in the Antarctic island; and in the gradually-revealed horror of the inhabitants of the *colour white;* or in the ingenuity of the perusal of the torn letter by phosphorus; or in such probably inexplicable psychological facts as the long ocean travelling voyager, in his delirium, beholding every creation of his "mind's-eye" in *motion*—movement being the all-predominant idea. Our remarks on "Arthur Gordon Pym" are purposely directed more towards bringing prominently forward certain commonly unnoted characteristics of the tale, than to recalling attention to its generally appreciated, and frequently commented upon, more salient features.

Another of Poe's productions for this year was " Siope: A Fable. [In the manner of the Psychological Autobiographists]." " Siope," which appeared in the *Baltimore Book* for 1838, is the weird prose poem now styled " Silence," and is paralleled in many passages by its author's sonnet to " Silence " and other later poems. Poe's inventive genius, indeed, was much more limited than is generally supposed, leading him to frequently repeat and repolish, rather than to originate, over and over again : the same favourite quotation, or pet idea, may be found doing duty in several places. Those readers well acquainted with his earlier as well as later publications, will be able to recall to mind many instances of such repetition.

CHAPTER XI.

IN THE CITY OF PENN.

LATE in 1838 Poe removed to Philadelphia. The reason of his removal is uncertain, but it has been suggested that regular literary employment was proffered him in the Quaker city, wherefore, as the independence he had sought to earn by his pen was not obtainable in New York, he migrated thither with his *lares et penates*. That, or the constitutional restlessness, which like a fiend goaded him hither and thither, may have been the motive power. The whole burden of the household now falling upon his shoulders, for Mrs. Clemm relinquished the New York house and accompanied the Poes to Philadelphia, the poet sought engagements in various quarters. Among other magazines for which he agreed to write was the *American Museum*, a new publication projected and edited by Dr. N. C. Brooks of Baltimore. Requested by the proprietor to furnish a critique on Washington Irving, Poe replied in the following terms :—

"PHILADELPHIA, *September* 4, 1838.

"MY DEAR SIR,—I duly received your favour with the $10. Touching the review, I am forced to decline it just now. I should be most unwilling not to execute such a task well, and this I could not do at so short notice, at least now. I have two other engagements which it would be ruinous to defer. Besides this, I am just leaving Arch Street for a small house, and, of course, am somewhat in confusion.

"My main reason, however, for declining is what I first

alleged, viz.: I could not do the review well at short notice. The truth is, I can hardly say that I am conversant with Irving's writings, having read nothing of his since I was a boy, save his ' Granada.' It would be necessary to give his entire works a reperusal. You see, therefore, the difficulty at once. It is a theme upon which I would like very much to write, for there is a vast deal to be said upon it. Irving is much overrated, and a nice distinction might be drawn between his just and his surreptitious and adventitious reputation—between what is due to the pioneer solely, and what to the writer.

" The merit, too, of his tame propriety and faultlessness of style should be candidly weighed. He should be compared with Addison, something being hinted about imitation, and Sir Roger de Coverley should be brought up in judgment. A bold and *a priori* investigation of Irving's claims would strike home, take my word for it. The American literary world never saw anything of the kind yet. Seeing, therefore, the opportunity of making a fine hit, I am unwilling to hazard your fame by a failure, and a failure would assuredly be the event were I to undertake the task at present.

" The difficulty with you is nothing—for I fancy you are conversant with Irving's works, old and new, and would not have to read for the task. Had you spoken decidedly when I first saw you, I would have adventured. If you can delay the review until the second number I would be most happy to do my best. But this, I presume, is impossible.

" I have gotten nearly out of my late embarrassments. ―― would not aid me, being much pushed himself. He would, no doubt, have aided me, if possible. Present my respects if you see him.—Very truly yours,

" Edgar A. Poe.

" Suppose you send me proofs of my articles ; it might be as well—that is, if you have time. I look anxiously for the first number, from which I date the dawn of a fine literary day in Baltimore.

" After the 15th, I shall be more at leisure, and will be happy to do you any literary service in my power. You have but to hint. E. A. P."

Whether Dr. Brooks made use of the suggestions thrown out, and attempted something that would make "a fine hit," matters little, but it is consolatory to think that he had not "spoken decidedly when" the poet first saw him, otherwise the world might have had a not too charitable critique on the "surreptitious and adventitious reputation" of Washington Irving, in lieu of the weird story of "Ligeia," which was Poe's contribution to the initial number of the periodical.

"Ligeia," the poet's favourite tale, was suggested, he says,[*] *by a dream*—a dream in which the eyes of the heroine produced the intense effect described in the fourth paragraph of the work. "Ligeia," heralded by one of those splendid passages which begem Joseph Glanvill's "Essays," assumes for its motto, "Man doth not yield himself to the angels, nor unto death utterly, save only through the weakness of his feeble will." A theme more congenial to the dream-haunted brain of Poe could scarcely be devised; and in his exposition of the thoughts suggested by its application he has been more than usually successful. The failure of Death to annihilate Will was, indeed, a suggestion that the poet—dreadingly, despairingly, familiar as he was with charnel secrets—could not fail to grasp at with the energy of hope, and adorn with the funereal flowers of his grave-nourished fantasy. In Poe's gradual and unnoted steps towards proving the impossible possible, his reader's reason is fettered, and his mind is blinded to the impassable limits of nature with such careful art, that he loses all hold on fact, and is ready and willing for the nonce to credit the reality of any mental chimera the wizard chooses

---

[*] In a MS. note, on a revised copy of the tale in my possession. —J. H. I.

to conjure up. At the *dénouement* of such a tale, one feels as if awakening from a nightmare : the knowledge that it is fiction is still for a while overclouded with the horrible thought that *it might be true.*

Like most of Poe's other tales, " Ligeia " was frequently revised and altered, and did not originally contain, as it does now, that most weird and most original of all his poems, " The Conqueror Worm."

The two other literary engagements to which the poet alluded in his letter to Dr. Brooks were with the Pittsburgh *Literary Examiner* and the Philadelphia *Gentleman's Magazine.* The latter was the property of Mr. W. E. Burton, an Englishman, who obtained some reputation in his days as a comedian, and then attempted to add to it as a *littérateur,* an attempt in which he was scarcely so successful. Poe appears to have contributed some odds and ends to the *Gentleman's Magazine* almost from his first arrival in Philadelphia, but it was not until July of the following year, when he was appointed editor, that he published anything of note in its pages. In the last month of 1838, he contributed to the *Museum* " The Signora Zenobia," and its pendant " The Scythe of Time," afterwards respectively renamed " How to Write a Blackwood Article," and " A Predicament."

In *The Gift* for 1839 appeared " William Wilson," one of the poet's finest tales, and one in many parts confessedly autobiographical. In an eulogistic but discriminative review of Hawthorne, published in *Graham's Magazine,* Poe drew attention to certain incidents in " Howe's Masquerade " that might be deemed to resemble plagiarism from " William Wilson," and "*might be* a very flattering coincidence of thought " by his

countryman ; but the strangest thing about it is, that
Poe's own tale is most closely paralleled in plot by a
rare drama, attributed to Calderon, called "El Encapo-
tado," which Washington Irving had called attention to.
The hero of the Spanish story, like "William Wilson,"
is throughout life thwarted in all his schemes for the
acquisition of wealth, pleasure, or love, by a mysterious
stranger, and when he ultimately forces the unknown,
at the point of the sword, to unmask, his "Fetch" or
double is beheld.* To accuse Poe of plagiarism in
this case would be unjust, for the idea of the *dual
man* permeates all civilised literatures, but it is a
severe commentary upon some of his own ill-con-
sidered critiques—which, however, have been most
bitterly avenged.

The portions of "William Wilson" referring to the
hero's school-days in England have already been transferred to these pages, but there are other passages—
evidently intended to be included in the writer's confessions—of interest here. Is it not Poe himself who
says, "I long for the sympathy—I had nearly said
for the pity—of my fellow-men. I would fain have
them believe that I have been, in some measure, the
slave of circumstances beyond human control. I would
wish them to seek out for me some little oasis of
fatality amid a wilderness of error. I would have
them allow—what they cannot refrain from allowing
—that although temptation may have erewhile
existed as great, man was never *thus*, at least, tempted
before." The usual exaggerations of boyhood's reminiscences—those days all deem they remember so distinctly, yet as a rule describe so indefinitely—are well

* *Vide* Medwin's *Life of Shelley*, vol. ii. pp. 300, 301.

marked in the portrayal of the old Stoke Newington house and its accessories ; but it is in the shadowy suggestiveness of the two "William Wilsons' " similarity that the author's power is displayed. The "singular whisper" of the one boy which grew to be "the very echo" of his namesake's ; the coincidence of birthdays and of names ; the non-observance of the resemblance by the other pupils ; the gradually increasing aversion for the wise monitions proffered by his *alter ego*, and the terrible signification of the one "William Wilson" *being asleep*, when his bedside was visited by the other, on the last night of his stay in the Academy, are all strokes of a master's hand——of a master who stands alone and incomparable in the realm he has himself constructed.

To the *Museum* for January and February Poe contributed "Literary Small Talk," and to the April number his much-admired lyric, "The Haunted Palace." With respect to this latter arose a controversy similar to that suggested by "Howe's Masquerade :" as with that, so with this, Poe, it is alleged, deemed he had been copied, and that Longfellow's "Beleaguered City" was a plagiarism of his idea, and is stated to have referred to the undeniable fact that his poem appeared first, Longfellow's not being published until November 1839, when it appeared in the *Southern Literary Messenger*. Of all men *literati* should be the first to recognise the fact that human invention is not infinite, and that similar ideas frequently occur almost simultaneously to different persons, it is, therefore, both rational and just to assume the resemblance between the poems of Poe and Longfellow to have been accidental. At all events, a similar fantasy to theirs had

I

been embodied in Tennyson's " Deserted House," published as early as 1830.

"The House of Usher," another of the poet's *chefs
d'œuvre,* illustrative of belief—a belief shared by
many of the good and great—in the sentience of all
matter, was published in the September number of
the *Gentleman's Magazine,* to which publication, as
already remarked, Poe had been appointed editor.
Mr. White, of the *Literary Messenger,* alluding in his
October issue to the tale and its author, remarks—
" We are pleased to find that our old assistant,
Edgar A. Poe, is connected with Burton in the editorial management of the *Gentleman's Magazine.* Mr.
Poe is favourably known to the readers of the
Messenger as a gentleman of fine endowment ; possessing a taste classical and refined. . . We always pre-
dicted that Mr. Poe would reach a high grade in
American literature;" only, adds his former employer,
" we wish Mr. Poe would stick to the department of
criticism ; *there,* he is an able professor." It was this
" sticking to criticism," to oblige publishers, instead
of following the true bent of his genius, that ruined
Poe's personal reputation, and lost the world many a
priceless poem and wondrous tale.

In the " Fall of the House of Usher," is developed
one of its author's favourite methods of riveting his
reader's attention. As in so many of his stories, instead
of soliciting sympathy for himself as the hero, he the
rather would appear to repel it, by assuming the
rôle, in his person of narrator, of a somewhat matter-
of-fact, even commonplace, practical character, in no
way *en rapport* with the eccentric or visionary friend
who is the real hero. He, Poe, pretends to come

before the stage, or to remain on it only in the minor
character of " Chorus," and thus casts a further air
of reality on the personages he introduces, by deluding
his readers into the belief that they are but fellow
spectators with him. Nevertheless, in the character
of " Roderick Usher"—a character upon which the
poet lavished his most consummate art, and upon
whose surroundings he bestowed the wealth of his
own desires—is sought to be depictured what Poe
wished the world to believe he resembled, as Byron
did with his " Corsairs " and "Laras." The opium-
eating hypochondriac, the *Fear*-fearing monomaniac,
is less unlike the veritable author of "Ulalume"
than is the friend of " Usher;" the mesmeriser of
" Valdemar;" the associate of " Legrand" of "the
Gold Bug;" the cool man of the world, who only
represents the conventional half—*the side turned to
the public.*

Poe's other contributions to the *Gentleman's Magazine*, during the remainder of 1839, were not of an
important character, consisting chiefly of short book
notices, slight sketches to accompany engravings, and
reprints of his shorter poems. " William Wilson"
and "Morella" were also republished in its pages, and
in the December number appeared " The Conversation
of Eiros and Charmion." This tale, in some respects
resembling one entitled " The Comet," which had
appeared in *The Token* for 1839, describes the history
of this earth's destruction by a comet, and is supposed
to be told in Aidenn by Eiros to Charmion. The
final catastrophe is assumed to take place through the
total extraction of the nitrogen from our atmosphere,
and the consequent immediate and omnipresent

combustion of the world. The whole story is most weirdly suggestive, and the climax startling in the extreme.

Under the title of *Tales of the Grotesque and Arabesque*, Poe now published a collection of his stories, in two volumes. These tales were copyrighted in 1839, but the title-page is dated 1840, and bears upon it the motto from Goethe :—

> " Seltsamen Tochter Jovis,
> Seinem Schosskinde, der Phantasie."

The volumes are inscribed to " Colonel William Drayton, of Philadelphia, with every sentiment of respect, gratitude, and esteem," and contain this *Preface :*— " The epithets ' Grotesque ' and ' Arabesque ' will be found to indicate, with sufficient precision, the prevalent tenor of the tales here published. But from the fact that, during a period of some two or three years, I have written five-and-twenty short stories, whose general character may be so briefly defined, it cannot be fairly inferred—at all events it is not truly inferred —that I have for this species of writing any inordinate, or indeed any peculiar, taste or prepossession. I may have written with an eye to this republication in volume form, and may, therefore, have desired to preserve, as far as a certain point, a certain unity of design. This is, indeed, the fact ; and it may even happen that, in this manner, I shall never compose anything again. I speak of these things here, because I am led to think it is the prevalence of the ' Arabesque ' in my serious tales, which has induced one or two critics to tax me, in all friendliness, with what they have been pleased to term ' Germanism ' and

gloom. The charge is in bad taste, and the grounds
of the accusation have not been sufficiently considered.
Let us admit, for the moment, that the 'phantasy-
pieces' now given *are* Germanic, or what not. Then
'Germanism' is the vein for the time being. To-morrow I may be anything but German, as yesterday I
was everything else. These many pieces are yet one
book. My friends would be quite as wise in taxing
an astronomer with too much astronomy, or an ethical
author with treating too largely of morals. But the
truth is that, with a single exception, there is no one
of these stories in which the scholar should recognise
the distinctive features of that species of pseudo-horror
which we are taught to call Germanic, for no better
reason than some of the secondary names of German
literature have become identified with its folly. If
in many of my productions terror has been the thesis,
I maintain that terror is not of Germany, but of the
soul,—that I have deduced this terror only from its
legitimate sources, and urged it only to its legitimate
results.

"There are one or two of the articles here [conceived
and executed in the purest spirit of extravaganza], to
which I expect no serious attention, and of which I
shall speak no farther. But for the rest I cannot
conscientiously claim indulgence on the score of hasty
effort. I think it best becomes me to say, therefore,
that if I have sinned, I have deliberately sinned.
These brief compositions are, in chief part, the results
of matured purpose and very careful elaboration."

Besides the tales already referred to in these pages,
this two volume collection contains the inferior
humoristic pieces, " The man that was used up," " The

Devil in the Belfry," " Von Jung "—now known as
" Mystification "—and " Why the little Frenchman
wears his hand in a sling." This collection does not
appear to have received much notice from the press,
or to have made any impression upon the public : the
edition, which was probably very small, disappeared,
and copies of it are of the most extreme rarity.

*Among the various publications Poe was now
writing for may be mentioned *Alexander's Weekly
Messenger*, in which he was airing his theory respecting
cryptology, to the effect that human ingenuity could
not construct any cryptograph human ingenuity could
not decipher. Tested by several correspondents with
specimens of their skill in the art of secret writing,
the poet actually took the trouble to examine and
solve them in triumphant proof, apparently, of the
truth of his theory. Another, and scarcely more
literary, labour in which he engaged at this time, in
the ceaseless effort " to keep the wolf from the door,"
was the production of a conchological manual for the
use of schools. Anent this work slander and malice
have said their worst; an enemy, evidently he whose
calumnies, under the guise of " a Memoir," have overclouded the poet's memory ever since his death,
spoke these words in the columns of the Philadelphia
Saturday Evening Post :—" One of the most remarkable
plagiarisms was perpetrated by Mr. Poe. . . . This
gentleman, a few years ago, in Philadelphia, published
a work on Conchology as original, when in reality it
was a copy, nearly verbatim, of ' The Text-Book of
Conchology,' by Captain Thomas Brown, printed in
Glasgow in 1833, a duplicate of which we have in
our library. Mr. Poe actually took out a copyright

for the American edition of Captain Brown's work,
and, omitting all mention of the English original, pretended, in the preface, to have been under great
obligations to several scientific gentlemen of this city.
It is but justice to add, that in the second edition of
this book, published lately in Philadelphia, the name
of Mr. Poe is withdrawn from the title-page, and his
initials only affixed to the preface. But the affair is
one of the most curious on record."

Having allowed the slanderer his say, the poet's
own response, *not* included in the above-mentioned
"Memoir," shall be given; but it may be stated that
Poe's work is *not* a plagiarism of Captain Brown's;
that he alluded to obligations to two persons only,
one at least of whom, Professor Wyatt, a Scotchman
—unaware that the calumny had ever reached Poe's
eyes, and not hearing of it himself until ten years
after the poet's death—gave an independent, but
similar explanatory denial of the accusation in the
Home Journal; that Poe's name was *not* withdrawn
from the title-page of the second edition, which was
called for immediately after the publication of the
first, and not after an interval of several years as
suggested by the paragraphist.

The poet's letter reads thus :—

"NEW YORK, *Feb.* 16, '47.

"MY DEAR SIR,—Some weeks ago I mailed you two
newspapers which, from what you say in your last letter,
I see you have not received. I now enclose some slips which
will save me the necessity of writing on painful topics. By
and by I will write you more at length.

"*Please reinclose the slips when read.*

"What you tell me about the accusation of plagiarism
made by the *Phil. Sat. Ev. Post* surprises me. It is the

first I heard of it—with the exception of a hint in one of your previous letters—but which I did not then comprehend. Please let me know as many *particulars* as you can remember —for I must see into the charge. Who edits the paper? who publishes it? &c. &c. &c. About what time was the accusation made? I assure you that it is *totally* false. In 1840 I published a book with this title—'The Conchologist's First Book: A system of Testacious Malacology, arranged especially for the use of Schools, in which the animals, *according to Cuvier*, are given with the shells, a great number of new species added, and the whole brought up, as accurately as possible, to the present condition of the science. By Edgar A. Poe. With illustrations of 215 shells, presenting a correct type of each genus.'

"This, I presume, is the work referred to. I wrote it in conjunction with Professor Thomas Wyatt, and Professor McMurtrie, of Philadelphia—my name being put to the work, as best known and most likely to aid its circulation. I wrote the Preface and Introduction, and translated from Cuvier the accounts of the animals, &c. *All* school-books are necessarily made in a similar way. The very title-page acknowledges that the animals are given 'according to Cuvier.' This charge is infamous, and I shall prosecute for it, as soon as I settle my accounts with 'The Mirror.' *
—Truly your friend,   E. A. POE."

The poet's letter having given the title-page minus only the words, "Published for the Author by Haswell, Barrington, and Haswell," and "Second Edition" added to the title of second issue, it need not be repeated, but the "Prefaces" to the first and second editions are worth recapitulation. The first is:—

"The term 'Malacology,' an abbreviation of 'Malacozoology,' from the greek μαλακος, *soft*, ζωον, *an animal*, and λογος, *a discourse*, was first employed by the French naturalist, De Blainville, to designate an important division of Natural

---

* *Vide* Account of "Action for Libel, Poe *v. Evening Mirror*," vol. ii. p. 113.

History, in which the leading feature of the animals discussed was the *softness* of the flesh, or, to speak with greater accuracy, of the general envelope. This division comprehends not only the *Mollusca*, but also the *Testacea* of Aristotle and of Pliny, and of course, had reference to molluscous animals in general,—of which the greater portion have shells.

"A treatise concerning the shells, exclusively, of this greater portion, is termed, in accordance with general usage, a treatise upon Conchology or Conchyliology ; although the word is somewhat improperly applied, as the Greek *conchylion*, from which it is derived, embraces in its signification both the animal and the shell. Ostracology would have been more definite.

"The common works upon this subject, however, will appear to every person of science very essentially defective, inasmuch as the *relation* of the animal and shell, with their dependence upon each other, is a radically important consideration in the examination of either. Neither in the attempt to obviate this difficulty is a work upon Malacology at large necessarily included. Shells, it is true, form, and, for many obvious reasons, will continue to form, the subject of chief interest, whether with regard to the school or the cabinet; still there is no good reason why a book upon *Conchology* (using the common term) may not be malacological as far as it proceeds.

"In this view of the subject, the present little work is offered to the public. Beyond the ruling feature—that of giving an anatomical account of each animal, together with a description of the shell which it inhabits,—I have aimed at little more than accuracy and simplicity, as far as the latter quality can be thought consistent with the rigid exactions of science.

"No attention has been given to the mere *History* of the subject ; it is conceived that any disquisition on this head would more properly appertain to works of ultimate research, than to one whose sole intention is to make the pupil acquainted, in as tangible a form as possible, with results. To afford, at a cheap rate, a concise, yet a sufficiently comprehensive, and especially a well illustrated school-book, has been the principal design.

"In conclusion, I have only to acknowledge my great indebtedness to the valuable public labours, as well as private assistance, of Mr. Isaac Lea, of Philadelphia.   To Mr. Thomas Wyatt, and his excellent *Manual of Conchology*, I am also under many obligations.   No better work, perhaps, could be put into the hands of the student as a secondary text-book. Its beautiful and perfectly well-coloured illustrations afford an aid in the collection of a cabinet scarcely to be met with elsewhere.   E. A. P."

The Preface to the second edition is :—

"In issuing a second edition of this 'Conchology,' in so very brief a period since the publication of the first large impression, the author has little more to do than to express the high pleasure with which he has seen his labours well received.   The success of the work has been decided ; and the entire design has been accomplished in its general introduction into schools.

"Many important alterations and additions are now made ; errors of the press carefully corrected ; and the work, upon the whole, is rendered more worthy of the public approbation.
                                                              "E. A. P."

For the novice, Captain Brown's "Text Book" may bear some resemblance to Poe's "First Book," from the simple fact that both treatises are founded upon one and the same system ; but the absurd charge, that one is, therefore, a plagiarism of the other, can only have been made through gross ignorance or wilful falsehood.   As a sequence of these scientific studies, Poe published a translation and digest of Lemonnier's "Natural History," and some other kindred writings.

On the title-page of the *Gentleman's Magazine* for 1840 appear the names of Burton and Poe as joint-editors, although the duties of the former were merely nominal, all the editorial labour devolving upon the poet.   For the new volume Poe agreed to write a romance, to be published in serial form, and the first instalment of this story appeared in the

January number. "The Journal of Julius Rodman: being an Account of the First Passage across the Rocky Mountains of North America ever achieved by Civilised Man." The projected work was never completed in Burton's Magazine, for reasons that will be seen further on, and its authorship was never hinted at by the various journalists who have published "Memoirs of Poe," until the happy discovery of a letter from the poet to Burton first gave us the clue to its existence. The publication of "Rodman's Journal" in the complete form in which, there is some reason for believing, Poe left the story, would certainly sustain, if it could not increase, its author's reputation. It is written in the realistic manner of "Arthur Gordon Pym," and although the fragment at present published breaks off at the moment when the "Journal" first begins to grow exciting, there is every probability that the remainder of the work was calculated to prove of absorbing interest. The non-publication in a complete form of the tale was, doubtless, due to the subsidence of public interest in exploration of the district to which the "Journal" refers. The tale was carried on through the six first numbers of the *Gentleman's* for 1840, and even in its present fragmentary state, is well worthy perusal on account of the idiosyncratic manner in which its author identifies himself with his hero—a hero who suffers from "hereditary hypochondria;" "was possessed with a burning love of nature; and worshipped her, perhaps, more in her dreary and savage aspects, than in her manifestations of placidity and joy." It is unnecessary to furnish an analysis of the work, but some comments upon it by Mr. William

Sawyer,* one of Poe's staunchest admirers and a poet himself, are apposite here:—"Without being one of Poe's most striking, this is certainly one of his most remarkable works," he observes. "It displays singular learning of a varied and exhaustive nature, and is a peculiar example of his unique power of giving his fancies the air of reality. Julius Rodman is placed before us as a real flesh-and-blood adventurer, and the early part of the narrative is occupied with details of the preparations for the journey, told to the minutest particular, as if seen to, and set down at the moment by one engaged in making them. The companions of the expedition are all described in detail, so that we seem to live among the persons with whom we are setting out; and after we are once on the journey the incidents, big and little, are recorded day by day as in a log, without literary effort, so that the *vraisemblance* is perfect. . . . The narrative is left unfinished. The Rocky Mountains are not crossed so far as we are permitted to accompany the party, and it is doubtful whether the hand which worked so deftly so far, ever added another line to what would, if carried to completion, have been a work of the type of 'Robinson Crusoe'—a fictitious personal narrative, with the stamp of reality set upon it by the creative power of genius, aided by exceptional capacity for observation and knowledge."

Poe's only other contribution to the *Gentleman's* for January calling for notice, is a review of Moore's "Alciphron." In the course of this critique he advanced the proposition—not a very novel one, perhaps—that the mind of man can *imagine* nothing

* In the London *Mirror* for November 3rd, 1877.

which has not really existed. Granting, "we can imagine a *griffin*, and that a griffin does not exist," he says in summing up, "not the griffin certainly, but its component parts. It is a mere compendium of known limbs and features—of known qualities. Thus with all that seems to be *new*—which appears to be a *creation* of intellect—it is resolvable into the old. The wildest and most vigorous effort of mind cannot stand the test of this analysis." This same critique also contains Poe's views, in opposition to those of Coleridge, on the suggested difference between *Fancy* and *Imagination*, he citing, as example of the merely fanciful, some lines from "The Culprit Fay"—a then popular American piece—and, as of the loftiest imagination, a piece from Shelley's "Queen Mab."

The February and March issues of the magazine contained little of value by Poe beyond "Rodman's Journal;" there was his sketch, in the former, of "The Business Man"—then headed "Peter Pendulum;"—various odds and ends, and a portion—some being by another hand—of the book notices. These latter included a review of Longfellow's "Voices of the Night," in which, whilst awarding his countryman very high praise as a poet, he charged him with plagiarising the conception of "The Midnight Mass for the Dying Year" from Tennyson's "Death of the Old Year." Beyond instalments of "Rodman's Journal," the April and May numbers did not contain much noticeable writing by Poe, but the former included "Silence: a sonnet," with the burden of "No more" —the germ of a refrain to be so famous hereafter— and the latter a critique on Bryant, and an essay on "The Philosophy of Furniture." The last sketch was subsequently revised and enlarged, but even then portrayed its author's artistic love of the luxurious and beautiful. With the June number the *Gentleman's Magazine* passed from Mr. Burton's hands into the possession of Mr. George R. Graham, and, at the same time, Edgar Poe's editorial duties came to an end. The following letter from the poet to Mr. Burton will throw some light upon the affair :—

"Sir,—I find myself at leisure this Monday morning, June 1, to notice your very singular letter of Saturday. . . . I have followed the example of Victorine and slept upon the matter, and you shall now hear what I have to say. In the first place, your attempts to bully me excite in my mind scarcely any other sentiment than mirth. When you address me again preserve, if you can, the dignity of a gentleman. . . I shall feel myself more at liberty to be explicit. As for the rest, you do me gross injustice ; and you know it. As usual, you have wrought yourself into a passion with me on account of some imaginary wrong ; for no real injury, or attempt at injury, have you ever received at my hands. As I live, I am utterly unable to say why you are angry, or what true grounds of complaint you have against me. You are a man of impulses ; have made yourself, in consequence, some enemies ; have been in many respects ill-treated by those whom you had looked upon as friends—and these things have rendered you suspicious. You once wrote in your magazine a sharp critique upon a book of mine—a very silly book—Pym. Had I written a similar criticism upon a book of yours, you feel that you would have been my enemy for life, and you therefore imagine in my bosom a latent hostility towards yourself. This has been a mainspring in your whole conduct towards me since our first acquaintance. It has acted to prevent all cordiality. In a general view of human nature your idea is just—but you will find yourself puzzled in judging me by ordinary motives. Your criticism was essentially correct, and therefore, although severe, it did not occasion in me one solitary emotion either of anger or dislike. But even while I write these words, I am sure you will not believe

them. Did I not still think you, in spite of the exceed-
ing littleness of some of your hurried actions, a man of
many honorable impulses, I should not now take the
trouble to send you this letter. I cannot permit myself
to suppose that you would say to me in cool blood what
you said in your letter of yesterday. You are, of course,
only mistaken, in asserting that I owe you a hundred dollars,
and you will rectify the mistake at once when you come to
look at your accounts.

Soon after I joined you, you made me an offer of money,
and I accepted $20. Upon another occasion, at my request,
you sent me enclosed in a letter $30. Of this 30, I repaid
20 within the next fortnight (drawing no salary for that
period). I was thus still in your debt $30, when not long
ago I again asked a loan of $30, which you promptly handed
to me at your own house. Within the last three weeks, three
dollars each week have been retained from my salary, an
indignity which I have felt deeply but did not resent. You
state the sum retained as $8, but this I believe is through a
mistake of Mr. Morrell. My postage bill, at a guess, might
be $9 or $10—and I therefore am indebted to you, upon the
whole, in the amount of about $60. More than this sum I
shall not pay. You state that you can no longer afford to
pay $50 per month for 2 or 3 pp. of MS. Your error here
can be shown by reference to the Magazine. During my
year with you I have written—

In July	5 pp.
,, August	9 ,,
,, Sept.	16 ,,
,, Oct.	4 ,,
,, Nov.	5 ,,
,, Dec.	12 ,,
,, Jan.	9 ,,
,, Feb.	12 ,,
,, March	11 ,,
,, April	17 ,,
,, May	14 ,, + 5 copied—Miss McMichael's MS.
,, June	9 ,, + 3 ,, Chandlers.

132 (*sic*)

"Dividing this sum by 12, we have an average of 11 pp.
per month—not 2 or 3. And this estimate leaves out of

question everything in the way of extract or compilation. Nothing is counted but *bonâ fide* composition. 11 pp. at \$3 per p. would be \$33, at the usual Magazine prices. Deduct this from \$50, my monthly salary, and we have left \$17 per month, or \$4 $\frac{25}{100}$ per week, for the services of proof-reading ; general superintendence at the printing office; reading, altera- tion, and preparation of MSS., with compilation of various articles, such as Plate articles, Field Sports, &c. Neither has anything been said of my name upon your title-page, a small item, you will say — but still something, as you know. Snowden pays his editresses \$2 per week each for their names *solely.* Upon the whole, I am not willing to admit that you have greatly overpaid me. That I did not do four times as much as I did for the Magazine was your own fault. At first I wrote long articles, which you deemed inadmissible, and never did I suggest any to which you had not some im- mediate and decided objection. Of course I grew discouraged, and could feel no interest in the journal.

"I am at a loss to know why you call me selfish. If you mean that I borrowed money of you—you know that you offered it, and you know that I am poor. In what instance has any one ever found me selfish ? Was there selfishness in the affront I offered Benjamin (whom I respect, and who spoke well of me) because I deemed it a duty not to receive from any one commendation at your expense ? . . . I have said that I could not tell why you were angry. Place yourself in my situation, and see whether you would not have acted as I have done. You first 'enforced,' as you say, a deduction of salary : giving me to understand thereby that you thought of parting company. You next spoke disrespectfully of me be- hind my back—this as an habitual thing—to those whom you supposed your friends, and who punctually retailed me, as a matter of course, every ill-natured word which you uttered. Lastly, you advertised your magazine for sale without saying a word to me about it. I felt no anger at what you did— none in the world. Had I not firmly believed it your design to give up your journal, with a view of attending to the Theatre, I should never have dreamed of attempting one of my own. The opportunity of doing something for myself seemed a good one—(and I was about to be thrown out of business)—and I embraced it. Now I ask you, as a man of honor and as a man of sense—what is there wrong in all this? What have I done at which you have any right to take offence? I can give you no definitive answer (respecting the continuation of Rodman's Journal) until I hear from you again. The charge of $100 I shall not admit for an instant. If you persist in it our intercourse is at an end, and we can each adopt our own measures.

"In the meantime, I am,

"Yr. Obt. St.,

"EDGAR A. POE.

"WM. E. BURTON, Esq."

Whatever soreness there may have been at this time between the co-editors, it appears to have ultimately worn away, for Poe spoke in friendly terms of Burton in his subsequent papers on "Autography," and Burton wrote defending the poet when, upon his decease, his character was assailed. Doubtless an amicable arrangement was subsequently arrived at, and, in all probability, Poe repaid his indebtedness— set forth in this letter with all his habitual carefulness—by a certain amount of "copy" to be used, and which was used, apparently, in the magazine after it passed out of the possession of its founder into the hands of Mr. Graham.

After his severance from the *Gentleman's,* Poe endeavoured to found a new monthly journal of his own, to be called the *Penn Magazine,* but the project fell through after the prospectus had been circulated among the members of the publishing world. The chief wording of this prospectus was subsequently adopted for the basis of a later project, to be adverted to hereafter, and need not, therefore, be cited from. Want of the necessary funds, and inability to secure a sufficient number of subscribers doubtless caused the failure of the poet's scheme.

K

CHAPTER XII.

EDITOR OF GRAHAM'S MAGAZINE.

FOR the five months following Poe's secession, nothing of his of any consequence appeared in the *Gentleman's Magazine.* The purchaser, Mr. Graham, was not only a man of literary proclivities but also a shrewd man of business, and he speedily recognised the value of the ex-editor's services. In November, therefore, he arranged with Poe to resume his former post on the magazine, which from the beginning of the forthcoming new year was to be amalgamated with another periodical styled the *Casket,* and henceforward was to be known as *Graham's Magazine.* To the last—the December—number of the *Gentleman's,* Poe contributed his gruesome sketch, "The Man of the Crowd." This weird record of the solitude-dreading mortal—this impersonation of La Bruyere's "*grand malheur de ne pouvoir être seul* "—appeals more strongly to the human heart than any of its author's other prose works, the majority of which, as is so generally acknowledged, subdue the intellect only. What a fascination for the thoughtful, whose thinking is prompted by heart as well as brain, lurks in these opening sentences of the tale !

"It was well said of a certain German book that ' *es läszt sich nicht lesen* '—it does not permit itself to be read. There are some secrets which do not permit themselves to be told. Men die nightly in their beds, wringing the hands of ghostly confessors, and looking them piteously in the eyes, die with despair of heart and convulsion in throat, on account of the hideousness of mysteries which will not *suffer themselves* to be revealed. Now and then, alas, the conscience of man takes up a burthen so heavy in horror that it can be thrown down only into the grave. And thus the essence of all crime is undivulged."

The description of a convalescent's feelings of serene contentment in the return of health, when he finds himself "in one of those happy moods which are so precisely the converse of *ennui*—moods of the keenest appetency, when the film from the mental vision departs," is a faithful portrayal of the experience of many, and is, therefore, widely different from Poe's usual psychological observations, which are mostly based upon the *outrè* and the abnormal. "The Man of the Crowd" stands forth as a specimen of its author's real genius—his masterly powers of combined suggestiveness and description.

From the beginning of 1841, and for some time henceforward, the history of Edgar Poe is merged into, and becomes chiefly, the recital of his literary labours, the most remarkable of which now consisted of contributions to *Graham's Magazine.* The worthy proprietor of that publication speedily received due reward for his appreciation of Poe's talents. Indeed, it is declared that in a little less than two years the number of subscribers to the magazine increased from five to fifty-two thousand, and this, although aided by Mr. Graham's liberality to his contributors, was mainly due to the new editor. His daring critiques, his analytic essays, and his weird stories, following one another in rapid succession, startled the public, and compelled it to an acknowledgment of his powers. New enemies were created, however, by the dauntless intrepidity with which he assailed the fragile reputations of the small bookmakers, especially in his pungent papers on " Autography."

In the April number of *Graham's* appeared Poe's world-famed story of " The Murders in the Rue Morgue." It was the first of a series—the series aptly termed by Baudelaire, *" une espéce de trilogie "*— illustrative of an analytic phase of its author's complex mind. The particular idiosyncrasy in which the tale germinated is thus introduced in the exordium :—

" The mental features discoursed of as the analytical are, in themselves, but little susceptible of analysis. We appreciate them only in their effects. We know of them, among other things, that they are always to their possessor, when inordinately possessed, a source of the liveliest enjoyment. As the strong man exults in his physical ability, delighting in such exercises as call his muscles into action, so glories the analyst in that moral activity which *disentangles.* He derives pleasure from even the most trivial occupations bringing his talent into play. He is fond of enigmas, of conundrums, of hieroglyphics ; exhibiting in his solutions of each a degree of *acumen* which appears to the ordinary apprehension preternatural. His results, brought about by the very soul and essence of method, have, in truth, the whole air of intuition.

" The faculty of re-solution is possibly much invigorated by mathematical study, and especially by that highest branch of it which, unjustly, and merely on account of its retrograde operations, has been called, as if *par excellence*, analysis. Yet to calculate is not in itself to analyse. A chess-player, for example, does the one without effort at the other. It follows that the game of chess, in its effects upon mental character, is greatly misunderstood. . . . I will, therefore, take occasion to assert that the higher powers of the reflective intellect are more decidedly and more usefully tasked by the unostentatious game of draughts than by all the elaborate frivolity of chess. In this latter, where the pieces have different and *bizarre* motions, with various and variable values, what is only complex is mistaken (a not unusual error) for what is profound. The *attention* is here called powerfully into play. If it flag for an instant, an oversight is committed, resulting in injury or defeat. The possible moves being not only manifold but involute, the chances of such oversights are multiplied; and in nine cases out of ten it is the more concentrative rather than the more acute player who conquers. In draughts, on the contrary, where the moves are *unique* and have but little variation, the probabilities of inadvertence are diminished, and the mere attention being left comparatively unemployed, what advantages are obtained by either party are obtained by superior *acumen*. To be less abstract—let us suppose a game of draughts where the pieces are reduced to four kings, and where, of course, no oversight is to be expected. It is obvious that here the victory can be decided (the players being at all equal) only by some *recherché* movement, the result of some strong exertion of the intellect. Deprived of ordinary resources, the analyst throws himself into the spirit of his opponent, identifies himself therewith, and not unfrequently sees thus, at a glance, the sole methods (sometimes indeed absurdly simple ones) by which he may seduce into error or hurry into miscalculation.

"Whist has long been noted for its influence upon what is termed the calculating power; and men of the highest order of intellect have been known to take an apparently unaccountable delight in it, while eschewing chess as frivolous. Beyond doubt there is nothing of a similar nature so greatly tasking the faculty of analysis. The best chess-player in Christendom *may* be little more than the best player of chess; but proficiency in whist implies capacity for success in all those more important undertakings where mind struggles with mind. When I say proficiency, I mean that perfection in the game which includes a comprehension of *all* the sources whence legitimate advantage may be derived. These are not only manifold but multiform, and lie frequently among recesses of thought altogether inaccessible to the ordinary understanding. To observe attentively is to remember distinctly; and, so far, the concentrative chess-player will do very well at whist; while the rules of Hoyle (themselves based upon the mere mechanism of the game) are sufficiently and generally comprehensible. Thus to have a retentive memory, and to proceed by 'the book,' are points commonly regarded as the sum total of good playing. But it is in matters beyond the limits of mere rule that the skill of the analyst is evinced. He makes, in silence, a host of observations and inferences. So, perhaps, do his companions; and the difference in the extent of the information obtained lies not so much in the validity of the inference as in the quality of the observation. The necessary knowledge is that of *what* to observe. Our player confines himself not at all; nor, because the game is the object, does he reject deductions from things external to the game. He examines the countenance of his partner, comparing it carefully with that of each of his opponents. He considers the mode of assorting the cards in each hand; often counting trump by trump, and honour by honour, through the glances bestowed by their holders upon each. He notes every variation of face as the play progresses, gathering a fund of thought from the differences in the expression of certainty, of surprise, of triumph, or of chagrin. From the manner of gathering up a trick he judges whether the person taking it can make another in the suit. He recognises what is played through feint, by the air with which it is thrown upon the table. A casual or inadvertent word; the accidental dropping or turning of a card, with the accompanying anxiety or carelessness in regard to its concealment; the counting of the tricks, with the order of their arrangement; embarrassment, hesitation, eagerness or trepidation—all afford, to his apparently intuitive perception, indications of the true state of affairs. The first two or three rounds having been played, he is in full possession of the contents of each hand, and thenceforward puts down his cards with as absolute a precision of purpose as if the rest of the party had turned outward the faces of their own.

"The analytical power should not be confounded with simple ingenuity; for while the analyst is necessarily ingenious, the ingenious man is often remarkably incapable of analysis. The constructive or combining power, by which ingenuity is usually manifested, and to which the phreno-logists (I believe erroneously) have assigned a separate organ, supposing it a primitive faculty, has been so frequently seen in those whose intellect bordered otherwise upon idiocy, as to have attracted general observation among writers on morals. Between ingenuity and the analytic ability there exists a difference far greater indeed than that between the fancy and the imagination, but of a character very strictly analogous. It will be found, in fact, that the ingenious are always fanciful, and the *truly* imaginative never otherwise than analytic."

" The Murders in the Rue Morgue " (as also the two narratives in a similar strain which shortly followed), are desired by their author to be read somewhat in the light of commentaries upon the propositions advanced in the preceding remarks. Accepted as fic-tion merely, their merit is pre-eminently conspicuous, but as demonstrations of the mental problems to which they refer, they deserve the earnest attention of the psychologist and moral philosopher, and entitle Poe's works to study in quarters where the produc-tions of the mere romancist are rarely or never known.

Poe's name was first introduced to the French public by " The Murders in the Rue Morgue," the tale, shortly after its appearance in *Graham's*, being copied with complimentary comment into the Paris *Charivari*, the translator objecting, however, that no such street as the *Rue Morgue* existed (" so far as he knew," says Poe) in Paris. This circumstance was also cited in after years by Baudelaire as one of a series of proofs that the poet had never visited the French metropolis ! Some years later the tale reappeared in *Le Commerce*, as an original *feuilleton*, under the title of " L'Orang-

Otang," and shortly afterwards *La Quotidienne*, aware, apparently, of the source whence the work had been obtained, transferred it bodily to its own columns. This being noticed by a third journal as a case of gross plagiarism, a lawsuit was instituted, during the hearing of which *Le Commerce* proved that Edgar Poe was the real and sole author of the story in question. The interest created by this legal inquiry induced Madame Isabella Meunier to translate several of Poe's tales for the *Democratic Pacifique* and other French journals.

In the May number of *Graham's* appeared another of Poe's prose *chefs d'œuvre*, the weird narrative entitled "A Descent into the Maelström." Scientific truth and poetic invention have never been more artistically blended than in this most marvellous and idiosyncratic tale : its author having learned the natural secret that a cylindrical body, revolving in a vortex, offers more resistance to its suction, and is consequently drawn into it with greater difficulty than bodies of any other form of equal bulk, instead of inditing a chapter on mechanics, charms all readers with a story of weird and fascinating power.

On the first of the same month he contributed to the Philadelphia *Saturday Evening Post*—a paper belonging to Mr. Graham, and for which Poe wrote critiques—another startling manifestation of his analytic capabilities, in a *prospective* review of Dickens's story of "Barnaby Rudge." In this review the poet explained with mathematical exactitude what should be the plot of the as-yet-unwritten story, and the correctness of his solution drew from Dickens a letter of flattering acknowledgment, in which he inquired whether Mr. Poe had dealings with the devil. Alluding to the poet's wonderful analysis of his plot, Dickens says, " By the way, are you aware that Godwin wrote his ' Caleb Williams ' backwards ? He first involved his hero in a web of difficulties, forming the second volume, and then, for the first, cast about him for some mode of accounting for what had been done." Some years later, Poe, commenting upon this remark, after noting that this was not the *precise* mode of procedure on Godwin's part, says, " But the author of ' Caleb Williams ' was too good an artist not to perceive the advantage derivable from at least a somewhat similar process," a process, indeed, not altogether divergent from Poe's own acknowledged method of retaining the *dénouement* of his work always before him, and subordinating all incident, tone, even verbal combination, to the development of this idea. But for deficiency in construction of plot he criticised the author of " Pickwick," deeming that he had no positive *genius* for *adaptation*, and still less, in Poe's judgment, " for that metaphysical art in which the souls of all *mysteries* lie," yet apart from this drawback, he expressed an intense reverence for Dickens, deeming him England's greatest living novelist.

In the July number of *Graham's* Poe reverted to his favourite theme of cryptography, in an article styled " A few Words on Secret Writing." It was a subject to which he had already devoted some time, both at home and in the papers of New York and Philadelphia, and this magazine article was the result of, and in connection with, his challenges to the public to produce a cryptographic riddle he should not be able to resolve. " The facility with which he would unravel the most dark and perplexing ciphers," writes a clerical friend, "was really supernatural. Out of a most confused medley of letters, figures, and cabalistic characters, in any of the seven different languages, the English, German, French, Spanish, Italian, Latin and Greek, his wonderful power of analysis would, almost at once, evolve sense, order, and beauty; and of the hundreds of cryptographs which he received while editor of one of our popular periodicals, he never failed to solve one unless it was illegitimate, that is, unless its author put it together not intending to have it made sense. During a visit which he paid to Lowell, designing to test his cryptographical skill, I wrote a short paragraph somewhat in the following fashion.* . . . The sentence was this:—

"'The patient was severely attacked with spasms and acute pain in the hypogastric region; remedial agents were employed; but without effect, and death soon ensued.' This rendered into cipher in the manner shown * above would be:— 'Gurengvragjuffrireryl nggnpxrgjigufonfzfnaqnqhgrcnvavagurulcbtnf gevpertvb aerzrqrnyntragfjrerrzcybirqohgjigubhgrssrpgnaqqrngufb bararafirq.'

"Mr. Poe solved this cipher in one-fifth of the time it took me to write it. This, however, is one of the most simple forms of cryptography."

In his magazine article, Poe deemed it scarcely possible to "imagine a time when there did not exist a necessity, or at least a desire, of transmitting information from one individual to another in such manner as to elude general comprehension," and, whilst tracing the history of the art of secret writing from dim anti-

* The process need not be described in these pages.—J. H. I.

quity, he propounds the dictum, that " means of secret
intercommunication must have existed almost contemporaneously with the invention of letters." Further
dilating upon the congenial theme, he says:—

" Few persons can be made to believe that it is not quite
an easy thing to invent a method of secret writing which
shall baffle investigation. Yet it may be roundly asserted
that human ingenuity cannot concoct a cipher which human
ingenuity cannot resolve. In the facility with which such
writing is deciphered, however, there exist very remarkable
differences in different intellects. Often, in the case of two
individuals of acknowledged equality as regards ordinary
mental efforts, it will be found that, while one cannot
unriddle the commonest cipher, the other will scarcely be
puzzled by the most abstruse. It may be observed generally that in such investigations the analytic ability is very
forcibly called into action ; and, for this reason, cryptographical solutions might with great propriety be introduced
into academies as the means of giving tone to the most
important of the powers of mind. . . .

" At a cursory glance, these various modes of constructing a cipher seem to have about them an air of inscrutable
secrecy. It appears almost an impossibility to unriddle
what has been put together by so complex a method. And
to some persons the difficulty might be great ; but to others
—to those skilled in deciphering—such enigmas are very
simple indeed. The reader should bear in mind that the
basis of the whole art of solution, as far as regards these
matters, is found in the general principles of the formation
of language itself, and thus is altogether independent of the
particular laws which govern any cipher, or the construction of its key. The difficulty of reading a cryptographical
puzzle is by no means always in accordance with the
labour or ingenuity with which it has been constructed.
The sole use of the key, indeed, is for those *au fait* to the
cipher ; in its perusal by a third party, no reference is had
to it at all. The lock of the secret is picked. In the
different methods of cryptography specified above,* it will be

_____

* In *Graham's Magazine.*—J. H. I.

observed that there is a gradually increasing complexity. But this complexity is only in shadow. It has no substance whatever. It appertains merely to the formation, and has no bearing upon the solution of the cipher. The last mode mentioned is not in the least degree more difficult to be deciphered than the first, whatever may be the difficulty of either."

Some amusing incidents growing out of Poe's dealings with cryptology are thus reverted to:—

"In the discussion of an analogous subject, in one of the weekly papers * of this city, about eighteen months ago, the writer of this article had occasion to speak of the application of a rigorous *method* in all forms of thought — of its advantages — of the extension of its use even to what is considered the operation of pure fancy — and thus, subsequently, of the solution of cipher. He even ventured to assert that no cipher, of the character above specified, could be sent to the address of the paper, which he would not be able to resolve. This challenge excited, most unexpectedly, a very lively interest among the numerous readers of the journal. Letters were poured in upon the editor from all parts of the country; and many of the writers of these epistles were so convinced of the impenetrability of their mysteries, as to be at great pains to draw him into wagers on the subject. At the same time, they were not always scrupulous about sticking to the point. The cryptographs were, in numerous instances, altogether beyond the limits defined in the beginning. Foreign languages were employed. Words and sentences were run together without interval. Several alphabets were used in the same cipher. One gentleman, but moderately endowed with conscientiousness, inditing us a puzzle composed of pot-hooks and hangers to which the wildest typography of the office could afford nothing similar, went even so far as to jumble together no less than *seven distinct alphabets*, without intervals between the letters *or between the lines*. Many of the cryptographs were dated in Philadelphia, and several

* Philadelphia *Saturday Evening Post.*—J. H. I.

of those which urged the subject of a bet were written by
gentlemen of this city. Out of, perhaps, one hundred
ciphers altogether received, there was only one which we
did not immediately succeed in resolving. This one we
demonstrated to be an imposition ; that is to say, we fully
proved it a jargon of random characters, having no meaning whatever. In respect to the epistle of the seven
alphabets, we had the pleasure of completely *nonpluss*-ing its
inditer by a prompt and satisfactory translation.

"The weekly paper mentioned was, for a period of some
months, greatly occupied with the hieroglyphic and caba-
listic-looking solutions of the cryptographs sent us from all
quarters. Yet, with the exception of the writers of the
ciphers, we do not believe that any individuals could have
been found among the readers of the journal who regarded
the matter in any other light than in that of a desperate
humbug. We mean to say that no one really believed in
the authenticity of the answers. One party averred that
the mysterious figures were only inserted to give a *queer*
air to the paper, for the purpose of attracting attention.
Another thought it more probable that we not only solved
the ciphers, but put them together ourselves for solution.
This having been the state of affairs at the period when it
was thought expedient to decline further dealings in necromancy, the writer of this article avails himself of the present opportunity to maintain the truth of the journal in
question—to repel the charges of rigmarole by which it was
assailed—and to declare, in his own name, that the ciphers
were all written in good faith, and solved in the same spirit."

The interest and excitement created by this public
discussion on secret writing continually increased; and
Poe, not liking to be conquered, continually wasted
valuable time and labour on the, to him, unprofitable
occupation of correspondence there anent, until, in the
August number of *Graham's Magazine*, the following
correspondence and comments commenced :—

"Just as we were going to press with the last sheet of
this number," writes the editor, "we received the following

letter from the well-known author of 'Clinton Bradshawe,' 'Howard Pinckney,' &c., &c. :—

"'My Dear Sir,—The enclosed cryptograph is from a friend of mine [Dr. Frailey], who thinks he can puzzle you. If you decipher it, then you are a magician ; for he has used, as I think, the greatest art in making it.—Your friend,
                                                'F. W. Thomas.'"

There is no necessity to cite the intricate puzzle which followed this note, in reply to which Poe said : " By return of mail we sent the solution to Mr. Thomas ; but as the cipher is an exceedingly ingenious one, we forbear publishing its translation here, and prefer testing the ability of our readers to solve it. *We will give a year's subscription to the magazine, and also a year's subscription to the "Saturday Evening Post," to any person, or rather to the first person, who shall read us this riddle.* We have no expectation that it will be read ; and therefore, should the month pass without an answer forthcoming, we will furnish the key to the cipher, and again offer a year's subscription to the magazine, to any person—who shall solve it *with the key*." To this Poe appended the statement that, in the magazine, he had only undertaken to decipher a certain class of cryptographs, and to this limit he must hold his correspondents, adding, " To be sure, we said that 'human ingenuity could not construct a cipher which human ingenuity could not resolve ;' but then we do not propose, just now, to make ourselves individually the test of 'human ingenuity' in general. We do not propose to solve *all* ciphers. Whether we can or cannot do this is a question for another day—a day when we have more leisure than at present we have any hope of enjoying. The most simple cryptograph requires, in its solution, labour, patience, and much time. We therefore abide by the limits of our cartel. It is true that in attempting the perusal of Dr. Frailey's we have exceeded these limits by very much; but we were seduced into the endeavour to read it by the decided manner in which an opinion was expressed that we could not."

Of *Graham's* many thousands of readers none had solved the puzzle by the time stated; its solution was, therefore, furnished in the October number, together with a letter from Dr. Frailey of Washington, as an evidence not only of its correctness but also of its attendant difficulties, not that such proof seemed requisite, after the failure of the public to decipher the enigma. It will be seen that, in order to increase the embarrassment of the would-be elucidator, the doctor had used arbitrary characters to represent *whole words*, which, taken in connection with the other difficulties mentioned in his note, and the extraordinary phraseology employed, enables us to better appreciate the work accomplished :—

"WASHINGTON, *July* 6, 1841.

"DEAR SIR,—It gives me pleasure to state that the reading by Mr. Poe, of the cryptograph which I gave you a few days since for transmission to him, is correct.

"I am the more astonished at this, since for various words. of two, three, and four letters, a distinct character was used for each, in order to prevent the discovery of some of those words, by their frequent repetition in a cryptograph of any length, and applying them to other words. I also used a distinct character for the terminations *tion* and *sion*, and substituted in every word where it was possible, some of the characters above alluded to. Where the same word of two of those letters occurred frequently, the letters of the key-phrase

and the characters were alternately used, to increase the difficulty.—As ever, yours, &c.,   Charles S. Frailey.
   "To F. W. Thomas, Esq."

This note from the propounder of the cryptograph was enclosed in the following letter from Poe's friend, Thomas:—

"Washington, *July* 6, 1841.

"My Dear Sir,—This morning I received yours of yesterday, deciphering the 'cryptograph' which I sent you last week from my friend, Doctor Frailey. You request that I would obtain the Doctor's acknowledgment of your solution; I have just received the enclosed from him.

"Doctor Frailey had heard me speak of your having deciphered a letter which our mutual friend, Dow, wrote upon a challenge from you last year, at my lodgings in your city, when Aaron Burr's correspondence in cipher was the subject of our conversation. You laughed at what you termed Burr's shallow artifice, and said you could decipher any such cryptography easily. To test you on the spot, Dow withdrew to the corner of the room, and wrote a letter in cipher, which you solved in a much shorter time than it took him to indite it.

"As Doctor Frailey seemed to doubt your skill to the extent of my belief in it, when your article on 'Secret Writing' appeared in the last number of your Magazine, I showed it to him. After reading it, he remarked that he thought he could puzzle you, and the next day he handed me the cryptograph which I transmitted to you. He did not tell me the key. The uncommon nature of his article, of which I gave you not the slightest hint, made me express to you my strong doubts of your ability to make the solution. I confess that your solution, so speedily and correctly made, surprised me. I congratulate myself that I do not live in an age when the black art is believed in, for, innocent as I am of all knowledge of cryptography, I should be arrested as an accessory before the fact, and, though I escaped, it is certain that you would have to die the death, and, alas! I fear upon my testimony. Your friend,   F. W. Thomas.

"Edgar A. Poe, Esq."

A transcript of the " solution " will afford an idea of some of the difficulties to be overcome in its discovery :—

" In one of those peripatetic circumrotations I obviated a rustic whom I subjected to catechetical interrogation respecting the nosocomical characteristics of the edifice to which I was approximate. With a volubility uncongealed by the frigorific powers of villatic bashfulness, he ejaculated a voluminous replication from the universal tenor of whose contents I deduce the subsequent amalgamation of heterogeneous facts. Without dubiety incipient pretension is apt to terminate in final vulgarity, as parturient mountains have been fabulated to produce muscupular abortions. The institution the subject of my remarks, has not been without cause the theme of the ephemeral columns of quotidian journals, and enthusiastic encomiations in conversational intercourse."

The key to this cipher is as follows :—" *But find this out, and I give it up.*"

Poe was not permitted to drop this subject so readily as he desired, at least as regards publicity. In publishing a long letter, in the December number of *Graham's*, from a Mr. Tyler—who stated that he had been practically conversant with secret writing for several years, and must admit that, in the solution of the intricate hieroglyphics submitted to him, Poe had exhibited a power of analytical and synthetical reasoning he had never seen equalled — the poet, whilst commenting upon several misapprehensions in his correspondent's communication, pointed out that his time was much occupied ; and as, notwithstanding the limits he had originally assigned to the challenged, they still continued to overwhelm him with correspondence, he must, perforce, in future decline to say anything further on the subject, deeply interesting though he found it to be.

L

Meanwhile, in addition to this cryptographic matter, and the strain of editorial duties, Poe was also contributing reviews and book notices to the monthly issues of *Graham's Magazine;* in July, amongst other matters, was a very eulogistic critique on Bolingbroke, and some remarkable utterances on the Temperance Movement. This latter, Poe declared, was the most important reformation the world had ever known, but that " its *great* feature had never yet been made a subject of comment. We mean," he explained, " that of adding to man's happiness . . . by the simple and most effectual process of exalting his capacity for enjoyment. The temperate man," he opined, " carries within his own bosom, under all circumstances, the true, the only elements of bliss."

The weird " Colloquy of Monos and Una," already alluded to in connection with the Stannard episode, appeared in the August number of *Graham's.* This tale, in its attempt to search out the secrets of mortality *beyond death*—to define the indefinable —is most masterful; nor Coleridge, nor De Quincey, nor any man, ever wrought the like; and, as a literary work, it is simply unique. The early portion of the " Colloquy " is an attack upon certain utilitarian and democratic tendencies of the time, the value and ultimate results of which were by no means perceptible to the poet. " At long intervals," one of his ultra-mortal characters remarks, "some master-minds appeared, looking upon each advance in practical science as a retrogradation in the true utility; . . . that knowledge was not meet for man in the infant condition of his soul. . . . The poets—living and perishing amid the scorn of the ' utilitarians '—

of rough pedants, who arrogated to themselves a title
which could have been properly applied only to the
scorned—these men, the poets, pondered piningly, yet
not unwisely, upon the ancient days when our wants
were not more simple than our enjoyments were keen;
—days when *mirth* was a word unknown, so solemnly
deep-toned was happiness;—holy, august, and blissful
days, when blue rivers ran undammed, between hills
unknown, into far-forest solitudes, primeval, odorous,
and unexplored. . . . Alas! we had fallen upon the
most evil of all our evil days. The great 'movement'—that was the cant term—went on: a dis-
eased commotion, moral and physical. . . . Among
other odd ideas, that of universal equality gained
ground; and in the face of analogy and of God—
in despite of the loud warning voice of the laws of
gradation so visibly pervading all things — wild
attempts at an omniprevalent democracy were made."
From this vain and vague outbreak at the nature of
surrounding things, the poet passes on to the true theme
of his imagination, to that strange attempt to pierce
the impenetrable veil which overshrouds the visage of
death made in this "Colloquy."

The same month that this tale appeared, appeared
also several reviews by Poe. In the most important
of these, that on Mr. Wilmer's "Quacks of Helicon,"
the poet's discontent at the contemporary state of
affairs is strongly expressed, and it is easy to comprehend, after perusal of this philippic, why certain
members of the American literary republic are still
so sore when Poe or Wilmer are on the *tapis.* The
former welcomes the work under review because,
among other reasons, " in the universal corruption and

rigmarole amid which we gasp for breath, it is really a pleasant thing to get even one accidental whiff of the unadulterated air of *truth*." The reviewer, after reprimanding Mr. Wilmer for the indecency of his satire, which he considers has done the work irreparable injury, without in any way enhancing its value on the score of sarcasm, vigour, or wit, as nothing vulgar should "*ever* be said or conceived," proceeds to commend the author for, above all his other merits, the far loftier merit of speaking fearlessly the truth, at an epoch when truth is out of fashion, and under circumstances of social position which would have deterred almost any man in our community from a similar Quixotism. "For the publication of the 'Quacks of Helicon,'—a poem which brings under review, by name, most of our prominent *literati*, and treats them, generally, as they deserve (what treatment could be more bitter?)—for the publication of this attack, Mr. Wilmer, whose subsistence lies in his pen, has little to look for—apart from the silent respect of those at once honest and timid—but the most malignant open or covert persecution. For this reason, and because it is the truth which he has spoken, do we say to him from the bottom of our hearts, God speed!"

" We repeat it : *it is* the truth which he has spoken ; and who shall contradict us? He has said unscrupulously what every reasonable man among us has long known to be 'as true as the Pentateuch'—that, as a literary people, we are one vast perambulating humbug. He has asserted that we are *clique*-ridden ; and who does not smile at the obvious truism of that assertion? He maintains that chicanery is, with us, a far surer road than talent to distinction in letters. Who gainsays this? The corrupt nature of our ordinary criticism has become notorious. Its powers have been prostrated by its own arm. The intercourse between critic and publisher, as it now almost universally stands, is comprised either in the paying and pocketing of black-mail, as the price of a simple forbearance, or in a direct system of petty and contemptible bribery, properly so called—a system even more injurious than the former to the true interests of the public, and more degrading to the buyers and sellers of good opinion, on account of the more positive character of the service here rendered for the consideration received. We laugh at the idea of any denial of our assertions upon this topic ; they are infamously true. In the charge of general corruption, there are undoubtedly many noble exceptions to be made. There are, indeed, some very few editors, who, maintaining an entire independence, will receive no books from publishers at all, or who receive them with a perfect understanding, on the part of these latter, that an unbiassed *critique* will be given. But these cases are insufficient to have much effect on the popular mistrust : a mistrust heightened by late exposure of the machinations of *coteries* in New York—*coteries* which, at the bidding of leading booksellers, manufacture, as required from time to time, a pseudo-public opinion by wholesale, for the benefit of any little hanger-on of the party, or pettifogging protector of the firm."

It is impossible to avoid sympathising with Poe's scornful bitterness, in respect to this matter, and to help feeling that the existing evil—for the evil did exist then, and does exist now—could only be met by such outspoken language ; and it is a remarkable commentary on the poet's words that Mr. Wilmer, in 1859,[*] is found declaring that when he published an article on " Edgar A. Poe and his Calumniators," not a single paper noticed the vindicatory work, " whereas the whole press of the country seemed desirous of giving circulation and authenticity to the slanders."

[*] *Vide* " *Our Press Gang ; or, a Complete Exposition of the Corruption and Crimes of the American Newspapers.*"

These facts—for *facts they are*—speak for themselves.

Noticeable reviews from the poet's pen in August were upon the Lives and Poetic Works of Margaret Davidson (one of Southey's *protégées*), and " L. E. L." The September number of *Graham's* contained the tale of " Never Bet the Devil your Head "—a skit at the " Moral "-mongers—and various book notices, the most interesting being a severe critique on Campbell for his " Life of Petrarch." Whilst deeming the Italian poet entitled to the highest consideration as a patriot, and for his zeal and judgment in the preservation of priceless literary treasures, Poe cannot refrain from confessing that he does not " regard the genius of Petrarch as a subject for enthusiastic admiration," nor the characteristics of his poetry as displaying traits of the highest, or even of a high, order. " Grace and tenderness " he grants him ; "but these qualities are surely insufficient to establish his poetical apotheosis." A temporary absence from Philadelphia prevented Poe contributing to *Graham's* for October; but in November he commenced, and continued through three consecutive numbers, a series of papers on " Autography." These analyses of character were new, and different from the articles bearing a similar title published previously in the *Southern Literary Messenger ;* they were more critical, more caustic, their author now more widely known, whilst the publication in which they appeared had a far larger and far more influential circulation, and, consequently, they created many more fresh enemies for their inditer.

CHAPTER XIII

REVERSES.

THE closing month of 1841 left Edgar Poe in one of
the most brilliant and prosperous periods of his literary
career. The current volume of *Graham's Magazine*
ended in a blaze of triumph, the final page containing the statement that, " Perhaps the editors of no
magazine, either in America or Europe, ever sat
down at the close of a year to contemplate the progress of their work with more satisfaction than we do
now. Our success has been unexampled, almost incredible. We may assert, without fear of contradiction,
that no periodical ever witnessed the same increase
during so short a period. We began the year almost
unknown; certainly, far behind our contemporaries
in numbers; we close it with a list of twenty-five
thousand subscribers, and the insurance on every
hand that our popularity has as yet seen only its
dawning. But if such is the orient, what will our
noonday be ? " Few can doubt but that this success—
unparalleled for those days—was due chiefly to the
talents of Edgar Poe. His tales, his essays, and, above
all, his undaunted critiques, inaugurated a series of
literary and pecuniary triumphs for the magazine and
its proprietor, although for the editor—the real creator
of this fortunate enterprise—little would seem to
have been gained beyond daily bread ; and misery
and misfortune, although temporarily repulsed, still

dogged his steps, ready to make him their prey once more.

Poe's literary labours for 1842 began with the publication of " Eleanora," in the *Gift* for the current year. This tale, so replete with personal revelations, has already been adverted to in connection with the poet's marriage. In *Graham's* for January appeared, besides the last of the " Autography " articles, several reviews, heralded by a vigorous *exordium* upon the condition of contemporary criticism in America. After condemning anonymous reviewing, the prevalent generalising, and other vicious practices of the critics, Poe argued with Bulwer that the reviewer " must have courage to blame boldly, magnanimity to eschew envy, genius to appreciate, learning to compare, an eye for beauty, an ear for music, and a heart for feeling," to all of which requirements Poe added, " a talent for analysis, and a solemn indifference to abuse." In a notice of the " Vicar of Wakefield," described as " one of the most admirable fictions in the language," some admirable remarks upon the subject of illustrating books are made, and various characteristic utterances —utterances as yet not reproduced—are given, upon Heber, Walpole, " Christopher North," and other more or less known writers. The February number of the magazine contained an article on Brainard, one of the pioneers of American literature, and a fresh and eulogistic review of " Barnaby Rudge," whilst the number for March included, amongst minor notices, analyses of new books by or about Lever, Longfellow, Howitt, and Brougham. In *Graham's* for April appeared the tale of " Life in Death," or " The Oval Portrait," as it was subsequently renamed. The thesis of this story is somewhat similar to one of Hawthorne's "Twice-Told Tales," and although containing a few Poësque touches, such as the hero's embarrassment as to the quantity of opium to be eaten, it does not call for extended comment. A far more important contribution to this number was a lengthy review of Longfellow's "Ballads," in the course of which Poe took occasion to propound his fixed idea that BEAUTY, and Beauty *only*, should be the theme of Art. If Truth were the chief object, the highest aim of Art, then, as he truly declares, "Jan Steen was a greater artist than Angelo, and Crabbe is a nobler poet than Milton." In uttering an earnest protest against those who deem the work should be subservient to its moral, he reproaches his brother poet for the confirmed didacticism of his tone; "that this mode of procedure will find stern defenders," he says, "should never excite surprise, so long as the world is full to overflowing with cant and conventicles. There are men who will scramble on all fours through the muddiest sloughs of vice to pick up a single apple of virtue." What may be termed the articles of his artistic creed are simply and severely summed up in these remarks, which will call forth a sympathetic echo in the hearts of all true worshippers of the Beautiful:—

"Now, with as deep a reverence for 'the true' as ever inspired the bosom of mortal man, we would limit, in many respects, its modes of inculcation. We would limit to enforce them. We would not render them impotent by dissipation. The demands of truth are severe. She has no sympathy with the myrtles. All that is indispensable in song is all with which she has nothing to do. To deck her in gay robes is to render her a harlot. It is but making her a flaunting paradox to wreathe her in gems and flowers.

Even in stating this our present proposition, we verify our own words—we feel the necessity, in enforcing this *truth*, of descending from metaphor. Let us then be simple and distinct. To convey 'the true' we are required to dismiss from the attention all inessentials. We must be perspicuous, precise, terse. We need concentration rather than expansion of mind. We must be calm, unimpassioned, unexcited— in a word, we must be in that peculiar mood which, as nearly as possible, is the exact converse of the poetical. He must be blind indeed who cannot perceive the radical and chasmal difference between the truthful and the poetical modes of inculcation. He must be grossly wedded to conventionalisms who, in spite of this difference, shall still attempt to reconcile the obstinate oils and waters of Poetry and Truth. . . .

"We would define in brief the Poetry of words as the *Rhythmical Creation of Beauty*. Beyond the limits of Beauty its province does not extend. Its sole arbiter is Taste. With the Intellect or with the Conscience it has only collateral relations. It has no dependence, unless incidentally, upon either Duty or *Truth*. That our definition will necessarily exclude much of what, through a supine toleration, has been hitherto ranked as poetical, is a matter which affords us not even momentary concern. We address but the thoughtful, and heed only their approval—with our own. If our suggestions are truthful, then 'after many days' shall they be understood as truth, even though found in contradiction of *all* that has been hitherto so understood. If false, shall we not be the first to bid them die?"

In summing up his observations upon the aims of true Art, Poe deems that, of the poets who have appeared most fully instinct with the principles he enunciates, Keats should be mentioned as the most remarkable; "he is," he declares, "the sole British poet who has never erred in his themes. Beauty is always his aim."

Much as the present, or the forthcoming generation may be inclined to accept these *dicta* as the veritable gospel of Poesy, they are scarcely likely to have gained Poe much κυδος from the half-educated critics, moral-mongers, and petty poetasters, amid whom he had to earn his daily bread; and their triumph was at hand. With this April number of *Graham's*, his editorial connection with the magazine ceased, although the following issue contained several book notices from his pen, as well as a characteristic tale, " The Masque of the Red Death"—well named " a Fantasy" by its author. A review of Hawthorne, commenced in this and completed in the next number, contains some noteworthy passages, especially if they be read in the knowledge that they were published when their subject was almost unknown, and yet was then designated by Poe as the highest and most meritorious prose writer of America. He says :—

" The style of Mr. Hawthorne is purity itself. His *tone* is singularly effective—wild, plaintive, thoughtful, and in full accordance with his themes. We have only to object that there is insufficient diversity in these themes themselves, or rather in their character. His *originality* both of incident and of reflection is very remarkable; and this trait alone would ensure him at least *our* warmest regard and commendation. . . . We look upon him as one of the few men of indisputable genius to whom our country has as yet given birth."

And again, with complete self-abnegation and absence of all jealousy :—" Of Mr. Hawthorne's Tales we would say, emphatically, that they belong to the highest region of Art—an Art subservient to genius of a very lofty order. We know of few compositions which the critic can more honestly commend than these ' Twice-Told Tales.' As Americans, we feel proud of the book." Another paragraph, in praise

of these productions, doubtless, excited a flutter of
indignant expostulation from the thousand and one
forgotten notorieties who beheld themselves so scorn-
fully overlooked by the critic:—"We have very few
American tales of real merit; we may say, indeed,
none, with the exception of ' The Tales of a Traveller'
of Washington Irving, and these ' Twice-Told Tales'
of Mr. Hawthorne. Some of the pieces of Mr. John
Neal abound in vigor and originality; but, in general,
his compositions of this class are excessively diffuse,
extravagant, and indicative of an imperfect sentiment
of Art."

For months the poet's story has been little more
than a record of his literary labour, but once again
his personal history—"unmerciful disaster"—inter-
venes, and henceforth his career is one of anguish
and terror.   With the April number, as above stated,
Poe's editorial management of *Graham's Magazine*
ceased.   During the eighteen months that he had
directed the destinies of the publication, its circulation
had increased from five to fifty-two thousand, and
its reputation had spread even across the Atlantic,
English and French *literati* both contributing to and
drawing allusions from its pages.   This being so, and
the poet's *régime* productive of such brilliant results,
why was the connection severed ?   Mr. Graham, the
magazine's proprietor, says of Poe—and his words
prove no quarrel terminated the editorship :—"He
had the docility and kind-heartedness of a child.   No
man was more quickly touched by a kindness, none
more prompt to atone for an injury.   For three or
four years I knew him intimately, and for eighteen
months saw him almost daily ; much of the time

writing or conversing at the same desk; knowing all his hopes, his fears, and little annoyances of life, as well as his high-hearted struggle with adverse fate—yet he was always the same polished gentleman—the quiet, unobtrusive, thoughtful scholar — the devoted husband—frugal in his personal expenses—punctual and unwearied in his industry — and the *soul of honour* in all his transactions. This, of course, was in his better days, and by them *we* judge the man. But even after his habits had changed, there was no literary man to whom I would more readily advance money for labour to be done."

Probably the whole truth as to Poe's resignation of this editorship will never be known; doubtless, it was due to a combination of causes. There was the constitutional restlessness—the " nervous restlessness —which," as he acknowledges, "haunted me as a fiend," and which at times overpowered him, and drove him from place to place in a vain search for the El Dorado of his hopes; there was the ever-lingering desire to found a magazine of his own, and, what must be confessed, the beginning of those "irregularities" which, during the remainder of his life, at certain more or less lengthy intervals, destroyed his hopes and placed his reputation in the power of implacable foes. The origin of this fearsome scourge—which was not the outcome of youthful excesses, as maliciously asserted —is to be traced to the most terrible episode in the unfortunate poet's career. In a letter to an old and esteemed correspondent, dated January 4, 1848, Poe thus unbosoms himself of his secret—a secret as gruesome as any told of in the most terrible of his tales :—

"You say, 'Can you *hint* to me what was the 'terrible evil' which caused the 'irregularities' so profoundly lamented?'* Yes, I can do more than hint. This 'evil' was the greatest which can befall a man. Six years ago, a wife, whom I loved as no man ever loved before, ruptured a blood-vessel in singing. Her life was despaired of. I took leave of her forever, and underwent all the agonies of her death. She recovered partially, and I again hoped. At the end of a year, the vessel broke again. I went through precisely the same scene. . . . Then again—again—and even once again, at varying intervals. Each time I felt all the agonies of her death—and at each accession of the disorder I loved her more dearly and clung to her life with more desperate pertinacity. But I am constitutionally sensitive—nervous in a very unusual degree. I became insane, with long intervals of horrible sanity. During these fits of absolute unconsciousness, I drank—God only knows how often or how much. As a matter of course, my enemies referred the insanity to the drink, rather than the drink to the insanity. I had, indeed, nearly abandoned all hope of a permanent cure, when I found one in the *death* of my wife. This I can and do endure as becomes a man. It was the horrible never-ending oscillation between hope and despair which I could *not* longer have endured, without total loss of reason. In the death of what was my life, then, I receive a new, but—Oh God!—how melancholy an existence."

Although the unveiling this terrible mystery in the poet's life almost resembles sacrilege, it is better that the truth be bared, than that the false impressions—purposely or unintentionally created—should continue as to Poe's accredited habits of dissipation. No one who really knew the man, either personally or through his works, but will believe him when he asserted, " I have absolutely *no* pleasure in the stimulants in which I sometimes so madly indulge. It has not been in the pursuit of pleasure that I have perilled life and

* *Vide* the Reply to Thomas Dunn English, p. 302.

reputation and reason. It has been in the desperate attempt to escape from torturing memories." * Doubtless, there are weighty reasons why this moral cancer, which ate so deeply into the poet's health and happiness, should have remained unrevealed; but, in this history of his life, concealment is as impossible as it is, apparently, needless,—he only has been the sufferer, personally and posthumously.

Previous, however, to Poe's resignation of the *Graham Magazine* editorship, the unhappy catastrophe had already happened to his idolised wife, and the hoping against hope, and relapses into fits of maddening despair, had already begun to exert their deleterious effects upon him, causing a gradual but slow deterioration of his whole moral, physical, and intellectual nature. Mr. Graham, in his eloquent defence of the poet against the defamation of Griswold,† thus alludes to domestic ties and troubles:—

"I shall never forget how solicitous of the happiness of his wife and mother-in law he was, whilst one of the editors of *Graham's Magazine ;* his whole efforts seemed to be to procure the comfort and welfare of his home. Except for their happiness, and the natural ambition of having a magazine of his own, I never heard him deplore the want of wealth. The truth is, he cared little for money, and knew less of its value, for he seemed to have no personal expenses. What he received from me in regular monthly instalments went directly into the hands of his mother-in-law for family comforts ; and *twice* only I remember his purchasing some rather expensive luxuries for his house, and then

---

* Letter to Mrs. S. H. Whitman.

† R. W. Griswold was an employé of Mr. Graham, and, it is alleged, was dismissed for dishonesty. Thackeray, when in America, detected him in deliberate lying, and it was through his falsehoods that Messrs. Harper & Brothers had to pay Charles Dickens a larger sum than anticipated for "advance sheets" of "Bleak House."—J. H. I.

he was nervous to the degree of misery until he had, by extra articles, covered what he considered an imprudent indebtedness. His love for his wife was a sort of rapturous worship of the spirit of beauty, which he felt was fading before his eyes. I have seen him hovering around her when she was ill, with all the fond fear and tender anxiety of a mother for her first-born—her slightest cough causing in him a shudder, a heart chill, that was visible. I rode out one summer evening with them, and the remembrance of his watchful eyes, eagerly bent upon the slightest change of hue in that loved face, haunts me yet as the memory of a sad strain. It was this hourly *anticipation* of her loss, that made him a sad and thoughtful man, and lent a mournful melody to his undying song." *

This adoration of and fidelity to his youthful wife is a trait in Poe's character that no one *personally* acquainted with the hapless pair ever denied, even the poet's most inveterate enemies acknowledged the fact. But when he was dead, and helpless to repudiate the slander, persons who assume to have had his confidence, and to have been his friends, yet knew him only in the last moments of his life, declare that the union with Virginia Clemm was only a marriage of convenience, and that Poe never had any real affection for her. Mrs. Osgood, who, undoubtedly, knew more of the poet's innermost feelings during the last five years of his life than any person outside his domestic circle, said of his wife, "I believe she was the only woman whom he ever truly loved; and this is evidenced by the exquisite pathos of the little poem lately written, called 'Annabel Lee,' of which she was the subject, and which is by far the most natural, simple, tender, and touchingly beautiful of all his songs. I have heard it said that it was intended to

* *Graham's Magazine,* March 1850.

illustrate a late love affair of the author; but they who believe this have, in their dulness, evidently misunderstood or missed the beautiful meaning latent in the most lovely of all its verses, where he says,—

> ' A wind blew out of a cloud, chilling
> My beautiful Annabel Lee,
> So that her *highborn kinsmen* came,
> And bore her away from me.'

There seems a strange and almost profane disregard of the sacred purity and spiritual tenderness of this delicious ballad, in thus overlooking the allusion to the *kindred angels* and the heavenly *Father* of the lost and loved and unforgotten wife."

The long-tried affection displayed for each other by the poet and Mrs. Clemm was, undoubtedly, the result of the mutual love they bore, and knew each other bore, for the departed Virginia. In the well-known sonnet addressed to his mother-in-law—his " more than mother "—Poe says, in language we hold no evidence to question the truth and earnestness of,—

> " My mother—my own mother, who died early,
> Was but the mother of myself; but you
> Are mother to the one I loved so dearly,
> And thus are dearer than the mother I knew
> By that infinity with which my wife
> Was dearer to my soul than its soul-life."

Mrs. Clemm clung to the poet, and watched and waited upon him after her daughter's death, because *she knew* how devoted a husband he had been. "It is utterly false," she asserted at the first promulgation of this slander—lately revived, for easily apparent purposes —" It is utterly false the report of his being faithless or unkind to her (Virginia). He was devoted to her

M

until the last hour of her death, as all our friends can testify. . . . I enclose you two of Eddie's letters. . . . The other was written at the time you generously offered to take my darling Virginia. I wrote to Eddie asking his advice, and this is his answer. Does the affection then expressed look as if he could ever cease to love her? And he never did."[*]

A writer in a New York journal, and, apparently, a personal acquaintance of Poe, says, " It was one of the saddest things in his sad history that the two dearest to him were sharers of his hardships and sufferings—his beautiful young wife and her devoted mother. He married his cousin, who was brought up at the South, and was as unused to toil as she was unfit for it. She hardly looked more than fourteen, fair, soft, and graceful and girlish. Every one who saw her was won by her. Poe was very proud and very fond of her, and used to delight in the round, childlike face and plump little figure, which he contrasted with himself, so thin and half-melancholy looking, and she in turn idolised him. She had a voice of wonderful sweetness, and was an exquisite singer, and in some of their more prosperous days, when they were living in a pretty little rose-covered cottage on the outskirts of Philadelphia, she had her harp and piano."[†]

At the time to which this writer refers the Poes appear to have resided in Coates Street, Fairmount, whence they removed to North Seven Street, Spring Garden, in the suburbs of the city. Some pleasant reminiscences of the poet and his family, as the house-

[*] Letter from Maria Clemm to Neilson Poe, August 26, 1860.
[†] A. B. Harris, in *Hearth and Home*, 1870.

hold was in this pretty Pennsylvanian home, have been furnished to us by Captain Mayne Reid and others. After describing the charming little suburban dwelling, with its floral bedecked porch, and its tasteful although inexpensive furniture, Captain Reid proceeds to describe its inmates, as he knew them, personally as well as by repute. " Poe," he says, " I have known for a whole month closeted in his house, all the time hard at work with his pen, poorly paid, and hard driven to keep the wolf from his slightly-fastened door; intruded on only by a few select friends, who always found him, what they knew him to be, a generous host, an affectionate son-in-law and husband,—in short, a respectable gentleman. . . . In the list of literary men there has been no such spiteful biographer as Rufus Griswold, and never such a victim of posthumous spite as poor Edgar Allan Poe." *

The poet's wife is referred to by the Captain as, " A lady angelically beautiful in person, and not less beautiful in spirit. No one who remembers that dark-eyed, dark-haired daughter of Virginia,†—her own name—her grace, her facial beauty, her demeanour, so modest as to be remarkable ; no one who has ever spent an hour in her company, but will endorse what I have said. I remember how we, the friends of the poet, used to talk of her high qualities, and when we talked of her beauty, I well knew that the rose-tint upon her cheek was too bright, too pure to be of earth. It was consumption's colour, that sadly beautiful light that beckons to an early tomb."

Mrs. Clemm, the poet's aunt, the mother of his wife,

---

* " A Dead Man Defended," in *Onward* for April 1869.
† Virginia Poe was a native of Maryland.—J. H. I.

was still the presiding spirit of their little domicile, and of her the Englishman says, " Besides the poet and his interesting wife, there was but one other dweller. It was a woman of middle age and almost masculine aspect. She had the size and figure of a man, with a countenance that, at first sight, seemed scarce feminine. A stranger would have been incredulous, surprised, as I was, when introduced to her as the mother of that angelic creature who had accepted Edgar Poe as the partner of her life. She was the ever vigilant guardian of the house, watching it against the ever silent but continuous sap of necessity, that appeared every day to be approaching closer and nearer. She was the sole servant, keeping everything clean ; the sole messenger, doing the errands, making pilgrimages between the poet and his publishers, frequently bringing back such chilling responses as, ' The article not accepted,' or, ' The cheque not to be given until such and such a day '—often too late for his necessities."

Mr. A. B. Harris, the author already quoted from, proceeds to relate of the residence in Spring Garden, that " It was during their stay there that Mrs. Poe, while singing one evening, ruptured a blood-vessel, and after that she suffered a hundred deaths. She could not bear the slightest exposure, and needed the utmost care ; and all those conveniences as to apartment and surroundings which are so important in the case of an invalid were almost matters of life and death to her. And yet the room where she lay for weeks, hardly able to breathe, except as she was fanned, was a little place with the ceiling so low over the narrow bed that her head almost touched it. But no one dared to speak, Mr. Poe was so sensitive and irritable ; ' quick as steel and flint,' said one who knew him in those days. And he would not allow a word about the danger of her dying; the mention of it drove him wild."

Not only did the mention of the danger of his wife's death drive Poe wild, but the thoughts of it evidently rendered him unfit for literary work. Unable to provide the comforts needed for her dearest to him, to have to see his anxieties and privations shared by her, drove the poet to the brink of madness. Powerless to provide for the necessities at home, " he would steal out of the house at night," says Mr. Harris, " and go off and wander about the streets for hours, proud, heartsick, despairing, not knowing which way to turn, or what to do, while Mrs. Clemm would endure the anxiety at home as long as she could and then start off in search of him.

" So they lived, bound together in tender bonds of love and sorrow—their love making their lot more tolerable—the three clinging to each other; and the mother was the good angel who strove to shield the poet and save him. This way their lives went on in those dark days; he trying desperately at times to earn money, writing a little, and fitfully fighting against himself, sustained only by their solace and sympathy, and by the helping hand of the self-sacrificing mother, who loved him as if he had been, indeed, her own son."

Unable to secure a certain income by literature— for it must be remembered that even in his best days his receipts were but small, and, at best, chiefly dependent upon the caprice or continuous goodwill of an employer—the unfortunate poet appears to have

thought the attainment of a government post would at
least secure him from utter dependence.   His literary
correspondent, Mr. F. W. Thomas, had recently obtained
a situation under government, and Poe hoped, through
the influence of his various friends and acquaintances,
to be able to do the same; at any rate he determined
to try, and the following letter to John Neal would
appear to refer to this attempt :—

" PHILADELPHIA, *June* 4.

" MY DEAR SIR,—As you gave me the first jog in my literary
career, you are in a manner bound to protect me and keep
me rolling.   I therefore now ask you to aid me with your
influence in whatever manner your experience shall suggest.
It strikes me that I never write to you except to ask a favour,
but my friend Thomas will assure you that I bear you always
in mind, holding you in the highest respect and esteem.—
Most truly yours,   EDGAR A. POE.

"JOHN NEAL, Esq."

Several of the poet's influential friends were, doubtless, appealed to, and the following extracts have been
given by an American journalist as portions of two
letters written on the 26th of June and 4th of July
respectively to the late F. W. Thomas : *—

"Would to God I could do as you have done ! Do you
seriously think that an application to Tyler would have a
good result ? My claims, to be sure, are few.   I am a
Virginian, at least I call myself one, for I have resided all
my life, until within the last few years, in Richmond.   My
political principles have always been, as nearly as may be,
with the existing administration, and I battled with right
good will for Harrison when opportunity offered.   With Mr.
Tyler I have some slight personal acquaintance—although
this is a matter which he has possibly forgotten.   For the

* " Memoir of Edgar Allan Poe," by R. H. Stoddard, pp. 66–69.

rest, I am a literary man, and I see a disposition in Government to cherish letters. Have I any chance ? "

Mr. Thomas probably held forth some kind of hope to the distracted poet, as this second communication followed fast upon the above :—

" I wish to God I could visit Washington—but the old story, you know—I have no money—not even enough to take me there, saying nothing of getting back. It is a hard thing to be poor—but as I am kept so by an honest motive, I dare not complain. Your suggestion about Mr. Kennedy is well timed ; and here, Thomas, you can do me a true service. Call upon Kennedy—you know him I believe—if not, introduce yourself, he is a perfect gentleman, and will give you a cordial welcome. Speak to him of my wishes, and urge him to see the Secretary of War in my behalf—or one of the other Secretaries, or President Tyler. I mention in particular the Secretary of War, because I have been to W. Point, and this may stand me in some stead. I would be glad to get almost any appointment—even a $500 one—so that I may have something independent of letters for a subsistence. To coin one's brain into silver, at the nod of a master, is to my thinking the hardest task in the world. Mr. Kennedy has been at all times a true friend to me—he was the first true friend I ever had—I am indebted to him *for life itself.* He will be willing to help me, I know—but *needs urging,* for he is always head and ears in business. Thomas, may I depend upon you ? "

Whether Mr. Thomas found time and inclination to prosecute his friend's desires or not, is, of course, unknown, but that the unfortunate poet did not obtain an appointment is but too well known. Could he have procured a permanent government post, it would have lifted him above the most galling petty pecuniary anxieties of the hour, and have left him some leisure, some power, to produce more of his highly-polished and more artistic labours, instead of leaving him to

fritter away his genius in hasty and crude work. After
Poe's severance from *Graham's,* his wife's illness, and,
during its height, his own inability to write, are
declared to have reduced the little household almost
to starvation. "There was then," says Mr. Harris,
"some kind of a society under the care of ladies for
helping in a delicate way those who were in need,
and would signify it by depositing some articles at
the rooms—persons whom common charity could not
reach; and to that Mrs. Clemm, the mother, made
application. Yet so sensitive and proud was the little
family, that it was almost impossible to aid them to
any extent, even when they were suffering for the
common comforts of life." Of course these terrible
struggles with illness and poverty were not continuous;
occasional bursts of hope broke through the clouds of
"unmerciful disaster," and whenever the prospects
brightened, the poet plied his pen with renewed vigour.
In October, Mr. Graham's magazine published a critique
by Poe on " Rufus Dawes," one of the forgotten two
hundred celebrities of Mr. Griswold's pantheon. Of him
—the then famous now forgotten " poet "—Poe said,
"We hesitate not to say that no man in America has
been more shamefully over-estimated." "We say shamefully," he adds, " for . . . the laudation in this instance,
as it stands upon record, must be regarded as a laugh-
able although bitter satire upon the general zeal,
accuracy, and independence of that critical spirit
which, but a few years ago, pervaded and degraded
the land." After a stringent review of the works of
Mr. Dawes, the poet proceeds to remark that that
gentleman is known for his amiability and for his
many friends, which may have enhanced his literary

reputation. " We shall not here insist upon the fact that *we*," says Poe, " bear him no personal ill-will. With those who know us, such a declaration would appear supererogatory ; and by those who know us not it would, doubtless, be received with incredulity. What we have said, however, is *not* in opposition to Mr. Dawes, nor even so much in opposition to the poems of Mr. Dawes, as in defence of the many true souls which, in Mr. Dawes's apotheosis, are aggrieved. The laudation of the unworthy is to the worthy the most bitter of all wrong. But it is unbecoming in him who merely demonstrates a truth to offer reason or apology for the demonstration."

These critiques were, of course, continually enlarging the circle of the poet's foes and shutting him out from publications where, had he been contented to, or, perhaps, permitted by publishers to, have written only tales and poems, his services would have been eagerly sought for. After having been long promised to the reading public as about to write for Snowden's *Lady's Companion*, that journal at last, in October 1842, published "The Landscape Garden," subsequently enlarged and called " The Domain of Arnheim," from his admired but dreaded pen. This essay, for it can scarcely be styled a tale, is used as a medium by the poet for the expression of his views on the employment of personal wealth in the pursuit of happiness. As the peg whereon to hang several of his own views of society he selects the common idea—" a grossly exaggerated one," as he admits—as to the amount of property accumulated in the celebrated Thelluson case, and proceeds to depict the ideas and aims of the presumed inheritor of this immense fortune,

this fabled "ninety millions of pounds." In the contemplation of this enormous wealth the mind of Edgar
Poe could find at once scope for his imagination and
solace for his cravings after splendour. The opinions
and idiosyncrasies of the hero of the sketch are the
barely hidden opinions and idiosyncrasies of the poet
himself, and as such are doubly interesting to his readers.
A believer in the reality of happiness, although never
the possessor of that chimera, he thus discourses on the
theme:—" In the brief existence of Ellison I fancy that
I have seen refuted the dogma, that in man's very
nature lies some hidden principle, the antagonist of
bliss. An anxious examination of his career has given
me to understand that, in general, from the violation
of a few simple laws of humanity arises the wretchedness of mankind ; that as a species we have in our
possession the as yet unwrought elements of content ;
and that, even now, in the present darkness and
madness of all thought on the great question of the
social condition, it is not impossible that man, the
individual, under certain unusual and highly fortuitous
conditions, may be happy."

To refute this proposition—the premises providing
for the indefinite " unusual and highly fortuitous conditions "—may be difficult ; but a palpable fallacy
appears to lurk in the poet's further suggestion that
" while a high order of genius is necessarily ambitious,
the highest is above that which is termed ambition.
And may it not thus happen," he demands, " that many
far greater than Milton have contentedly remained
mute and inglorious ? "   " I believe," is his avowed
conclusion, " that the world has never seen—and that,
unless through some series of accidents goading the

noblest order of mind into distasteful exertion, the
world will never see—that full extent of triumphant
execution in the richer domains of art, of which the
human nature is absolutely capable." Of course, as in
the previous case, the poet has allowed himself a
certain loophole of escape, in the apparent fact that
the greatest genius being contented to remain unknown,
the existence of his superior capability cannot be dis-
proved, but to us it appears self-evident that genius
is itself the motive power that impels to production,
and the greater the genius the stronger the impulse
to produce, irrespective of "distasteful exertion" or
impediment.

The elements of happiness, as propounded by the
creator of Arnheim's gorgeous domain, apply more
strictly to the seeker after physical rather than mental
enjoyment, and his third elementary principle might
seem to be contradictory to the fourth ; these are his
conditions of earthly bliss:—" That which he considered chief was the simple and purely physical one
of free exercise in the open air. . . . His second condition was the love of woman. His third, and most
difficult of realisation, was the contempt of ambition.
His fourth was an object of unceasing pursuit." That
Ellison, or, rather, his *alter ego*, Poe, should have little
or no faith in the possibility of the improvement of
the general condition of man, is scarcely surprising,
although it hardly accords with the doctrines he is
presupposed to have imbibed from Condorcet and other
Human Perfectibility advocates. In his proposition
that the elements of beauty in art are as certain and
as unchangeable, although not so demonstrable, as
the rules of mathematics, he will have the credence

and sympathy of all his brethren. His suggestion that genius cannot be gained by study of rules, although rules may be adduced from works of genius —that " we may be instructed to build a ' Cato ' (*i.e.*, Addison's), but we are in vain told *how* to conceive a Parthenon or an ' Inferno' "—is, indeed, little more than a new application of the old adage *poeta nascitur non fit.* But " The Domain of Arnheim," apart from any interest it may derive from its author's personal views, will always charm the intelligent reader by its gorgeous and glowing scenery—the comprehensive realisation of a poet's vast and most exuberant imagination.

In November Snowden's *Lady's Companion* began the publication of " The Mystery of Marie Roget," one of the most marvellous examples of Poe's capability of dealing with, and analysing, the mysteries of the human mind. This tale, which occupied a large portion of three monthly numbers of the journal in which it was first issued, made a profound impression upon the public, not that it was so interesting as a work of art as many of its predecessors from the same pen, but from the fact that it referred to real and widely-known circumstances. To some extent the story is a sequel, or rather sequence, of " The Murders in the Rue Morgue," and purports to be carried on, so far as the mere spectators of the tragedy are concerned, by the same personages ; but whilst that was pure fiction from beginning to end, this recital refers to fact, that is to say, to fact but slightly veiled. The author furnishes the following preliminary words in explanation of the general design of his narrative :—

" A young girl, Mary Cecilia Rogers, was murdered in the vicinity of New York ; and although her death occasioned an intense and long-enduring excitement, the mystery attending it had remained unsolved at the period when the present paper was written and published. Herein, under pretence of relating the fate of a Parisian *grisette*, the author has followed in minute detail the essential, while merely paralleling the inessential, facts of the real murder of Mary Rogers. Thus all argument founded upon the fiction is applicable to the truth ; and the investigation of truth was the object. 'The Mystery of Marie Roget' was composed at a distance from the scene of the atrocity, and with no other means of investigation than the newspapers afforded. Thus much escaped the writer of which he could have availed himself, had he been on the spot, and visited the localities. It may not be improper to record, nevertheless, that the confessions of *two* persons (one of them the 'Madame Deluc' of the narrative), made at different periods, long subsequent to the publication, confirmed in full, not only the general conclusion, but absolutely *all* the chief hypothetical details by which that conclusion was attained."

Poe, under the garb of the magazine's editor, concludes the narrative thus : " For reasons which we shall not specify, but which to many readers will appear obvious, we have taken the liberty of here omitting, from the MSS. placed in our hands [by Mr. Poe], such portion as details the *following up* of the apparently slight clue obtained !" Latterly it has been the fashion (especially by foreigners) to disbelieve that Marie Roget's mystery had any real existence, and that the whole recital was the coinage of the poet's brain, and the notes only appended to give it an air of *vraisem-*

blance. Nevertheless, such was not the case; the narrative *was* founded on fact, although the incidents of the tragedy differed widely from those recounted in the tale. The naval officer implicated was named Spencer. In a letter to a literary friend asking about the omitted portions of the manuscript, above referred to, Poe says, "Nothing was omitted in 'Marie Roget' but what I omitted myself—all *that* is mystification. . . . The 'naval officer,' who committed the murder (rather the accidental death arising from an attempt at abortion) *confessed* it; and the whole matter is now well understood; but, for the sake of relatives, I must not speak further."

This narrative, or rather this analysis of the Unknown by ratiocination, is, presumedly, based upon the fact that even *chance* may be made a matter of absolute calculation. The subject was peculiarly suited to the mind of Poe, a mind in which mathematical accuracy was balanced by lofty imagination tinged by superstition. "There are few persons," he remarks, "even among the calmest thinkers, who have not occasionally been startled into a vague yet thrilling half-credence in the supernatural *by coincidences* of so seemingly marvellous a character that, as *mere* coincidences, the intellect has been unable to receive them. Such sentiments—for the half-credences of which I speak have never the full force of *thought*—such sentiments are seldom thoroughly stifled unless by reference to the doctrine of chance, or, as it is technically termed, the Calculus of Probabilities. Now this calculus is in its essence purely mathematical; and thus we have the anomaly of the most rigidly exact in science applied to the shadow and spirituality of the most intangible in speculation."

Recurring to this doctrine, he continues :—

"Experience has shown, and a true philosophy will always show, that a vast, perhaps the larger portion of truth, arises from the seemingly irrelevant. It is through the spirit of this principle, if not precisely through its letter, that modern science has resolved to *calculate upon the unforeseen.* But perhaps you do not comprehend me. The history of human knowledge has so uninterruptedly shown that to collateral, or incidental, or accidental events, we are indebted for the most numerous and most valuable discoveries, that it has at length become necessary, in any prospective view of improvement, to make not only large, but the largest allowances for inventions that shall arise by chance, and quite out of the range of ordinary expectation. It is no longer philosophical to base upon what has been a vision of what is to be. *Accident* is admitted as a portion of the substructure. We make chance a matter of absolute calculation. We subject the unlooked for and unimagined to the mathematical *formulæ* of the schools. I repeat that it is no more than fact that the *larger* portion of all truth has sprung from the collateral."

Analogous speculations form the bases of other succeeding stories, such as "The Purloined Letter" and "The Gold Bug," hereafter to be referred to. There is, however, another reference in "The Mystery of Marie Roget" to an all-important and but-too-rarely-alluded-to truth, the vital importance of which cannot be over-estimated—the effects of which, however, are beheld and experienced much more injuriously in America than in the Old World :—

"We should bear in mind," is the commentary, "that in general it is the object of our newspapers rather to create a sensation—to make a point—than to further the cause of truth. The latter end is only pursued when it seems coincident with the former. The print which merely falls in with ordinary opinion (however well founded this opinion may be), earns for itself no credit with the mob. The mass of the people regard as profound only him who suggests *pungent contradictions* of the general idea. In ratiocination, not less than in literature, it is the *epigram* which is the most immediately and the most universally appreciated. In both, it is of the lowest order of merit."

The Gift for 1843 contained "The Pit and the Pendulum," a tale of less philosophical value, perhaps, than the class of works just alluded to, but of intense fascination to the general reader. It is founded upon, or rather suggested by, the terrible sufferings of a Spanish refugee, who closed his miserable career amid the company of actors to which Poe's mother belonged, and it would be interesting to discover how the story reached the poet's knowledge. The author of this tale of the Inquisition's tortures, reproduces in its earliest sentences somewhat similar psychological fancies to those found in the "Colloquy of Monos and Una," but richer in tone and riper in experience. There is a truth and suggestiveness in the following passages which can be recognised and appreciated by many who would fail to grasp the shadowy hints of the earlier work :—

"Even in the grave all *is not* lost. Else there is no immortality for man. Arousing from the most profound of slumbers, we break the gossamer web of *some* dream. Yet in a second afterwards (so frail may that web have been) we remember not that we have dreamed. In the return to life from the swoon there are two stages : first, that of the sense of mental or spiritual; secondly, that of the sense of physical existence. It seems probable that if, upon reaching the second stage, we could recall the impressions of the first, we should find these impressions eloquent in memories of the gulf beyond. And that gulf is—what ? How at least shall we distinguish its shadows from those of the tomb ? But if the impressions of what I have termed the first stage are not at will recalled, yet, after long interval, do they not come unbidden, while we marvel whence they come? He who has never swooned is not he who finds strange palaces and wildly familiar faces in coals that glow; is not he who beholds floating in mid-air the sad visions that the many may not view; is not he who ponders over the perfume of some novel flower; is not he whose brain grows bewildered with the meaning of some musical cadence which has never before arrested his attention.

"Amid frequent and thoughtful endeavours to remember, amid earnest struggles to regather some token of the state of seeming nothingness into which my soul had lapsed, there have been moments when I have dreamed of success; there have been brief, very brief periods when I have conjured up remembrances which the lucid reason of a later epoch assures me could have had reference only to that condition of seeming unconsciousness."

Another noteworthy point about this story is the artistic accuracy of taste displayed in what may be regarded by some as mere minor details; for instance, instead of a description of the concrete horrors, such as a commonplace mind would have given, of the interior of the *pit*, the imagination only is appealed to and all its terror is *suggested* but left untold. What a far finer instinct, and more profound knowledge of art, does this restraint imply, than if the narrator had afforded a circumstantial account of some such loathsome mediæval pit as is the one, for instance, shown at Baden-Baden. The idea of the collapsing chamber, also, unlike in other tales in which that oft-told-of apparatus of torture plays a part, is made subservient to the other purposes of the work, rather than they to it.

Upon leaving Mr. Graham, Poe once more exerted himself towards carrying into execution his life-long scheme of a magazine of his own. He wrote to his

N

friends in various parts of the States, issued prospectuses from time to time, and for a long while did his best, but in vain, to resuscitate his embryo periodical. Ultimately he induced Mr. Thomas C. Clarke, a Philadelphia publisher, and founder and editor of several well-known publications, to join him in his speculation. Poe, as literary and art critic for the *Saturday Evening Post*——for many years one of the most popular and flourishing journals of its kind in the country—— had already afforded Mr. Clarke, who was the proprietor, evidence of his literary and editorial ability. Accordingly, on January 31, 1843, Mr. Clarke took Edgar Poe into partnership, so far, at least, as the projected periodical was concerned, and issued a prospectus and other publications connected with it signed "Clarke and Poe." The address to the journals and anticipated contributors, alluding to the prospectus which had already been circulated of the proposed *Penn Magazine*, stated that that project had been suspended through circumstances of no interest to the public, and that it had now been resumed, under the best auspices, subject only to a change of title. The name given to the stillborn journal had been deemed too local in its suggestions, it was, therefore, proposed to adopt that of *The Stylus* for the new speculation. Allusion was made to "the general knowledge, on the part of the public," of Poe's former connection with the *Southern Literary Messenger*, and *Graham's Magazine*, and such knowledge, it was pre-supposed, obviated the necessity for any very rigid definition of the literary character or aims of the new publication. "In many important points, however," said Poe, "the new magazine will differ widely from either of those named. It will endeavour to be more varied, more vigorous, more pungent, more original, more individual, and more independent." Again, referring to the two periodicals with which his connections had been best known, he said:—

"I shall be pardoned for speaking more directly of the two magazines in question. Having in neither of them any proprietary right, the objects of their very worthy owners, too, being in many respects at variance with my own, I found it not only impossible to effect anything on the score of taste for their mechanical or external appearance, but difficult to stamp upon them internally that *individuality* which I believed essential to their success. In regard to the extensive and permanent influence of such publications, it appears to me that continuity, distinctness, and a marked certainty of purpose, are requisites of vital importance; but attainable only when one mind alone has at least the general direction and control. Experience, to be brief, has shown me that in founding a journal wherein my interest should not be merely editorial, lies my sole chance of carrying out to completion whatever peculiar intentions I may have entertained."

Despite the wide diffusion of the prospectus containing these paragraphs, and the exertions of the poet, a sufficient number of subscribers to start the projected publication on a sound basis could not be obtained, and the scheme fell through, or, rather, was deferred for a time. It has been stated that some numbers of *The Stylus* were, indeed, published; but this assertion, it is believed, was only founded on the fact of a "dummy" copy having been printed as a specimen of what it was intended to offer the public.

Notwithstanding the failure of the magazine project, Mr. Clarke and Poe remained on a very amicable footing, the former doing all his limited powers permitted to befriend the latter, and assist him in his literary plans. In a vindication of the poet from the slanders of his first biographer, Mr. Clarke says, with reference to "Poe and the wife he so tenderly loved . . . I have some singular revelations which throw a strong light on the causes that darkened the life, and made most unhappy the death, of one of the most remarkable of all our literary men." "During his engagement in my office," continues this authority, " I published a life of Mr. Poe, with a portrait from a daguerreotype. Both the life and the portrait are utterly unlike the gross caricatures manufactured since his death ; . . . the portrait prefixed to a recent volume of Poe's poems bears no resemblance to the fine, intellectual head of Poe." "Why," indignantly demands Mr. Clarke —"why are such wrongs perpetrated upon the dead ? why are they permitted ? " The life published by Mr. Clarke is stated by Griswold to have been prepared "in Philadelphia, in 1843," by Poe himself, for a paper called *The Museum,* and he pretends to quote from it in order to prove that "many parts of it are untrue." The second paragraph is assumed to be a citation from a letter of Miss Barrett (Mrs. Browning), referring to "The Raven," a poem *not then written,* much less published !

During 1843 Poe continued contributing, chiefly critiques, to *Graham's Magazine.* Amongst other writings he completed the tale of "The Gold Bug," and sold it to Mr. Graham for fifty-two dollars. *The Dollar* newspaper, a publication edited by N. P. Willis, offering a premium of $100 for the best tale, Poe obtained his manuscript back from Mr. Graham, submitted it to the adjudicators, and, for it, was awarded the prize. The history of this practical illustration of the poet's cipher theory that human ingenuity cannot construct an enigma human ingenuity cannot resolve, is a further proof of the frequent inability of publishers to gauge the pecuniary value of literary works. In an unpublished letter, Poe, referring to this—in America—most popular of his productions, says, "'The Gold Bug' was originally sent to Graham; but he not liking it, I got him to take some critical papers instead, and sent it to 'The Dollar Newspaper,' which had offered $100 for the best story. It obtained the premium, and made a great noise."

This tale, although founded upon trite and threadbare worn incidents, has an air of freshness and originality from the novelty of the scientific theory by which it is permeated: Poe may not have been the first to discover, but he certainly was the first to popularise, the discovery of the mathematical ratio in which the letters of the alphabet recur. In enshrining this technicality in the story of a hidden treasure, he adopted the very best method of fascinating the attention " of the greatest number." In his two favourite and, *apparently*, contradictory styles of art, simplicity and suggestiveness, this tale is decidedly its author's *chef d'œuvre*.

Despite the timely aid of the one hundred dollar prize, Poe's pecuniary affairs appear to have reached a very trying stage by this period, and nothing but incessant labour enabled him to keep himself and family from utter destitution. For *The Pioneer*, a monthly magazine edited by Mr. J. R. Lowell, and which Poe says "was an excellent work, but had a *very* limited circulation," he wrote some reviews, including one on one of Griswold's compilations, the principal paragraphs of which were subsequently embodied in an article on the " Rationale of Verse." During the year he also contributed various critiques to *Graham's Magazine* on " Channing " (a nephew of Dr. Channing), " Halleck," " Cooper," and other somewhat forgotten celebrities.   In his article on Channing Poe thus alluded to Tennyson, a not very "popular" poet at that time :—

" For Tennyson, as for a man imbued with the richest and rarest poetic impulses, we have an admiration—a reverence unbounded.   His ' Morte d'Arthur,' his ' Locksley Hall,' his ' Sleeping Beauty,' his ' Lady of Shalott,' his ' Lotos Eaters,' his ' Œnone,' and many other poems, are not surpassed, in all that gives to Poetry its distinctive value, by the compositions of any one living or dead.   And his leading error—that error which renders him unpopular—a point, to be sure, of no particular importance—that very error, we say, is founded in truth—in a keen perception of the elements of poetic beauty. We allude to his quaintness—to what the world chooses to term his affectation.   No true poet—no critic whose approbation is worth even a copy of the volume we now hold in our hand—will deny that he feels impressed, sometimes even to tears, by many of those very affectations which he is impelled by the prejudice of his education, or by the cant of his reason, to condemn.   He should thus be led to examine the extent of the one, and to be wary of the deductions of the other.   In fact, the profound intuition of Lord Bacon has supplied, in one of his immortal apothegms, the whole philosophy of the point at issue.   ' There is no exquisite beauty,' he truly says, ' without some *strangeness* in its proportions.' We maintain, then, that Tennyson errs, not in his occasional quaintness, but in its continual and obtrusive excess.   And, in accusing Mr. Channing of having been inoculated with *virus* from Tennyson, we merely mean to say that he has adopted and exaggerated that noble poet's characteristic defect, having mistaken it for his principal merit ! "

The article on "Fitz-Greene Halleck" contained some very pertinent remarks on the adventitious reputations acquired by the pioneers of a country's literature. "Those rank first who were first known," declares Poe, adding that among the literary pioneers of America "there is not one whose productions have not been grossly overrated by his countrymen." Such home truths were scarcely calculated to gain the poet "golden opinions" from his contemporaries, nor increase his popularity with his brother journalists. But he dared all *published* opinion, and in the very teeth of Cooper's supreme popularity ventured upon saying, in reviewing one of that author's forest stories :—

"The interest, as usual, has no reference to *plot*, of which, indeed, our novelist seems altogether regardless, or incapable ; but depends, first, upon the nature of the theme ; secondly, upon a Robinson-Crusoe-like detail in its management ; and thirdly, upon the frequently repeated portraiture of the half-civilised Indian. In saying that the interest depends, first, upon the nature of the theme, we mean to suggest that this theme—life in the wilderness—is one of intrinsic and universal interest, appealing to the heart of man in all phases ; a theme, like that of life upon the ocean, so unfailingly omni-prevalent in its power of arresting and absorbing attention, that while success or popularity is, with such a subject, expected as a matter of course, a failure might be properly regarded as conclusive evidence of imbecility on the part of the author. The two theses in question have been handled *usque ad nauseam*—and this through the instinctive perception of the universal interest which appertains to them. A writer, distrustful of his powers, can scarcely do better than discuss either one or the other. A man of genius will rarely, and should never, undertake either ; first, because both are excessively hackneyed ; and, secondly, because the reader never fails, in forming his opinion of a book, to make discount, either wittingly or unwittingly, for that intrinsic interest which is inseparable from the subject and independent of the manner in which it is treated. Very few, and very dull indeed, are those who do not instantaneously perceive the distinction ; and thus there are two great classes of fictions—a popular and widely-circulated class, read with pleasure, but without admiration—in which the author is lost or forgotten; or remembered, if at all, with something very nearly akin to contempt ; and then, a class, not so popular, nor so widely diffused, in which, at every paragraph, arises a distinctive and highly pleasurable interest, springing from our perception and appreciation of the skill employed, or the genius evinced in the composition. After perusal of the one class, we think solely of the book ; after reading the other, chiefly of the author. The former class leads to popularity ; the latter to fame. In the former case, the books sometimes live, while the authors usually die ; in the latter, even when the works perish, the man survives. Among American writers of the less generally circulated, but more worthy and more artistic fictions, we may mention Mr. Brockden Brown, Mr. John Neal, Mr. Simms, Mr. Hawthorne ; at the head of the more popular division we may place Mr. Cooper."

These caustic critiques notwithstanding, Poe's literary labours for 1843 and the following year, taken altogether, were poorer in quality and quantity, and, doubtless, in remuneration, than in any succeeding, or preceding, year since his first adoption of literature as a profession. But these years were, it must be remembered, those in which the poet was first awakened to the fell certainty of his darling wife's mortal illness— the dreadful years in which he first really succumbed to the temptations of temporary oblivion proffered by drugs and stimulants.

In speaking of the "quantity" of his writings referable to this melancholy epoch of the poet's career, *original* matter only must be considered as alluded to. In his mental incapacity to produce anything of his own, Poe appears to have resorted to translating from the French. From April 1843, until the beginning of 1845, a constant, an almost weekly, supply of translated tales and sketches appear over his initials in the pages of the New York *New Mirror*, and its successor, the *Evening Mirror*. This bread-and-butter work, executed under high pressure, must have been a most terrible infliction for Poe's morbidly sensitive temperament, and, despite the few reviews taken by *Graham's*, have barely sufficed to maintain the unfortunate man and his household above veritable starvation. Among the various schemes he endeavoured to plan during his leisure—his lucid—intervals, was the republication of his tales in periodic parts, but we have no evidence that anything more appeared than number one of "The Prose Romances of Edgar A. Poe," containing "The Murders in the Rue Morgue," and "The Man that was Used Up."

In the winter of 1843, he delivered a lecture at the "William Wirt" Institution, on the "Poets and Poetry of America," and, in the course of the evening, took occasion to deliver some very severe remarks upon Mr. Griswold's compilation, recently published under a title similar to that given by Poe to his discourse. This trenchant attack upon the new and much belauded volume created no little excitement at the time in the literary coteries of Philadelphia, and by the book's compiler was never forgiven, and was terribly avenged. Mr. Griswold, it should be mentioned, for a short time occupied the editorial chair in Mr. Graham's publishing office which Poe had vacated. To the March number of *Graham's Magazine* Poe contributed a lengthy and appreciative review of Horne's magnificent epic, "Orion." Criticism was scarcely the poet's *forte;* and although the instincts of his own genius invariably prompted him to recognise and acknowledge the productions of kindred spirits, his critiques more closely resemble the unravelling an intricate riddle, than the sympathetic or antipathetic discussion of a propounded subject. And yet when we peruse Poe's definition of the rules of Art—as furnished by Nature—we cannot refuse to acknowledge their truth. Some of his more remarkable utterances in this review of "Orion," as embodying the theories he believed, and strove to follow out in poesy, may be reproduced here : —

"Although we agree, for example, with Coleridge, that poetry and *passion* are discordant, yet we are willing to permit Tennyson to bring to the intense *passion* which prompted his 'Locksley Hall,' the aid of that terseness and pungency which are derivable from rhythm and from rhyme. The effect he produces, however, is a purely passionate, and not, unless in detached passages of this magnificent philippic, a properly poetic effect. His ' Œnone,' on the other hand, exalts the soul not into passion, but into a conception of pure *beauty*, which in its elevation—its calm and intense rapture—has in it a foreshadowing of the future and spiritual life, and as far transcends earthly passion as the holy radiance of the sun does the glimmering and feeble phosphorescence of the glow-worm. His ' Morte d'Arthur ' is in the same majestic vein. The 'Sensitive Plant ' of Shelley is in the same sublime spirit. Nor, if the passionate poems of Byron excite more intensely a greater number of readers than either the ' Œnone,' or the 'Sensitive Plant,' does this indisputable fact prove anything more than that the majority of mankind are more susceptible of the impulses of passion than of the impressions of beauty ? Readers do exist, however, and always will exist, who, to hearts of maddening fervour, unite in perfection the sentiment of the beautiful—that divine sixth sense which is yet so faintly understood—that sense which phrenology has attempted to embody in its organ of *ideality*—that sense which is the basis of all Cousin's dreams—that sense which speaks of GOD through His purest, if not His *sole* attribute—which proves, and which alone proves His existence.

" To readers such as these—and only to such as these— must be left the decision of what the true Poesy is. And these—with *no* hesitation—will decide that the origin of Poetry lies in a thirst for a wilder Beauty than Earth supplies —that Poetry itself is the imperfect effort to quench this im- mortal thirst by novel combinations of beautiful forms (col- locations of forms), physical or spiritual, and that this thirst when even partially allayed—this sentiment when even feebly meeting response—produces emotion to which all other human emotions are vapid and insignificant.

" We shall now be fully understood. If, with Coleridge, and, however erring at times, his was precisely the mind fitted to decide a question such as this—if, with him, we reject *passion* from the true—from the pure poetry—if we reject even passion—if we discard as feeble, as unworthy the high spirituality of the theme (which has its origin in a sense of the Godhead), if we dismiss even the nearly divine emotion of human *love*—that emotion which, merely to name, causes the pen to tremble—with how much greater reason shall we dismiss all else ? And yet there are men who would mingle with the august theme the merest questions of expediency— the cant topics of the day—the doggerel æsthetics of the time—who would trammel the soul in its flight to an ideal Helusion, by the quirks and quibbles of chopped logic. There are men who do this—lately there are a set of men who make a practice of doing this—and who defend it on the score of the advancement of what they suppose to be *truth*. Truth is, in its own essence, sublime ; but her loftiest sublimity, as derived from man's clouded and erratic reason, is valueless— is pulseless—is utterly ineffective when brought into compari- son with the unerring *sense* of which we speak; yet grant this *truth* to be all which its seekers and worshippers pretend— they forget that it is not truth, *per se*, which is made their thesis, but an *argumentation*, often maudlin and pedantic, always shallow and unsatisfactory (as from the mere inadapta- tion of the vehicle it *must* be) by which this *truth*, in casual and indeterminate glimpses, is, *or is not*, rendered manifest."

After pointing out the matters in which he deemed Horne had departed from the proper standard—the standard which he, Poe, assumed to be the true one—he concluded by acknowledging that "Orion" "will be admitted by every man of genius to be one of the noblest, if not the very noblest, poetical works of the age. Its defects are trivial and conventional; its beauties intrinsic and supreme."

Consequent, apparently, upon this critique, some correspondence took place between the two poets. "During a certain period of Poe's * troubled circumstances," writes Horne, "he wrote to me, I being then in London, and inclosed a manuscript, saying that he had singled me out, though personally a stranger, to ask the friendly service of handing a certain story to the editor of one of the magazines, with a view, of course, to some remittance. Without waiting to read the story I replied at once that I considered his application to me a great compliment, and that I would certainly do the best I could in the business. But when I read the story, my heart of hope sank within me : it was 'The Spectacles.' I tried several magazines, not an editor would touch it. In vain I represented the remarkable tact with which the old lady, under the very trying task she had set herself, did, nevertheless, maintain her female delicacy and dignity. I met with nothing beyond a deaf ear, an uplifted eyebrow, or the ejaculations of a gentleman pretending to feel quite shocked. It may be that false modesty, and social, as well as religious, hypocrisy, are the concomitant and counterpart of our present equivocal

* Edgar Allan Poe. A Memorial Volume. Baltimore, 1877. pp. 82, 83.

state of civilisation; but if I were not an Englishman,
it is more than probable I should say that those
qualities were more glaringly conspicuous in England
than in any other country." No comment is needed
here upon the fact that any imagination could be discovered so ultraprurient, and utterly ridiculous, as to
perceive anything contrary to the most rigid and puri-
tanic delicacy in the playful, but not very powerful,
badinage of "The Spectacles."

One day in April of this year, 1844, the good folks
of New York were startled by a *jeu d'esprit,* or hoax, on
the subject of Ballooning, and Poe was the author.
The *Sun,* in which this amusing sally appeared, had
already a reputation for information not elsewhere
obtainable, in consequence of its publication of the
notorious "Moon Hoax" article,* when one morning
its readers—and their number increased that day with
much celerity—were astounded by reading the following wonderful communication:—

" Astounding News by Express, *via* Norfolk !
" The Atlantic crossed in Three Days !!
"Signal Triumph of Mr. Monck Mason's Flying
Machine !!!

" *Arrival at Sullivan's Island, near Charleston, S.C., of
Mr. Mason, Mr. Robert Holland, Mr. Henson, Mr. Harrison Ainsworth, and four others, in the Steering Balloon,
' Victoria,' after a passage of seventy-five hours from Land
to Land! Full Particulars of the Voyage!* "

This wonderful record of unparalleled adventure
was originally published, as its concocter, indeed, confessed, " with the preceding heading in magnificent
capitals, well interspersed with notes of admiration,

* *Vide* pp. 97–100.

as a matter of fact, in the *New York Sun,* a daily newspaper, and therein fully subserved the purpose of creating indigestible aliment for the *quidnuncs* during the few hours intervening between a couple of the Charleston mails. The rush for the 'sole paper which had the news' was something beyond even the prodigious; and, in fact, if (as some assert) the 'Victoria' *did* not absolutely accomplish the voyage recorded, it will be difficult to assign a reason why she *should* not have accomplished it."

As a *jeu d'esprit,* this trick on public credulity was a splendid success, but such jests are scarcely the class of productions one would desire to obtain from a poetic genius. Doubtless, for the immediate needs of the hour, these clever impositions paid their author much better than did the best of his poems, whilst they also furnished more ample food for his cravings for reputation, and his insatiable love of hoaxing. Poe's readers and admirers must, in point of fact, always be upon their guard against his inveterate habit of attempting to gauge their gullibility; his passion for this propensity frequently led him into indulging in the practice when least expected—into giving way to the desire of befooling his readers when apparently most in earnest.

In the same month as "The Balloon Hoax," Godey published in his *Lady's Book,* a literary magazine of Philadelphia, "A Tale of the Ragged Mountains." It was one of its author's favourite stories, and the scene of it is laid in the vicinity where his college days were spent, that is to say, in the neighbourhood of Charlottesville. Taken in connection with mesmeric theories—and at this period Poe appears to have been investigating such theories with the most steadfast interest—this tale is a singular manifestation, but, beyond some Poësque *traits* of thought and diction, contains nothing very remarkable. The Death Fetch, Doppelgänger, and similar dual creations of superstition have always been numerous enough in literature, and this revivification, although treated in a suggestively original manner, calls for no lengthy comment. Perhaps, when Poe's own habits are considered, and his love of mystification fully allowed for, the most interesting passages in the tale will be found in these allusions to its hero's use of drugs :—" His imagination was singularly vigorous and creative ; and no doubt it derived additional force from the habitual use of morphine, which he swallowed in great quantity, and without which he would have found it impossible to exist. It was his practice to take a very large dose of it immediately after breakfast each morning—or rather, immediately after a cup of strong coffee, for he ate nothing in the forenoon—and then set forth alone, or attended only by a dog, upon a long ramble. . . . In the meantime," that is to say, after some hours walking, "the morphine had its customary effect— that of enduing all the external world with an intensity of interest. In the quivering of a leaf—in the hue of a blade of grass—in the shape of a trefoil—in the humming of a bee—in the gleaming of a dewdrop— in the breathing of the wind—in the faint odours that came from the forest—there came a whole universe of suggestion—a gay and motley train of rhapsodical and immethodical thought."

Scarcely any original composition is again discernible until the end of the year. A review, already alluded to, in *The Pioneer*, and the quaintly beautiful verses, "Dreamland," published in the June number of *Graham's*, are all we can trace before the following September. The poem is replete with words—thoughts —expressions—that have appeared again, and again, in others of their author's poems, but is, nevertheless, most idiosyncratic and original. Those who have thus far followed Poe's "route, obscure and lonely," need not ask who is "the traveller" that

> " Meets aghast
> Sheeted Memories of the Past—
> Shrouded forms that start and sigh
> As they pass the wanderer by—
> White-robed forms of friends long given,
> In agony, to the Earth—and Heaven."

"The Oblong Box" appeared in Godey's *Lady's Book* for September. It is a tale of no particular merit, for Poe, and is chiefly remarkable for some somewhat curious mental analyses. In this same month the *New Mirror* perished, and with it, of course, the unfortunate poet's chief, although slender, source of livelihood. Thoroughly adrift, something decided had now to be done, and done at once. A living was not to be had, apparently, from literature in Philadelphia, and the conclusion was arrived at, probably through some intimation from Willis, to seek New York once more.

CHAPTER XIV.

NEW YORK ONCE MORE.

EDGAR POE'S reputation had already preceded him to New York, where, indeed, the publications of N. P. Willis, and other literary correspondents and friends, had kept his name for some time before the public.

" Our first knowledge of Mr. Poe's removal to this city," says Willis, * " was by a call which we received from a lady who introduced herself to us as the mother of his wife. She was in search of employment for him, and she excused her errand by mentioning that he was ill, that her daughter was a confirmed invalid, and that their circumstances were such as compelled her taking it upon herself. The countenance of this lady, made beautiful and saintly by an evidently complete giving up of her life to privation and sorrowful tenderness, her gentle and mournful voice urging its plea, her long-forgotten but habitually and unconsciously refined manners, and her appealing yet appreciative mention of the claims and abilities of her son, disclosed at once the presence of one of those angels upon earth that women in adversity can be. It was a hard fate that she was watching over. Mr. Poe wrote with fastidious difficulty, and in a style too much above the popular level to be well paid. He was always in pecuniary difficulty, and, with his sick

* *Home Journal*, Saturday, October 13, 1849.

wife, frequently in want of the merest necessities of life."

The immediate result of that interview with Mrs. Clemm is not told; but, eventually, Edgar Poe was engaged as sub-editor on the *Evening Mirror.* Willis, writing to his former partner Morris,* when called upon to make some remarks respecting his acquaintance with the deceased poet, says, in language that would give greater gratification were it a little less self-glorifying :—

" In our harassing and exhausting days of ' daily ' editorship, Poe, *for a long time,* was our assistant—the constant and industrious occupant of a desk in our office. . . . Poe came to us quite incidentally, neither of us having been *personally* acquainted with him till that time ; and his position towards us, and connection with us, of course unaffected by claims of previous friendship, were a fair average of his general intercourse and impressions. As he was a man who never smiled, and never said a propitiatory or deprecating word, we were not likely to have been seized with any sudden partiality or wayward caprice in his favour.

" *I should* preface my avowal of an *almost reverence* for the man, as I knew him, by reminding the reader of the strange double, common to the presence and magnetism of a man of genius, the mysterious electricity of mind. . . .

" It was rather a step downward, after being the chief editor of several monthlies, as Poe had been, to come into the office of a daily journal as a mechanical paragraphist. It was his business to sit at a desk, in a corner of the editorial room, ready to be called upon for any of the miscellaneous work of the day ; yet you remember how absolutely and how good-humouredly ready he was for any suggestion ; how punctually and industriously reliable in the following out of the wish once expressed ; how cheerful and present-minded his work when he might excusably have been so listless and abstracted. *We loved the man* for the entireness of fidelity

---

* From Idlewild, October 17, 1859.

with which he served us. When he left us, we were very reluctant to part with him."

Again, in the letter to the *Home Journal* already referred to, Willis says :—

" Poe was employed by us, for several months, as critic and sub-editor. This was our first personal acquaintance with him. He resided with his wife and mother at Fordham,* a few miles out of town, but was at his desk in the office from nine in the morning till the evening paper went to press. With the highest admiration for his genius, and a willingness to let it atone for more than ordinary irregularity, we were led by common report to expect a very capricious attention to his duties, and, occasionally, a scene of violence and difficulty. Time went on, however, and he was invariably punctual and industrious. With his pale, beautiful, and intellectual face, as a reminder of what genius was in him, it was impossible, of course, not to treat him always with deferential courtesy, and, to our occasional request that he would not probe too deep in a criticism, or that he would erase a passage coloured too highly with his resentments against society and mankind, he readily and courteously assented—far more yielding than most men, we thought, on points so excusably sensitive. With a prospect of taking the lead in another periodical, he, at last, voluntarily gave up his employment with us, and, through all this considerable period, we had seen but one presentment of the man—a quiet, patient, industrious, and most gentlemanly person, commanding the utmost respect and good feeling by his unvarying deportment and ability."

This characterisation of the poet is not of much importance, save that it affords another link in the chain of evidence as to Poe's general behaviour. Mr. Willis's fondness for patronising his betters is somewhat ludicrous, and he quite forgets to remark that the profits of his grandiloquent paper scarcely sufficed to pay *his*

* This is a mistake : Poe did not remove to Fordham until 1846. —J. H. I.

"critic and sub-editor" an *honorarium* large enough to keep body and spirit together. Poe's contributions to the *Evening Mirror* were not great either in quality or quantity, and soon after his resignation of his post upon it, the paper passed from Messrs. Willis and Morris into the hands of new proprietors. At first, beyond those of a "mechanical paragraphist," Poe's duties in his new position had not called for much activity. In October he appears to have resumed his translations from the French, and to have continued them in the columns of this paper for several months, but it is not until the beginning of the following January that any original writing therein can be traced to his pen.

Meanwhile, in Godey's magazine for November, was published his tale, "Thou Art the Man,"—one of the most conventional of his fictions ; and in the *Southern Literary Messenger* for December, a caustic satire on the "Mutual Admiration Society" system among editors, entitled "The Literary Life of Thingum Bob, Esq., late Editor of the *Goosetherumfoodle.*" More important than these were the initial papers of "Marginalia," contributed to the *Democratic Review*, during the last two months of the year. From the introduction to these pungent, pithy, paragraphs, which were continued in the pages of various publications up to the very day of their author's death, and which, despite their idiosyncratic powers, have not yet all been collected — these sentences may be fittingly reproduced :—

" In getting my books I have been always solicitous of an ample margin ; this not so much through any love of the thing in itself, however agreeable, as for the facility it affords me of pencilling suggested thoughts, agreements, and differences of opinion, or brief critical comments in general. Where what I have to note is too much to be included within the narrow limits of a margin, I commit it to a slip of paper, and deposit it between the leaves; taking care to secure it by an imperceptible portion of gum tragacanth paste.

" All this may be whim; it may be not only a very hackneyed, but a very idle practice, yet I persist in it still; and it affords me pleasure—which is profit, in despite of Mr. Bentham with Mr. Mill on his back.

" This making of notes, however, is by no means the making of mere *memoranda*—a custom which has its disadvantages, beyond doubt. ' *Ce que je mets sur papier,*' says Bernardin de St. Pierre, '*je remets de ma mémoire, et par consequence je l'oublie;*' and, in fact, if you wish to forget anything on the spot, make a note that this thing is to be remembered.

" But the purely marginal jottings, done with no eye to the Memorandum Book, have a distinct complexion, and not only a distinct purpose, but none at all; this it is which imparts to them a value. They have a rank somewhat above the chance and desultory comments of literary chit-chat—for these latter are not unfrequently ' talk for talk's sake,' hurried out of the mouth; while the *marginalia* are deliberately pencilled, because the mind of the reader wishes to unburthen itself of a *thought*—however flippant—however silly—however trivial—still a thought indeed, not merely a thing that might have been a thought in time, and under more favourable circumstances. In the *marginalia*, too, we talk only to ourselves; we therefore talk freshly—boldly—originally— with *abandonnement* — without conceit — much after the fashion of Jeremy Taylor, and Sir Thomas Browne, and Sir William Temple, and the anatomical Burton, and that most logical analogist Butler, and some other people of the old day, who were too full of their matter to have any room for their manner, which being thus left out of question was a capital manner indeed—a model of manners, with a richly marginallic air. The circumscription of space, too, in these pencillings, has in it something more of advantage than inconvenience. It compels us (whatever diffuseness of idea we may clandestinely entertain) into Montesquieu-ism, into Tacitus-ism (here I leave out of view the concluding portion of the 'Annals'). . . . .

"During a rainy afternoon, not long ago, being in a mood too listless for continuous study, I sought relief from *ennui* in dipping here and there at random among the volumes of my library—no very large one certainly, but sufficiently miscellaneous, and, I flatter myself, not a little *recherché*.

"Perhaps it was what the Germans call the 'brain-scattering' humour of the moment; but, while the picturesqueness of the numerous pencil-scratches arrested my attention, their helter-skelteriness of commentary amused me. I found myself at length forming a wish that it had been some other hand than my own which had so bedevilled the books, and fancying that, in such case, I might have derived no inconsiderable pleasure from turning them over. From this the transition-thought (as Mr. Lyell, or Mr. Murchison, or Mr. Featherstonhaugh would have it) was natural enough—there might be something even in *my* scribblings which, for the mere sake of scribbling, would have interest for others.

"The main difficulty respected the mode of transferring the notes from the volumes—the context from the text—without detriment to that exceedingly frail fabric of intelligibility in which the context was imbedded. With all appliances to boot, with the printed pages at their back, the commentaries were too often like Dodona's oracles—or those of Lycophron Tenebrosus—or the essays of the pedant's pupils in Quintillian, which were 'necessarily excellent, since even he (the pedant) found it impossible to comprehend them :' what, then, would become of it—this context—if transferred—if translated? Would it not rather be *traduit* (traduced) which is the French synonyme, or *overzezet* (turned topsy-turvy) which is the Dutch one?

"I concluded at length to put extensive faith in the acumen and imagination of the reader—this as a general rule. But, in some instances, where even faith would not remove mountains, there seemed no safer plan than so to remodel the note as to convey at least the ghost of a conception as to what it was all about. Where, for such conception, the text itself was absolutely necessary, I could quote it; where the title of the book commented upon was indispensable, I could name it. In short, like a novel-hero dilemma'd, I made up my mind

' to be guided by circumstances,' in default of more satisfactory rules of conduct.

" As for the multitudinous opinion expressed in the subjoined *farrago*—as for my present assent to all, or dissent
from any portion of it—as to the possibility of my having in
some instances altered my mind—or as to the impossibility
of my not having altered it often—these are points upon
which I say nothing, because upon these there can be nothing
cleverly said. It may be as well to observe, however, that
just as the goodness of your true pun is in the direct ratio of
its intolerability, so is nonsense the essential sense of the
Marginal Note."

Following this introduction are various specimens
of Poe's ideas, grave and gay, on all kinds of topics.
The puns and jests are no better than such light ware
is generally, but his opinions on certain books and
their authors, and on some of the arts and sciences,
deserve preservation. Music is a frequent theme with
him, for of music he was a passionate devotee, and a
capable student. Speaking in commendatory terms of
the late H. F. Chorley, he says, " But the philosophy of
music is beyond his depth, and of its physics he, unquestionably, has no conception. By the way," he
adds, " of all the so-called scientific musicians, how
many may we suppose cognisant of the acoustic facts
and mathematical deductions ? To be sure, my acquaintance with eminent composers is quite limited ;
but I have never met *one* who did not stare and say
' yes,' ' no,' ' hum !' ' ha !' ' eh ?' when I mentioned
the mechanism of the *Siréne*, or made allusion to the
oval vibrations at right angles."

A lengthy note is devoted to a presumed omission
in all the Bridgewater treatises, in their failure to
notice " *the great* idiosyncrasy in the Divine system of
adaptation — that idiosyncrasy which stamps the

adaptation as Divine, in distinction from that which is the work of merely human constructiveness. I speak," he asserts, " of the complete *mutuality* of adaptation," and then proceeds to furnish examples, needless to cite here, concluding in drawing a contrast between human and divine inventions, " the plots of God are perfect. The Universe is a plot of God."

Referring to his favourite author, Dickens, he remarks that his " serious (minor) compositions have been lost in the blaze of his comic reputation. One of the most forcible things ever written," he opines, " is a short story of his, called ' The Black Veil ;' a strangely-pathetic and richly-imaginative production, replete with the loftiest tragic power." That Dickens's head must puzzle the phrenologists then occurs to him, for in it, he observes, " the organs of ideality are small ; and the conclusion of the ' Curiosity Shop' is more truly ideal (in both phrenological senses) than any composition of equal length in the English language."

Some ideas are then hazarded as to the treatment to be awarded dunces ; " where the gentler sex is concerned," says the chivalrous poet, " there seems but one course for the critic—speak if you can commend ; be silent, if not." Frequently his opinions run counter to those of the immense majority of his republican brethren, as in the note, " The sense of high birth is a moral force whose value the democrats are never in condition to calculate : ' *Pour savoir ce qu'est Dieu,*' says the Baron de Bielfeld, ' *il faut être Dieu même.*' " His views and reviews of things in general, as set forth in these original and entertaining Margin-

alia, supply ample literary food for interest and imagination, but scarcely need lengthy notice in their
author's biography, albeit they open many unsuspected
sidelights upon the darker recesses of his mental story.
When, for instance, he declares, " I am far more than
half-serious in all that I have ever said about manuscript, as affording indication of character," we feel that
he is really confiding in us, as also in the sequence,
" I by no means shrink from acknowledging that I
act, hourly, upon estimates of character derived from
chirography." " How many good books suffer neglect
through the inefficiency of their beginnings," is a
thought, indeed, likely to have been in the mind of
him who invariably acts up to his advice here given,
of " at all risks, let there be a few vivid sentences,
imprimis, by way of the electric bell to the telegraph."
A large portion of his misfortunes—the rôle of critic
he was compelled to play being really compulsory—
are suggested by the assertion that " a man of genius,
if not permitted to choose his own subject, will do
worse, in letters, than if he had talents none at all.
And *here* how imperatively is he controlled ! "   " To be
sure ! " exclaimed Poe, " he can write to suit himself, but
in the same manner his publishers print."   Whilst the
accusation in the following paragraph is too surely
pointed to be taken for any one else than self-reference :
—" It is the curse of a certain order of mind, that it
can never rest satisfied with the consciousness of its
ability to do a thing.   Still less is it content with
doing it.   It must both know and show how it was
done."

With 1845 was inaugurated the most brilliant
epoch of Poe's literary career, although the continually

increasing weakness of his wife flung a cloud of gloom over its brightness. In *The Gift* for the new year appeared " The Purloined Letter," the last of the famous detective trilogy, of which the " Rue Morgue " and " Marie Roget " mysteries form parts. The three tales should always be read in conjunction with one another, because, although published separately, and each complete in itself, the one is but a sequence of the analytic reasoning of the other, and all are but varied examples of the futility of over acuteness, or rather cunning, when opposed by extraordinary combinations, or by the calculations of genius.

On January 4th was published the first number of a new periodical, entitled *The Broadway Journal*. " It was not until No. 10 that I had anything to do with this journal as editor," is Poe's endorsement upon our copy, but from its commencement he wrote for it. To the first, and the following number, he contributed a review of Mrs. Browning's " Drama of Exile and other Poems," and, whilst not forgetful of his critical severities, he found enough in the work to call forth his most enthusiastic admiration and poetic sympathy. That she had, even then, done more in poetry than any woman, living or dead, was a decision Poe could not fail to arrive at ; neither was he singular nor original in deeming that she had " surpassed all her poetical contemporaries of either sex, with a single exception," that exception being Tennyson. What Mrs. Browning thought of her transatlantic reviewer's strictures on her presumed want of due knowledge of the mechanism of verse may be gathered from this extract out of a letter to Mr. Horne :—

" Mr. Poe seems to me in a great mist on the subject of
metre. You yourself have skipped all the philosophy of the
subject in your excellent treatise on ' Chaucer Modernised,'
and you shut your ears when I tried to dun you about it one
day. But Chaucer wrote on precisely the same principles
(eternal principles) as the Greek poets did, I believe, unalter-
ably; and you, who are a musician, ought to have sung it
out loud in the ears of the public. There is no ' pedantic
verbiage' in Longinus. But Mr. Poe, who attributes the
' Œdipus Colonos' to Æschylus (*vide* review on me), sits
somewhat loosely, probably, on his classics."

Poe, certainly, was not a profound Greek scholar;
but he had been to classical schools, and was a well-
read man, and could not, therefore, have ascribed the
dramas of Sophocles to Æschylus, save in a fit of
oblivious haste, such as, indeed, the somewhat involved nature of the passage in question suggests must
have been the case in this instance.

A critique on N. P. Willis constituted Poe's sole contribution to the third number of the *Broadway Journal*,
and it contained nothing very original or striking, but
was chiefly occupied by an elaborate discussion as to the
boundaries between Fancy and Imagination, travelling
over much the same ground that had been traversed
five years previously, in a review of Moore's poetry.

On the 29th of January the first published version
of Poe's poetic *chef d'œuvre*, the far-famed " Raven,"
appeared in the *Evening Mirror*, with these introductory
words by Willis :—

" We are permitted to copy, (in advance of publication,)
from the second No. of the *American Review*, the following
remarkable poem by Edgar Poe. In our opinion, it is the
most effective single example of ' fugitive poetry ' ever published in this country ; and unsurpassed in English poetry
for subtle conception, masterly ingenuity of versification, and

consistent sustaining of imaginative lift. . . . It is one of those 'dainties bred in a book,' which we feed on. It will stick to the memory of everybody who reads it."

This publication with the author's name, and the immediate reproduction of the poem in the journals of nearly every town in the United States, prevented any attempt at concealment, had Poe really thought to make one. Certain it is that " The Raven " appeared in the *American Review* for February, as by " Quarles," preceded by the following note, the inspiration, evidently, of the poet himself :—

" The following lines from a correspondent, besides the deep quaint strain of the sentiment, and the curious introduction of some ludicrous touches amidst the serious and impressive, as was doubtless intended by the author—appear to us one of the most felicitous specimens of unique rhyming which has for some time met our eye. The resources of English rhythm for varieties of melody, measure, and sound, producing corresponding diversities of effect, have been thoroughly studied, much more perceived, by very few poets in the language. While the classic tongues, especially the Greek, possess, by power of accent, several advantages for versification over our own, chiefly through greater abundance of spondaic feet, we have other, and very great advantages of sound, by the modern usage of rhyme. Alliteration is nearly the only effect of that kind which the ancients had in common with us. It will be seen that much of the melody of " The Raven " arises from alliteration, and the studious use of similar sounds in unusual places. In regard to its measure, it may be noted, that if all the verses were like the second, they might properly be placed merely in short lines, producing a not uncommon form ; but the presence in all the others of one line—mostly the second in the verse—which flows continuously, with *only* an aspirate pause in the middle, like that before the short line in the Sapphic Adonic, while the fifth has at the middle pause no similarity of sound with any part beside, give the versification an entirely different effect.

We could wish the capacities of our noble language, in prosody, were better understood."

No single "fugitive" poem ever caused such a *furor;* in the course of a few weeks it spread over the whole of the United States, calling into existence parodies and imitations innumerable, and, indeed, creating quite a literature of its own; it carried its author's name and fame from shore to shore, inducing veritable poets in other lands—last but not least, Monsieur Mallarmè, — to attempt to transmute its magical charms into their tongues; it drew admiring testimony from some of the finest spirits of the age, and, finally, made Poe the lion of the season. And for this masterpiece of genius—this poem which has, probably, done more for the renown of American letters than any other single work—it is alleged that Poe, then in the heyday of his intellect and reputation, received the sum of *ten* dollars!

Mrs. Browning, then Miss Barrett, in a letter written some time after publication of this poem, says: "This vivid writing!—this power *which* is felt! 'The Raven' has produced a sensation—a 'fit horror' here in England. Some of my friends are taken by the fear of it, and some by the music. I hear of persons *haunted* by the Nevermore, and one acquaintance of mine, who has the misfortune of possessing a 'bust of Pallas,' never can bear to look at it in the twilight. Our great poet, Mr. Browning, author of 'Paracelsus,' &c., is enthusiastic in his admiration of the rhythm."

Poe himself, although extremely proud of the profound impression "The Raven" had made on the public, had no particular fondness for it, and preferred, far more, many of his juvenile pieces; they, he could not

but feel, were the offspring of inspiration, whilst this
was but the product of art—of art, of course, control-
ling and controlled by genius. Writing to a favourite
correspondent upon this subject, he remarks :—

"What you say about the blundering criticism of 'the
Hartford Review man' is just. For the purposes of poetry it
is quite sufficient that a thing is possible, or at least that
the improbability be not offensively glaring. It is true that
in several ways, as you say, the lamp might have thrown the
bird's shadow on the floor. *My* conception was that of the
bracket candelabrum affixed against the wall, high up above
the door and bust, as is often seen in the English palaces,
and even in some of the better houses of New York.

"Your objection to the *tinkling* of the footfalls is far more
pointed, and in the course of composition occurred so forcibly
to myself that I hesitated to use the term. I finally used it,
because I saw that it had, in its first conception, been suggested to my mind by the sense of the *supernatural* with
which it was, at the moment, filled. No human or physical
foot could tinkle on a soft carpet, therefore, the tinkling of
feet would vividly convey the supernatural impression. This
was the idea, and it is good within itself; but if it fails, (as
I fear it does,) to make itself immediately and generally *felt*,
according to my intention, then in so much is it badly conveyed, or expressed.

"Your appreciation of 'The Sleeper' delights me. In the
higher qualities of poetry it is better than 'The Raven;' but
there is not one man in a million who could be brought to
agree with me in this opinion. 'The Raven,' of course, is
far the better as a work of art; but in the true basis of all
art, 'The Sleeper' is the superior. I wrote the latter when
quite a boy.

"You quote, I think, the two *best* lines in 'The Valley of
Unrest'—those about the palpitating trees."

Whence Poe drew the first idea of "The Raven"
is a much mooted point. The late Buchanan Read
informed Robert Browning that Poe described to him,
(*i.e.*, Read,) the whole process of the construction of his

poem, and declared that the suggestion of it lay wholly in a line from " Lady Geraldine's Courtship : "—

" With a murmurous stir uncertain, in the air the purple curtain," &c.

This account necessarily involves some misunderstanding : that Poe did derive certain hints, unconsciously or otherwise, from Mrs. Browning's poem cannot be doubted, as, for instance, in his parallel line to the above :—

" And the silken, sad, uncertain rustling of each purple curtain ; "

but the germ of " The Raven " is most assuredly discoverable elsewhere. Does not the following explanation offer more tangible evidence as to its origin than anything yet published ? Does it not, indeed, tear the veil from the mystery, and prove that the first suggestion was derived from an American theme ?

It has been seen that in 1843 Poe was writing for the *New Mirror*. The number for October 14th contained some verses entitled " Isadore," by Mr. Albert Pike, a well-known American *littérateur*. Amongst some introductory remarks by the irrepressible editor, N. P. Willis, these words occur : " We do not understand why we should not tell what we chance to know —that these lines were written after sitting up late at study—the thought of losing her who slept near him at his toil having suddenly crossed his mind in the stillness of midnight." This statement really establishes a first coincidence between the poems of Poe and Pike ; both write a poem lamenting a lost love, when, in point of fact, neither one nor the other had lost either his "Isadore," or his "Lenore," save in imagination; and in his half-hoaxing, half-serious, "Philosophy of Composition" Poe states that the theme adopted for the projected poem was "a lover lamenting his deceased mistress." Far more important, however, than the subject of his verse, so he suggests, was the effect to be obtained from the refrain, and in Mr. Pike's composition the most distinctive—the only salient—feature is the refrain of "forever, Isadore," with which each stanza concludes. A still more remarkable coincidence follows : in his search for a suitable refrain Poe would have his to-be-mystified readers believe that he was irresistibly impelled to select the word "Nevermore." Evidently there are plenty of equally eligible words in the English language—words embodying the long sonorous $\bar{o}$ in connection with r as the most producible consonant; but a perusal of Mr. Pike's poem rendered research needless, for not only does the refrain contain the antithetic word to *never*, and end with the -$\bar{o}re$ syllable, but in *one* line are found the words "never," and "more," and in others the words "no more," "evermore," and "forever more"—quite sufficient, all must admit, for the analytic mind of Poe.

Thus far the subject, the refrain, and the word selected for the refrain, have been easily paralleled, and over the transmutation of the heroine's name from Isadore into Lenore no words need be wasted. In concluding this section of our argument, it is but just that some specimen of Mr. Pike's work should be shown; two stanzas, therefore, of his poem—which contains six stanzas fewer than Poe's — shall be cited :—

" Thou art lost to me forever—I have lost thee, Isadore,—
Thy head will never rest upon my loyal bosom more.
Thy tender eyes will never more gaze fondly into mine,
Nor thine arms around me lovingly, and trustingly entwine.
Thou art lost to me forever, Isadore.

" My footsteps through the rooms resound all sadly and
forlore ;
The garish sun shines flauntingly upon the unswept floor ;
The mocking-bird still sits and sings a melancholy strain,
For my heart is like a heavy cloud that overflows with rain.
Thou art lost to me forever, Isadore."

Mr. Pike's metre and rhythm are, as might be
expected, very much less dexterously managed than
Poe's, although the *intention* was evidently to produce
an effect similar to that afterwards carried out in
" The Raven ; " but the irregularities are so eccentric
that one sees that the prototype poem was that of a
writer unable to get beyond the intention—one unacquainted with metrical laws. " Of course, I pretend to
no originality in either the rhythm, or the metre of
' The Raven,' " said Poe, adding, " what originality ' The
Raven,' has, is in their " (the forms of verse employed)
" *combination into stanza,* nothing even remotely approaching this combination has ever been attempted."

But " Isadore " contains no allusion to the " ghastly
grim and ancient Raven," unless its " melancholy
burden " be shadowed forth by the " melancholy
strain " of " the *mocking*-bird." Whence, then, did
Poe import his sable auxiliary, the pretext, as he tells
us, for the natural repetition of the refrain ? " Naturally, a parrot, in the first instance, suggested itself,"
he remarks, and as a favourite work with him was
Gresset's *chef d'œuvre,* it is not improbable that a reminiscence of " Ver-Vert "—not " Vert-Vert," as many

P

persist in miscalling that immortal bird—*may* have given him the first hint, but that it was in "Barnaby Rudge" he finally found the needed fowl seems clear to us. Upon the conclusion of that story Poe, referring to a prospective review he had formerly published of it,[*] called attention to certain points he deemed Dickens had failed to make: the raven therein, for instance, he considered, "might have been made more than we now see it, a portion of the conception of the fantastic Barnaby. Its croakings might have been prophetically heard in the course of the drama. Its character might have performed, in regard to that of the idiot, much the same part as does, in music, the accompaniment in respect to the air." Here, indeed, beyond question, is seen shadowed forth the poet's own raven and its duty.

A few additional links in the chain may be added. The story following Mr. Pike's verses in the *New Mirror* contains, many times repeated, the unusual name of "Eulalie." Till the appearance of "The Raven," for several years Poe had published but one new poem, "Dreamland," yet in the following July appeared—in *The American Review*—his "Eulalie," a poem which, in many passages, closely resembles "Isadore." Thus, Mr. Pike speaks of "thy sweet eyes radiant," and Poe, in "Eulalie," of "the eyes of the radiant girl." Mr. Pike says

——"thy face,
Which thou didst lovingly upturn with pure and trustful gaze,"

and Poe, "dear Eulalie upturns her matron eye;" and, be it noted, the gaze of both is *upturned* to the moon. There are other points of resemblance between the poems, needless to advert to here, as the genesis of "The Raven" is now, it is presumed, satisfactorily and unanswerably expounded.

This wonderful piece of poetic mechanism underwent, as did, indeed, nearly all of Poe's work, several alterations and revisions after its first publication. The very many more minute of these variations do not call for notice here, but the change made in the latter half of the eleventh stanza, from the original reading of—

> ' So, when Hope he would adjure,
> Stern Despair returned, instead of the sweet Hope he dared adjure,
> That sad answer, " Nevermore " '—

to its present masterly roll of melancholy music, is too radical to be passed by unnoted.

Poe's reputation now rested upon a firm basis. His society was sought for by the *élite* of American society, and the best houses of New York were ready to proffer a hearty welcome to him who stood even yet on the brink of poverty, dogged by all its attendant demons. "Although he had been connected with some of the leading magazines of the day," remarks Mrs. Whitman, " and had edited for a time with great ability several successful periodicals, his literary reputation at the North had been comparatively limited until his removal to New York, when he became personally known to a large circle of authors and literary people, whose interest in his writings was manifestly enhanced by the perplexing anomalies of his character and by the singular magnetism of his presence." But it was not until the publication of his poetic *chef d'œuvre* that he became a society lion. When "The Raven" appeared, as this same lady records, Poe one evening electrified the company assembled at the house of an accomplished poetess in Waverley Place—where a weekly *réunion* of artists and men of letters was held—by the recitation, at the request of his hostess, of the wonderful poem.

No longer merely a somewhat-to-be-dreaded reviewer but now a famous man, it became necessary to include the poet in the biographical critical laudations of " Our Contributors," published from time to time in *Graham's Magazine.* "Edgar Allan Poe" formed the seventeenth article in the series of American *literati,* so lowly had his merits been gauged, and to James Russell Lowell was intrusted the task of adjudicating upon his claims to a niche in the Pantheon. In many respects Lowell's critique, published in February 1845, is the best yet given upon certain characteristics of Poe's genius, and although the estimate formed of his poetic precocity is overdrawn, being founded upon incorrect *data,*—and although the reviewer evidently lacks sympathy with the reviewed—with the admirable analysis of our poet's tales, it would be difficult to find fault. In this article, as originally published—and it may be remarked that it has since been greatly revised— Professor Lowell, after styling Poe "the most discriminating, philosophical, and fearless critic upon imaginative works who has written in America," proceeds to qualify his remarks by adding:—

He *might be,* rather than he always *is,* for he seems sometimes to mistake his phial of prussic-acid for his inkstand. If we do not always agree with him in his premises, we are, at least, satisfied that his deductions are logical, and that we are reading the thoughts of a man who thinks for himself, and says what he thinks, and knows well what he is, talking about. . . . We do not know him personally, but we suspect him for a man who has one or two pet prejudices on which he prides himself. These sometimes allure him out of the strict path of criticism, but, where they do not interfere, we would put almost entire confidence in his judgments. Had Mr. Poe the control of a magazine of his own, in which to display his critical abilities, he would have been as autocratic, ere this, in America, as Professor Wilson has been in England ; and his criticisms, we are sure, would have been far more profound and philosophical than those of the Scotchman."

With reference to the poet's career apart from literature, Professor Lowell observes that " Remarkable experiences are usually confined to the inner life of imaginative men, but Mr. Poe's biography displays a vicissitude and peculiarity of interest such as is rarely met with," and he thereupon furnishes a short *résumé* of his hero's adventures. Of Poe's powers as a writer of fiction he remarks :—

" In his tales, he has chosen to exhibit his powers chiefly in that dim region which stretches from the very utmost limits of the probable into the weird confines of superstition and unreality. He combines in a very remarkable manner two faculties which are seldom found united ; a power of influencing the mind of the reader by the impalpable shadows of mystery, and a minuteness of detail which does not leave a pin, or a button unnoticed. . . . Even his mystery is mathematical to his own mind. To him x is a known quality. . . . However vague some of his figures may seem, however formless the shadows, to him the outline is as clear and distinct as that of a geometrical diagram. For this reason Mr. Poe has no sympathy with *mysticism*. The mystic dwells *in* the mystery, is enveloped with it ; it colours all his thoughts. . . , Mr. Poe, on the other hand, is a spectator *ab extrâ*. He analyses, he dissects, he watches

—— ' with an eye serene
The very pulse of the machine,'

for such it practically is to him, with wheels and cogs and piston-rods all working to produce a certain end. It is this that makes him so good a critic. Nothing baulks him, or throws him off the scent, *except now and then a prejudice.*

"A monomania he paints with great power. He loves to dissect these cancers of the mind, and to trace all the subtle ramifications of its roots. In raising images of horror, also, he has a strange success; conveying to us sometimes by a dusty hint some terrible *doubt* which is the secret of all horror. He leaves to imagination the task of finishing the picture, a task to which only she is competent :—

> " ' For much imaginary work was there ;
> Conceit deceitful, so compact, so kind,
> That for Achilles' image stood his spear,
> Gripp'd in an armed hand ; himself, behind,
> Was left unseen, save to the eye of mind.' "

Professor Lowell, alluding to the highly finished and classical *form* of Poe's writings, refers, as an example of his style, to "The Fall of the House of Usher," remarking, "It has a singular charm for us, and we think that no one could read it without being strongly moved by its serene and sombre beauty. Had its author written nothing else, it would alone have been enough to stamp him as a man of genius, and the master of a classic style. In this tale occurs one of the most beautiful of his poems " . . . (*i.e.,* "The Haunted Palace ")—" we know no modern poet who might not have been justly proud of it."

The publication of "The Raven" gave an immediate impetus to Poe's activity, and aided him to dispose of the result of his labours ; the press teemed with his work. The February number of Godey's magazine contained his "Thousand and Second Tale of Scheherazade," a satiric story made up chiefly of odds and ends of scientific wonders, and supposed to relate the ultimate fate of the vizier's daughter, to whom all the tales in "The Arabian Nights" are ascribed. The poet's love of hidden hoaxing is well exemplified by the names of the personages in this little romance; for instance, the heroine is "Scheherazade," (She her has said,) and the incidents are assumedly derived from the Oriental work, "Tellmenow Isitsoörnot," (Tell me now is it so or not,) which is compared, for its rarity, with the "Zohar," (So ah,) of "Jochaides," (Joke aides.) These trifles, and similar ones, occurring frequently in the poet's prose works, are emanations of the spirit which excelled in, and even delighted at, "The Balloon Hoax," the "Von Kempelen Discovery," and, in a higher degree, the analyses of "Marie Roget," the "Case of M. Valdemar," and others of that genus.

For the *Evening Mirror* of February 3rd Poe wrote an article on "Didacticism," in which he inveighed strongly against those who deemed poetry a fit medium for the dissemination of "morals ; " all the more salient portions of the essay were embodied in subsequent critiques. On the 8th of the month he reviewed, in the *Broadway Journal*, an American selection from the poems of Bulwer, and rated the editor of the book for giving a *selection* only ; he should, he considers, "in common justice, have either given us *all* the poems of the author, or something that should have worn at least the semblance of an argument in objection to the poems omitted," and concludes with the request that in any future edition this editor "will cut out his introduction, and give in place of it the poems of Bulwer which, whether rightfully or wrongfully, have been omitted." "Some Secrets of the Magazine Prison-House" appeared in the *Journal* for the 15th of February, and, undoubtedly, throw a lurid light upon the mys-

teries of the unfortunate poet's impecuniosity; that
the references *are* to himself no one acquainted with
his career can doubt.   As this short paper is unknown
to many of the poet's admirers, and as it is explanatory of some of the miseries of his life, we give it *in
extensô* :—

"The want of an International Copyright Law, by rendering it nearly impossible to obtain anything from the booksellers in the way of remuneration for literary labour, has
had the effect of forcing many of our very best writers into
the service of the Magazines and Reviews, which, with a
pertinacity that does them credit, keep up in a certain or uncertain degree the good old saying that even in the thankless
field of Letters the labourer is worthy of his hire.   How—by
dint of what dogged instinct of the honest and proper—these
journals have contrived to persist in their paying practices, in
the very teeth of the opposition got up by the Fosters and
Leonard Scotts, who furnish for eight dollars any four of the
British periodicals for a year, is a point we have had much
difficulty in settling to our satisfaction, and we have been
forced to settle it at last upon no more reasonable ground than
that of a still lingering *esprit de patrie*.   That Magazines
can live, and not only live but thrive, and not only thrive
but afford to disburse money for original contributions, are
facts which can only be solved, under the circumstances, by
the really fanciful, but still agreeable supposition, that there is
somewhere still existing an ember not altogether quenched
among the fires of good feeling for letters and literary men
that once animated the American bosom.

"It would *not do* (perhaps this is the idea) to let our poor
devil authors absolutely starve while we grow fat, in a literary sense, on the good things of which we unblushingly pick
the pocket of all Europe : it would not be exactly the thing,
comme il faut, to permit a positive atrocity of this kind ; and
hence we have Magazines, and hence we have a portion of
the public who subscribe to these Magazines (through sheer
pity), and hence we have Magazine publishers (who sometimes
take upon themselves the duplicate title of 'editor *and* proprietor'),—publishers, we say, who, under certain conditions

of good conduct, occasional puffs, and decent subserviency at all times, make it a point of conscience to encourage the poor-devil author with a dollar or two, more or less as he behaves himself properly, and abstains from the indecent habit of turning up his nose.

"We hope, however, that we are not so prejudiced, or so vindictive, as to insinuate that what certainly does look like illiberality on the part of them, (the Magazine publishers,) is really an illiberality chargeable to *them.* In fact, it will be seen at once that what we have said has a tendency directly the reverse of any such accusation. These publishers pay *something*—other publishers nothing at all. Here certainly is a difference—although a mathematician might contend that the difference might be infinitesimally small. Still, these Magazine editors and proprietors *pay* (that is the word), and with your true poor-devil author the smallest favours are sure to be thankfully received. No : the illiberality lies at the door of the demagogue-ridden public, who suffer their anointed delegates (or perhaps arointed—which is it ?) to insult the common sense of them (the public) by making orations in our national halls on the beauty and conveniency of robbing the Literary Europe on the highway, and on the gross absurdity in especial of admitting so unprincipled a principle that a man has any right and title either to his own brains, or the flimsy material that he chooses to spin out of them, like a confounded caterpillar as he is. If anything of this gossamer character stands in need of protection, why we have our hands full at once with the silkworms and the *morus multicaulis.*

"But if we cannot, under the circumstances, complain of the absolute illiberality of the Magazine publishers (since pay they do), there is at least one particular in which we have against them good grounds of accusation. Why, (since pay they must,) do they not pay with a good grace and *promptly ?* Were we in an ill-humour at this moment we could a tale unfold which would erect the hair on the head of Shylock. A young author, struggling with Despair itself in the shape of a ghastly poverty, which has no alleviation—no sympathy from an everyday world that cannot understand his necessities, and that would pretend not to understand them if it comprehended them ever so well—this young author is politely requested to compose an article, for which he will 'be handsomely paid.' Enraptured, he neglects perhaps for a month the sole employment which affords him the chance of a livelihood, and having starved through the month (he and his family) completes at length the month of starvation and the article, and despatches the latter, (with a broad hint about the former,) to the pursy 'editor' and bottle-nosed 'proprietor' who has condescended to honour him (the poor devil) with his patronage. A month (starving still), and no reply. Another month — still none. Two months more—still none. A second letter, modestly hinting that the article may not have reached its destination — still no reply. At the expiration of six additional months, personal application is made at the 'editor and proprietor's' office. Call again. The poor devil goes out, and does not fail to call again. Still call again;—and call again is the word for three or four months more. His patience exhausted, the article is demanded. No—he can't have it—(the truth is, it was too good to be given up so easily)—'it is in print,' and 'contributions of this character are never paid for (it is a *rule* we have) under six months after publication. Call in six months after the issue of your affair, and your money is ready for you—for we are business men ourselves—prompt.' With this the poor devil is satisfied, and makes up his mind that the 'editor and proprietor' is a gentleman, and that of course he (the poor devil) will wait as requested. And it is supposable that he would have waited if he could— but Death in the meantime would not. He dies, and by the good luck of his decease, (which came by starvation,) the fat 'editor and proprietor' is fatter henceforward, and for ever, to the amount of five and twenty dollars, very cleverly saved, to be spent generously in canvas-backs and champagne.

"There are two things which we hope the reader will not do as he runs over this article : first, we hope that he will not believe that we write from any personal experience of our own, for we have only the reports of actual sufferers to depend upon ; and second, that he will not make any personal application of our remarks to any Magazine publisher now living, it being well known that they are all as remarkable for their generosity and urbanity, as for their intelligence and appreciation of Genius."

On Friday, February 28th, Poe delivered a lecture in the Library of the New York Historical Society, on the "Poets and Poetry of America." The discourse attracted much attention, not only on account of the lecturer's eloquence, personal beauty, and the magnetic fascination of his presence, but, also, by the originality and courage of his remarks. He daringly attacked the ephemeral favourites of the day, and did not forbear from vigorous onslaughts upon the editors and compilers who had belauded them into temporary notoriety. The result of this lecture was that the attacked poured forth torrents of abuse, none the less annoying because anonymous, none the less effective because false. A few friends defended the poet in such publications as were open to them : the *American Review* referred to "the devoted spirit in which he advocated the claims and urged the responsibilities of literature. The necessity of a just and independent criticism," says this journal, "was his main topic. He made unmitigated war upon the prevalent Puffery, and dragged several popular idols from their pedestals. His closest critical remarks were given to an examination of the poetry of Mrs. Sigourney and the Davidsons. Bryant, Halleck, and Willis were spoken of briefly, but any neglect in this particular was compensated by several choicely delivered recitations from their verses. . . . There has been a great deal said about this lecture which should be either repeated or printed."

This lecture of the now famous Edgar Poe was a nine-days' wonder, and, on the 8th March following its delivery, the poet himself thus wrote about it :—

"In the late lecture on the 'Poets and Poetry of America,' delivered before an audience made up chiefly of editors and their connections, I took occasion to speak what I know to be the truth, and I endeavoured so to speak it that there should be no chance of misunderstanding what it was I intended to say. I told these gentlemen to their teeth, that, with a *very* few noble exceptions, they had been engaged for many years in a system of indiscriminate laudation of American books—a system which, more than any other one thing in the world, had tended to the depression of that 'American Literature' whose elevation it was designed to effect. I said this, and very much more of a similar tendency, with as thorough a distinctness as I could command. Could I, at the moment, have invented any terms *more* explicit, wherewith to express my contempt of our general editorial course of corruption and puffery, I should have employed them beyond the shadow of a doubt;—and should I think of anything more expressive *hereafter*, I will endeavour either to find or to make an opportunity for its introduction to the public.

"And what, for all this, had I to anticipate? In a very few cases the open, and, in several, the silent approval of the more chivalrous portion of the press;—but in a majority of instances, I should have been weak indeed to look for anything but abuse. To the Willises—the O'Sullivans—the Duyckincks—to the choice and magnanimous few who spoke promptly in my praise, and who have since taken my hand with a more cordial and a more impressive grasp than ever— to these, I return, of course, my acknowledgments, for that they have rendered me my due. To my vilifiers I return also such thanks as they deserve, inasmuch as without what they have done me the honour to say there would have been much of point wanting in the compliments of my friends. Had I, indeed, from the former received any less equivocal tokens of disapprobation, I should at this moment have been looking about me to discover what sad blunder I had committed.

"I am most sincere in what I say. I thank these, my opponents, for their goodwill,—manifested, of course, after their own fashion. No doubt they mean me well—if they could only be brought to believe it ; and I shall expect more reasonable things from them hereafter. In the meantime, I await patiently the period when they shall have fairly made an end of what they have to say—when they shall have sufficiently exalted themselves in their own opinion—and when, especially, they shall have brought *me* over to that precise view of the question which it is their endeavour to have me adopt.　　　　　　　　　　　　　　　　　E. A. P."

As a pleasing pendant to the whirlwind which some portions of this lecture aroused may be mentioned the fact that, during his discourse, Poe had recited, with approving comments, "Florence Vane," a beautiful lyric by Philip P. Cooke, a young Virginian, who died a few years later in his youthful and budding promise of fame. Poe's sympathetic delivery, and the warm encomia he awarded the poem and its author, excited considerable interest, and caused "Florence Vane" to take a place in American literary selections which, however deserved, it might not otherwise so readily have succeeded in obtaining.

On the same day that the above letter was written Poe associated himself with two journalists in the editorial management of the *Broadway Journal.* In consequence of this new undertaking, the poet resigned the position he had held on the *Evening Mirror,* but, in bidding farewell to its wretched drudgery, he entered into trials and troubles almost as bad, and commenced a series of episodes not only as romantic, but, also, quite as unfortunate, as the earlier years of his life.

CHAPTER XV.

THE "BROADWAY JOURNAL."

ON the 8th of March 1845, Edgar Poe became joint-editor, with two New York journalists, of the *Broadway Journal*, a publication of no particular influence or circulation. One of his coadjutors devoted himself to the musical and dramatic section of the paper, and the other shared the literary department with their new associate. The views of Poe and his literary companion being diametrically opposite, it was arranged that each should be free to enunciate his own opinions independently of the other—an arrangement that produced a somewhat novel, not to say unseemly, appearance, during the few weeks the system lasted.

No sooner was Poe reseated in an editorial chair than he resumed an unfortunate " Discussion with Outis," which he had commenced in Willis's paper, the *Evening Mirror*, on the unsavoury subject of plagiarism, and which he now continued, from week to week, in the columns of the *Broadway Journal*. How this unprofitable disputation arose was thus : In the *Evening Mirror* for the 14th of January, Poe had published a short notice of "The Waif," a collection of fugitive verses edited by Longfellow, observing in the course of his remarks :—

" We conclude our notes on the ' Waif' with the observation that, although full of beauties, it is infected with a *moral taint*—or is this a mere freak of our own fancy ? We shall be pleased if it be so; but there *does* appear, in this little volume, a very careful avoidance of all American poets who may be supposed especially to interfere with the claims of Mr. Longfellow. These men Mr. Longfellow can continually *imitate* (*is* that the word?), and yet never even incidentally commend."

"Much discussion ensued," says Poe, proceeding to narrate in the *Journal* that "a friend of Mr. Longfellow's penned a defence, which had at least the merit of being thoroughly impartial; for it defended Mr. Longfellow not only from the one-tenth of very moderate disapproval in which I had indulged, but from the nine-tenths of my enthusiastic admiration into the bargain. . . . This well-intended defence was published in the *Mirror* with a few words of preface by Mr. Willis, and of postscript by myself. Still dissatisfied, Mr. Longfellow, through a second friend, addressed to Mr. Willis an expostulatory letter, of which the *Mirror* printed only the following portion:—

"'It has been asked, perhaps, why Lowell was neglected in this collection? Might it not as well be asked why Bryant, Dana, and Halleck were neglected? The answer is obvious to any one who candidly considers the character of the collection. It professed to be, according to the Poem [*sic*, but query Proem.—J. H. I.], from the humbler poets; and it was intended to embrace pieces that were anonymous, or which were [*sic*, query not] easily accessible to the general reader—the *waifs* and *estrays* of literature. To put anything of Lowell's, for example, into a collection of *waifs*, would be a particular liberty with pieces which are all collected and christened.'"

"Not yet content," continues Poe, "or misunderstanding the tenor of some of the wittily-*put* comments which accompanied the quotation, the aggrieved poet, through one of the two friends, as before, or perhaps through a third, finally prevailed upon the good-nature of Mr. Willis to publish an explicit declaration of his disagreement with '*all* the disparagement of Longfellow' which had appeared in the criticism in question.

"Now when we consider that many of the points of censure made by me in this *critique* were absolutely as plain as the nose upon Mr. Longfellow's face, that it was impossible to gainsay them, that we defied him and his coadjutors to say a syllable in reply to them, and that they held their tongues and not a syllable said—when we consider all this, I say, then the satire of the '*all*' in Mr. Willis's manifesto becomes apparent at once. Mr. Longfellow did not see it; and I presume his friends did not see it. I did. In my mind's eye it expanded itself thus :—

" ' My dear sir, or sirs, what will you have? You are an insatiable set of cormorants, it is true; but if you will only let me know what you desire, I will satisfy you, if I die for it Be quick ! merely say what it is you wish me to admit, and (for the sake of getting rid of you) I will admit it upon the spot. Come ! I will grant at once that Mr. Longfellow is Jupiter Tonans, and that his three friends are the Graces, or the Furies, which ever you please. As for a fault to be found with either of you, *that* is impossible, and I say so. I disagree with *all*, with every syllable of the disparagement that ever has been whispered against you up to this date, and (not to stand upon trifles) with all that ever *shall* be whispered against you henceforward, for ever and for ever.' . . . In the meanwhile Mr. Briggs in this paper, in the *Broadway Journal*, did me the honour of taking me to task for what he supposed to be my insinuations against Mr. Aldrich."

In his reply in the *Mirror* (prefaced by a few words from Mr. Willis), the poet reiterated the charge that " *Somebody* is a thief," with reference to the palpable "parallelism " between Hood's beautiful poem " The Deathbed," and some verses entitled " A Death-bed," by Mr. J. Aldrich ; but, after a collation of the two pieces, and a demonstration that the resemblance was too close to be accidental, he left it to the public to form its own judgment upon the affair. " At this point the matter rested for a fortnight," continues the narration, " when a fourth friend of Mr. Longfellow took up the cudgels for him, in another communication to the *Mirror*," which communication, signed " Outis," Poe reprinted in full, and then proceeded to criticise thus :—

"What I admire in this letter is the gentlemanly grace of its manner, and the chivalry which has prompted its composition. What I do *not* admire is all the rest. In especial, I do not admire the desperation of the effort to make out a case. No gentleman should degrade himself, on any grounds, to the paltriness of *ex parte* argument; and I shall not insult Outis at the outset by assuming for a moment that he (Outis) is weak enough to suppose me (Poe) silly enough to look upon all this abominable rigmarole as anything better than a very respectable specimen of special pleading.

"As a general rule, in a case of this kind, I should wish to begin with the beginning, but as I have been unable, in running my eye over Outis' remarks, to discover that they have any beginning at all, I shall be pardoned for touching them in the order which suits me best. Outis need not have put himself to the trouble of informing his readers that he has 'some acquaintance with Mr. Longfellow.' It was needless, also, to mention that he did not know *me*. I thank him for his many flatteries, but of their inconsistency I complain. To speak of me in one breath as a poet, and in the next to insinuate charges of 'carping littleness,' is simply to put forth a flat paradox. When a plagiarism is committed and detected, the word 'littleness' and other similar words are immediately brought into play. To the words themselves I have no objection whatever; but their application might occasionally be improved.

"Is it altogether impossible that a critic be instigated to the exposure of a plagiarism, or still better, of plagiarism generally, wherever he meets it, by a strictly honourable and even charitable motive? Let us see. A theft of this kind is committed—for the present we will admit the *possibility* that a theft of this character can be committed. The chances, of course, are that an established author steals from an unknown one, rather than the converse; for in proportion to the circulation of the original is the risk of the plagiarism's detection. The person about to commit the theft hopes for impunity altogether on the ground of the reconditeness of the source from which he thieves. But this obvious consideration is rarely borne in mind. We read a certain passage in a certain book. We meet a passage nearly similar in another book. The first book is not at

Q

hand, and we cannot compare dates. We decide by what we fancy the probabilities of the case. The one author is a distinguished man—our sympathies are always in favour of distinction. ' It is not likely,' we say in our hearts, ' that so distinguished a personage as A would be guilty of plagiarism from this B, of whom nobody in the world has ever heard. We give judgment, therefore, at once against B of whom nobody in the world has ever heard ; and it is for the very reason that nobody in the world has ever heard of him that, in ninety-nine cases out of the hundred, the judgment so precipitously given is erroneous. Now, then, the plagiarist has not merely committed a wrong in itself—a wrong whose incomparable meanness would deserve exposure on absolute grounds—but he, the guilty, the successful, the eminent, has fastened the degradation of his crime—the retribution which should have overtaken it in his own person—upon the guilt-less, the toiling, the unfriended struggler up the mountainous path of Fame. Is not sympathy for the plagiarist, then, about as sagacious and about as generous as would be the sympathy for the murderer, whose exultant escape from the noose of the hangman should be the cause of an innocent man's being hung? And because I, for one, should wish to throttle the guilty, with a view of letting the innocent go, could it be considered proper on the part of any ' acquaintance of Mr. Longfellow's ' who came to witness the execution— could it be thought, I say, either chivalrous or decorous, on the part of this ' acquaintance,' to get up against me a charge of ' carping littleness,' while we stood amicably together at the foot of the gallows?

" In all this I have taken it for granted that such a sin as plagiarism exists. We are informed by Outis, however, that it does *not*. ' I shall not charge Mr. Poe with plagiarism,' he says, ' for, as I have said, such charges are perfectly absurd.' An assertion of this kind is certainly *funny* (I am aware of no other epithet which precisely applies to it) ; and I have much curiosity to know if Outis is prepared to swear to its truth—holding right aloft in his hand, of course, and kissing the back of Disraeli's ' Curiosities,' or the ' Mélanges ' of Suard and André. But if the assertion is funny (and it *is*), it is by no means an original thing. It is precisely, in fact, what all the plagiarists and all the ' acquaintances ' of plagiarists, since the flood, have maintained with a very praiseworthy resolution."

The poet continues, for several more paragraphs, in a similar strain; and in the following number of the *Journal* resumed what he styled "The Voluminous History of the little Longfellow War," by a further reply to the " Letter of Outis." This continuation is wiredrawn, and far from brilliant, and deferred till the following week "interesting developments," evidently with the intention of prolonging and increasing any excitement the discussion may have aroused. A few paragraphs may be cited, however:—

"Here is a gentleman," says Poe, "who writes, in certain respects, as a gentleman should, and who yet has the effrontery to base a defence of a friend from the charge of plagiarism, on the broad ground that no such thing as plagiarism ever existed. I confess that to an assertion of this nature there is no little difficulty in getting up a reply. . . . What could any judge, on any bench in the country, do but laugh or swear at the attorney who should begin his defence of a petty-larceny client with an oration demonstrating, *à priori*, that no such thing as petty-larceny ever had been, or, in the nature of things, ever could be, committed ? . . . 'What is plagiarism ?' demands Outis at the outset, *avec l'air d'un Romain qui sauve sa patrie*—' what is plagiarism, and what constitutes a good ground for the charge ?'. . . He answers the two questions by two others. . . . 'Did no two men,' he says, 'ever think alike without stealing one from the other ? Or, thinking alike, did no two men ever use the same or similar words to convey the thoughts, and that without any communication with each other ? To deny it is absurd.' Of course it is—very absurd ; and the only thing *more* absurd that I can call to mind, at present, is the supposition that any person ever entertained an idea of denying it. . . .

"But let me aid Outis to a distinct conception of his own irrelevance. I accuse his friend, specifically, of a plagiarism.

This accusation Outis rebuts by asking me with a grave face—not whether the friend might not, in this individual case, and in the compass of eight short lines, have happened upon ten or twelve peculiar identities of thought, and identities of expression, with the author from whom I charge him with plagiarising—but simply whether I do not admit the *possibility* that once, in the course of eternity, some two individuals might not happen upon a single identity of thought, and give it voice in a single identity of expression. Now, frankly, I admit the possibility in question, and would request my friends to get ready for me a strait-jacket if I did not. . . .

"I put no faith in the *nil admirari*, and am apt to be amazed at every second thing which I see. One of the most amazing things I have yet seen is the complacency with which Outis throws to the right and left his anonymous assertions, taking it for granted that because he (Nobody) asserts them, I must believe them as a matter of course. However, he is quite in the right. I am perfectly ready to admit anything that he pleases, and am prepared to put as implicit faith in his *ipse dixit* as the Bishop of Autun did in the Bible—on the ground that he knew nothing about it at all. . . .

"He wishes to show, then, that Mr. Longfellow is innocent of the imitation with which I have charged him, and that Mr. Aldrich is innocent of the plagiarism with which I have *not* charged him; and this duplicate innocence is expected to be proved *by* showing the possibility that a certain, or that any uncertain, series of coincidences may be the result of pure accident. Now, of course, I cannot be sure that Outis will regard my admission as a service or a disservice, but I admit the possibility at once. . . . But, in admitting this, I admit just nothing at all, so far as the advancement of Outis' proper argument is concerned. The affair is one of *probabilities* altogether, and can be satisfactorily settled only by reference to their calculus."

The following week a still more voluminous budget appeared from Poe's pen, in continuation of this interminable discussion, but from it only these lines—of biographical import—require citation:—

"If Outis has his own private reasons for being disgusted with what he terms the 'wholesale mangling of victims without rhyme or reason,' there is not a man living, of common sense and common honesty, who has not better reason (if possible) to be disgusted with the insufferable cant and shameless misrepresentations practised by just such persons as Outis, with the view of decrying by sheer strength of lungs—of trampling down—of rioting down—of mobbing down any man with a soul that bids him come out from among the general corruption of our public press, and take his stand upon the open ground of rectitude and honour.

"The Outises who practise this species of bullyism are, as a matter of course, anonymous. . . . Their low artifices are insinuated calumnies, and indefatigable whispers of regret from post to pillar, that 'Mr. So-and-so, or Mr. This-and-that, *will* persist in rendering himself so dreadfully unpopular'— no one, in the meantime, being more thoroughly and painfully aware than these very Outises that the unpopularity of the just critic who reasons his way, guiltless of dogmatism, is confined altogether within the limits of the influence of the victims, without rhyme and reason, who have been mangled by wholesale. Even the manifest injustice of a Gifford is, I grieve to say, an exceedingly popular thing; and there is *no* literary element of popularity more absolutely and more universally effective than the pungent impartiality of a Wilson or a Macaulay. In regard to my own course—without daring to arrogate to myself a single other quality of either of these eminent men than that pure contempt for mere prejudice and conventionality which actuated them all, I will now unscrupulously call the attention of the Outises to the fact that it was during what they (the Outises) would insinuate to be the unpopularity of my 'wholesale mangling of the victims without rhyme and reason,' that, in one year, the circulation of the *Southern Messenger* (a five-dollar journal) extended itself from seven hundred to nearly five thousand—and that, in little more than twice the same time, *Graham's Magazine* swelled its list from five to fifty-two thousand subscribers.

"I make no apology for these egotisms, and I proceed with them without hesitation—for, in myself, I am but defending a set of principles which no honest man need be ashamed of defending, and for whose defence no honest man will consider an apology required. . . . Not even an Outis can accuse me, with even a decent show of verisimilitude, of having ever descended, in the most condemnatory of my reviews, to that personal abuse which, upon one or two occasions, has indeed been levelled at myself, in the spasmodic endeavours of aggrieved authors to rebut what I have ventured to demonstrate. . . . What I have written remains, and is readily accessible in any of our public libraries. I have had one or two impotent enemies and a multitude of cherished friends—and both friends and enemies have been, for the most part, literary people ; yet no man can point to a single *critique*, among the very numerous ones which I have written during the last ten years, which is either wholly fault-finding or wholly in approbation ; nor is there an instance to be discovered, among all that I have published, of my having set forth, either in praise or censure, a single opinion upon any critical topic of moment, without attempting, at least, to give it authority by something that wore the semblance of a reason. . . . Very many of the most eminent men in America, whom I am proud to number among the sincerest of my friends, have been rendered so solely by their approbation of my comments upon their own works—comments in great measure directed *against* themselves as authors —belonging altogether to that very class of criticism which it is the petty policy of the Outises to cry down."

To this terribly lengthy discussion anent plagiarism a postscript was subsequently indited by the poet, in which he sought to prove that *unconscious* plagiarism "is in the direct ratio of the poetic sentiment—of the susceptibility to the poetic impression ; and, in fact," he concluded, "all literary history demonstrates that, for the most frequent and palpable plagiarisms, we must search the works of the most eminent poets."

That the results of this "Discussion" were far from beneficial to the contemporary fame and fortune of Poe few can doubt ; that it added to the number of his enemies—who were scarcely so few or so impotent as he affected to believe—is equally certain; whilst that it could in no way increase the presumed "multitude of cherished friends," whatever it may have effected in the quantity of his readers, needs no demonstration.

It is pleasant to turn from this bitter repast to the more genial topic of the poet's more literary work, although his gall was by no means all expended in the above profitless warfare. In the *Broadway Journal* for March, for instance, he contrived to deliver some very severe and, that they were true, ill-endured blows at certain national foibles, in a short article on "Satirical Poems." In the following month he returned to his more natural manner, contributing revised versions of "The Valley Nis" and "The Doomed City," and a new tale, "Some Words with a Mummy," to the *American Review.*

"Some Words with a Mummy" is written in that humorous style which was so unnatural with Poe, and which his sombre—his ultra-poetic temperament—would have prevented him from ever becoming proficient in. It is, perhaps, his best effort in that direction, and contains many of those cutting satiric touches which he bandied about so freely, if unwisely, at this transition period of his life—the period when constant collisions with journalistic sharpshooters and jealous cliques caused a more decided deterioration of his *morale* than did any preceding or succeeding calamities. It was his frequent misfortune to attempt to fight men of the world with their own weapons, and with the invariable consequences that happen to those who touch pitch. A single paragraph from the last-named

tale will show why it is that Poe's writings are so unpopular with some of his countrymen ; the Americans
being, as a general rule, too susceptible to relish a
joke at their own expense.   The hero, Count Alla-
mistakeo [all-a-mistake-o], the resuscitated Egyptian
mummy, is informed of the benefits of the democratic
institutions enjoyed by the Yankees; their advantages
of having universal suffrage, and no king.   "He listened
with marked interest, and, in fact, seemed not a little
amused.   When we had done," continues the narrator,
"he said that a great while ago there had occurred
something of a very similar sort.   Thirteen Egyptian
provinces determined all at once to be free, and so
set a magnificent example to the rest of mankind.
They assembled their wise men, and concocted the
most ingenious constitution it is possible to conceive.
For a while they managed remarkably well, only their
habit of bragging was prodigious.   The thing ended,
however, in the consolidation of the thirteen states,
with some fifteen or twenty others, in the most odious
and insupportable despotism that ever was heard of
upon the face of the earth.   I asked what was the
name of the usurping tyrant.   As well as the Count
could recollect, it was *Mob.*"

The April number of the *Southern Literary Messenger*
contained an announcement to the effect that its old
conductor and contributor was about to resume writing
for its pages.   "It needs an Argus to guard and watch
the press," says the editor, "and, to enable the *Messenger*
to discharge its part, we have engaged the services of
Mr. E. A. Poe, who will contribute a monthly *critique
raisonnée* of the most important forthcoming works in
this country and Europe."   The poet's multifarious

labours, however, prevented him carrying out this projected scheme, although he subsequently recommenced writing for the *Messenger*, and continued a contributor during the rest of his life.

During April and May Poe published several minor articles and book notices in the *Broadway Journal*, and as many of these are uncollected, and their paternity unknown, the more interesting will be alluded to, and quoted from, in these pages. It may, indeed, be remarked here, that the poet's own revised copy of the *Journal* being in our possession, and his articles therein which were published anonymously, or over *noms de plume*, having his initials appended in pencil, we are enabled to rescue much interesting matter from oblivion.

" Human Magnetism " was a subject Poe was now deeply interested in, although he was not to be deceived by many of the impostures prevalent. Noticing a work on this subject, and pointing out certain views in which he differed from its author, he took occasion to say—" Most especially do we disagree with him in his (implied) disparagement of the work of Chauncey Hare Townshend, which we regard as one of the most truly profound and philosophical works of the day—a work to be valued properly only in a day to come." " Anastatic Printing " was also a subject that attracted his attention, and upon which he wrote a short article, replete with idiosyncratic remarks. The invention was one that greatly excited his imagination, and caused him to foresee a palmy future for authors; to anticipate the time when writers would be enabled to publish their works " without the expensive interference of the type-setter, and the often

ruinous intervention of the publisher." This literary
millennium was to produce, among other unfulfilled
blessings, " some attention to legibility of manuscript "
by men of letters ; and " the cultivation of accuracy
in manuscript," opined the poet, would " tend, with an
inevitable impetus, to every species of improvement
in style ; more especially in the points of concision
and distinctness ; and this again, in a degree even
more noticeable, to precision of thought and luminous
arrangement of matter ; " and his conclusion was, that
" at present the literary world is a species of anomalous congress, in which the majority of the members
are constrained to listen in silence, while all the eloquence proceeds from a privileged few. In the new
régime the humblest will speak as often and as freely
as the most exalted, and will be sure of receiving just
that amount of attention which the intrinsic merit of
their speeches may deserve."

A revival of the " Antigone" of Sophocles having
been attempted in New York, in imitation of similar re-
vivals in Europe, Poe, in commenting very severely upon
the performance, said—" Apart from all this, there is
about the ' Antigone,' as well as about all the ancient
plays, an insufferable *baldness*, or platitude, the inevitable
result of inexperience in art—but a baldness, nevertheless, which pedantry would force us to believe the
result of a studied and supremely artistic simplicity
alone. Simplicity is, indeed, a very lofty and very
effective feature in all true art—but *not* the simplicity which we see in the Greek drama. The simplicity of the Greek sculpture is everything that can
be desired, because here the art in itself is the simplicity in itself, and in its elements. The Greek

sculptor chiselled his forms from what he saw before him every day, in a beauty far nearer to perfection than any work of any Cleomenes in the world. But in the drama, the *direct* — the straightforward, *un-German* Greek had no Nature so directly presented, from which to copy his conceptions. . . . To the Greeks, beyond doubt, their drama *seemed* perfection —and this fact is absurdly urged as proof of their drama's perfection in itself. It need only be said, in reply, that their art and their sense of art must have been necessarily on a level."

Adverting to the absurdity of attempting to reproduce a Greek play before a modern audience, especially with such a want of all the requisite appliances as this little New York theatre displayed, Poe paused to bestow his praise upon the successful manner in which Mendelssohn has wedded his music to the Hellenic drama : he must, he says, " have been inspired when he conceived the plan. . . . He had," remarked Poe, " many difficulties to contend with; his own natural style must be abandoned, and the cramped and unmelodious system of the Greek unisonous singing adopted. To preserve that distinctive character, and still render the music acceptable to modern ears, must have taxed the utmost ingenuity of the composer. But he has succeeded to a marvel."

Some of Poe's strictures on the performance and the performers of " Antigone " aroused the anger of the manager, or director, or whatever he was, of the theatre, and he indited an amusingly pompous epistle to the poet, addressed to " Edgar Poe, Esq., &c., &c., &c., Author of THE RAVEN," in which, after stating that he deemed his *critique* " *characterised* much *more* by *ill-nature* and an *illiberal* spirit, than by fair and candid, or even *just* criticism," and that, therefore, he, the great Somebody, " in *justice* to *myself*, have withdrawn your (Poe's) name *from* the free list." On this display of " Achilles' wrath " Poe wrote an amusing paper in the *Broadway Journal*, from which this paragraph may be cited :—

" We are not wrong (are we ?) in conceiving that Mr. —— is in a passion. We are not accustomed to compositions of precisely this character—(that is to say, notes written in large capitals, with admiration notes for commas,—the whole varied occasionally with lowercase) — but still we think ourselves justified in imagining that Mr. —— was in a passion when he sent us this note from his suite of *boudoirs* at the Astor House. In fact, we fancy that we can trace the gradations of his wrath in the number and impressiveness of his underscoring. The SIRS ! ! for example, are exceedingly bitter ; and in THE RAVEN, which has five black lines beneath it, each one blacker than the preceding, we can only consider ourselves as devoted to the infernal gods."

Among more serious subjects which followed in the *Journal* from Poe's pen, may be mentioned, as amongst his uncollected writings, an article on the science of Street Paving ; a review of Leigh Hunt, in which the conclusion was arrived at that *taste* was his *forte*, but that of critical analysis he was utterly deficient ; a sympathetic notice of " Eothen," then recently issued, drew forth the remark that its author "brings the East to us more vividly than any other Eastern traveller has done." A *critique* on Old English Poetry, replete with Poësque passages, and noticeable for its glowing enthusiasm for " The Ancient Mariner," followed, and from among old poems singled out for especial commendation, was Marvell's exquisitely tender lines on

the " Maiden's Lamentation for her Fawn." A scarification of " Poems" by a Mr. Lord, and a friendly
notice of "Philothea"—in which were some significant
allusions to "Zanoni"—concluded the week's number.

In May the tale of " Three Sundays in a Week "
appeared in the *Journal,* in the insatiable pages of
which periodical were republished, all more or less
revised, and frequently over *noms de plume,* nearly the
whole of Poe's stories, and a large portion of his poems.
As an extract from *The New World,* some stanzas in
parody of " The Raven" appeared in this month's issue,
under the title of " A Gentle Puff;" and were republished with the editorial remark that this one only,
out of the many complimentary notices they received,
would be reprinted, and it because of its uniqueness.
As the opinion of a contemporary journalist on Poe's
non-respect of persons in his critical capacity, one
stanza may be worth citation :—

"Neither rank nor station heeding, with his foes around him
     bleeding,
  Sternly, singly, and alone, his course he kept upon that floor ;
  While the countless foes attacking, neither strength nor valour
     lacking,
  On his goodly armour hacking, wrought no change his visage o'er,
  As with high and honest aim he still his falchion proudly bore,
            Resisting error evermore."

Amid critical notices by the poet, other than those
adverted to already, are many interesting opinions upon
literature and kindred topics ; and his indignation is
particularly aroused by some deprecatory comments
of certain reviewers of "the august works of Tennyson
and Miss Barrett." " It is worse than sacrilege," exclaims Poe, " to intrust to *such hands* poems which, if
we are entitled to estimate the merit of anything by

its effect on the greatest intellects and the noblest hearts, are *divine*, if there be any divinity within the soul of man."

"The Power of Words," one of the best of Poe's prose poems, appeared in the *Democratic Review* for June. The tale, if such it may be termed, for it is utterly devoid of incident, is merely the conversation of two disembodied spirits as they soar through the infinite vistas of space. Their discourse on such syllogisms as that only the acquiring, and not the possessing, knowledge, produces happiness, passes by natural transitions into a discussion—every line of which is pregnant with poetic suggestion—on the *physical power of words*, and concludes with a *dénouement* as startling as that of any of its author's works.

In the *Broadway Journal* for this month Poe published a sketch of a very different description, on Magazine-writing, entitled "Peter Snooks." It was called forth as a commentary on a paper by Mr. Duyckinck on Magazine Literature; is replete with excellent remarks and, it might almost be said, with prophecies that have already been fulfilled. Alluding to the relative value of European and American magazine articles, and to some of the disadvantages under which contributors of the latter *then* laboured, Poe said :—

"We are so circumstanced as to be unable to pay for elaborate compositions—and, after all, the true invention is elaborate. There is no greater mistake than the supposition that a true originality is a mere matter of impulse or inspiration. To originate, is carefully, patiently, and understandingly, to combine. The few American magazinists who ever think of this elaboration at all, cannot afford to carry it into practice for the paltry prices offered them by our periodical publishers. For this, and other glaring reasons, we are behind the age in a *very* important branch of literature, a branch which, moreover, is daily growing in importance, and which, in the end (not far distant), will be the *most* influential of all the departments of letters.

"We are lamentably deficient not only in invention proper, but in that which is more strictly *art*. What American, for instance, in penning a criticism, ever supposes himself called upon to present his readers with more than the exact stipulation of his title—to present them with a criticism, and *something beyond ?* Who thinks of making his *critique* a work of art in itself, independently of its critical opinions ? a work of art, such as are all the more elaborate and most effective reviews of Macaulay ? Yet these reviews we have evinced no incapacity to appreciate when presented. The best American review ever penned is miserably ineffective when compared with the notice of Montagu's ' Bacon,' and yet this latter is, in general, a piece of tawdry sophistry, owing everything to a consummate, to an exquisite arrangement—to a thorough and just sufficiently comprehensive diffuseness, to a masterly *climacing* of points—to a style which dazzles the understanding with its brilliancy, but not more than it misleads it by its perspicuity, causing us so distinctly to comprehend that we fancy we coincide—in a word, to the perfection of art—of all the art which a Macaulay can wield, or which is applicable to any criticism that a Macaulay could write."

Hereafter follows an analysis of "Peter Snooks," that tale being referred to as a specimen of the artistic manner in which an experienced English magazinist constructs *his* story, a most remarkable deficiency in that branch of literature being ascribed to Americans of the period. Poe declared, indeed, that except Hawthorne and one or two others, there " was not even a respectable skilful tale-writer on that side the Atlantic."

In July, Messrs. Wiley & Putnam announced for publication, in their *Library of American Books*, a volume of "Tales by Edgar A. Poe" himself. This collection was made for the publishers by Mr. E. A. Duyckinck, editor of the well-known *Cyclopedia of American Literature.* Besides many of the poet's previously published tales, the book contained the new story of "Mesmeric Revelation," a story issued soon afterwards in the *Columbian Magazine.* Poe was somewhat annoyed at the selection made, and wrote to a correspondent:—

"It may be some years before I publish the rest of my tales, essays, &c. The publishers cheat—and I must wait till I can be my own publisher. The collection of tales issued by Wiley & Putnam were selected by a gentleman whose taste does not coincide with my own, from seventy-two written by me at various times —and those chosen are *not* my best, nor do they fairly represent me in any respect."

Subsequently the author seems to have somewhat modified his views as to the nature of this collection— for the editor of which he always expressed a high opinion. Small as was the volume, and limited its contents in quantity, the quality elicited a large amount of admiration and respect, not only in the United States but also in Europe. The "Tales" were published simultaneously in New York and London, and from the latter city Mr. Martin F. Tupper wrote to the publisher, "Shall we make Edgar Poe famous by a notice in the *Literary Gazette?*" Mr. Putnam does not state whether he accepted this generous offer; it is, therefore, difficult to say how much of the poet's renown is due to the mediation of the "Proverbial Philosopher." Probably the most important of the foreign reviews of these "Tales" was the appreciative *critique* by Monsieur E. D. Forgues that appeared in the *Revue des Deux Mondes.* The reviewer, after an analysis of the various stories, proceeds to comment upon their shortness, and the greater probability of fame such writings possess over the wire-drawn inanities of our novelists, concluding with real prescience, that "*il sera opportun de les comparer quand le temps aura consolidé la reputation naissante du conteur étranger et——qui sait ? —ébranle quelque peu celles de nos romanciers féconds.*" This, and other highly flattering notices of the young foreigner, gave an impetus to his reputation in Europe, which may be deemed to have culminated in the *vrai-semblant* translations of Baudelaire, who, indeed, spent many years of his life in an endeavour to thoroughly identify his mind with that of his favourite *littéra-teur,* Edgar Poe, and who has reproduced many of Poe's finest tales with but little, if any, loss of vigour and originality. Indeed, it is chiefly due to the efforts of Baudelaire——to the, in some respects, kindred genius of him to whom Victor Hugo wrote :——" *Vous avez doté le ciel de l'art d'on ne sait quel rayon macabre——vous avez créé un frisson nouveau* "——that Poe's works have become standard classics in France. Edgar Poe, it may be pointed out, is the only American writer really well known and popular in that country. In Spain his " Historias Extraordinarias " speedily acquired fame, and have been thoroughly nationalised ; whilst in Germany his poems and tales both have been frequently translated ; also in Italy three or four separate translations of the latter have been published.

Poe forwarded a copy of his " Tales " to Mrs. Browning, then Miss Barrett, who, writing to a correspondent shortly afterwards, remarked——" There is a tale of his

R

which I do not find in this volume, but which is going the rounds of the newspapers, about mesmerism, throwing us all into most admired disorder, or dreadful doubts as to whether it can be true, as the children say of ghost-stories. The certain thing in the tale in question is the power of the writer, and the faculty he has of making horrible improbabilities seem near and familiar." The story to which Mrs. Browning referred was " The Facts in the Case of M. Valdemar," not published until December of that year.

In July, the sole management of the *Broadway Journal* devolved upon Poe, although the publication did not become his own property for some months later. The new volume opened with the usual flourish of trumpets from the publisher, who, after thanking his numerous friends for their aid in " the very difficult task of establishing a literary and critical weekly," informs them that " the success of the work, in the brief period of its existence, has been, he truly believes, beyond precedent, and that from a brilliant past he looks confidently to a triumphant future."

To the *Journal* for this month Poe contributed, besides revisions of his earlier tales and poems, a lengthy review of Mr. Hirst's poems, a sympathetic one of Mr. Hoyt's quaint " Chaunt of Life," several voluminous *critiques* on *The Drama,* and many shorter notices and notes, of more or less interest. His dramatic *critiques* were chiefly occupied with the acting of Mrs. Mowatt—of whose grace and beauty he spoke in terms of enthusiastic admiration—and from the first of them these significant sentences may be cited:—

" We have no sympathies with the prejudices which would have dissuaded Mrs. Mowatt from the stage. There is no

cant more contemptible than that which habitually decries
the theatrical profession—a profession which, in itself,
embraces all that can elevate and ennoble, and absolutely
nothing to degrade. If some, if many, or if even nearly all
of its members are dissolute, this is an evil arising not from
the profession itself, but from the unhappy circumstances
which surround it. . . . In the mere name of *actress* she
can surely find nothing to dread—nothing, or she would be
unworthy of the profession, not the profession unworthy
her. The theatre is ennobled by its high facilities for the
development of genius—facilities not afforded elsewhere in
equal degree. By the spirit of genius, we say, it is ennobled,
it is sanctified beyond the sneer of the fool or the cant of
the hypocrite. The actor of talent is poor of heart, indeed,
if he do not look with contempt upon the mediocrity even
of a king. The writer of this article is himself the son of an
actress, has invariably made it his boast, and no earl was
ever prouder of his earldom than he of his descent from a
woman who, although well born, hesitated not to consecrate
to the drama her brief career of genius and of beauty."

Poe's contribution to the *American Review* for this
month was the poem of "Eulalie," and to *Graham's
Magazine* that most suggestive story, "The Imp of
the Perverse." Probably in no other tale of this author
will such originality of investigation, and such acu-
menical analysis of a monomania, be discoverable,
as in this one. The field of research would appear
to have been quite unexplored in this direction, and
had, perchance, been left so, because hitherto no one
had at once combined in his own person the power
to analyse, and the morbid "sixth sense" of *perversity*
analysable. Many, most persons, have, undoubtedly,
to some extent, and at certain times, felt promptings
to act in a manner they know to be diametrically
opposed to their own interests, and that for no reasonable reason; yet few, whose mental equilibrium is

invariably unshaken, come within the morbid circle of
those depicted by Poe, with whom "the assurance of
the wrong, or error, of any action is often the one un-
conquerable *force* which impels us, and alone impels
us, to its prosecution." Whether this "overwhelming
tendency to do wrong for the wrong's sake" will not,
as the poet declares, " admit of analysis, or resolution,
into ulterior elements," or whether it really " is a
radical, a primitive, impulse," may safely be left to the
professed *psychologist* to discuss; but no thoughtful
person will refuse to admit the truth of the illustrations
Poe offers in corroboration of his theory. The love,
inherent in human nature, to dally with danger, is
faithfully rendered in these words :—

" We stand upon the brink of a precipice. We peer into
the abyss—we grow sick and dizzy. Our first impulse is
to shrink from the danger. Unaccountably, we remain.
By slow degrees our sickness, and dizziness, and horror,
become merged in a cloud of unnameable feeling. By
gradations, still more imperceptible, this cloud assumes
shape, as did the vapour from the bottle out of which arose
the genius in the Arabian Nights. But out of this, *our*
cloud upon the precipice's edge, there grows into palpability
a shape far more terrible than any genius or any demon of
a tale, and yet it is but a thought, although a fearful one,
and one which chills the very marrow of our bones with
the fierceness of the delight of its horror. It is merely the
idea of what would be our sensations during the sweeping
precipitancy of a fall from such a height; and this fall—
this rushing annihilation—for the very reason that it
involves that one most ghastly and loathsome of all the
most ghastly and loathsome images of death and suffering
which have ever presented themselves to our imagination—
for this very cause do we now the most vividly desire it ;
and because our reason violently deters us from the brink,
therefore do we the more impetuously approach it. There
is no passion in nature so demoniacally impatient as that of

nim who, shuddering upon the edge of a precipice, thus meditates a plunge. To indulge for a moment in any attempt at *thought* is to be inevitably lost; for reflection but urges us to forbear, and *therefore* it is, I say, that we *cannot.* If there be no friendly arm to check us, or if we fail in a sudden effort to prostrate ourselves backward from the abyss, we plunge and are destroyed.

"Examine these and similar actions as we will, we shall find them resulting solely from the spirit of the *perverse.* We perpetrate them merely because we feel that we should *not.* Beyond or behind this there is no intelligible principle; and we might indeed deem this perverseness a direct instigation of the arch-fiend, were it not occasionally known to operate in furtherance of good."

Thoughts and investigations like these are not the stock of a conventional writer; even if they be not original discovery, they are the result of personal research, and are handled with a power, and clearness, and fascination, that no attempt at depreciation can dissever from true genius.

In August, Poe published in the *American Review* a crucial examination of certain native dramatic works, under the title of "The American Drama." The poet advances some very strong arguments to prove the fallacy of the often made assertion that "the Drama has declined;" but if the specimens of contemporary native art he proceeds thereupon to criticise might be deemed a fair sample of the efforts of To-day, it would have to be confessed that, in this instance, the *vox populi* is in the right. The article affords occasion for adducing some very pungent and forcible reasoning. "The great opponent to Progress is Conservatism," says the poet, "in other words—the great adversary of Invention is Imitation: the propositions are in spirit identical. Just as an art is imitative, it is stationary. The most imitative arts are the most prone to repose—and the converse."

In this and the following month, a series of " Marginal Notes," in continuation of the " Marginalia " of the *Democratic Review*, were issued in the *Lady's Book*. They vary in value, but embody in a condensed and pithy manner many of Poe's idiosyncratic ideas. Some of the sayings, indeed, as in the following sentences, are of real autobiographic application :—" So vitally important is this last (*i.e.*, industry), that it may well be doubted if anything to which we have been accustomed to give the title of ' a work of genius ' was ever accomplished without it ; and it is chiefly because this quality and genius are nearly incompatible, that ' works of genius ' are few, while mere men of genius are, as I say, abundant." But although, as Poe points out, industry must combine with genius to produce a *chef-d'œuvre*, he is very careful to warn his readers against the ancient error that industry itself *is* genius.

The *Broadway Journal* during these two months manifested numerous proofs of its editor's industry, and no lack of his genius. In a running commentary, evidently written in great haste, on Thomas Hood's works, he took occasion to express his admiration of many of that poet's exquisite lyrics, restraining, however, his enthusiasm until he came to " The Haunted House," which struck kindred fire from him ; calling forth the remark, that had Hood written nothing else, " it would have sufficed to render him immortal." Many *critiques* of books and authors—native and foreign —and all more or less marked by his distinguishing traits of thought, appeared in the weekly columns of the *Journal.* On the 16th August "Lenore," a most musical chaunt, founded upon its author's juvenile poem of "The Pæan," was published, and in the following number the weird story of "The Tell-Tale Heart." This tale well deserves to rank amid Poe's best works, not only on account of its able construction, and masterly delineation of a homicidal monomania, but because it embodies within its few short pages some of those hitherto undescribed, but universally experienced, "touches of nature" which make the whole world kin. How true—terribly true—is the description of the old man's agony, while he is listening in the silent night for the uplifting of the door-latch, and seeks, but vainly, to persuade himself that his fears are groundless; whilst he says to himself, " It is nothing but the wind in the chimney;" "It is only a mouse crossing the floor;" or, " It is merely a cricket which has made a single chirp." There is more of real horror in the hints of such a narration, than in all the imaginary bloodshed with which tragedy has drenched the stage.

The same issue of the *Journal* contained an editorial note defending the editor against an allegation by a contemporary, anent "The American Drama " *critique*, that he, Poe, could never find anything to admire in Longfellow's writings. " Now this is doing us the grossest injustice," says Poe, for "from Mr. Longfellow's first appearance in the literary world until the present moment, we have been, if not his warmest admirer and most steadfast defender, at least *one* of his warmest and most steadfast. We even so far committed ourselves, in a late public lecture, as to place him at the very head of American poets. Yet, because upon several occasions we have thought proper to *demon-*

strate the sins, while displaying the virtues, of Professor Longfellow, is it just or proper, or even courteous, on the part of *The Gazette,* to accuse us, in round terms, of uncompromising hostility to this poet?" Poe had made too many enemies not to find these anonymous insinuations and misrepresentations of daily occurrence, and it is a somewhat pitiable sight to see him stooping, although often unavoidably, to defend himself against such scurrilities. One of these charges was somewhat amusingly put, and noticed in the *Broadway* in a not unfriendly manner. The *jeu d'esprit* may be cited here, by way of contrast to the generally but too dark shades in the story of the "Raven," as his friends liked to style the poet:—

"The Rev. Arthur Coxe's 'Saul, a Mystery,' having been condemned in no measured terms by Poe of the *Broadway Journal,* and Green of the *Emporium,* a writer in the Hartford *Columbian* retorts as follows :—

> An entertaining history,
> Entitled 'Saul, a Mystery,'
> Has recently been published by the Reverend Arthur Coxe.
> The poem is dramatic,
> And the wit of it is Attic,
> And its teachings are emphatic of the doctrines orthodox.
>
> But Mr. Poe, the poet,
> Declares he cannot go it—
> That the book is very stupid—or something of that sort :
> And Green, of *The Empori-*
> *Um,* tells a kindred story,
> And swears like any Tory that it isn't worth a groat.
>
> But maugre all the croaking
> Of the 'Raven,' and the joking
> Of the verdant little fellow of the used-to-be review,
> THE PEOPLE, in derision
> Of their impudent decision,
> Have declared, without division, that the 'Mystery will do.'

"The *truth,* of course, rather injures an epigram than other-wise; and nobody will think the worse of the one above

when we say that we have expressed *no opinion whatever* of
'Saul.' 'Give a dog a bad name,' &c. Whenever a book
is abused, it is taken for granted that it is we who have been
abusing it. Mr. Coxe has written some very beautiful
poems, and 'Saul' may be one of them for anything that we
know to the contrary."

Other noteworthy things by Poe, which appeared in
the *Journal* during the two months referred to, were
a laudatory review of Mrs. Oakes Smith's "Poems;"
a trenchant *critique* on "Christopher North," and an
analysis of his critical powers; a defence of Machiavelli
—spoken of as "a man of profound thought, of great
sagacity, of indomitable will, and unrivalled during
his time, if not in knowledge of the human, at least in
knowledge of the Italian, heart;"—new remarks on
"Leigh Hunt," "Festus," and the effects of travel on
literary wares. With respect to this last item, "it is
astonishing to see how a magazine article," said the
poet, "like a traveller, spruces up after crossing the
sea. We ourselves have had the honour of being
pirated without mercy—but as we found our articles
improved by the process (at least in the opinion of
our countrymen), we said nothing, as a matter of
course. We have written paper after paper which
attracted no notice at all until it appeared as original
in *Bentley's Miscellany* or the Paris *Charivari*. The
Boston *Notion* * once abused us very lustily for having
written 'The House of Usher.' Not long afterwards
Bentley published it anonymously, as original with
itself,—whereupon the *Notion*, having forgotten that
we wrote it, not only lauded it *ad nauseam*, but copied
it *in toto*."

* Edited by R. W. Griswold.

Charles Lamb next comes under the poet's critical notice, on account of his " Essays of Elia," and he is, opined Poe, the most original of all the British essay-ists. " Of all original men, too, Lamb," said his re-viewer, " has the fewest demerits. Of gross faults he has none at all. His merest extravagances have about them a symmetry which entitles them to critical re-spect. And his innumerable good qualities who shall attempt to depict ? "

But literary squabbles still occupied a large portion of the poet's time and his journal—the *literary* world was too much with him, either for his comfort or reputation. A certain Mr. Jones now excited his wrath by his [published] opinions on " American Humour," or rather his attacks on authors he deemed deficient of that element. " The French," said this Mr. Jones, " have no humour ; " to which Poe retorted, " Let him pray Heaven that in Hades he fall not into the clutches of Molière, of Rabelais, of Voltaire ! " and forthwith proceeded to administer a severe castiga-tion to the offending journalist. The following week the skirmishing was resumed, but nothing very des-perate appears to have taken place in this case ; although a regular hornet's nest of pilferers were stirred up by an exposure, in the same number, of their plagiarisms. From these miserable petty matters it is pleasant to pass to some truly noble thoughts on Milton, aroused by the publication of his " Prose Works," the language of which, said the American poet, after due allowance has been made for the time in which they were written, " no man has ever sur-passed, if, indeed, any man has ever equalled, in purity, in force, in copiousness, in majesty, or, in what may be termed, without the least exaggeration, a gorgeous magnificence of style." In the course of this article occasion was taken to defend Bacon from the accusation of being "the meanest of mankind." "We would undertake to show *à priori,*" said Poe, "that no man, with Bacon's thorough appreciation of the true and beautiful, could, by any possibility, be 'the meanest,' although his very sensibility might make him the weakest 'of mankind.'"

Week after week this work of reviewing books, authors, drama, and fine arts, and attacking or defending people and opinions, went on with more or less skill, as if the poet were aided by some hundred-handed demon. Much parade was made in editorial notes of the literary help received from well-known *littérateurs,* but, beyond a few verses, little was contributed by any of the persons named. In the last week of October Poe became proprietor as well as editor of the *Journal,* and inaugurated his assumption of the sole control of the publication by the commencement of an absurd disputation with some Boston newspapers. This petty but lengthy journalistic warfare arose thus: In consequence of the *furor* excited by the lecture the poet gave in New York, in the early part of the year, he was invited to Boston to deliver a poem in the Lyceum of that city. It is stated that the lecture-course of this institution was waning in popularity, and that Poe's fame being at its zenith, he was invited as a great attraction for the opening of the winter session. Unfortunately the poet accepted the invitation, having the intention, his earliest biographer avers, of writing an original poem for the occasion, upon a subject which had haunted his imagination for years, but his manifold cares and anxieties prevented the accomplishment of the purpose —if such he had—and he contented himself with the recitation of his juvenile poem of " Al Aaraaf."

"I remember him well, as he came on the platform," says one who was present. " He was the best realisation of a poet in feature, air, and manner, that I had ever seen, and the unusual paleness of his face added to its aspect of melancholy interest. He delivered a poem that no one understood, but at its conclusion gave the audience a treat which almost redeemed their disappointment. This was the recitation of his own ' Raven,' which he repeated with thrilling effect. It was something well worth treasuring in memory. . . . Poe," adds this authority, "after he returned to New York, was much incensed at Boston criticism on his poem."

Probably the poet was not incensed to any very great extent at what was said about him, but doubtless deemed it a favourable opportunity, for his journal's sake, to make what he termed " a bobbery." A just view of the case was taken by a contemporary publication, the Charlestown *Patriot*, when it remarked that for a man endowed with such a genius, and constituted as was Poe, "it was a blunder to accept the appointment which called him to deliver himself in poetry before the Boston Lyceum. Highly imaginative men," as it says truly, " can scarcely succeed in such exhibitions. . . . In obeying this call to Boston," it continues, " Mr. Poe committed another mistake. He had been mercilessly exercising himself as a critic at the expense of some of their favourite writers. The swans of New England, under his delineation, had been described as

mere geese, and those, too, of none of the whitest. . . .
Poe had dealt with favourites of Boston unsparingly,
and they hankered after their revenge.   In an evil
hour, then, did he consent to commit himself, in verse,
to their tender mercies.   It is positively amusing to
see how eagerly all the little witlings of the press, in
the old purlieus of the Puritan, flourish the critical
tomahawk about the head of their critic.   In their
eagerness for retribution, one of the papers before us
actually congratulates itself and readers on the (asserted)
failure of the poet. . . . Mr. Poe committed an error in
consenting to address an audience in verse, who, for
three mortal hours, had been compelled to sit and hear
Mr. Caleb Cushing in prose.   The attempt to speak,
after this, in poetry, and fanciful poetry, too, was sheer
madness.   The most patient audience in the world
must have been utterly exhausted by the previous
infliction.   But it is denied that Mr. Poe failed at all.
He had been summoned to recite poetry.   It is asserted
that he did so.   The Boston *Courier*, one of the most
thoughtful of the journals of that city, gives us a very
favourable opinion of the performance which has been
so harshly treated.   'The poem,' says that journal,
'called "The Messenger Star," was an eloquent and
classic production, based on the right principles, containing the essence of *true* poetry, mingled with a
gorgeous imagination, exquisite painting, every charm
of metre, and a graceful delivery.' "

A week after the recitation of his poem Poe began
to comment, in a tone of badinage, upon the remarks
made by some of the Bostonian papers with respect to
his recent performance : " We have been quizzing the
Bostonians," was his assertion, " and one or two of the

more stupid of their editors and editresses have taken
it in high dudgeon." In the next issue of the *Broadway Journal*, the poet, after quoting a vindicatory
paragraph from the Boston *Sunday Times*, proceeds:—

"Our excellent friend Major Noah has suffered himself to
be cajoled by that most beguiling of all little divinities, Miss
Walters of the *Transcript*. We have been looking all over
her article, with the aid of a taper, to see if we could discover
a single syllable of truth in it, and really blush to acknowledge that we cannot. The adorable creature has been
telling a parcel of fibs about us, by way of revenge for
something that we did to Mr. Longfellow (who admires her
very much), and for calling her 'a pretty little witch' into
the bargain.

"The facts of the case seem to be these :—We *were* invited
to 'deliver' (stand and deliver) a poem before the Boston
Lyceum. As a matter of course, we accepted the invitation.
The audience *was* 'large and distinguished.' Mr. Cushing
preceded us with a very capital discourse. He was much
applauded. On arising we were most cordially received. We
occupied some fifteen minutes with an apology for not
'delivering,' as is usual in such cases, a didactic poem—a
didactic poem, in our opinion, being precisely no poem at all.
After some further words—still of apology—for the 'in-
definitiveness' and 'general imbecility' of what we had to
offer—all so unworthy a Bostonian audience—we commenced, and, with many interruptions of applause, concluded.
Upon the whole, the approbation was considerably more
(the more the pity too) than that bestowed upon Mr.
Cushing.

"When we had made an end, the audience of course arose
to depart—and about one-tenth of them, probably, had
really departed, when Mr. Coffin, one of the managing committee, arrested those who remained by the announcement
that we had been requested to deliver 'The Raven.' We
delivered 'The Raven' forthwith — (without taking a
receipt)—were very cordially applauded again—and this
was the end of it, with the exception of the sad tale invented to suit her own purposes by that amiable little enemy

of ours, Miss Walters. We shall never call a woman 'a pretty little witch' again, as long as we live.

"We like Boston. We were born there—and perhaps it is just as well not to mention that we are heartily ashamed of the fact. The Bostonians are very well in their way. Their hotels are bad. Their pumpkin-pies are delicious. Their poetry is not so good. Their common is no common thing—and the duck-pond might answer, if its answer could be heard, for the frogs.

"But with all these good qualities the Bostonians have no soul. They have always evinced towards us the basest ingratitude for the services we rendered them. . . . When we accepted, therefore, an invitation to 'deliver' a poem in Boston, we accepted it simply and solely because we had a curiosity to know how it felt to be publicly hissed, and because we wished to see what effect we could produce by a neat little *impromptu* speech in reply. Perhaps, however, we overrated our own importance, or the Bostonian want of common civility—which is not quite so manifest as one or two of their editors would wish the public to believe: We assure Major Noah that he is wrong. The Bostonians are well-bred—as *very* dull persons very generally are.

"It could scarcely be supposed that we would put ourselves to the trouble of composing for the Bostonians anything in the shape of an *original* poem. We did not. We had a poem (of about five hundred lines) lying by us—one quite as good as new—one, at all events, that we considered would answer sufficiently well for an audience of Transcendentalists. *That* we gave them—it was the best that we had—for the price—and it *did* answer remarkably well. Its name was *not* 'The Messenger Star'—who but Miss Walters would ever think of so delicious a little bit of invention as that? We had *no* name for it at all. The poem is what is occasionally called a 'juvenile poem'—but the fact is, it is anything but juvenile now, for we wrote it, printed it, and published it, in book form, before we had fairly completed our tenth year. We read it *verbatim*, from a copy now in our possession, and which we shall be happy to show at any moment to any of our inquisitive friends. . . .

"As regards the anger of the Boston *Times* and one or two other absurdities—as regards, we say, the wrath of Achilles—

we incurred it—or rather its manifestation—by letting some of our cat out of the bag a few hours sooner than we had intended. Over a bottle of champagne that night, we confessed to Messrs. Cushing, Whipple, Hudson, Field, and a few other natives who swear not altogether by the frog-pond —we confessed, we say, the soft impeachment of the hoax. *Et hinc illæ iræ.* We should have waited a couple of days."

This lengthy letter did not conclude Poe's comments upon the matter; for three weeks he permitted the affair to remain dormant, so far as his own journal was concerned, but at the expiration of that period he issued another long editorial, beginning with the remark, " As we very confidently expected, our friends in the southern and western country (*true* friends and *tried*) are taking up arms in our cause—and more especially in the cause of a national as distinguished from a sectional literature. They cannot see (it appears) any further necessity for being ridden to death by New England." After quoting certain opinions of the press, the poet goes on to say, that if asked " What is the most exquisite of sublunary pleasures ? " the reply would be " the making a fuss, or, in the classical words of a Western friend, the 'kicking up a bobbery;'" adding, " never was a ' bobbery ' more delightful than that which we have just succeeded in 'kicking up' all round about Boston Common. We never saw the Frogpondians so lively in our lives. They seem absolutely to be upon the point of waking up . . . to certain facts which have long been obvious to all the world except themselves—the facts that there exist other cities than Boston . . . other vehicles of literary information than the ' Down-East Review.' "

Other newspaper opinions are then cited, and other over-wrought banterings indulged in, and then what was really the gist of the article was given in these words :—

"We knew very well that, among a certain *clique* of the Frogpondians, there existed a predetermination to abuse us under *any* circumstances. We knew that write what we would they would swear it to be worthless. We knew that were we to compose for them a ' Paradise Lost ' they would pronounce it an indifferent poem. It would have been very weak in us, then, to put ourselves to the trouble of attempting to please these people. We preferred pleasing ourselves. We read before them a 'juvenile,' a *very* 'juvenile ' poem —and thus the Frogpondians were *had*—were delivered up to the enemy bound hand and foot. Never were a set of people more completely demolished. They have blustered and flustered, but what have they done or said that has not made them more thoroughly ridiculous? what, in the name of Momus, is it *possible* for them to do or to say?

"We 'delivered' them the 'juvenile poem,' and they received it with applause. This is accounted for by the fact that the *clique* (contemptible in numbers as in everything else) were overruled by the rest of the assembly. These malignants did not *dare* to interrupt by their preconcerted hisses the respectful and profound attention of the majority. . . . The poem being thus well received, in spite of this ridiculous little cabal—the next thing to be done was to abuse it in the papers. Here, they imagined, they were sure of their game. But what have they accomplished? The poem, they say, is bad. We admit it. We insisted upon this fact in our prefatory remarks, and we insist upon it now, over and over again.

"Repelled at these points, the Frogpondian faction hire a thing they call the ' Washingtonian Reformer ' (or something of that kind), to insinuate that we must have been 'intoxicated' to have become possessed of sufficient audacity to 'deliver' such a poem to the Frogpondians. In the first place, why cannot these miserable hypocrites say ' drunk ' at once, and be done with it? In the second place, we are perfectly willing to admit that we *were* drunk—in the face of at least eleven or twelve hundred Frogpondians who will be willing to take oath that we were *not*. We are willing to

S

admit either that we were drunk, or that we set fire to the Frogpond, or that once upon a time we cut the throat of our grandmother. The fact is, we are perfectly ready to admit anything at all—but what has cutting the throat of our grandmother to do with our poem, or the Frogpondian stupidity? We shall get drunk when we please. As for the editor of the ' Jeffersonian Teetotaler' (or whatever it is), we advise her to get drunk too, as soon as possible—for when sober she is a disgrace to the sex, on account of being so awfully stupid.

" *N.B.* The ' Washingtonian Teetotaler' is edited by a little old lady in a mobcap and spectacles—at least we presume so, for every second paper in Boston *is.*"

Here it should be explained, for those who, know-ing Poe's invariable courtesy towards women, fail to recognise the subject of his satire, that the publica-tion alluded to was edited by *Mr.* Edmund Burke, who, said the poet, " assured us, with tears in *her* eyes, that *she* was not a little old lady in a mobcap and spectacles."

From the *postscriptum* to this editorial may be cited these few more sentences :—" Miss Walters (the Siren !) has seen cause, we find, to recant all the ill-natured little insinuations she has been making against us (mere white lies—she need not take them so much to heart), and is now overwhelming us with apologies —things which we have never yet been able to with-stand. She defends our poem on the ground of its being ' juvenile,' and we think the more of her defence because she herself has been juvenile so long as to be a judge of juvenility."

During the following weeks Poe delivered a few more Parthian darts at these Bostonian editors, but, so far as the *Broadway Journal* was concerned, this was the end of the far-famed attack on Frogpondium.

The whole squabble was petty, and little worthy of the strenuous exertions it aroused against the poet. Those hurried jocular, although overstrained, newspaper jottings,—thrown off in the midst of cares and anxieties of all kinds, and whilst their unfortunate writer, suffering under almost chronic impecuniosity, and unable to pay for literary aid, was obliged to supply " copy " for nearly the whole of the *Journal*,—have been referred to, and adduced from, as evidence of Poe's irretrievably bad nature. Work of a more pleasing nature, however, was now occupying his attention and time. In October he published in his journal ˙ the poetically worded sketch of " The Island of the Fay," in which some of his most salient *traits* of thoughts are expressed. In this composition he pointed out how human figures disfigure a landscape ; reiterated his oft-told love of solitude ; and affected to believe, with the old geographer Pomponious Mela, that the earth is a living *sentient* being. In this same prose poem Poe, in drawing attention to the palpable fact that *space* is an object in our universe, laid down a proposition that really contained the germ of his subsequent great work " Eureka."

In the following month of November, the tale of " Spectacles " appeared in the *Broadway Journal*, which also contained the announcement that Poe was now its " sole proprietor and editor ; " *Graham's Magazine* contained " The System of Dr. Tarr and Professor Fether," and " Mesmeric Revelations" was published in the *Columbian Magazine*. This last story, and its sequel of " The Facts in the Case of M. Valdemar "— published next month in the *American Review*— created a more profound and wider-spread excitement

than any other of his previous works. He was overwhelmed with inquiries as to their being fact or fiction,
and carefully avoided giving the public a definite
answer. Commenting upon *The Tribune's* remarks
about the latter tale—that terrible tale of mesmer-
ising a man *in articulo mortis*—Poe said, " For our
part, we find it difficult to understand how any dispassionate *transcendentalist* can doubt the facts as we
state them ; they are by no means so incredible as
the marvels which are hourly narrated, and believed, on
the topic of mesmerism. *Why* cannot a man's death
be postponed indefinitely by mesmerism ? *why* cannot
a man talk after he is dead ? *why ?*—*why ?*—that is
the question ; and as soon as the *Tribune* has answered
it to our satisfaction we will talk to it further."
And in reprinting " The Facts " in his journal, he
notes that the article " has given rise to some discussion—especially in regard to the truth or falsity of
the statement made. It does not become *us*, of
course," he adds, " to offer one word on the point at
issue. We have been requested to reprint the article,
and do so with pleasure. We leave it to speak for
itself. We may observe, however, that there are a
certain class of people who pride themselves upon
Doubt as a profession."

The wordy warfare as to the facts of " The Facts "
being a record of real circumstance or not, waxed
warmer, and even people who should have known
better took the side of the believers. Dr. Collyer,
a well-known mesmerist, was among the many who
expressed their belief as to the " case of Monsieur
Valdemar " being a true one, and he wrote this letter
to Poe on the subject :—

" BOSTON, *December* 16, 1845.

" DEAR SIR—Your account of M. Valdemar's case has been universally copied in this city, and has created a very great sensation. It requires from me no apology, in stating, that I have not the least doubt of the *possibility* of such a phenomenon ; for I did actually restore to active animation a person who died from excessive drinking of ardent spirits. He was placed in his coffin ready for interment.

" You are aware that death very often follows excessive excitement of the nervous system ; this arising from the extreme prostration which follows ; so that the vital powers have not sufficient energy to react.

" I will give you the detailed account on your reply to this, which I require for publication, in order to put at rest the growing impression that your account is merely a *splendid creation* of your own brain, not having any truth in fact. My dear sir, I have battled the storm of public derision too long on the subject of Mesmerism, to be now found in the rear ranks—though I have not publicly lectured for more than two years, I have steadily made it a subject of deep investigation.

" I sent the account to my friend Dr. Elliotson of London ; also to *The Zoist*—to which journal I have regularly contributed.

" Your early reply will oblige, which I will publish, with your consent, in connection with the case I have referred to. Believe me yours, most respectfully,

" ROBERT H. COLLYER."

In public allusion to this communication, Poe humorously said, " We have no doubt that Dr. Collyer is perfectly correct in all that he says, and all that he desires us to say ; but the truth is, there is a very small modicum of truth in the case of M. Valdemar, which, in consequence, may be called a hard case— *very* hard for M. Valdemar, for Dr. Collyer, and ourselves. If the story was not true, however, it should have been, and perhaps *The Zoist* may discover that it *is* true, after all."

In England " Valdemar's Case " also startled the public, and actually found certain *pseudo* scientific writers ready to accept it as a narration of facts. *The Popular Record of Modern Science,* a London weekly paper sub-styling itself " A Journal of Philosophy and General Information," reprinted the tale with the comment, " It bears internal evidence of authenticity ! " and in criticising the remarks of the *Morning Post*— which also reprinted the narration—took occasion to say :

" Credence is understood to be given to it at New York, within a few miles of which city the affair took place, and where, consequently, the most ready means must be found for its authentication or disproval. The initials of the medical men, and of the young medical student, must be sufficient in the immediate locality to establish their identity, especially as M. Valdemar was well known, and had been so long ill as to render it out of the question that there should be any difficulty in ascertaining the names of the physicians by whom he had been attended. In the same way the nurses and servants, under whose cognisance the case must have come during the seven months which it occupied, are of course accessible to all sorts of inquiries. It will therefore appear that there must have been too many parties concerned to render prolonged deception practicable. The angry excitement and various rumours, which have at length rendered a public statement necessary, are also sufficient to show that *something* extraordinary must have taken place. No steamer will leave England for America till the 3rd of February, but within a few weeks of that time, we doubt not, it will be possible to lay before the readers of *The Record* information which will enable them to come to a pretty accurate conclusion."

It is easy to imagine the delight with which Poe chuckled over the absurd sophistry of these *pseudo* scientists, and over the success, in an English self-titled philosophical paper, of his "'Valdemar Case' hoax," as he called it in a letter to a friend. He would find more true gratification, however, in these allusions to the work in a letter of Mrs. Browning's:—"Then there is a tale of his which I do not find in this volume,* but which is going the rounds of the newspapers, about mesmerism, throwing us all into most admired disorder, or dreadful doubts as to whether it can be true, as the children say of ghost stories. The certain thing in the tale in question is the power of the writer, and the faculty he has of making horrible improbabilities seem near and familiar."

To Mrs. Browning Poe now dedicated, in most enthusiastic terms, a new collection of his poems, published in November by Messrs. Wiley and Putnam, as "The Raven and other Poems." In the *Preface* to the volume the poet pathetically remarks, "Events not to be controlled have prevented me from making, at any time, any serious effort in what, under happier circumstances, would have been the field of my choice. With me poetry has been not a purpose, but a passion; and the passions should be held in reverence; they must not—they cannot at will be excited with an eye to the paltry compensations, or the more paltry commendations, of mankind." And, in a note to the *Poems written in Youth*, he says,—chiefly with reference to the remark of Charles Dickens in the *Foreign Quarterly Review*, that Poe "had all Tennyson's spirituality, and might be considered as the best of his imitators"— "Private reasons—some of which have reference to the sin of plagiarism, and others to the date of Tennyson's first poems—have induced me, after some hesita-

* *I.e.,* the 1845 edition of "Tales."

tion, to republish these, the crude compositions of my earliest boyhood." The volume of poetry did not appear to make such a deep impression upon the public as did the volume of "Tales," partly, perchance, on account of the contents being already well known through reprints, and partly because it contained little beyond "The Raven" likely to earn the approbation of the multitude.

On turning to the less literary, although scarcely less public, life of Poe at this period, he is seen mixing in the best society New York could boast of, and charming every one by the fascination of his manners and the brilliancy of his conversational powers. Mrs. Oakes Smith informs us, that "It was in the brilliant circles that assembled in the winter of 1845–46 at the houses of Dr. Dewey, Miss Anna C. Lynch, Mr. Lawson, and others, that we first met Edgar Poe. His manners were, at these reunions, refined and pleasing, and his style and scope of conversation that of a gentleman and a scholar. Whatever may have been his previous career, there was nothing in his appearance or manner to indicate his excesses. He delighted in the society of superior women, and had an exquisite perception of all the graces of manner and shades of expression. He was an admiring listener, and an unobtrusive observer. We all recollect the interest felt at the time in everything emanating from his pen—the relief it was from the dulness of ordinary writers, the certainty of something fresh and suggestive. His critiques were read with avidity; not that he convinced the judgment, but that people felt their ability and courage. Right or wrong he was terribly in earnest."

" Like De Quincey," as Mrs. Whitman remarks, " he never *supposed* anything, he always knew."

This last named lady, in her beautiful monograph on " Poe and his Critics," instances, as evidence of the habitual kindliness and courtesy of the poet's nature, an incident that occurred at one of the soirées above alluded to :— " A lady, noted for her great lingual attainments, wishing to apply a wholesome check to the vanity of a young author, proposed inviting him to translate for the company a difficult passage in Greek, of which language she knew him to be profoundly ignorant, although given to a rather pretentious display of Greek quotations in his published writings. Poe's earnest and persistent remonstrance against this piece of *méchanceté* alone averted the embarrassing test." Trifling as this anecdote may appear, it is good proof of that generous and charitable disposition which they who knew him only from the scandalous calumnies of his detractors have so unwarrantably denied him the possession of.

Those who have thus far followed Poe's story through these pages, will know what a passionate adoration he bore towards the beautiful sharer of his luckless lot. " Sometimes," says Mrs. Whitman, " his fair young wife was seen with him at the weekly assemblages in Waverley Place. She seldom took part in the conversation, but the memory of her sweet and girlish face, always animated and vivacious, repels the assertion, afterwards so cruelly and recklessly made, that she died a victim to the neglect and unkindness of her husband, ' who,' as it has been said, ' deliberately sought her death that he might embalm her memory in immortal dirges.' . . . We might cite the testimony alike of friends and enemies," continues Mrs. Whitman, " to Poe's unvarying kindness towards his young wife and cousin, if other testimony were needed than that of the tender love still cherished for his memory, by one whose life was made doubly desolate by his death—the sister of his father, and the mother of his Virginia. It is well known to those acquainted with the parties," Mrs. Whitman proceeds to narrate, " that all who have had opportunities for observation in the matter have noticed her husband's tender devotion to her during her prolonged illness. Even Dr. Griswold speaks of having visited him during a period of illness caused by protracted anxiety and watching by the side of his sick wife. It is true that, notwithstanding her vivacity and cheerfulness at the time we have alluded to, her health was, even then, rapidly sinking ; and it was for her dear sake, and the recovery of that peace which had been so fatally perilled amid the irritations and anxieties of his New York life, that Poe left the city and removed to the little Dutch cottage in Fordham, where he passed the remaining three years of his life."

Returning to the poet's labours on the *Broadway Journal,* we find some noteworthy critiques in the last November number, on various works of contemporary and permanent interest. Professor Raumer's book on America is noticed, chiefly as an instance of the difficulties experienced by foreigners to obtain correct information about American literature, and the fact that the author professedly derived his knowledge of their poets from Griswold's compilation is commented upon in stinging terms. Victor Hugo is next alluded to, his fictions being referred to as unequalled, whilst his "Notre Dame" calls forth Poe's enthusiastic sympathy, as "a work of high genius controlled by consummate art." Tennyson's "Poems" then come under review, and their creator is spoken of as "a poet who (in our own humble, but sincere opinion) is *the greatest* that ever lived. We are perfectly willing to undergo all the censure," subjoins Poe, "which so heretical an opinion may draw down upon us." This month's literary labours were concluded by the publication, in *Graham's Magazine*, of the "System of Dr. Tarr and Professor Fether," a tale of no particular value.

In the December numbers of his *Journal* Poe gave a lengthy review of the Poems of Mrs. Osgood, of whom more will be heard later on, some appropriate remarks on Mrs. Norton's "Child of the Isles," sympathetic allusions to Prescott, reference to "Love and Mesmerism" by Horace Smith, as the work of "an author who never did anything ill," and manifold minor reviews and notices, including one on the works of Shelley, opined to be "a poet whom all poets, and whom poets only, appreciate."

The days of his periodical were numbered, but before resigning the control of its columns, the poet contrived to enliven the "Editorial Miscellany" with another small skirmish. "The Brook-Farm" folk, now best remembered by their embalmment in Hawthorne's "Blithedale Romance," went out of their way to find fault with Poe, whose fame, their chief journal alleged, was degenerating into "notoriety, through a certain blackguard warfare which he had been waging against the poets and newspaper critics of New England, and which it would be most charitable to impute to insanity." After this last insinuation—a somewhat awkward one for a people so situated as were the " Farmers "—its propounders, reviewing Poe's recent volume of poems, concluded their animadversions by declaring that the author " does not write for Humanity; he has more of the art than the soul of poetry. He affects to despise the world while he writes for it. He certainly has struck out a remarkable course: the style and imagery of his earliest poems mark a very singular culture, a judgment most severe for a young writer, and a familiarity with the less hackneyed portions of classic lore and nomenclature. He seems to have had an idea of working out his forms from pure white marble. But the poet's humanity is wanting ; a morbid egotism repels you. He can affect you with wonder, but rarely with the thrill of any passion, except, perhaps, of pride, which might be dignity, and which therefore always is interesting. We fear this writer even courts the state described by Tennyson :—

> " ' A glorious devil, large in heart and brain,
>   That did love beauty only.' "

Of these final not altogether unflattering, and in some respects not quite unfaithful, remarks, Poe took no note ; but the innuendoes as to his insanity, insulting a Boston audience, ill motives, plagiarism of Tennyson, and so forth, he accompanied by a running commentary as caustic as it was pertinent, introducing the subject in this fashion :—

" *The Harbinger*—edited by ' The Brook-Farm Phalanx ' —is, beyond doubt, the most reputable organ of the Crazyites. We sincerely respect it—odd as this assertion may appear. It is conducted by an assemblage of well read persons who mean no harm, and who, perhaps, can do less. Their objects are honourable, and so forth—all that anybody can understand of them—and we really believe that Mr. Albert Brisbane, and one or two other ladies and gentlemen, under-stand all about them that is necessary to be understood. But what we, individually, have done to *The Harbinger*, or what we have done to 'The Brook-Farm Phalanx,' that 'The Brook-Farm Phalanx' should stop the ordinary opera-tions at Brook Farm, for the purpose of abusing us, is a point we are unable to comprehend. If we have done anything to affront 'The Brook-Farm Phalanx' we will make an apology forthwith—provided 'The Brook-Farm Phalanx' (which we have a great curiosity to see) will just step into our office, which is 304 Broadway."

With this farewell volley Poe's connection with the periodical may be said to have ceased, for although it did not expire until the following month, and the latest number contained some noteworthy remarks by the poet on Cromwell and on Faber's Speaking Autom-aton, the editorial management had then passed into the hands of a certain "Thomas Dunn English," of whom more will be heard presently. In his *Valedic-tory*, the ex-editorial proprietor stated, "Unexpected engagements demanding my whole attention, and the objects being fulfilled, so far as regards myself person-ally, for which the *Broadway Journal* was established, I now, as its editor, bid farewell as cordially to foes as to friends."

CHAPTER XVI.

THE LITERATI OF NEW YORK.

It is time that a lady who exercised no slight influence over Edgar Poe, during one portion of his short
career, should now be introduced to the reader.
Frances Sargent Locke, afterwards Osgood, was one of
a literary family, both her sisters and her brother
having attained some celebrity, in their days, as authors.
She was the daughter of a prosperous American merchant, who took a pride in encouraging the poetic
efforts of his children. Whilst Frances was still a
girl in years, but already noted for her beauty, Mr. S.
Osgood, an artist of reputation, undertook to paint her
portrait, and during the sittings is stated to have
charmed the fair maiden—as Othello did Desdemona
—by a recital of his adventures at home and abroad.
As might be imagined, the result of these sittings was
the formation of an attachment between the youthful
poetess and her portrait painter, and, eventually, their
marriage.

In 1834 the Osgoods visited Europe, and took up
their residence in London, of the Royal Academy of
which city the artist had formerly been a pupil. The
talents of the husband, and the grace and beauty of
the wife, appear to have interested the good people of
the British metropolis in their favour. Portraits of the
Hon. Mrs. Norton, the poet Rogers, and other persons of
celebrity, were painted by Mr. Osgood, whilst his young

bride earned her moiety of reputation by a graceful volume of verse, published as " A Wreath of Wild Flowers from New England." A drama written by the fair authoress at the instigation of Sheridan Knowles, was accepted for representation at Drury Lane, but indefinitely postponed performance in consequence of the recall of the Osgoods to America, on account of the illness and death of the authoress' father.

The gifted pair returned to their native land in 1840, and speedily took a foremost station in literary and artistic society, Mr. Osgood, however, occasionally going away on lengthy tours in search of that Beautiful which he might have found at home. Meanwhile, the poetess became a frequent contributor of graceful *vers de société*, and literary sketches, to the leading American magazines and annuals, and in this capacity attracted the notice of Edgar Poe. He reviewed her poems with that chivalrous rather than critical enthusiasm he reserved for female authors, and deemed for her " *Not* to write poetry, not to act it, think it, dream it, and be it, is entirely out of her power." Upon the poet's removal to New York he found the Osgoods already resident there. It was impossible for the two families to mix in the same circles, as they did, without meeting, and Poe's first interview with the fair authoress has been thus described in Mrs. Osgood's own words :—

" My first meeting with the poet was at the Astor House. A few days previous, Mr. Willis had handed me, at the *table d'hôte*, that strange and thrilling poem entitled *The Raven*, saying that the author wanted my opinion of it. Its effect upon me was so singular, so like that of ' weird, unearthly music,' that it was with a feeling almost of dread I heard he desired an introduction. Yet I could not refuse without seeming ungrateful, because I had just heard of his

enthusiastic and partial eulogy of my writings, in his lecture
on American Literature. *I shall never forget the morning*
when I was summoned to the drawing-room by Mr. Willis to
receive him. With his proud and beautiful head erect, his
dark eyes flashing with the electric light of feeling and
thought, a peculiar, an inimitable blending of sweetness and
hauteur in his expression and manner, he greeted me calmly,
gravely, almost coldly ; yet with so marked an earnestness
that I could not help being deeply impressed by it. From
that moment until his death we were friends."

The friendship thus inaugurated between the two
poets exercised an undoubted influence upon both of
them. In the sympathetic society of Frances Osgood
the unfortunate and harassed editor found some
nepenthë for his troubles, whilst under his skilful
guidance the poetess learned how to produce " a
bolder note " and a more impassioned song. If she
now composed with less rapidity than of heretofore, a
deeper tone and a more profound pathos is beheld in
her later writings, as if the " few additional years,
with their inevitable sorrow," which Poe considered " to
have stirred the depths of her heart," were, indeed, no
poetic fiction. But to the dominating influence of
Edgar Poe himself, more than to anything else, must
be ascribed the change in Frances Osgood's feelings.
In what light she now regarded her poetic Mentor may
be best comprehended from these lines to him, published in his own periodical, the *Broadway Journal* :—

To———.

" In Heaven a spirit doth dwell
    ' Whose heart-strings are a lute.' "—Edgar Poe.

" I cannot tell *the world* how thrills my heart
    To every touch that flies thy lyre along ;
How the wild Nature and the wondrous Art,
    Blend into Beauty in thy passionate song—

" But this *I know*—in thine enchanted slumbers,
    Heaven's poet, Israfel—with minstrel fire—
Taught the music of his own sweet numbers,
    And tuned—to chord with his—thy glorious lyre ! "

Well known as is Poe's exquisite response to these
lines, it will still bear repetition here :—

To F——s S. O——d.

" Thou wouldst be loved ?—then let thy heart
        From its present pathway part not !
    Being everything which now thou art,
        Be nothing which thou art not.
    So with the world thy gentle ways,
        Thy grace—thy more than beauty—
    Shall be an endless theme of praise,
        And love—a simple duty."—EDGAR POE.

Shortly after this reciprocation of sentiments, and
the exchange of certain other poems and letters of a
similar character, Poe was engaged to write a series of
critiques on the " Literati of New York," for Mr.
Godey's magazine, *The Lady's Book,* and how Frances
Osgood was interested in them will be best gathered
from her own pleasant account :—

" It was in his own simple yet poetical home, that to me
the character of Edgar Poe appeared in its most beautiful light.
Playful, affectionate, witty, alternately docile and wayward
as a petted child—for his young, gentle, and idolised wife,
and for all who came, he had, even in the midst of his most
harassing literary duties, a kind word, a pleasant smile, a
graceful and courteous attention. At his desk, beneath the
romantic picture of his loved and lost Lenore, he would sit,
hour after hour, patient, assiduous, and uncomplaining,
tracing in an exquisitely clear chirography, and with almost
superhuman swiftness, the lightning thoughts—the ' rare and
radiant ' fancies—as they flashed through his wonderful and
ever-wakeful brain. I recollect one morning towards the

T

close of his residence in this city, when he seemed unusually gay and light-hearted. Virginia, his sweet wife, had written me a pressing invitation to come to them; and I, who never could resist her affectionate summons, and who enjoyed his society far more in his own home than elsewhere, hastened to Amity Street. I found him just completing his series of papers entitled *The Literati of New York.* ' See,' said he, displaying, in laughing triumph, several little rolls of narrow paper, ' I am going to show you, by the difference in length of these, the different degrees of estimation in which I hold all you literary people. In each of these, one of you is rolled up and fully discussed. Come, Virginia, help me!' And one by one they unfolded them. At last they came to one which seemed interminable. Virginia laughingly ran to one corner of the room with one end, and her husband to the opposite with the other. ' And whose lengthened sweetness long drawn out is that?' said I. ' Hear her!' he cried, ' just as if her little vain heart didn't tell her it's herself!'"

Subsequently, when requested to furnish her reminiscences of the unfortunate poet, Mrs. Osgood replied:—

"For you, who knew and understood my affectionate interest in him, and my frank acknowledgment of that interest to all who had a claim upon my confidence, for you, I will willingly do so. I think no one could know him—no one *has* known him personally—certainly no woman—without feeling the same interest. I can sincerely say, that although I have frequently *heard* of aberrations on his part from ' the straight and narrow path,' I have never *seen* him otherwise than gentle, generous, well-bred, and fastidiously refined. To a sensitive and delicately nurtured woman, there was a peculiar and irresistible charm in the chivalric, graceful, and almost tender reverence with which he invariably approached all women who won his respect. It was this which first commanded and always retained my regard for him.

" *I have been told* that when his sorrows and pecuniary embarrassments had driven him to the use of stimulants, which a less delicate organisation might have borne without injury, he was in the habit of speaking disrespectfully of the ladies of his acquaintance. *It is difficult for me to believe this ;*

for to *me*, to whom he came during the year of our acquaintance for counsel and kindness in all his many anxieties and
griefs, he never spoke irreverently of any woman save one,
and then only in *my* defence; and though I rebuked him for
his momentary forgetfulness of the respect due to himself
and to me, I could not but forgive the offence for the sake of
the generous impulse which prompted it. Yet, even were
these sad rumours true of him, the wise and well informed
knew how to regard, as they would the impetuous anger of a
spoiled infant, baulked of its capricious will, the equally
harmless and unmeaning phrenzy of that stray child of Poetry
and Passion. For the few unwomanly and slander-loving
gossips who have injured *him* and *themselves* only by repeating his ravings, when in such moods they have accepted his
society, I have only to vouchsafe my wonder and my pity.
They cannot surely harm the true and pure, who, reverencing
his genius and pitying his misfortunes and his errors,
endeavoured, by their timely kindness and sympathy, to
soothe his sad career."

Such were the impressions left upon Mrs. Osgood
by Edgar Poe, and how she, in her turn, appeared to
him is told in these words of the poet. "In character
she is ardent, sensitive, impulsive. . . the very soul
of truth and honour; a worshipper of the beautiful,
with a heart so radically artless as to seem abundant
in art; universally admired, respected, and beloved.
In person she is about the medium height, slender
even to fragility, graceful whether in action or repose;
complexion usually pale, hair black and glossy, eyes
a clear, luminous grey, large, and with singular capacity
for expression."

Although the personal acquaintance of the two
poets lasted only for one year, Mrs. Osgood having to
travel for her health's sake, "I maintained a correspondence with Mr. Poe," says the lady, "in accordance
with the earnest entreaties of his wife, who imagined

that my influence over him had a restraining and
beneficial effect. It *had,* as far as this—that having
solemnly promised me to give up the use of stimulants, he so firmly respected his promise and me,
as never once, during our whole acquaintance, to
appear in my presence when in the slightest degree
affected by them." "The charming love and confidence that existed between his wife and himself,"
Mrs. Osgood's testimony has already been cited in
corroboration of. It was, she declares, "always delight-
fully apparent to me, in spite of the many little poetical
episodes in which the impassioned romance of his
temperament impelled him to indulge ; of this I cannot
speak too earnestly, too warmly."

But an uncharitable and censorious public, fed by
the jealous whisperings of envious men, and, sadder
still, of jealous women, chose to regard these "poetical
episodes" in another light. One of the victims of the
scandals and calumnies accumulated upon the poet's
devoted head, was his warm friend and defender,
Frances Osgood. Alluding to his epistolary and conversational powers, she had remarked to a correspondent,
"His letters were divinely beautiful, and for hours I
have listened to him, entranced by strains of pure and
almost celestial eloquence such as I have never read
or heard elsewhere." By means of this correspondence
it was sought to crush, or, at all events, inflict a cruel
vengeance upon Poe, for slighted advances and critical
contempt. One implacable woman, whose name death
and her sex forbid us to mention, chanced to see at Poe's
house an open note or letter from Mrs. Osgood, which
she assumed to consider called for interference. This
same woman, whose own advances to the poet were

anything but pleasant, so busied herself that a committee
of ladies was actually appointed to call upon Mrs.
Osgood, and remonstrate with her upon the imprudence
of such a correspondence. In consequence of their
representations, the poetess consented that they should
act on her behalf and request the return of her letters.
The late Margaret Fuller, afterwards Countess D'Ossoli,
was, it is understood, one of the ladies who acted upon
this occasion, and a well-known literary lady of New
York another, but the acknowledged instigator and
"wire puller" of the movement was Mrs. E——, the
woman above referred to. The story has been told us
thus :—

"The ladies repaired to Fordham, presented their creden-
tials, and made their demand. The poor Raven, driven to
desperation, ruffled his plumage, called the fair ambassa-
dresses 'busy-bodies,' and added injury to insult by saying
that 'Mrs. E—— had better come and look after her *own*
letters.' Now this was very indiscreet of him, and *very*
reprehensible, and no one knew this better than himself.
But you shall hear what he himself says about it in a letter :
—'In the heat of passion, stung to madness by her inconceivable perfidy, and by the grossness of the injury which
her jealousy prompted her to inflict upon *all of us*—upon
both families—I permitted myself to say what I should not
have said. I had no sooner uttered the words than I *felt*
their dishonour. I felt, too, that although *she* must be
damningly conscious of her own baseness, she would still
have a right to reproach me for having betrayed, under *any*
circumstances, her confidence.

" 'Full of these thoughts, and terrified almost to death lest
I should again, in a moment of madness, be similarly tempted,
I went immediately to my secretary—(when those two ladies
went away),—made a package of her letters, addressed them to
her, and with my own hands left them at her door. Now
you cannot be prepared for the diabolical malignity which
followed. Instead of feeling that I had done all I could to

repair an unpremeditated wrong; instead of feeling that almost any other person would have retained the letters to make good (if occasion required), the assertion that I possessed them; instead of this, she urged her brothers and brother-in-law to *demand of me the letters.* The position in which she thus placed me you may imagine. Is it any wonder that I was driven *mad* by the intolerable sense of wrong? . . . You will now comprehend what I mean in saying that the *only* thing which I found it impossible to forgive Mrs. Osgood, was her reception of Mrs. E——.'"

Such is the account furnished by Poe himself of one of the most deplorable incidents in his life, and one which has been misrepresented, exaggerated, and distorted in a hundred different ways by foes and thoughtless retailers of scandal. The guileless nature of Mrs. Osgood, and the passionate, proud spirit of Poe, rendered both easy prey to craft and calculating cold duplicity. It is satisfactory to learn that, despite the intervention of "busybodies," the two poets remained friendly to the close of their contemporaneously ended careers, and whilst Poe frequently alludes in his correspondence with affectionate interest to Mrs. Osgood, the final poem of that lady's last volume, published just as she died—a few months after Poe— was inscribed to him, and was of him, as "Israfel."*

The poet's literary labours during the early half of 1846, after his relinquishment of the *Broadway Journal,* do not appear to have been either voluminous or valuable. To *Graham's Magazine,* and the *Democratic Review,* he contributed a certain quantum of "Marginalia," but his own and his wife's ill health rendered him little able to wield his pen with any of the readiness he had so lately displayed. The settlement of various

* *Vide* Appendix D.

matters connected with his defunct periodical occupied a considerable portion of his time, and as an example of the honourable manner in which he strove to perform the pecuniary engagements—despite the difficulties under which he laboured—that arose out of his recent publishership, this little note may be cited:—

> "NEW YORK, *April* 16, '46.
>
> "MY DEAR SIR,—You seem to take matters very easily, and I really wonder at your patience under the circumstances. But the truth is, I am in no degree to blame. Your letters, one and all, reached me in due course of mail, and I attended to them *as far as I could.* The business, in fact, was none of mine, but of the person to whom I transferred the Journal, and in whose hands it perished.
>
> "Of course, I feel no less in honour bound to refund you your money, and now do so, with many thanks for your promptness and courtesy.—Very cordially yours,
>
> "EDGAR A. POE."

During the months of February, March, and April, the poet contributed notices of leading American authors to the pages of Godey's *Lady's Book,* and in May commenced in the same magazine a series of critical studies on "The Literati of New York." These essays, which were continued from month to month until October, were immensely successful, so far as creating a sensation was concerned, but in some respects they greatly injured Poe's prospects, both by enlarging still further the number of his foes, and even by causing the intimidation of the less courageous of his friends, who foresaw and dreaded the decrease of his popularity in many influential places. The causticity of these critiques, indeed, produced a terrible commotion in the ranks of mediocrity, and no effort was left untried to put a stop to their publication. Poe himself was alternately threatened and cajoled, but of course to no purpose ; similar efforts were made with Mr. Godey, but with what little success this letter from the Philadelphian publisher will show :—

"*The Authors and Mr. Poe.*
"*June* 1846.

"We have received several letters from New York, anonymous and from personal friends, requesting us to be careful what we allow Mr. Poe to say of the New York authors, many of whom are our personal friends. We reply to one and all, that we have nothing to do but publish Mr. Poe's opinions, *not our own.* Whether we agree with Mr. Poe or not, is another matter. *We are not to be intimidated* by a threat of the loss of friends, or turned from our purpose by honeyed words. . . . Many attempts have been made, and are making, by various persons to forestall public opinion. *We have the name of one person,*—others are busy with reports of Mr. Poe's illness. Mr. Poe has been ill, but we have letters from him of very recent dates, also a new batch of *The Literati,* which show anything but feebleness either of body or mind. Almost every paper that we exchange with has praised our new enterprise, and spoken in high terms of Mr. Poe's opinion."

Highly successful as Poe's " opinions " may have been for the publisher's pocket—and some of the *Lady's Book* issues ran through three editions—the unfortunates of whom they were expressed were scarcely so contented. One of them, duplicately named " Thomas Dunn English " and " Thomas Dunn Brown," dissatisfied with the manner in which his literary shortcomings had been dissected by the critic, or, as Poe suggests, hankering after wider notoriety, obtained the use of the *Evening Mirror* from its new proprietors, Fuller and Company, and inserted therein a grossly personal attack upon the poet, who thereupon instituted

a libel suit against the newspaper, and recovered heavy
damages for defamation of character. From the so-
called " Reply of Mr. English," some of the more
relevant paragraphs may be cited, but the " card " is
too lengthy and too indecent to be quoted *in extenso*.
It was editorially introduced with the plea that " As
Mr. Godey, ' for a consideration,' lends the use of his
battery for an attack on the one side, it is but fair
that we allow our friends an opportunity to exercise
a little ' self-defence ' on the other." As Poe's critique
was purely directed against the literary weaknesses
of " English," the personalities of the " Reply " were
utterly uncalled for ; it began thus :—

" As I have not, of late, replied to attacks made upon me
through the public press, I can easily afford to make an
exception, and still keep my rule a general one. A Mr.
Edgar A. Poe has been engaged for some time past in giving
to the public, through the medium of the *Lady's Book*,
sketches of what he facetiously calls the ' Literati of New
York.' These names, by way of distinction, I presume,
from his ordinary writings, ' *honest* opinions.' He honours
me by including me in the very numerous and remarkably
august body he affects to describe. . . . As he seems to covet
a notice from me, he shall be gratified.

" Mr. Poe states in his article, ' I do not personally know
Mr. English.' . . . I know Mr. Poe by a succession of his
acts—one of which is rather costly. I hold Mr. Poe's
acknowledgment for a sum of money which he obtained of
me under false pretences. As I stand in need of it at this
time, I am content he should forget to know me, provided he
acquits himself of the money he owes me. I ask no interest,
in lieu of which I am willing to credit him with the sound
cuffing I gave him when I last saw him.

" Another act of his gave me some knowledge of him. A
merchant of this city had accused him of committing forgery.
He consulted me on the mode of punishing his accuser, and
as he was afraid to challenge him to the field, or chastise him

personally, I suggested a legal prosecution as his sole remedy. At his request I obtained a counsellor who was willing, as a compliment to me, to conduct his suit without the customary retaining fee. But, though so eager at first to commence proceedings, he dropped the matter altogether when the time came for him to act—thus virtually admitting the truth of the charge.

"Some time before this, if I mistake not, Mr. Poe accepted an invitation to deliver a poem before a society of the New York University. About a week before the time when this poem was to be pronounced, he called on me, appearing to be much troubled—said he could not write the poem, and begged me to help him out with some idea of the course to pursue. I suggested that he had better write a note to the society, and frankly state his inability to compose a poem on a stated subject. He did not do this, but—*as he always does when troubled*—drank until intoxicated; and remained in a state of intoxication during the week. When the night of exhibition came, it was gravely announced that Mr. Poe could not deliver his poem, on account of severe indisposition !

"His next affair of a similar kind, was still more discreditable. Unmindful of his former act, he accepted an invitation to deliver a poem before a Boston institution—the Lyceum, I think. When I remonstrated with him on undertaking a task he could not perform, he alleged that he was in want of the money they would pay him, and would contrive to 'cook up something.' Want of ability prevented him from performing his intention, and he insulted his audience, and rendered himself a laughing-stock, by reciting a mass of ridiculous stuff, written by some one, and printed under his name when he was about eighteen years of age. It had a peculiar effect upon his audience, who dispersed under its infliction ; and when he was rebuked for his fraud, he asserted that he had intended a hoax. . . . His lamentation over my lack of a common English education is heart-rending to hear. I will acknowledge my deficiencies with pleasure. It is a great pity that he is not equally candid.

"He really does not possess one tithe of that greatness which he seems to regard as an uncomfortable burden. He mistakes coarse abuse for polished invective, and vulgar insinuation for sly satire. He is not alone thoroughly unprin-

cipled, base, and depraved, but silly, vain, and ignorant,—
not alone an assassin in morals, but a quack in literature.
His frequent quotations from languages of which he is entirely
ignorant, and his consequent blunders, expose him to ridi-
cule; while his cool plagiarisms, from known or forgotten
writers, excite the public amazement. He is a complete
evidence of his own assertion, that 'no spectacle can be more
pitiable than that of a man without the commonest school
education, busying himself in attempts to instruct mankind
on topics of polite literature.'"

Mr. English next proceeds to furnish his version of
the Mrs. E——'s letters case—alleges a chastisement
he had inflicted on Poe was so violent that it had
caused the poet's confinement to his bed for a day or
two, and winds up his diatribe by declaring his reviewer "overrates his own powers."

That any newspaper could be found to insert such
a communication in its columns, appears extraordinary,
even although the proprietors made no concealment
of their hatred for the person attacked, but what was
still more lamentable was the fact that Poe, not
content to leave to public justice the exoneration
of his character from all charges not self-evidently
false, foolishly increased the importance of the attack
by publishing a refutation of it. The slanders signed
with the name of "English," but generally believed to
have been the joint composition of various persons,
appeared in the *Evening Mirror* of the 23d of June,
and on the 28th inst. Poe's answer appeared in the
Philadelphia *Saturday Gazette.* The editor of the
latter paper, remarking that, at the "particular request
of some of Mr. Poe's friends in this city," he publishes
that gentleman's reply to the attack made upon him
in the *Mirror,* adding justly, " Mr. English's letter was

very severe upon the private character of Mr. Poe, and
the latter retaliates in the same spirit.   All this is, to
our notion, in bad taste, yet we cannot well refuse the
assailed an opportunity to exculpate himself."

Of the poet's voluminous *Reply to Mr. English and
Others*, only a small portion can possibly be quoted, as
the letter, which would fill a small volume, deals not
only with " English," but with the "Others."   It is
dated New York, June 27th, and begins in this
wise :—

" *To the Public.*—A long and serious illness of such character as to render quiet and perfect seclusion in the country
of vital importance, has hitherto prevented me from seeing an
article headed ' The War of the Literati,' signed ' Thomas
Dunn English.' . . . This article I might, and should, indeed,
never have seen, but for the kindness of Mr. Godey, who
enclosed it to me with a suggestion that certain portions of it
might be thought on my part to demand a reply.

" I had some difficulty in comprehending what *that was*,
said or written by Mr. English, that could be deemed
answerable by any human being ; but I had not taken into
consideration that I had been, for many months, absent and
dangerously ill—that I had no longer a journal in which to
defend myself—that these facts were well known to Mr.
English—that he is a blackguard of the lowest order—that
it would be a silly truism, if not unpardonable flattery, to
term him either a coward or a liar—and, lastly, that the
magnitude of a slander is usually in the direct ratio of the
littleness of the slanderer, but, above all things, of the
impunity with which he fancies it may be uttered.

" Of the series of papers which have called down upon me,
while supposed defenceless, the animadversions of the pensive
Fuller, the cultivated Clark, the 'indignant Briggs,'* and
the animalcula with moustaches for antennæ, that is in the
capital habit of signing itself in full 'Thomas Dunn English'

---

* Proprietors of the New York *Evening Mirror*, in which the libel
appeared.—J. H. I.

—of this series of papers all have been long since written, and *three* have been already given to the public. The circulation of the Magazine in which they appear cannot be much less than 50,000, and, admitting but four readers to each copy, I may congratulate myself on a monthly audience of *at* least 200,000 from amongst the most refined and intellectual classes of American society. Of course, it will be difficult on the part of *The Mirror* (I am not sure whether five hundred or six hundred be the precise number of copies it *now* circulates)—difficult, I say, to convince the 200,000 readers in question that, individually and collectively, they are blockheads—that they do not rightly comprehend the unpretending words which I have addressed to them in this series—and that, as for myself, I have no other design in the world than misrepresentation, scurrility, and the indulgence of personal spleen. What has been printed is before my readers; what I have written besides is in the hands of Mr. Godey, and shall remain unaltered. . . . In sketching individuals, every candid reader will admit that, while my general aim has been accuracy, I have yielded to delicacy even a little too much of verisimilitude. Indeed, on this score, should I not have credit for running my pen through certain sentences referring, for example, to the brandy nose of Mr. Briggs (since Mr. Briggs is only one-third described when this nose is omitted), and to the family resemblance between the whole visage of Mr. English and that of the best looking but most unprincipled of Mr. Barnum's baboons?

"It will not be supposed, from anything here said, that I myself attach any importance to this series of papers. The public, however, is the best judge of its own taste; and that the spasms of one or two enemies have given the articles a notoriety far surpassing their merit or my expectation, is possibly no fault of mine. In a preface their very narrow scope is defined. They are loosely and inconsiderately written—aiming at nothing beyond the gossip of criticism—unless, indeed, at the relief of those '*necessities*' which I have never blushed to admit, and which the editor of *The Mirror*—the quondam associate of gentlemen—has, in the same manner, never blushed publicly to insult and to record.

"But let me return to Mr. English's attack—and, in so

returning, let me not permit any profundity of disgust to induce, even for an instant, a violation of the dignity of truth. What is *not false* amid the scurrility of this man's statements, it is not in my nature to brand as false. . . . The errors and frailties which I deplore, it cannot at least be asserted that I have been the coward to deny. Never, even, have I made attempt at *extenuating* a weakness which is (or, by the blessing of God, *was*) a calamity, although those who did not know me intimately had little reason to regard it otherwise than as a crime. For, indeed, had my pride, or that of my family, permitted, there was much—very much—there was everything—to be offered in extenuation. Perhaps, even, there was an epoch of which it might not have been wrong in me to hint—what by the testimony of Dr. Francis and other medical men, I might have demonstrated, had the public, indeed, cared for the demonstration—that the irregularities so profoundly lamented were the *effect* of a terrible evil rather than its cause. . . .

" It is not, then, my purpose to deny any part of the conversation represented to have been held *privately* between this person and myself. . . . The *details* of the ' conversation,' as asserted, I shall not busy myself in attempting to understand. . . .

" I shall not think it necessary to maintain that I am *no* ' coward.' On a point such as this a man should speak only through the acts, moral and physical, of his whole public career. But it is a matter of common observation that your *real* coward never fails to make it a primary point to accuse all his enemies of cowardice. . . . Now, the origin of the nickname, ' Thomas Done Brown,' is, in Philadelphia, quite as thoroughly understood as Mr. English could desire. With even the inconceivable amount of brass in his possession, I doubt if he *could*, in that city, pronounce aloud that simple word ' coward,' if his most saintly soul depended upon the issue. . . .

" His primary thrashing, of any note, was bestowed upon him, I believe, by Mr. John S. Du Solle, the editor of the *Spirit of the Times*, who could not very well get over acting with this indecorum, on account of Mr. E.'s amiable weakness—a propensity for violating the privacy of a publisher's MSS. I have not heard that there was any resentment on the part of Mr. English."

A record of several other chastisements inflicted by various known and named individuals on Mr. English's person follows, and then the poet proceeds to deal *seriatim* with the charges against himself :—

"About the one or two other *unimportant* points in this gentleman's attack upon myself, there is, I believe, very little to be said. He asserts that I have complimented his literary performances. . . . I solemnly say that in no paper of mine did there ever appear one word about this gentleman—unless of the broadest and most unmistakable irony—that was not printed from the MS. of the gentleman himself. The last number of the *Broadway Journal* (the work having been turned over by me to another publisher) was edited by Mr. English. The editorial portion was wholly his, and was one interminable pæan of his own praises. The truth of all this—if any one is weak enough to care a penny about *who* praises or who damns Mr. English—will no doubt be corroborated by Mr. Jennings, the printer.

"I am charged, too, unspecifically, with being a plagiarist on a very extensive scale. He who accuses another of what all the world knows to be *especially* false, is merely rendering the accused a service by calling attention to the *converse* of the fact, and should never be helped out of his ridiculous position by any denial on the part of the accused. We want a magazine paper on 'The Philosophy of Billingsgate.' But I am really ashamed of indulging even in a sneer at this poor miserable fool, on any mere topic of literature alone.

"As a matter of course I should have been satisfied to follow the good example of Mr. Wise,* when insulted by Mr. English (if this be, indeed, the person's name), had there been nothing more serious in the blatherskite's attack than the particulars to which I have hitherto alluded. The two passages which follow, however, are to be found in the article referred to :—

'I hold Mr. Poe's acknowledgment for a sum of money which he obtained from me under false pretences.'

---

* The Hon. Henry A. Wise, then United States Minister to France, who entirely ignored his libeller.—J. H. I.

And again :—

'A merchant of this city,' &c. (*vide* paragraph ending, 'thus virtually admitting the truth of the charge,' page 75).

"It will be admitted by the most patient that these accusations are of such a character as to justify me in rebutting them in the most public manner possible, even when they are found to be urged by a Thomas Dunn English. The charges are criminal, and, with the aid of the *Mirror*, I can have them investigated before a criminal tribunal. In the meantime, I must not lie under these imputations a moment longer than necessary. To the first charge I reply, then, simply that Mr. English is indebted *to me* in what (to me) is a considerable sum—that I owe him nothing—that in the assertion that he holds my acknowledgment for a sum of money under *any* pretence obtained, he lies—and that I defy him to produce such acknowledgment.

"In regard to the second charge, I must necessarily be a little more explicit. 'The merchant of New York' alluded to, is a gentleman of high respectability—Mr. Edward J. Thomas, of Broad Street. I have now the honour of his acquaintance, but some time previous to this acquaintance, he had remarked to a common friend that he had heard whispered against me an accusation of forgery. The friend, as in duty bound, reported this matter to me. I called at once on Mr. Thomas, who gave me no very thorough explanation, but promised to make inquiry, and confer with me hereafter. Not hearing from him in what I thought due time, however, I sent him (unfortunately by Mr. English, who was always in my office for the purpose of doing himself honour in running my errands) a note, of which the following is a copy :—

'OFFICE OF THE *Broadway Journal*, &c.

EDWARD J. THOMAS, ESQ.

'SIR,—As I have not had the pleasure of hearing from you since our interview at your office, may I ask of you to state to me distinctly, whether I am to consider the charge of *forgery* urged by you against myself, in the presence of a common friend, as originating with yourself or MR. Benjamin?—Your obedient servant,

'(Signed) EDGAR A. POE.'

"The reply brought me was verbal and somewhat vague. As usual my messenger had played the bully, and, as *very* usual, had been treated with contempt. The idea of *challenging* a man for a charge of *forgery* could only have entered the head of an owl or an English : of course I had no resource but in a suit which one of Mr. E.'s friends offered to conduct for me. I left town to procure evidence, and on my return found at my house a letter from Mr. Thomas. It ran thus :—

'New York, *July* 5, 1845.

'E. A. Poe, Esq., New York.

'Dear Sir,—I had hoped ere this to have seen you, but as you have not called, and as I may soon be out of the city, I desire to say to you that, after repeated efforts, I saw the person, on Friday evening last, from whom the report origi- nated to which you referred in your call at my office. He denies it *in toto*—says he does *not know it* and never said so —and it undoubtedly arose from the misunderstanding of some word used. It gives me pleasure thus to trace it, and still more to find it destitute of foundation in truth, as I thought would be the case. I have told Mr. Benjamin the result of my inquiries, and shall do so to ———* by a very early opportunity—the only two persons who know any- thing of the matter, as far as I know.—I am, Sir, very truly your friend and obedient servant,

'(Signed) Edward J. Thomas.'

"Now, as this note was most satisfactory and most kind —as I neither wished nor could have accepted Mr. Thomas' money—as the motives which had actuated him did not seem to me malevolent—as I had heard him spoken of in the most flattering manner by one whom, above all others, I most profoundly respect and esteem—it does really appear to me hard to comprehend how even so malignant a villain as this English could have wished me to proceed with the suit.

"In the presence of witnesses I handed him the letter, and requested his opinion. In lieu of it he gave me his advice : *it was that I should deny having received such a letter and urge the prosecution to extremity.* I promptly

---

* The person referred to here was Mrs. Osgood.—J. H. I.

U

ordered him to quit the house. In his capacity of hound, he obeyed.

"These are the facts which, in a court of justice, I propose to demonstrate; and, having demonstrated them, shall I not have a right to demand of a generous public that it brand with eternal infamy that wretch, who, with a full knowledge of my exculpation from so heinous a charge, has not been ashamed to take advantage of my supposed inability to defend myself, for the purpose of stigmatising me as a felon?

"And of the gentleman who (also with a thorough knowledge of the facts, as I can and will show) prostituted his sheets to the circulation of this calumny—of *him* what is it necessary to say? At present—nothing. . . . Not even in taking vengeance on a Fuller can I stoop to become a Fuller myself. . . .   EDGAR A. POE."

This rejoinder appears to have been the most foolish act of Poe's life; for it was as difficult for him, as for any one else, to descend into the arena and combat blackguards with any other than their own weapons. To a friend who remonstrated with him, however, on the manner of the above communication, he wrote:—

"I do not well see how I could have otherwise replied to English. You must know him (English) before you can well estimate my reply. He is so thorough a 'blatherskite' that to have replied to him with *dignity* would have been the extreme of the ludicrous. The only true plan—not to have answered him at all—was precluded on account of the nature of some of his accusations—forgery, for instance. To such charges, even from the Autocrat of all the Asses, a man is *compelled* to answer. There he had me. Answer him I must. But how? Believe me, there exists no such dilemma as that in which a gentleman is placed when he is forced to reply to a blackguard. If he have any genius, then is the time for its display. I confess to you that I rather *like* that reply of mine, in a literary sense; and so do a great many of my friends. It fully answered its purpose, beyond a doubt. Would to Heaven every work of Art did as much! You err in supposing me to have been 'peevish' when I wrote the reply. The peevishness was all 'put on' as a part of my argument—of my plan; so was the 'indignation' with which I wound up. *How* could I be either peevish or indignant about a matter so well adapted to further my purposes? Were I able to afford so expensive a luxury as personal—especially, as *refutable*—abuse, I would willingly pay any man $2000 per annum to hammer away at me all the year round."

And, in another letter to the same correspondent, Poe, referring to the action for libel he had successfully carried out against the New York publisher of the slanders, says of English :—

"The vagabond, at the period of the suit's coming on, ran off to Washington, for fear of being criminally prosecuted. The 'acknowledgment' referred to was not forthcoming, and the *Mirror* could not get *a single witness* to testify *one word* against my character. . . . My suit against the *Mirror* was terminated by a verdict of $225 in my favour. The costs and all will make them a bill of $492. Pretty well—considering that there was *no* actual 'damage' done to me."

Early in the summer of 1846 Poe removed from Amity Street, New York, to Fordham, Westchester County, at that time quite out in the country, but now become almost a suburb of the city. His darling wife's health was rapidly failing, and it was, Mrs. Whitman remarks, "for her dear sake, and for the recovery of that peace which had been so fatally perilled. amid the irritations and anxieties of his New York life, that Poe left the city and removed to the little Dutch cottage in Fordham, where he passed the three remaining years of his life. It was to this quiet haven in the beautiful spring or early summer of 1846, when the fruit-trees were all in bloom and the grass in its freshest verdure, that he brought his Virginia to die."

His literary engagements occasionally called the poet to New York, but in such cases it was usual for his mother-in-law, Mrs. Clemm, to accompany him. Once, soon after the removal to Fordham, being detained all night in town, he sent the following tender lines to his wife, to reassure her. As the note—written on a rough page of his pocket-book—is the only one known to have been addressed by Poe to his wife, it is deserving citation :—

"*June* 12, 1846.

"My DEAR HEART—My DEAR VIRGINIA—Our mother will explain to you why I stay away from you this night. I trust the interview I am promised will result in some *substantial good* for me—for your dear sake and hers—keep up your heart in all hopefulness, and trust yet a little longer. On my last great disappointment I should have lost my courage *but for you*—my little darling wife. You are my *greatest* and *only* stimulus now, to battle with this uncongenial, unsatisfactory, and ungrateful life.

"I shall be with you to-morrow (illegible) P.M., and be assured until I see you I will keep in *loving remembrance* your *last words*, and your fervent prayer !

"Sleep well, and may God grant you a peaceful summer with your devoted   EDGAR."

What was the promised good, and whether the promise was fulfilled, are unknown. During the sad summer months the poet alternately occupied his time, when anxiety about his wife permitted him to work, in writing out his pithy "Marginalia" for *Graham's Magazine* and the *Democratic Review*, and the "Literati" for the *Lady's Book*, and in beautifying the green sward about his little cottage—"the sweetest little cottage imaginable," says Mrs. Clemm ; adding :—

"Oh, how supremely happy we were in our dear cottage home ! We three lived only for each other. Eddie rarely left his beautiful home. I attended to his literary business, for he, poor fellow, knew nothing about money transactions. How should he, brought up in luxury and extravagance ?

" He passed the greater part of the morning in his study, and, after he had finished his task for the day, he worked in our beautiful flower garden, or read and recited poetry to us. Every one who knew him *intimately* loved him. Judges pronounced him the best conversationalist *living*. We had very little society except among the *literati*, but this was exceedingly pleasant."*

Among the literary friends who visited the Poes at their pleasant country home was Mrs. Gove-Nichols. Of her first excursion to Fordham, she records :—

" I found the poet, and his wife, and his wife's mother—who was his aunt—living in a little cottage at the top of a hill. There was an acre or two of green sward, fenced in about the house, as smooth as velvet and as clean as the best kept carpet.† There were some grand old cherry-trees in the yard, that threw a massive shade around them. The house had three rooms—a kitchen, a sitting-room, and a bed-chamber over the sitting-room. ‡ There was a piazza in front of the house that was a lovely place to sit in in summer, with the shade of cherry-trees before it. There was no cultivation, no flowers—nothing but the smooth green sward and the majestic trees.

" On the occasion of this, my first, visit to the poet, I was a good deal plagued—Poe had somehow caught a full-grown bob-o'-link. He had put him in a cage, which he had hung on a nail driven into the trunk of a cherry-tree. The poor bird was as unfit to live in a cage as his captor was to live in the world. He was as restless as his jailer, and sprang

---

* To Judge Neilson Poe. August 19th, 1860.

† Compare with description of grass in "Domain of Arnheim" and "Landor's Cottage."—J. H. I.

‡ This is a mistake ; there were, and still are, two rooms on each floor.—J. H. I.

continually, in a fierce, frightened way, from one side of the cage to the other. I pitied him, but Poe was bent on taming him. There he stood with his arms crossed before the imprisoned bird, his sublime trust in attaining the impossible apparent in his whole self. So handsome, so impassive in his wonderful intellectual beauty, so proud and so reserved, and yet so confidentially communicative, so entirely a gentleman upon all occasions that I ever saw him—so tasteful, so good a talker was Poe, that he impressed himself and his wishes, even without words, upon those with whom he spoke. However, I remonstrated against the imprisonment of 'Robert of Lincoln Green.'

" ' You are wrong,' said he quietly, 'in wishing me to free the bird. He is a splendid songster, and as soon as he is tamed he will delight our home with his musical gifts. You should hear him ring out like a chime of joy-bells his wonderful song.'

" Poe's voice was melody itself. He always spoke low, when in a violent discussion, compelling his hearers to listen if they would know his opinion, his facts, fancies, or philosophy, or his weird imaginings. These last usually flowed from his pen, seldom from his tongue.

" On this occasion I was introduced to the young wife of the poet, and to the mother, then more than sixty years of age. She was a tall, dignified old lady, with a most ladylike manner, and her black dress, though old and much worn, looked really elegant on her. She wore a widow's cap, of the genuine pattern, and it suited excellently with her snow-white hair. Her features were large, and corresponded with her stature, and it seemed strange how such a stalwart and queenly woman could be the mother of her *petite* daughter. Mrs. Poe looked very young; she had large black eyes, and a pearly whiteness of complexion, which was a perfect pallor. Her pale face, her brilliant eyes, and her raven hair, gave her an unearthly look. One felt that she was almost a dissolved spirit, and when she coughed it was made certain that she was rapidly passing away.

" The mother seemed hale and strong, and appeared to be a sort of universal Providence for her strange children.

" The cottage had an air of taste and gentility that must have been lent to it by the presence of its inmates. So neat,

so poor, so unfurnished, and yet so charming, a dwelling I
never saw. The floor of the kitchen was white as wheaten
flour. A table, a chair, and a little stove that it contained,
seemed to furnish it completely. The sitting-room floor was
laid with check matting; four chairs, a light stand, and a
hanging book-shelf, composed its furniture. There were
pretty presentation copies of books on the little shelves, and
the Brownings had posts of honour on the stand. With
quiet exultation Poe drew from his side-pocket a letter he
had recently received from Elizabeth Barrett (Browning).
He read it to us. It was very flattering. She told Poe
that his 'poem of the Raven had awakened a fit of horror
in England.'* This was what he loved to do. To make
the flesh creep, to make one shudder and freeze with horror,
was more to his relish (I cannot say more to his mind or
heart) than to touch the tenderest chords of sympathy or
sadness.

"On the book-shelf there lay a volume of Poe's poems.
He took it down, wrote my name in it, and gave it to me.
I think he did this from a feeling of sympathy, for I could
not be of advantage to him, as my two companions could.†
I had sent him an article when he edited the *Broadway
Journal*, which had pleased him. It was a sort of wonder
article, and he published it without knowing the authorship,
and he was pleased to find his anonymous contributor in
me. He was at this time greatly depressed. Their extreme
poverty, the sickness of his wife, and his own inability to
write, sufficiently accounted for this. We spent half an hour
in the house, when some more company came, which included
ladies, and then we all went out for a walk.

"We strolled away into the woods, and had a very cheerful time, till some one proposed a game at leaping. I think
it must have been Poe, as he was expert in the exercise. Two
or three gentlemen agreed to leap with him, and although
one of them was tall, and had been a hunter in times past,
Poe still distanced them all. But, alas! his gaiters (*i.e.*, gaiter-
shoes), long worn and carefully kept, were both burst in the

---

* "A fit horror," *vide* p. 221.

† A reviewer one ; "the other, a person who wrote laudatory notices
of books, and borrowed money or favours from their flattered authors
afterwards."—J. H. I.

grand leap that made him victor. I had pitied the poor bob-o'-link in his hard and hopeless imprisonment, but I pitied poor Poe more now. I was certain he had no other shoes, boots, or gaiters. Who among us could offer him money to buy another pair? If any one had money, who had the effrontery to offer it to the poet? When we reached the cottage, I think all felt that we must not go in, to see the shoeless unfortunate sitting or standing in our midst. I had an errand, however; I had left the volume of Poe's poems, and I entered the house to get it. The poor old mother looked at his feet, with a dismay that I shall never forget.

"'O Eddie!' said she, 'how *did* you burst your gaiters?'

"Poe seemed to have fallen into a semi-torpid state as soon as he saw his mother. . . .

"I related the cause of the mishap, and she drew me into the kitchen.

"'Will you speak to Mr. —— ' (the reviewer), she said, 'about Eddie's last poem?'

"'If he will only take the poem, Eddie can have a pair of shoes. He has it—I carried it last week, and Eddie says it is his best. You will speak to him about it, *won't you?*'

"We had already read the poem in conclave, and, Heaven forgive us, we could not make head or tail of it. It might as well have been in any of the lost languages, for any meaning we could extract from its melodious numbers. I remember saying that I believed it was only a hoax that Poe was passing off for poetry, to see how far his name would go in imposing upon people. But here was a situation. The reviewer had been actively instrumental in the demolition of the gaiters.

"'Of course they will publish the poem,' said I, 'and I will ask C—— to be quick about it.'

"The poem was paid for at once, and published soon after. I presume it is regarded as genuine poetry in the collected poems of its author, but then it brought the poet a pair of gaiters and twelve shillings over."

Upon Mrs. Gove-Nichols' next visit to Fordham, the poet became very confidential with her:—

" 'I write,' he said, 'from a mental necessity— to satisfy my taste and my love of art. Fame forms no motive power with me. What can I care for the judgment of a multitude, every individual of which I despise ?'

" 'But, Mr. Poe,' said I, 'there are individuals whose judgment you respect.'

" 'Certainly, and I would choose to have their esteem unmixed with the mean adulation of the mob.'

" 'But the multitude may be honestly and legitimately pleased,' said I.

" 'That may be *possible*,' said Poe, musingly, 'because they may have an honest and legitimate leader, and not a poor man who has been paid a hundred dollars to manufacture opinions for them and fame for an author.'

" 'Do reviewers sell their literary conscience thus unconscionably ?' said I.

" 'A literary critic must be loth to violate his taste, his sense of the fit and the beautiful. To sin against these and praise an unworthy author, is to him an unpardonable sin. But if he were placed on the rack, or if one he loved better than his own life were writhing there, I can conceive of his forging a note against the Bank of Fame, in favour of some would-be poet, who is able and willing to buy his poems and his opinions.'

" He turned almost fiercely upon me, his fine eyes piercing me. 'Would you blame a man for not allowing his sick wife to starve ?' said he.

" I changed the subject, and he became quiet, and we walked along, noting beauties of flowers and foliage, of hill and dale, 'till we reached the cottage.'

" At my next visit," resumes Mrs. Gove-Nichols, " Poe said, as we walked along the brow of the hill, 'I can't look out on this loveliness till I have made a confession to you. I said to you, when you were last here, that I despised Fame.'

" 'I remember,' said I.

" 'It was false,' said he; 'I love Fame. I dote on it; I idolise it; I would drink to the very dregs the glorious intoxication. I would have incense ascend in my honour from every hill and hamlet, from every town and city on this earth. Fame ! glory ! they are life-giving breath and living blood. No man lives unless he is famous ! How bitterly I belied my nature, and my aspirations, when I said I did not desire fame, and that I despised it.'

"I suggested that the utterance on both occasions might be true to the mood that suggested them. But he declared that there was no truth in his first assertion. I was not as severe with him as he was with himself."

The summer months flew by, taking with them the strength of his beloved young wife, and unnerving and unfitting the poet for all literary exertion. He was unable to work, and, even if he had been able, the but too successful career of his "Literati" sketches had caused many magazines, edited by the reviewed or their allies, to close their pages to him. The dangerous censorship he had assumed in this series, says Mrs. Whitman, " exposed him to frequent indignant criticism, while, by his personal errors and indiscretions, he drew upon himself much social censure and *espionage*, and became the victim of dishonouring accusations from which honour itself had forbidden him to exculpate himself." The worse his wife became, the less able became the poet to labour with his pen, so that the situation of the family grew more deplorable daily. The dreary months dragged along, and no help appeared. "The autumn came, and Mrs. Poe sank rapidly in consumption," resumes the narrative of Mrs. Gove-Nichols.

"I saw her in her bed-chamber," she relates. "Everything here was so neat, so purely clean, so scant and poverty-stricken, that I saw the poor sufferer with such a heart-ache . . . There was no clothing on the bed, which was only straw, but a snow-white counterpane and sheets. The weather was cold, and the sick lady had the dreadful chills that accompany the hectic fever of consumption. She lay on the straw bed, wrapped in her husband's greatcoat, with a large tortoiseshell cat in her bosom. The wonderful cat seemed conscious of her great usefulness. The coat and the cat were the sufferer's only means of warmth, except as her husband held her hands, and her mother her feet.

"Mrs. Clemm was passionately fond of her daughter, and her distress on account of her illness and poverty and misery was dreadful to see.

"As soon as I was made aware of these painful facts, I came to New York and enlisted the sympathies and services of a lady, whose heart and hand were ever open to the poor and miserable. A feather bed and abundance of bed clothing and other comforts were the first-fruits of my labour of love. The lady headed a private subscription, and carried them sixty dollars the next week. From the day this kind lady first saw the suffering family of the poet, she watched over them as a mother watches over her babe. She saw them often, and ministered to the comfort of the dying and the living."

Mrs. Shew (afterwards Houghton), the lady whose unostentatious sympathy Mrs. Nichols had so happily invoked, knew nothing of the poet or his family, save that they were helpless and needed aid; but that was all that was necessary to call forth her friendly services.

CHAPTER XVII.

MARIE LOUISE SHEW.

The facts of Poe's poverty, illness, and inability to write soon became public property. One consequence of these circumstances being published was the outbreak in the papers of an epidemic of literary and personal abuse of the unprotected poet. In another instance, an implacable woman, still smarting under a hastily-uttered and bitterly-repented remark of Poe's,* actually tortured his dying wife by sending her some of the scurrilous attacks on her unfortunate husband, and by so doing, so the poet firmly believed, shortened her life. But there was a bright side to this too gloomy picture. Commenting upon a paragraph in the columns of a daily contemporary that, without Poe's knowledge or connivance, had brought the poor proud poet's unhappy circumstances before the world, N. P. Willis made an appeal to the public on his friend's behalf. In this article, which appeared in the *Home Journal,* he took the opportunity of suggesting that the poet's case was a strong argument in favour of founding an hospital for well-educated persons in reduced circumstances. Some of Willis's remarks are worth repetition, although it is to be believed that, at the time, they had little other effect than making Poe's misery still more notorious. He said :—

"The feeling we have long entertained on this subject has been freshened by a recent paragraph in the *Express,* an-

* *Vide,* p. 292.

nouncing that Mr. Edgar Allan Poe and his wife were both dangerously ill, and suffering for want of the common necessaries of life. Here is one of the finest scholars, one of the most original men of genius, and one of the most industrious of the literary profession of our country, whose temporary suspension of labour, from bodily illness, drops him immediately to a level with the common objects of public charity. There is no intermediate stopping-place — no respectful shelter where, with the delicacy due to genius and culture, he might secure aid, unadvertised, till, with returning health, he could resume his labours and his unmortified sense of independence. He must either apply to individual friends—(a resource to which death is sometimes almost preferable)—or *suffer down* to the level where Charity receives claimants, but where Rags and Humiliation are the only recognised Ushers to her presence. Is this right? Should there not be, in all highly-civilised communities, an institution designed expressly for educated and refined objects of charity —a hospital, a retreat, a home of seclusion and comfort, the sufficient claims to which would be such susceptibilities as are violated by the above-mentioned appeal in a daily paper?"

This suggestive article of Willis speedily reached Poe's hands. He was intensely horrified at having his private matters thus thrust before the public, and immediately sent the following letter to the editor of the *Home Journal*, in which publication it appeared, within a week after the article that had called it forth:—

"MY DEAR WILLIS,—The paragraph which has been put in circulation respecting my wife's illness, my own, my poverty, &c., is now lying before me ; together with the beautiful lines by Mrs. Locke and those by Mrs. ——, to which the paragraph has given rise, as well as your kind and manly comments in the *Home Journal*.

"The motive of the paragraph I leave to the conscience of him or her who wrote it or suggested it. Since the thing is done, however, and since the concerns of my family are thus pitilessly thrust before the public, I perceive no mode of escape from a public statement of what is true and what is erroneous in the report alluded to.

"That my wife is ill, then, is true ; and you may imagine with what feelings I add that this illness, hopeless from the first, has been heightened and precipitated by the reception, at two different periods, of anonymous letters—one enclosing the paragraph now in question ; the other, those published calumnies of Messrs. ——, for which I yet hope to find redress in a court of justice. *

"Of the facts, that I myself have been long and dangerously ill, and that my illness has been a well understood thing among my brethren of the press, the best evidence is afforded by the innumerable paragraphs of personal and of literary abuse with which I have been latterly assailed. This matter, however, will remedy itself. At the very first blush of my new prosperity, the gentlemen who toadied me in the old will recollect themselves and toady me again. You, who know me, will comprehend that I speak of these things only as having served, in a measure, to lighten the gloom of unhappiness, by a gentle and not unpleasant sentiment of mingled pity, merriment, and contempt.

"That, as the inevitable consequence of so long an illness, I have been in want of money, it would be folly in me to deny—but that I have ever materially suffered from privation, beyond the extent of my capacity for suffering, is not altogether true. That I am 'without friends' is a gross calumny, which I am sure *you* never could have believed, and which a thousand noble-hearted men would have good right never to forgive me for permitting to pass unnoticed and undenied. Even in the city of New York I could have no difficulty in naming a hundred persons, to each of whom—when the hour for speaking had arrived—I could and would have applied for aid and with unbounded confidence, and with absolutely *no* sense of humiliation.

"I do not think, my dear Willis, that there is any need of my saying more. I am getting better, and may add—if it be any comfort to my enemies—that I have little fear of getting worse. The truth is, I have a great deal to do ; and I have made up my mind not to die till it is done.—Sincerely yours,

"EDGAR A. POE.

"*December* 30th, 1846."

---

* The libel suit against the *Evening Mirror* had not yet commenced.—J. H. I.

Whilst the paragraph which invoked this protest from the proud, unfortunate poet, was running the usual newspaper rounds—during all those dreadful days whilst his wife's life was ebbing so rapidly—Poe himself was ill, and utterly unable to write anything but the most urgent and imperative letters, such as the above. The few papers of his which were published during this sad interval, as, for instance, the "Marginalia," had been completed and sold several months before publication to the respective magazines, as, indeed, appears to have been the fate pretty generally of all his later articles. The last of the "Literati" was issued in the October number of the *Lady's Book*, and "The Cask of Amontillado," a tale of deep-studied, implacable revenge, was the poet's contribution for November to that magazine.

It was Poe's intention—an intention he never lived to carry out—to republish the critical sketches from the *Lady's Book*, but greatly revised, in book form, as:—

THE LITERATI:

Some honest opinions about

AUTORIAL MERITS AND DEMERITS,

with

OCCASIONAL WORDS OF PERSONALITY.

Together with

MARGINALIA, SUGGESTIONS, AND ESSAYS

by

EDGAR A. POE.

" If I have in any point receded from what is commonly received, it hath been for the purpose of proceeding *melius* and not *in aliud.*" —*Lord Bacon.*

" Truth, peradventure, by force, may for a time be trodden *down*, but never, by any means, whatsoever, can it be trodden *out.*" —*Lord Coke.*

In an extremely interesting letter which Poe wrote on the 15th of December, to a rare and valued correspondent, he thus, amongst other matters, alludes to some of these literary projects:—

"My dear ——,—By way of beginning this letter, let me say a word or two of apology for not having sooner replied to your letters of June 9th and October 13th. For more than six months I have been ill—for the greater part of that time, dangerously so, and quite unable to write even an ordinary letter. My magazine papers appearing in this interval were all in the publisher's hands before I was taken sick. Since getting better, I have been, as a matter of course, overwhelmed with the business accumulating during my illness.

"It always gives me true pleasure to hear from you, and I wish you could spare time to write me more frequently. I am gratified by your good opinion of my writings, because what you say evinces the keenest discrimination. Ten times the praise you bestow on me would not please me half so much, were it not for the intermingled scraps of censure, or of objection, which show me that you well know what you are talking about. . . .

"Let me now advert to the points of your two last letters:—

"The criticism on Rogers is not mine—although, when it appeared, I observed a similarity to my ordinary manner.

"The notice of Lowell's 'Brittany' *is* mine. You will see that it was merely a preparatory notice—I had designed repeating it in full, but something prevented me.

"The criticism on Shelley is *not* mine; is the work of Parke Godwin. I never saw it.

"The critic alluded to by Willis as connected with the *Mirror*, and as having found a parallel between Hood and Aldrich, *is* myself. See my reply to 'Outis,' in the early numbers of the *Broadway Journal*.

"My reference to L. G. Clark, in spirit but not in letter, is what you suppose. He *abused* me in his criticism—but so feebly—with such a parade of intention and effort, but with so little effect or power, that I—forgave him:—that is to say, I had little difficulty in pardoning him. His strong point was that I ought to write well, because I had asserted

her sweetest kiss of love and will die blessing you. But come—oh come to-morrow ! Yes, I *will* be calm—everything you so nobly wish to see me. My mother sends you, also, her 'warmest love and thanks.' She begs me to ask you, if possible, to make arrangements at home so that you may stay with us to-morrow night. I enclose the order to the Postmaster.

"Heaven bless you and farewell.

"EDGAR A. POE.

"FORDHAM, *Jan.* 29. 47."

The very day these lines were written Mrs. Shew called at the cottage, but soon afterwards left it, in order to see after certain comforts for the sick wife. When bidding Mrs. Shew good-bye, the invalid took from her pillow a portrait of her husband and presented it to her kind friend,* together with a little jewel-case that had belonged to the poet's mother, and which he had preserved religiously through all his troubles. She also asked Mrs. Shew to read an old worn letter, and the fragment of another, from the second wife of Poe's adoptive father, Mr. Allan, which she, Virginia, had carefully preserved, as the means of exonerating her husband from the responsibility of having caused dissension in his godfather's home.

Another day, and the poet was wifeless. . . .

For the dear sake of her who was no more—for the sake of "the one *he* loved so dearly "—the poor heartbroken man kept his promise, and bore up bravely until after his youthful bride had been borne to her sepulchre.

The last days of the poet's wife had been soothed by Mrs. Shew, and the final care of the dead lady's remains was undertaken by that same friend.

* Subsequently stolen from Mrs. Shew.—J. H. I.

"Mrs. Shew was *so* good to her," said Mrs. Clemm. "She tended her while she lived, as if she had been her dear sister, and when she was dead she dressed her for the grave in beautiful linen. If it had not been for her, my darling Virginia would have been laid in her grave in cotton. I can never tell my gratitude that my darling was entombed in lovely linen."

"It seemed to soothe the mother's sorrow in a wonderful way," remarks Mrs. Gove-Nichols, "that her daughter had been buried in fine linen. How this delicate raiment could add so much to her happiness, I was not able to see, but so it was."

It is recorded that the day of the funeral was a desolate, dreary day—"the skies they were ashen and sober"—and the bereaved husband was forced to assume his old military cloak, which Mrs. Shew had been at pains to hide out of sight, fearing the memories it must arouse, it having, erstwhile, and in the days of their greatest tribulation, served as a covering for Virginia's bed. The deceased lady was entombed in the old family vault of the Valentines,[*] in the Reformed church at Fordham, by permission of the owner.

Everyone who knew the poet's wife describes her as charming in both manners and features. A portrait of her is in the possession of her half-sister, Mrs. Neilson Poe, and is said to be a good likeness. "From it it is clear that she was very beautiful."[†]

After all was over, and the hapless poet left to face the world once more, exhausted nature gave way, and he fell ill again; in fact, for some days he sank into

---

[*] Probably a branch of the Virginian Valentines, of which family the first Mrs. Allan was a member.—J. H. I.

[†] Letter from John P. Poe, Esq.—J. H. I.

an apathetic stupor, unconscious of all around him. In faithful pursuance of her promise to his dying wife, Mrs. Shew still continued to befriend Poe. The following letter to her from Mrs. Clemm—who continued her watchful care of her unfortunate nephew—showed how much her aid was still depended upon:—

" Friday Evening.

"MY DEAR SWEET FRIEND,—I write to say that the medicines arrived the next train after you left to-day, and a kind friend brought them up to us that same hour. The cooling application was very grateful to my poor Eddie's head, and the flowers were lovely—not 'frozen,' as you feared they would be. I very much fear this illness is to be a serious one. The fever came on at the *same time* to-day (as you said it would), and I am giving the sedative mixture. He did not rouse up to talk to Mr. C——, as he would naturally do to so kind a friend. . . . Eddie made me promise to write you a note about the wine (which I neglected to tell you about this morning). He desires me to return the last box of wine you sent my sweet Virginia (there being some left of the first package, which I will put away for any emergency). The wine was a great blessing to us while *she needed* it, and by its cheering and tonic influence we were enabled to keep her a few days longer with us. The little darling always took it smiling, even when difficult to get it down. But for your timely aid, my dear Mrs. S., we should have had no last words—no loving messages— no *sweet farewells*, for she ceased to speak (from weakness) but with her beautiful eyes ! . . . Eddie has quite set his heart upon the wine *going back to you*, thinking and hoping you may find it useful for the *sick artist* you mentioned 'as convalescent and in need of delicacies.' God bless you, my sweet child, and come soon to your sorrowing and desolate friend,

"MARIA CLEMM.

"P.S.—We look for you in an early train to-morrow, and hope you will stay as long as possible. What we should do without you now is fearful to think of. Eddie says you promised Virginia to come every other day for a long time, or until he was able to go to work again. I hope and believe *you will not fail him;* and I pray that every blessing may be yours, and may follow you in life, as your angelic tenderness and compassion deserve.

"Mr. C—— will tell you of our condition, as he is going to call for this note in an hour's time; and, until we see you, farewell."

For a few days, Edgar Poe, under the careful nursing which he received, appeared to recover, and during this short period of temporary convalescence indited the lines "To M—— L—— S——" (Marie Louise Shew). In this overflowing of an intense gratitude to her to whom he owed

> " The resurrection of deep-buried faith
> In Truth—in Virtue—in Humanity,"

the poet poured forth his thanks with all the vehemence of his impassioned nature, and all untrammelled by the ordinary conventionalities of that everyday life which he so hated and so despised.

The poet's convalescence was of short duration, and was terminated by a vain attempt to grapple with the difficulties of his position. He endeavoured to resume his correspondence, which involved him in all kinds of worries and distressing themes. On the 16th of February he replied to a correspondent who had informed him of a gross charge of plagiarism, which had been set afloat during his disabled condition.* On the 17th of the same month, his suit against the *Mirror* for the publication of the Dunn-English libel terminated in the poet's favour, the jury awarding

* *Vide* pp. 135, 136, concerning the Conchology story.—J. H. I.

Poe $225 for defamation of his character, and this, notwithstanding the intemperate reply he had published. Of the award it appears probable that he never received a single dollar, the amount, if ever paid, apparently finding its way into the pockets of those who carried on the case for him.

Meanwhile, Poe suffered a relapse, and for some time his life was in danger. Mrs. Shew, however, did not forget her promise to his dead wife, and still continued her friendly exertions on the poet's behalf. Naturally, this kind lady could not provide for all the poet's requirements, she wrote, therefore, to a friend in the New York Union Club on the subject, and he brought the matter under the notice of some of the members, many of whom were personally acquainted with Poe. General Scott, who was present at the time, gave his five dollars, saying, " I wish I could make it five hundred," adding, that he believed "Poe to be much belied ; that he had noble and generous *traits*, which belonged to the old and better school," concluding what was quite a speech for the old hero, that "true-hearted Americans ought to take care of her poets as well as her soldiers." General Scott, it should be pointed out, was uncle to the second wife of Mr. Allan, Poe's adoptive father ; had known the poet from his childhood, and had obtained him his nomination to the West Point Military Academy. A private collection of about one hundred dollars was made, and with this, and certain amounts sent by "Stella" (Mrs. Lewis), and other literary friends, old debts were paid off, and all urgent necessities provided for.

During the height of this last attack Mrs. Shew, who was a doctor's only daughter, and had received a medical education, nursed the invalid herself, alternating her nights at the bedside with Mrs. Clemm. The diary which she kept at that time she generously placed at our disposal, so far as it related to Poe, and from it the following interesting particulars are extracted:—" I made my diagnosis, and went to the great Dr. Mott with it; I told him that at best, when Mr. Poe was well, his pulse beat only ten regular beats, after which it suspended, or intermitted (as doctors say). I decided that in his best health he had lesion of one side of the brain, and as he could not bear stimulants or tonics, without producing insanity, I did not feel much hope that he could be raised up from brain fever brought on by extreme suffering of mind and body—actual want, and hunger, and cold having been borne by this heroic husband in order to supply food, medicine, and comforts to his dying wife —until exhaustion and lifelessness were so near at every reaction of the fever, that even sedatives had to be administered with extreme caution. . . . From the time the fever came on until I could reduce his pulse to eighty beats, he talked to me incessantly of the past, which was all new to me, and often begged me to write his fancies for him, for he said he had promised so many greedy publishers his next efforts, that they would not only say that he did not keep his word, but would also revenge themselves by saying all sorts of evil of him if he should die."

The jottings taken down by Mrs. Shew at that time refer chiefly to Poe's early life, and have already been made use of in a former portion of this narrative.

As soon as the poet was enabled to get about again— for nature gradually reasserted her influence—he began to resume his wonted avocations. As yet, he was still unable to execute any continuous literary work, but, as a beginning, he attempted to pay off his epistolary debts. Upon the 10th of March he wrote to Mrs. Locke, of Lowell, Massachusetts, who, upon the publication of the newspaper paragraphs referring to his illness and poverty, had sent him some verses,* and a sympathetic letter proffering to assist him :—

"In answering your kind letter permit me in the very first place to absolve myself from a suspicion which, under the circumstances, you could scarcely have failed to entertain— a suspicion of discourtesy towards yourself, in not having more promptly replied to you. . . . I could not help fearing that should you see my letter to Mr. Willis—in which a natural pride, which I feel you could not blame, impelled me to shrink from public charity, even at the cost of truth, in denying those necessities which were but too real—I could not help fearing that, should you see this letter, you would yourself feel pained at having caused me pain—at having been the means of giving further publicity to an unfounded report—at all events to the report of a wretchedness which I had thought it prudent (since the world regards wretchedness as a crime) so publicly to disavow. In a word, venturing to judge your noble nature by my own, I felt grieved lest my published denial might cause you to regret what you had done ; and my first impulse was to write you, and assure you, even at the risk of doing so too warmly, of the sweet emotion, made up of respect and gratitude alone, with which my heart was filled to overflowing. While I was hesitating, however, in regard to the propriety of this step, I was overwhelmed by a sorrow so poignant as to deprive me for several weeks of all power of thought or action. Your letter, now lying before me, tells me that I had not been mistaken in your nature, and that I should not have hesitated to have addressed you ; but believe me, my dear Mrs.

* Now in my possession.—J. H. I.

Locke, that I am already ceasing to regard those difficulties or misfortunes which have led me to even this partial correspondence with yourself."

The New England lady was only too delighted to have elicited a response from the famous poet, and such a confidential one too — for Poe, like Byron, Burns, and other brother bards, was ready to bare the secrets of his heart of hearts to the veriest stranger— and at once drew him into a correspondence that grew into personal acquaintance, and, eventually, entangled him in one of the most troublesome *imbroglios* of his life.

On the day following that on which the letter cited from above was written, the poet sent this little note to the representatives of the "Philosophical Society" of Wittenberg College, Springfield, Ohio, in acknowledgment of their letter informing him of his election, on the preceding 9th of February, to the honorary membership of that institution :—

"NEW YORK, *March* 11, 1847.

"GENTLEMEN,—Very serious illness has hitherto prevented me from replying to your most flattering letter of the 24th ult.

"May I now beg you to express to your Society my grateful acceptance and appreciation of the honour they have conferred on me ?—With respect & esteem, I am, gentlemen, Yo. mo. ob. St.,   EDGAR A. POE."

This fair specimen of autograph hunters' success in "drawing out" a distinguished contemporary having been disposed of, the poet is also found writing on the same date to an esteemed correspondent, on various topics already referred to, such as the Philadelphia *Saturday Evening Post's* charge of plagiarising Captain

Brown's book on Conchology; the result of the suit against the *Mirror;* the projected *Stylus* magazine; the " Valdemar Case," and other matters. He remarks, " I am still quite sick, and overwhelmed with business—but snatch a few moments to reply to yours of the 21st ult. . . . I cannot tell why the review of Hawthorne does not appear—but I presume we shall have it by and by. He (Mr. Godey) paid me for it, when I sent it—so I have no business to ask about it."

During the remainder of 1847 the poet led a secluded life with his mother-in-law, Mrs. Clemm, receiving occasional visits from his friends and admirers, but rarely forsaking the precincts of his sorrow-hallowed cottage. Mrs. Shew continued to visit Ford-ham at such intervals as her active life allowed, and on certain yet unfrequent occasions her patient went to New York. In her diary of this year Mrs. Shew has the following interesting reminiscence :—

" Mr. Poe came to town to go to a midnight service with a lady friend and myself. He went with us and followed the service like a *churchman*, looking directly towards the chancel, and holding one side of my prayer-book ; sang the psalms with us, and to my astonishment struck up a tenor to our soprano ; and got along nicely during the *first part of the service*, which was on the subject of the sympathies of our soul with our wants. The passage being often repeated, ' He was a man of sorrows and acquainted with grief,' he begged me to remain quiet, and saying he would wait for us outside, he rushed out, *too excited to stay.* I knew he would not leave us to return home alone (although my friend thought it doubtful), and so, after the sermon, as I began to feel anxious—as we were in a strange church—I looked back and saw his pale face. As the congregation rose to sing the hymn, ' Jesus, Saviour of my soul,' he appeared at my side, and sang the hymn without looking at the book, in a fine, clear tenor. He looked inspired. . . I did not dare to ask him why he left, but he mentioned after we got home that the subject 'was marvellously handled.' "

Poe rarely forsook Fordham, however, during tne year following his lost Lenore's death, but spent his time in mourning over her memory, and in thinking out the plan of the great and crowning work of his life—his great philosophical "prose-poem" "Eureka." Whilst engaged upon this work, records Mrs. Shew, he was quite certain of success. She endeavoured to curb his over sanguine expectations, for, she remarks, " I did not expect him to live long; I knew that organic disease had been gaining upon his physical frame through the many trials and privations of his eventful life. I told him in all candour that nothing could or would save him from sudden death but a prudent life of calm, with a woman fond enough and strong enough to manage his affairs for him. I was often subjected to his irony for my lectures, coming, as they did, from a woman so little skilled in worldly troubles or cares as I was then. . . . He said I had never troubled myself to read his works, or poems; which was true, for my heart found so much sorrow to sympathise with in the griefs of those I came in contact with, that there was no need of resorting to ideal woe; . . . but ' I was a rest for his spirit,' for this very reason."

The quiet and studious life Poe lived at Fordham, meanwhile, was very different to that ascribed to him by the paragraph-mongers of the press, and the scari-fied victims of his pen. Many interesting recollections have been given by his visitors of the calm and soli-tary way in which he spent his time, during his resi-dence at the quaint little Dutch cottage, but none more valuable than these autobiographic glimpses afforded by one of his unpublished letters :—

" The editor of the *Weekly Universe* speaks kindly, and I find no fault with his representing my habits as ' shockingly irregular.' He could not have had the ' personal acquaintance ' with me, of which he writes, but has fallen into a very natural error. The fact is thus :—My *habits* are rigorously abstemious, and I omit nothing of the natural regimen requisite for health—*i.e.*, I rise early, eat moderately, drink nothing but water, and take abundant and regular exercise in the open air. But this is my private life—my studious and literary life—and of course escapes the eye of the world. The desire for society comes upon me only when I have become excited by drink. Then *only* I go—that is, at these times only I *have been* in the practice of going among my friends ; who seldom, or in fact never, having seen me unless excited, take it for granted that I am always so. Those who *really* know me, know better. In the meantime I shall turn the general error to account. But enough of this—the causes which maddened me to the drinking point are no more, and I am done with drinking for ever. I do *not* know the editors and contributors of the *Universe*, and was not aware of the existence of such a paper. Who are they? or is it a secret?"

This self-revelation, even if to be accepted *cum granô salis*, must be regarded as a most important contribution towards a thorough comprehension of the apparently complex and dual nature of Poe's existence. Further side-lights are flung upon his story, so far as this period of it is concerned, by the reminiscences of his various visitors at Fordham. An author who visited the poet's cottage during the summer of 1847, described it as "half buried in fruit-trees, and as having a thick grove of pines in its immediate neighbourhood ; but the proximity of the railroad, and the increasing population of the little village,

have since wrought great changes in the place.
Round an old cherry-tree, near the door, was a broad
bank of greenest turf. The neighbouring beds of
mignonette and heliotrope, and the pleasant shade
above, made this a favourite seat. Rising at four
o'clock in the morning, for a walk to the magnificent
aqueduct bridge over Harlem river, our informant
found the poet, with his mother (Mrs. Clemm), standing on the turf beneath the cherry-tree, eagerly watching the movements of two beautiful birds that seemed
contemplating a settlement in its branches. He had
some rare tropical birds in cages, which he cherished
and petted with assiduous care."

An English lady, as Mrs. Whitman further records,
"passed several weeks at the little cottage in Fordham,
in the early autumn of 1847, and described to us, with
a truly English appreciativeness, its unrivalled neatness, and the quaint simplicity of its interior and
surroundings. It was at the time bordered by a
flower-garden, whose clumps of rare dahlias and
brilliant beds of autumnal flowers showed, in the
careful culture bestowed upon them, the fine floral
taste of the inmates." "Our English friend described
the poet," resumes Mrs. Whitman, "as giving to his
birds and his flowers a delighted attention that seemed
quite inconsistent with the gloomy and grotesque
character of his writings. A favourite cat, too, enjoyed
his friendly patronage, and often when he was engaged
in composition it seated itself on his shoulder, purring
as if in complacent approval of the work proceeding
under its supervision."

"During Poe's residence at Fordham a walk to
High Bridge," continues our authority, "was one of

his favourite and habitual recreations. The water of the aqueduct is conveyed across the river on a range of lofty granite arches, which rise to the height of a hundred and forty-five feet above high-water level. On the top a turfed and grassy road, used only by foot-passengers, and flanked on either side by a low parapet of granite, makes one of the finest promenades imaginable.

" The winding river and the high rocky shores at the western extremity of the bridge are seen to great advantage from this lofty avenue. In the last melancholy years of his life—'the lonesome latter years'—Poe was accustomed to walk there at all times of the day and night; often pacing the then solitary pathway for hours without meeting a human being. A little to the east of the cottage rises a ledge of rocky ground, partly covered with pines and cedars, commanding a fine view of the surrounding country and of the picturesque College of St. John's, which had at that time in its neighbourhood an avenue of venerable old trees. This rocky ledge was also one of the poet's favourite resorts. Here, through long summer days, and through solitary, star-lit nights, he loved to sit, dreaming his gorgeous waking dreams, or pondering the deep problems of the *Universe*,— that grand ' prose-poem ' to which he devoted the last and maturest energies of his wonderful intellect."

In this way the poet lived—" in a world of things ideal "—spending his time in musing over the unforgotten past, and in devising schemes for a famous future. At times his solitude was broken in upon not only by his ever-welcome friends, but, also, by those most malignant pests of literary society, female

bores, who wanted to make the renowned poet's
acquaintance and engage his pen on their behalf in
friendly criticism.   Mrs. Shew records that she often
found such persons "sitting in Mrs. Clemm's little
room, waiting to see the man of genius who had
rushed out, to escape to the fields or forest, or to the
grounds of the Catholic school in the vicinity.   I
remember," she relates, "Mrs. Clemm one day sending
me after him in great secrecy, and I found him sitting
on a favourite rock muttering his desire to die, and
get rid of literary bores.   He liked me for my ignorance and indifference, no doubt, to worldly honours, and
lamented, in sincere sorrow, when I grew like the rest
of the world by my duties and position."

During this period of mental incubation the poet
published little, and that little had been chiefly
written previous to 1847.   "Eureka" greatly engaged
his mind, but, so he frequently alleged, its publication
was only to be regarded as the stepping-stone to the
furtherance of starting a magazine of his own, on a
safe and certain basis.   This life-long dream gradually
began to assume a more definite shape than it had
hitherto worn ; the name of the *Stylus* was permanently
adopted for the projected publication, and a well-
arranged plan devised for setting it afloat.   Besides
his "prose-poem," few literary compositions were
attempted, and of these, the weird monody of
"Ulalume" was the only one important.   It was towards the close of this "most immemorial year"—
this year in which he had lost his cousin-bride,—that
this "most musical, most melancholy" dirge was
written.   Like so much of his poetry, it was autobiographical, and, on his own authority we have it, was

in its basis, although not in the precise correspondence
of time, simply historical. " Such was the poet's lonely
midnight walk," says Mrs. Whitman ; " such, amid the
desolate memories and sceneries of the hour, was the
new-born hope enkindled within his heart at sight
of the morning star—

' Astarte's bediamonded crescent '—

coming up as the beautiful harbinger of love and
happiness yet awaiting him in the untried future, and
such the sudden transition of feeling, the boding
dread, that supervened on discovering that which had
at first been unnoted, that it shone, as if in mockery
or in warning, directly over the sepulchre of the lost
' Ulalume.' "

This marvellously melodious poem first appeared
anonymously, in Colton's *American Review* for
December 1847, as " Ulalume : a Ballad," and, being
reprinted in the *Home Journal*, was, by an absurd
mistake, on a subsequent republication, ascribed to
the then editor, N. P. Willis. The poem originally
possessed an additional stanza which, at the suggestion of Mrs. Whitman, Poe eventually omitted, and,
thereby, greatly strengthened the effect. In after
years, however, the lady regretted the suppression of
these final lines, deeming them essential to the comprehension of the entire poem. Few persons will be
likely to share this regret on reading the excluded
verses, which read thus :—

> " Said we then—the two, then—' Ah, can it
> Have been that the woodlandish ghouls—
> The pitiful, the merciful ghouls—
> To bar up our path and to ban it
> From the secret that lies in these wolds—

Had drawn up the spectre of a planet
From the limbo of lunary souls—
This sinfully scintillant planet
From the Hell of the planetary souls?' "

Another poetical essay belonging to this year was the fanciful little piece entitled " An Enigma," written for " Stella " (Mrs. Estelle Anna Lewis), a lady already alluded to as having among others assisted Poe in the hour of his extreme need. This little effusion of gratitude did not appear in public until its issue in March 1848, in the *Union Magazine*, although it had been sent off several months before, as the following notelet shows :—

" *November 27, 1847.*

" DEAR MRS. LEWIS—A thousand thanks for your repeated kindness, and, above all, for the comforting and cheering words of your note. Your advice I feel as a command which neither my heart nor my reason would venture to disobey. May Heaven for ever bless you and yours !

" A day or two ago I sent to one of the Magazines the sonnet enclosed. Its tone is somewhat too light ; but it embodies a riddle which I wish to put you to the trouble of expounding. Will you try ?

" My best regards, with those of Mrs. Clemm, to Mr. Lewis, and believe me, with all the affection of a brother.—Yours always, EDGAR A. POE."

CHAPTER XVIII.

EUREKA!

WITH the new year (1848) Edgar Poe's literary activity recommenced. In the first instance, he circulated as widely as possible the prospectus of his projected magazine, the *Stylus*, sending copies to all his friends and acquaintances in various parts of the States, and, generally, with an explanatory letter. This prospectus, which slightly varied, from time to time, at every reprint, is extremely interesting, as showing what were the poet's real views with respect to his life-long project, and what ideas he had formed as to the *beau ideal* of a journal. The prospectus reads:—

" THE STYLUS.

A Monthly Journal of Literature Proper, the Fine Arts, and the Drama.

To be Edited by

EDGAR A. POE.

" *To the Public.*—Since resigning the conduct of the *Southern Literary Messenger* at the beginning of its third year, and more especially since retiring from the Editorship of *Graham's Mazagine* soon after the commencement of its second, I have had always in view the establishment of a monthly journal which should retain one or two of the chief features of .the work first mentioned, abandoning or greatly modifying its general character;—but not until now have I felt at liberty to attempt the execution of this design.

"I shall be pardoned for speaking more directly of the two magazines in question. Having in neither of them any proprietary right; the objects of their worthy owners, too, being at variance with my own; I found it not only impossible to effect anything, on the score of taste, for their mechanical appearance, but difficult to stamp upon them internally that *individuality* which I believed essential to their success. In regard to the permanent influence of such publications, it appears to me that continuity and a marked certainty of purpose are requisites of vital importance; but attainable only where one mind alone has at least the general control. Experience, to be brief, has shown me that in founding a journal of my own, lies my sole chance of carrying out to completion whatever peculiar intentions I may have entertained.

"These intentions are now as heretofore. It shall be the chief purpose of the magazine proposed, to become known as one wherein may be found at all times, on all topics within its legitimate reach, a sincere and a fearless opinion. It shall be a leading object to assert in precept and to maintain in practice the rights, while in effect it demonstrates the advantages, of an absolutely independent criticism :—a criticism self-sustained; guiding itself only by intelligible laws of art; analysing these laws as it applies them; holding itself aloof from all personal bias, and acknowledging no fear save that of the Right.

"In the first number of the *Stylus* the Editor will commence the publication of a work on which he has been employed unremittingly for the last two years. It will be called 'Literary America,' and will endeavour to present, much in detail, that great desideratum, a faithful account of the literary productions, literary people, and literary affairs of the United States.

"There is no design, however, to make the journal a critical one solely, or even very especially. It will aim at something *more* than the usual magazine variety, and at affording a fair field for the *true* talent of the land, without reference to the mere *prestige* of name or the advantages of worldly position. But since the efficiency of the work must in great measure depend upon its definitiveness, the STYLUS will limit itself to *Literature Proper, the Fine Arts, and the Drama.*

" In regard to what is going on, within the limits assigned, throughout the civilised world, it will be a principal object of the magazine to keep its readers really *au courant.* For this end, accurate arrangements have been made at London, Paris, Rome and Vienna. The most distinguished of American scholars has agreed to superintend the department of classical letters.* At all points the most effective aid is secured."

The remainder of the prospectus · is devoted to the more technical portion of the project, being chiefly concerned with the matters of the journal's mechanical execution—which was promised to be far superior to the ordinary magazine style—with the quality of the paper, the rate of subscription, and so forth. Engravings, it may be noted, were promised not only to be of the highest art, but to be " only in obvious illustration of the text," which was in contradiction of the custom then pretty prevalent in America, of " cooking up " some kind of text, or the other, to illustrate the illustration. Altogether, if this prospectus—dated " New York City, January 1848," and signed by the poet—promised much, it only propounded a feasible scheme that, in more practical and more worldly-wise hands, should have and must have succeeded, when backed by so renowned and fascinating a reputation as was Poe's.

At this period the poet was so sanguine of the success of his project, that his conversation and correspondence both were filled with the subject. He wrote to all his friends to assist him, forwarding them the prospectus and endeavouring to galvanise them into enthusiasm. From a letter to an old and long-

---

* Professor Charles Anthon, *vide* p. 350.—J. H. I.

neglected correspondent he wrote on the 4th of January in these terms :—

"GOOD FRIEND :—Your last, dated July 26th, ends with— ' Write, will you not?' I have been living ever since in a constant state of intention to write, and finally concluded not to write at all, until I could say something definite about the *Stylus* and other matters. You perceive that I now send you a Prospectus. But before I speak farther on this topic, let me succinctly reply to various points in your letter.

"1. 'Hawthorne' is out. How do you like it?

"2. 'The Rationale of Verse' was found to come down too heavily (as I forewarned you it did) upon some of poor Colton's friends in Frogpondium—the 'pundits,' you know ; so I gave him 'a song' for it and took it back. The song was 'Ulalume—a Ballad,' published in the December number of the *American Review*. I enclose it, as copied by the *Home Journal* (Willis's paper), with the editor's remarks. Please let me know how you like 'Ulalume.' As for the 'Rat. of Verse,' I sold it to 'Graham' at a round advance on Colton's price, and in Graham's hands it is still—but not to remain even there ; for I mean to get it back, revise or rewrite it (since ' Evangeline ' has been published), and deliver it as a lecture when I go South and West on my Magazine expedition.

"3. I have been 'so still' on account of preparation for the Magazine campaign ; also, have been working at my book—nevertheless I have written some trifles not yet published—some which have been.

"4. My health is better—best. I have never been so well.

. . . . .

"6. The 'common friend' alluded to is Mrs. Frances S Osgood, the poetess.

"7. I agree with you only in part, as regards Miss Fuller.* She has some general, but no particular, critical powers. She belongs to a *school* of criticism—the Göthean, æsthetic, eulogistic. The creed of this school is that, in criticising an author, you must imitate him, ape him, out Herod - Herod. . . . For example, she abuses Lowell (the

---

* Margaret Fuller, afterwards Countess D'Ossoli.—J. H. I.

best of our poets, perhaps) on account of a personal quarrel with him. She has omitted all mention of me, for the same reason—although, a short time before the issue of her book, she praised me highly in the *Tribune*. I enclose you her criticism, that you may judge for yourself. She praised 'Witchcraft,' because Mathews . . . wrote it. In a word, she is an ill-tempered and very inconsistent *Old Maid*—avoid her. . . .

"And now, having replied to all your queries, let me refer to the *Stylus*. I am resolved to be my own publisher. To be controlled is to be ruined. My ambition is great. If I succeed, I put myself (within two years) in possession of a fortune and infinitely more. My plan is to go through the South and West, and endeavor to interest my friends so as *to commence with a list of at least five hundred subscribers.* With this list, I can take the matter into my own hands. There are some of my friends who have sufficient confidence in me to advance their subscription — but, at all events, succeed *I will*. Can you or will you help me? I have room to say no more. Truly yours,   E. A. POE."

If the poet expected his many acquaintances, and still more numerous admirers, to send him their dollars in advance, he speedily discovered his mistake, and saw that some other means must be adopted towards raising the amount requisite to defray his preliminary expenses. In order, therefore, to obtain sufficient capital to start him upon his tour in search of subscribers, he determined to deliver a series of lectures, and, in the subjoined letter to Mr. H. D. Chapin, thus expresses his ideas on the subject, and the helplessness of his position :—

"FORDHAM—*Jan.* 17——48.
"MY DEAR SIR,—Mrs. Shew intimated to me, not long ago, that you would, perhaps, lend me your aid in my endeavour to re-establish myself in the literary world ; and I now venture to ask your assistance. When I last spoke with you, I mentioned my design of going to see Mr. Neal

at Portland, and there, with his influence, deliver a Lecture —the proceeds of which might enable me to take the first steps towards my proposed Magazine:—that is to say, put, perhaps, $100 in my pocket; which would give me the necessary outfit and start me on my tour. But, since our conversation, I have been thinking that a better course would be to make interest among my friends here—in N. Y. city—and deliver a Lecture, in the first instance, at the Society Library. With this object in view, may I beg of you so far to assist me as to procure for me the use of the Lecture Room? The difficulty with me is that payment for the Room is demanded *in advance* and I have no money. I believe the price is $15. I think that, without being too sanguine, I may count upon an audience of some 3 or 4 hundreds—and if even 300 are present, I shall be enabled to proceed with my plans.

"Should you be so kind as to grant me the aid I request, I should like to engage the Room for the *first Thursday in February.*—Gratefully yours, EDGAR A. POE.

"I am deeply obliged to you for your note of introduction to Col. Webb. As yet I have not found an opportunity of presenting it—thinking it best to do so when I speak to him about the Lecture."

Mr. Chapin, or some other friend, apparently smoothed down all difficulties, for Poe made his definite arrangement for delivering the initial lecture of his campaign. Matters being thus far arranged, it became necessary to make the affair as public as possible, and in pursuance of this plan the aid of friendly editors had to be enlisted. N. P. Willis was, of course, applied to, and in these terms:—

"FORDHAM, *January 22, 1848.*
"MY DEAR MR. WILLIS,—I am about to make an effort at re-establishing myself in the literary world, and *feel* that I may depend upon your aid.

"My general aim is to start a Magazine, to be called the *Stylus;* but it would be useless to me, even when established, if not entirely out of the control of a publisher. I mean, therefore, to get up a Journal which shall be *my own*, at all points. With this end in view, I must get a list of, at least, five hundred subscribers to begin with :—nearly two hundred I have already. I propose, however, to go South and West, among my personal and literary friends—old College and West Point acquaintances—and see what I can do. In order to get the means of taking the first step, I propose to lecture at the Society Library, on Thursday, the 3rd of February—and, that there may be no cause of *squabbling*, my subject shall *not be literary* at all. I have chosen a broad text—'The Universe.'

"Having thus given you *the facts* of the case, I leave all the rest to the suggestions of your own tact and generosity. —Gratefully, *most* gratefully, your friend always,—

"EDGAR A. POE."

Upon receipt of this communication, or rather upon a reminder that he had not alluded to Poe's intimation, Willis announced in the *Home Journal* that he had " by accident omitted to mention—in our last week's paper—that our friend and former editorial associate, Mr. Poe, was to deliver a lecture, on Thursday evening, February 3rd, at the Society Library. The subject is rather a broad one, 'The Universe;' but, from a mind so original, no text could furnish any clue to what would probably be the sermon. There is but one thing certain about it, that it will be compact of thought most fresh, startling, and suggestive. Delivered under the warrant of our friend's purely intellectual features and expression, such a lecture as he must write would doubtless be, to the listeners, a mental treat of a very unusual relish and point.

" We understand that the purpose of Mr. Poe's lecture is to raise the necessary capital for the establishment of a magazine, which he proposes to call the *Stylus.* They who like literature without trammels, and criticism without gloves, should send in their names forthwith as subscribers. . . . The severe afflictions with which Mr. Poe has been visited within the last years have left him in a position to devote himself, self-sacrificingly, to his new task ; and, with energies that need the exercise, he will, doubtless, give that most complete attention which alone can make such an enterprise successful."

Although Poe had given Willis " the facts of the case," he neither wished nor expected that his quondam associate should make them *all* public : he wished the lecture to be announced, but not the *cause* of the lecture being given. However, he had now to make the best of it, and exert himself to the utmost to face the public. Whatever curiosity there may have been to see the poet after his lengthy seclusion, and the distressing causes of it, certain it is that far too few persons attended the lecture to have rendered it a success, at least from a pecuniary point of view. The address was delivered in the library of the New York Historical Society, and was on the Cosmogony of the Universe, being, with some variation, a *précis* of his subsequently published " Eureka."

But few journals had drawn attention to the forthcoming lecture, and its delivery, it is recorded, took place on a stormy night : these reasons may, perhaps, account for the smallness of the audience. " There were not more than sixty persons in the room," says Mr. M. B. Field, who was present. " The lecture was a rhapsody of the most intense brilliancy. Poe appeared inspired, and his inspiration affected the scant audience almost painfully. His eyes seemed to glow like these of his own ' Raven,' and he kept us entranced for two hours and a half."

Such scant audiences, despite the enthusiasm of the lecturer, or the lectured, could not give much material aid toward the furtherance of the poet's project. But, although poor and, for a time, baffled, he never for an instant gave up his hope, indeed, his *certainty*, of succeeding ultimately in starting his proposed periodical. For a time he had to return to his lonely Fordham home, to contemplate anew the complex problems of creation; or to discuss with stray, and often heedless, visitors, with an intensity of feeling and steadfastness of belief never surpassed, his unriddling of the secret of the Universe.

Writing to a correspondent on the 29th of February, he thus hopefully lays down his future plan of proceeding :—

"I mean to start for Richmond on the 10th March. Everything has gone as I wished it, and my final success is certain, or I abandon all claims to the title of Vates. The only contretemps of any moment, lately, has been Willis's somewhat premature announcement of my project :—but this will only force me into action a little sooner than I had proposed. Let me now answer the points of your last letter.

"C—— acted pretty much as all mere men of the world act. I think very little the worse of him for his endeavor to succeed with you at my expense. I always liked him, and I believe he liked me. His 'I understand the matter perfectly' amuses me. Certainly, then, it was the only matter he did understand. His intellect was *O*.

"'The Rationale of Verse' will appear in *Graham*, after all.* I will stop in Philadelphia to see the proofs.

"As for Godey, he is a good little man, and means as well as he knows how. . . .

---

* It did not though, *vide* p. 321.—J. H. I.

"The 'most distinguished of American scholars'[*] is Professor Charles Anthon, author of the 'Classical Dictionary.'

"I presume you have seen some newspaper notices of my late lecture on the Universe. You could have gleaned, however, no idea of what the lecture was, from what the papers said it was. All praised it—as far as I have yet seen—and all absurdly misrepresented it. The only report of it which approaches the truth is the one I enclose—from the *Express* —written by E. A. Hopkins, a gentleman of much scientific acquirement, son of Bishop Hopkins, of Vermont; but he conveys only my general idea, and his digest is full of inaccuracies. I enclose also a slip from the *Courier and Enquirer*. Please return them. To eke out a chance of your understanding what I really *did* say, I add a loose summary of my propositions and results:—

"The General Proposition is this—Because Nothing was, *therefore* All Things are.

"1. An inspection of the *universality* of Gravitation—*i.e.*, of the fact that each particle tends, *not* to any one common point, but to *every other* particle—suggests perfect totality, or *absolute* unity, as the source of the phenomenon.

"2. Gravity is but the mode in which is manifested the tendency of all things to return into their original unity—is but the reaction of the first Divine Act.

"3. The *law* regulating the return—*i.e.*, the *law* of Gravitation—is but a necessary result of the necessary and sole possible mode of equable *irradiation* of matter through space : this *equable* irradiation is necessary as a basis for the Nebular Theory of Laplace.

"4. The Universe of Stars (contradistinguished from the Universe of Space) is limited.

"5. Mind is cognisant of Matter *only* through its two properties, attraction and repulsion : therefore Matter *is* only attraction and repulsion : a finally consolidated globe-of-globes, being but one particle, would be without attraction— *i.e.*, gravitation : the existence of such a globe presupposes the expulsion of the separative ether which we know to exist between the particles as at present diffused : thus the final globe would be matter without attraction and repulsion : but

---

[*] *Vide* prospectus of the *Stylus*, p. 343.—J. H. I.

these *are* matter : then the final globe would be matter without matter—*i.e.*, no matter at all : it must disappear. Thus Unity is *Nothingness.*

"6. Matter, springing from Unity, sprang from Nothingness—*i.e.*, was *created.*

"7. All will return to Nothingness, in returning to Unity.

"Read these items *after* the Report. As to the Lecture, I am very quiet about it—but, if you have ever dealt with such topics, you will recognise the novelty and *moment* of my views. What I have propounded will (in good time) revolutionise the world of Physical and Metaphysical Science. I say this calmly—but I say it.

"I shall not go till I hear from you.—Cordially—

"E. A. Poe.

"By the by, lest you infer that my views, in detail, are the same with those advanced in the *Nebular Hypothesis,* * I venture to offer a few addenda, the substance of which was penned, though never printed, several years ago, under the head of—'A Prediction.'"

These *addenda* would occupy a dozen or so pages and are, therefore, clearly unsuitable for our citation; besides, Poe's theory is much better explained in "Eureka "—a work available for all. His unconscionably lengthy epistle concludes with the jocular remark, "How will *that* do for a postscript ?"

During the early part of 1848 the poet continued to exchange visits with a few of his friends, including Mrs. Shew, who still occasionally befriended him, and his "more than mother," Mrs. Clemm. It was at this time that his gratitude to the noble-hearted woman for her kindness to him, and to her who had been "dearer to *his* soul than its own soul-life," again, for the second time, vented itself in melodious verse. He indited some fresh lines "To Marie Louise," a

* Of Laplace.—J. H.

portion only of which were ever published, and then without a title. The following letter to the same lady refers to the project alluded to in the last-cited epistle, that is to say, his intention of delivering a series of lectures in the various chief cities of the States, beginning with Richmond, Virginia:—

"*Thursday, March* 30.

"DEAREST LOUISE,—You see that I am not yet off to Richmond as I proposed. I have been detained by some very unexpected and very important matters which I will explain to you when I see you. What *is* the reason that you have not been out ? I believe the *only* reason is that you suspect I am really anxious to see you.

"When you see Mr. H.—— I wish you would say to him that I would take it as an especial favor if he would pay me a visit at Fordham next Sunday. I have something to communicate to him *of the highest importance*, and about which I need his advice. Won't you get him to come—and come with him to show him the way ?—Sincerely yours,

"EDGAR A. POE."

As desired, the Mr. H——, referred to above, called upon the poet and found that his advice was wanted with respect to the proposed publication of "Eureka" in book form. "I had heard his brilliant lecture on the occasion of its first delivery, and was much interested in it," says this gentleman. "I did all I could to persuade him to omit the bold declaration of Pantheism at the close, which was not necessary to the completeness or beauty of the lecture. But I soon found that *that* was the dearest part of the whole to him; and we got into quite a discussion on the subject of Pantheism. For some time his tone and manner were very quiet, though slowly changing as we went on, until at last a look of scornful pride, worthy of Milton's Satan, flashed over his pale delicate face and broad brow, and a strange thrill nerved and dilated for an instant his slight figure, as he exclaimed, 'My whole nature utterly *revolts* at the idea that there is any Being in the Universe superior to *myself !* ' I knew then that there was no use in further argument. The subject was dropped, and there was nothing further in the interview that I can now recall. But that sentence, and the mode of its utterance, made an indelible impression. . . . There is one other incident that I recall concerning that visit. . . . He was speaking of his near neighbours, the Jesuit Fathers at Fordham College, and praised them warmly: 'They were highly-cultivated gentlemen and scholars,' he said, 'smoked, drank, and played cards like gentlemen, and never said a word about religion.' "

Having made his final revisions of the "Eureka," and, probably, hoping to derive sufficient for the copyright of a first edition to start him upon his lecturing tour, the poet went to town and saw Mr. George Putnam, the publisher, with a view of arranging for the publication of his work. Mr. Putnam's own account of the interview and its result is, doubtless, a somewhat imaginative one, but is interesting as affording renewed evidence of the intense belief which Poe had in the truth of his own theory. The publisher's account runs that a gentleman one day entered the office, and in a nervous and excited manner, requested his attention to a matter of the greatest importance :—

"Seated at my desk, and looking at me a full minute with his 'glittering eye,' he at length said, 'I am Mr. Poe.' I was 'all ear,' of course, and sincerely interested. It was

z

the author of 'The Raven' and of 'The Gold Bug!'* 'I hardly know,' said the poet, after a pause, 'how to begin what I have to say. It is a matter of profound importance.' After another pause, the poet seeming to be in a tremor of excitement, he at length went on to say that the publication he had to propose was of momentous interest. Newton's discovery of gravitation was a mere incident compared with the discoveries revealed in this book. It would at once command such unusual and intense interest that the publisher might give up all other enterprises, and make this one book the business of his lifetime. An edition of fifty thousand copies might be sufficient to begin with, but it would be but a small beginning. No other scientific event in the history of the world approached in importance the original developments of the book. All this and more, not in irony or jest, but in *intense* earnest—for he held me with his eye, like the Ancient Mariner. I was really impressed, but not overcome. Promising a decision on Monday (it was late Saturday), the poet had to rest so long in uncertainty, upon the *extent* of the edition, partly reconciled by a small loan meanwhile. We *did* venture, not upon fifty thousand, but five hundred."†

Accordingly, in the course of a few weeks, the work upon which Poe had spent so many months, and, indeed, in some respects, years of thought, was published in a handsomely-printed volume of 144 pages, as "Eureka: a Prose Poem; by Edgar A. Poe." The work was dedicated, "with very profound respect," to Alexander von Humboldt, and was heralded by this *Preface :*—

"To the few who love me and whom I love—to those who feel rather than to those who think—to the dreamers and those who put faith in dreams as in the only realities— I offer this Book of Truths, not in its character of Truth-Teller, but for the Beauty that abounds in its Truth ;

---

* It appears singular that Mr. Putnam did not know the poet at once, seeing that he had already, as representative of the firm of Wiley & Putnam, published two books by Poe.—J. H. I.

† *Putnam's Magazine*, second series, vol. iv. p. 471.

constituting it true. To these I present the composition as an Art-Product alone :—let us say as a Romance ; or, if I be not urging too lofty a claim, as a Poem.

" *What I here propound is true :*—therefore it cannot die :—or if by any means it be now trodden down so that it die, it will ' rise again to the Life Everlasting.'

" Nevertheless, it is as a Poem only that I wish this work to be judged after I am dead. E. A. P."

It was in a style perfectly in accordance with the magnitude and magnificence of the theme he had undertaken to dilate upon, that the poet commenced the *opus magnum* of his life : he begins thus—

" It is with humility really unassumed—it is with a senti- ment even of awe—that I pen the opening sentence of this work : for of all conceivable subjects I approach the reader with the most solemn—the most comprehensive—the most difficult—the most august.

" What terms shall I find sufficiently simple in their sublimity—sufficiently sublime in their simplicity—for the mere enunciation of my theme ?

" I design to speak of the *Physical, Metaphysical and Mathematical—of the Material and Spiritual Universe :— of its Essence, its Origin, its Creation, its Present Condition and its Destiny.* I shall be so rash, moreover, as to challenge the conclusions, and thus, in effect, to question the sagacity, of many of the greatest and most justly reverenced of men.

" In the beginning, let me as distinctly as possible an- nounce—not the theorem which I hope to demonstrate— for, whatever the mathematicians may assert, there is, in this world at least, *no such thing* as demonstration—but the ruling idea which, throughout this volume, I shall be con- tinually endeavouring to suggest.

" My general proposition, then, is this :—*In the Original Unity of the First Thing lies the Secondary Cause of All Things, with the Germ of their Inevitable Annihilation.*"

No comprehending reader can deny the grandeur and fascination of this work, although if—after the

mind has had time to recover from the spell which
has hurried it along through the all-absorbing theme
to the last startling climax—we begin to question and
to doubt, Poe's analysis of creation will, probably, be
found to be no more convincing than its thousand-and-
one predecessors. Yet a spell there is about it due
to something more than mere witchery of words ; due
to the fact that startling theories bearing all the
semblance of truths—truths hitherto untold, or dimly
guessed at—are frequently enunciated and demonstrated as nearly as verbal demonstration is capable of.
The only critical examination of the technical merits
of this work, with which we are acquainted, is contained
in a very remarkable article by Dr. William Hand
Browne, in the *New Eclectic Magazine*, on "Poe's
'Eureka' and Recent Scientific Speculations," wherein
is shown how the various theories advanced by the
poet have been singularly paralleled by those of the
most recent and distinguished scientists and corroborated by their discoveries.

A great hindrance to the acceptance of this work
by scientific inquirers is the absurd, and utterly-out-
of-place attempt at humour, displayed in the tirade
against the Aristotelian and Baconian schools of philosophy, at the commencement of the essay. This, and
the fact that the author is well known as a writer of
fiction and *poetry*, have combined to impede the influence of "Eureka" in the sphere where its value
could best be gauged.

Poe himself was a staunch believer in the truth of
his theory of creation, and was wont to discuss the
knotty points in "Eureka" with an eloquence that
temporarily persuaded, even if it did not permanently

convince, his hearers. He could not submit to hear
the merits of his work discussed by unsympathetic
and incompetent critics, and after it was published
in book form, and thus become public property,
addressed this thoroughly characteristic letter to Mr.
Charles Fenno Hoffmann, then editing the New York
Literary World, respecting a flippant critique of the
book which had appeared in the columns of that periodical :—

" DEAR SIR, — In your paper of July 29, I find some
comments on 'Eureka,' a late book of my own ; and I know
you too well to suppose, for a moment, that you will refuse
me the privilege of a few words in reply. I feel, even,
that I might safely claim, from Mr. Hoffman, the right,
which every author has, of replying to his critic *tone for
tone* — that is to say, of answering your correspondent,
flippancy by flippancy and sneer by sneer — but, in the
first place, I do not wish to disgrace the 'World'; and, in
the second, I feel that I should never be done sneering, in
the present instance, were I once to begin. Lamartine
blames Voltaire for the use which he made of (*ruse*)
misrepresentations, in his attacks on the priesthood ; but our
young students of Theology do not seem to be aware that in
defence, or what they fancy to be defence, of Christianity,
there is anything wrong in such gentlemanly peccadillos as
the deliberate perversion of an author's text—to say nothing
of the minor *indecora* of reviewing a book without reading it
and without having the faintest suspicion of what it is about.
" You will understand that it is merely the *misrepresentations* of the *critique* in question to which I claim the
privilege of reply :—the mere *opinions* of the writer can be
of no consequence to me—and I should imagine of very
little to himself — that is to say if he knows himself,
personally, so well as *I* have the honour of knowing him.
The first misrepresentation is contained in this sentence :—
'This letter is a keen burlesque on the Aristotelian or
Baconian methods of ascertaining Truth, both of which the
writer ridicules and despises, and pours forth his rhapsodical

ecstasies in a glorification of a third mode—the noble art of *guessing.*' What I *really* say is this :—' That there is no absolute *certainty* either in the Aristotelian or Baconian process—that, for this reason, neither Philosophy is so profound as it fancies itself—and that neither has a right to sneer at that *seemingly* imaginative process called Intuition (by which the great Kepler attained his laws) ; since ' Intuition,' after all, is but the conviction arising from those *in*ductions or *de*ductions of which the processes are so shadowy as to escape our consciousness, elude our reason, or defy our capacity of expression.' The second misrepresentation runs thus :—' The development of electricity and the formation of stars and suns, luminous and non-luminous, moons and planets, with their rings, &c., is deduced, very much according to the nebular theory of Laplace, from the principle propounded above.' Now the impression intended to be made here upon the reader's mind, by the ' Student of Theology,' is, evidently, that my theory may be all very well in its way, but that it is nothing but Laplace over again, with some modifications that he (the Student of Theology) cannot regard as at all important. I have only to say that no gentleman can accuse me of the disingenuousness here implied ; inasmuch as, having proceeded with my theory to that point at which Laplace's theory *meets it*, I then *give Laplace's theory in full*, with the expression of my firm conviction of its absolute truth *at all points*. The *ground* covered by the great French astronomer compares with that covered by my theory, as a bubble compares with the ocean on which it floats ; nor has he the slightest allusion to ' the principle propounded above,' the principle of Unity being the source of all things—the principle of Gravity being merely the Reaction of the Divine Act which irradiated all things from Unity. In fact, *no* point of *my* theory has been even so much as alluded to by Laplace. I have not considered it necessary, here, to speak of the astronomical knowledge displayed in the ' stars *and* suns ' of the Student of Theology, nor to hint that it would be better grammar to say that ' development and formation ' *are*, than that development and formation *is*. The third misrepresentation lies in a footnote, where the critic says, ' Further than this, Mr. Poe's claim that he can account for the existence of all organised beings, man included, merely from those principles on which the origin and present appearance of suns and worlds are explained, must be set down as mere bald assertion, without a particle of evidence. In other words, we should term it *arrant fudge.*' The perversion at this point is involved in a wilful misapplication of the word 'principles.' I say 'wilful,' because, at page 63, I am *particularly* careful to distinguish between the principles proper, Attraction and Repulsion, and those merely resultant *sub*-principles which control the universe in detail. To these sub-principles, swayed by the immediate spiritual influence of Deity, I leave, without examination, *all that* which the Student of Theology so roundly asserts I account for on the *principles* which account for the constitution of suns, &c. . . .

"Were these 'misrepresentations' (*is* that the name for them ?) made for any less serious a purpose than that of branding my book as 'impious,' and myself as a 'pantheist,' a 'polytheist,' a Pagan, or a God knows what (and indeed I care very little so it be not a 'Student of Theology'), I would have permitted their dishonesty to pass unnoticed, through pure contempt for the boyishness—for the *turn-down-shirt-collarness* of their tone :—but, as it is, you will pardon me, Mr. Editor, that I have been compelled to expose a 'critic,' who, courageously preserving his own *anonymosity*, takes advantage of my absence from the city to misrepresent, and thus vilify me, *by name.*   EDGAR A. POE.

"FORDHAM, *September 20,* 1848."

Some small pecuniary recompense, probably, accrued to Poe from the publication of "Eureka," for directly after that event, and some months previous to writing the above letter, he started on his long-projected tour, the object of which was to raise the means, by lectures and obtaining subscribers' names, to start the *Stylus*. He is first heard of at Richmond, Virginia, where he renewed several old, and made some new, acquaintanceships. Among the latter was Mr. John R. Thompson's, who had become proprietor of the

Southern Literary Messenger, the periodical upon which Poe's editorial career had commenced, and to the pages of which he now agreed to resume contributing. As they became more intimate, Mr. Thompson became much attached to the poet—as, indeed, did all who were personally acquainted with him—and recorded some pleasing reminiscences of their intercourse.

"It was not until within two years of his death," he remarks, "that I ever met Mr. Poe, but during that time" (the two years) "I saw him very often. When in Richmond he made the office of the *Messenger* a place of frequent resort. His conversation was always attractive, and at times very brilliant. Among modern authors his favourite was Tennyson, and he delighted to recite from the 'Princess' the song, 'Tears, idle tears'—a fragment of which—

"'When unto dying eyes
The casement slowly grows a glimmering square'—

he pronounced unsurpassed by any image expressed in writing."

From Richmond, Poe appears to have returned home to Fordham, and there to have laboured industriously for the magazines. He left home but rarely, and then only by special arrangement. A very characteristic letter to his constant friend, Mrs. Shew, is referable to this epoch; it reads thus:—

"*Sunday Night.*

"MY DEAR FRIEND LOUISE—Nothing for months has given me so much real pleasure as your note of last night. I have been engaged all day on some promised work, otherwise I should have replied immediately—as my heart inclined. I sincerely hope you may not drift out of my sight before I can thank you. How kind of you to let me do even *this small service* for you, in return for the great debt I owe you! Louise! —my brightest, most unselfish of all who ever loved me! . . . I shall have so much pleasure in thinking of you and yours in that music-room and library. Louise—I give you great credit for taste in these things, and I know I can please you in the purchases. During my first call at your house after my Virginia's death, I noticed with so much pleasure the large painting over the piano, which is a masterpiece, indeed ; and I noticed the size of all your paintings—the scrolls instead of set figures of the drawing-room carpet—the soft effect of the window shades—also the crimson and gold. . . . I was charmed to see the harp and piano uncovered. The pictures of Raphael and ' The Cavalier ' I shall never forget—their softness and beauty ! The guitar with the blue ribbon, musicstand, and antique jars. I wondered that a little country maiden like you had developed so classic a taste and atmosphere. Please present my kind regards to your uncle, and say that I am at his service any—or every—day this week ; and ask him, please, to specify time and place.—Yours sincerely, EDGAR A. POE."

In explanation of this communication, it should be stated that Mrs. Shew had requested the poet to assist her uncle in selecting furniture for a new house she had taken. " I gave him *carte blanche*," she remarks, "to furnish the music-room and library as he pleased. I had hung the pictures myself, . . . placing over the piano a large painting by Albano. Mr. Poe admired it for hours, and never seemed tired of gazing upon it. . . . Mr. Poe was much pleased at my request, and my uncle said he .had never seen him so cheerful and natural—' quite like other people.' "

It was shortly after this, during the summer,* that Poe wrote the first rough draft of " The Bells," and at Mrs. Shew's residence. " One .day he came in," she records, and said, " Marie Louise, I have to write a

* Not autumn, as has been incorrectly published.—J. H. I.

poem; I have no feeling, no sentiment, no inspiration." His hostess persuaded him to have some tea. It was served in the conservatory, the windows of which were open, and admitted the sound of neighbouring church bells. Mrs. Shew said, playfully, "Here is paper;" but the poet, declining it, declared, "I so dislike the noise of bells to-night, I cannot write. I have no subject—I am exhausted." The lady then took up the pen, and, pretending to mimic his style, wrote, "The Bells, by E. A. Poe;" and then, in pure sportiveness, "The Bells, the little silver Bells," Poe finishing off the stanza. She then suggested for the next verse, "The heavy iron Bells;" and this Poe also expanded into a stanza. He next copied out the complete poem, and headed it, "By Mrs. M. L. Shew," remarking that it was her poem; as she had suggested and composed so much of it.* Mrs. Shew continues, "My brother came in, and I sent him to Mrs. Clemm to tell her that 'her boy would stay in town, and was well.' My brother took Mr. Poe to his own room, where he slept twelve hours, and could hardly recall the evening's work. This showed his mind was injured," comments the lady, "nearly gone out for want of food, and from disappointment. He had not been drinking, and had only been a few hours from home. Evidently his vitality was low, and he was nearly insane. While he slept we studied his pulse, and found the same symptoms which I had so often noticed before. I called in Dr. Francis † (the old man was odd, but very skilful), who was one of our neighbours. His words were, 'He has

---

* This manuscript is now in my possession. —J. H. I.
† *Vide* Poe's Works, vol. iv. pp. 419-421. Edinburgh, 1874-5.

heart disease, and will die early in life.' We did not waken him, but let him sleep." The day following, records Mrs. Shew, "After he had breakfasted, I went down town with him, and drove him home to Fordham in my carriage. He did not seem to realise that he had been ill, and wondered why 'Madame Louise' had been so good as to bring him home."

This incident not only depicts the almost boyish simplicity of the poet in many matters, but also shows to what a debilitated and critical state his health had now been reduced. His contempt for the ordinary conventionalities of life rendered it difficult, at times, for his friends to maintain their relations with him. Mrs. Shew long continued to befriend him and his aunt, but, ultimately, his continually increasing eccentricities compelled her to define more closely the limits of their intercourse. Poe took umbrage at this, and in June of this year indited his last letter to her. With respect to some of the passages in this epistle Mrs. Shew makes these remarks:—"I believe I am the only correspondent of Mr. Poe to whom he called himself 'a lost soul.' He did not believe his soul was lost—it was only a sarcasm he liked to repeat to express his sufferings and despair. I never saw a quotation from 'The Raven' in any letter of his but this. . . . Mr. Poe's cat always left her cushion to rub my hand, and I had always to speak to it before it would retire to its place of rest again. He called her 'Catarina'—she seemed possessed. I was nervous and almost afraid of his wonderful cat. Mr. Poe would get up in the night to let her in or out of the house or room, and it would not eat when he was away."

This appeal to his kind-hearted friend ran thus:—

"Can it be true, Louise, that you have the idea fixed in your mind to desert your unhappy and unfortunate friend and patient? You did not say so, I know, but for months I have known you were deserting me, not willingly, but none the less surely—my destiny—

'Disaster, following fast and following faster, till his song one burden bore—
    Till the dirges of his Hope that melancholy burden bore—
            Of "Never—nevermore." '

So I have had premonitions of this for months. I repeat, my good spirit, my loyal heart! must this follow as a sequel to all the benefits and blessings you have so generously bestowed? Are you to vanish like all I love, or desire, from my darkened and 'lost soul?' I have read over your letter again and again, and cannot make it possible, with any degree of certainty, that you wrote it in your right mind. (*I know you did not without tears of anguish and regret.*) Is it possible your influence is lost to me? Such tender and true natures are ever loyal until death; but you are not dead, you are full of life and beauty! Louise, you came in . . . in your floating white robe—'Good morning, Edgar.' There was a touch of conventional coldness in your hurried manner, and your attitude as you opened the kitchen-door to find Muddie,* is *my last remembrance of you.* There was love, hope, and *sorrow* in your smile, instead of love, hope, and *courage,* as ever before. O Louise, how many sorrows are before you! Your ingenuous and sympathetic nature will be constantly wounded in its contact with the hollow, heartless world; and for me, alas! unless some true and tender, and pure womanly love saves me, I shall hardly last a year longer alive! A few short months will tell how far my strength (physical and moral) will carry me in life here. How can I believe in Providence when *you* look coldly upon me? Was it not you who renewed my hopes and faith in God? . . . and in humanity? Louise, I heard your voice as you passed out of my sight leaving me . . . ; but I still listened to your voice. I heard you say with a sob, 'Dear Muddie.' I

* Mrs. Clemm's pet name at home.—J. H. I.

heard you greet *my Catarina,* but it was only as a memory . . . nothing escaped *my ear,* and I was convinced it was not your generous self. . . repeating words so foreign to your nature—to your tender heart! I heard you sob out your sense of duty to my mother, and I heard her reply 'Yes, Loui . . . yes.' . . . Why turn your soul from its true work for the desolate to the thankless and miserly world? . . . I felt my heart stop, and I was sure I was then to die before your eyes. Louise, it is well—it is fortunate—you looked up with a tear in your dear eyes, and raised the window, and talked of the guava you had brought for my sore throat. Your instincts are better than a *strong man's reason for me*— I trust they may be for *yourself.* Louise, I feel I shall not prevail—a shadow has already fallen upon your soul, and is reflected in your eyes. It is *too late*—you are floating away with the cruel tide . . . it is not a common trial—it is a fearful one to me. Such rare souls as yours so beautify this earth! so relieve it of all that is repulsive and sordid. So brighten its toils and cares, it is hard to lose sight of them even for a short time . . . but you must know and *be assured* of my regret and my sorrow if aught I have ever written has hurt you. *My heart never wronged you.* I place you in *my esteem*—in *all solemnity*—beside the friend of my boyhood —the mother of my schoolfellow, of whom I told you, and as I have repeated in the poem . . . as the truest, tenderest of this world's most womanly souls, and an angel to my forlorn and darkened nature. I will not say 'lost soul' again, for your sake. I will try to overcome my grief for the sake of your unselfish care of me in the past, and in life or death, I am ever yours gratefully and devotedly,

"EDGAR A. POE."

With this characteristic communication the poet's correspondence with his disinterested and generous friend came to an end. They never met again.

CHAPTER XIX.

HELEN WHITMAN.

Poe had not been back in Fordham long before he once more started off on a lecturing engagement, and this time to Lowell, Massachusetts, whence flattering propositions had reached him. Upon his arrival there he lectured upon "The Female Poets of America." The subject was one which afforded him plenty of scope for awarding certain New England ladies their due meed of praise, and amongst those named he specially selected Mrs. Helen Whitman for "pre-eminence in refinement of art, enthusiasm, imagination, and genius, properly so-called." Personally, Poe was unacquainted with this lady, but she had been seen by him, so it is averred, "on his way from Boston, when he visited that city to deliver a poem before the Lyceum there. Restless, near midnight, he wandered from his hotel near where she lived, until he saw her walking in a garden. He related the incident afterwards in one of his most exquisite poems, worthy of himself, of her, and of the most exalted passion." *

There is no need to inquire into the truth of this romantic story, which Poe's poem, indeed, lends some colouring to, it sufficing to record that the poet had for some long time past expressed deep interest in Mrs. Whitman's poetic contributions to the magazines,

* Beginning, "I saw thee once—once only—years ago."

and had alluded to them, on several occasions, in the most flattering terms. Eventually, upon a so-called "Valentine" party being given to the literati of New York, in the winter of 1847-8, Mrs. Whitman, at a friend's request, contributed some anonymous verses to the author of "The Raven." The remainder of the story may be continued in Poe's own words in a long subsequent letter to the lady :—

"I have already told you that some few casual words spoken of you by —— ——, were the first in which I had ever heard your name mentioned. She alluded to what she called your 'eccentricities,' and hinted at your sorrows. Her description of the former strangely arrested—her allusion to the latter enchained and rivetted my attention.

"She had referred to thoughts, sentiments, traits, *moods*, which I knew to be my own, but which, until that moment, I had believed to be my own solely—unshared by any human being. A profound sympathy took immediate possession of my soul. I cannot better explain to you what I felt than by saying that your unknown heart seemed to pass into my bosom—there to dwell for ever—while mine, I thought, was translated into your own.

"From that hour I loved you. Since that period I have never seen nor heard your name without a shiver, half of delight, half of anxiety.—The impression left upon my mind was that you were still a wife, and it is only within the last few months that I have been undeceived in this respect.

"For this reason I shunned your presence and even the city in which you lived. You may remember that once when I passed through Providence with Mrs. Osgood I positively refused to accompany her to your house, and even provoked her into a quarrel by the obstinacy and seeming unreasonableness of my refusal. I dared neither go nor say why I could not. I dared not speak of you—much less see you. For years your name never passed my lips, while my soul drank in, with a delirious thirst, all that was uttered in my presence respecting you.

"The merest whisper that concerned you awoke in me a

shuddering sixth sense, vaguely compounded of fear, ecstatic happiness and a wild inexplicable sentiment that resembled nothing so nearly as a consciousness of guilt.

"Judge, then, with what wondering, unbelieving joy, I received, in your well-known MS., the Valentine which first gave me to see that you knew me to exist.

"The idea of what men call Fate lost then in my eyes its character of futility. I felt that nothing hereafter was to be doubted, and lost myself for many weeks in one continuous, delicious dream, where all was a vivid, yet indistinct bliss.—

"Immediately after reading the Valentine, I wished to contrive some mode of acknowledging—without wounding you by seeming directly to acknowledge—my sense—oh, my keen—my exulting—my ecstatic sense of the honour you had conferred on me. To accomplish as I wished it, precisely *what* I wished, seemed impossible, however ; and I was on the point of abandoning the idea, when my eyes fell upon a volume of my own poems ; and then the lines I had written, in my passionate boyhood, to the first purely ideal love of my soul—to the Helen Stannard of whom I told you— flashed upon my recollection. I turned to them. They expressed all—*all* that I would have said to you—so fully— so accurately and so exclusively, that a thrill of intense superstition ran at once through my frame. Read the verses and then take into consideration the peculiar need I had, at the moment, for just so seemingly an unattainable mode of communication with you as they afforded. Think of the absolute appositeness with which they fulfilled that need— expressing not only all that I would have said of your person, but all that of which I most wished to assure you, in the lines commencing—

"On desperate seas long wont to roam."

Think of the rare agreement of name, and you will no longer wonder that to one accustomed as I am to the Calculus of Probabilities, they wore an air of positive miracle. . . . I yielded at once to an overwhelming sense of Fatality. From that hour I have never been able to shake from my soul the belief that my Destiny, for good or for evil, either here or hereafter, is in some measure interwoven with your own.

"Of course I did not expect, on your part, any acknowledgment of the printed lines 'To Helen;' and yet, without confessing it even to myself, I experienced an indefinable sense of sorrow in your silence. At length, when I thought you had time fully to forget me (if, indeed, you had had ever really remembered) I sent you the anonymous lines in MS. I wrote, first, through a pining, burning desire to communicate with you in *some* way—even if you remained in ignorance of your correspondent. The mere thought that *your* dear fingers would press—*your* sweet eyes dwell upon characters which *I* had penned—characters which had welled out upon the paper from the depths of so devout a love—filled my soul with a rapture, which seemed, then, all sufficient for my human nature. It *then* appeared to me that merely this one thought involved so much of bliss that here on earth I could have no right ever to repine—no room for discontent. If ever, *then*, I dared to picture for myself a richer happiness, it was always connected with your image in Heaven. But there was yet another idea which impelled me to send you those lines :—I said to myself the sentiment —the holy passion which glows in my bosom *for her*, is of Heaven, heavenly, and has no taint of the earth. Thus then must lie in the recesses of her own pure bosom, at least the germ of a reciprocal love, and if this be indeed so, she will need no earthly clue—she will instinctively feel who is her correspondent—In this case, then, I may hope for some faint token at least, giving me to understand that the source of the poem is known and its sentiment comprehended even if disapproved.

"O God!—how long—*how long* I waited in *vain*—hoping against hope—until, at length, I became possessed with a spirit far sterner—far more reckless than despair—I explained to you—but without detailing the vital influences they wrought upon my fortune—the singular additional, yet seemingly trivial fatality by which you happened to address your anonymous stanzas to Fordham instead of New York— by which my aunt happened to get notice of their being in the West Farm post-office. But I have not yet told you that your lines reached me in Richmond on the very day in which I was about to enter on a course which would have borne me far, far away from *you*, sweet, sweet Helen, and from this divine dream of your love."

2 A

In the above words Poe has depicted his ideal feelings only, for, as yet, they do not portray any personal knowledge of Mrs. Whitman. The lady's poetic response, and a vivid lifelike dream Mrs. Osgood's verbal description of her had excited, determined the poet to seek an introduction to his unknown correspondent. In the meanwhile, he wrote to an English acquaintance visiting Providence, under date of June 10th, 1848, these words of inquiry :—

" Do you know Mrs. Whitman ? I feel deep interest in her poetry and character. I have never seen her—never but once. —— ——, however, told me many things about the romance of her character which singularly interested me and excited my curiosity. Her poetry is beyond question *poetry*—instinct with genius. Can you not tell me something about her—anything—everything you know—and *keep my secret*—that is to say, let no one know that I have asked you to do so ? *May* I *trust* you ? I can and will.—Believe me truly your friend,   EDGAR A. POE."

Soon after this letter reached its destination, its recipient visited Mrs. Whitman at her mother's house. Miss Maria McIntosh, the well-known authoress, was present, and, it being a bright moonlight night, she remarked to Mrs. Whitman, " ' On such a night as this,' one month ago, I met Mr. Poe for the first time, at the house of a gentleman in Fordham, and his whole talk was about you." Upon hearing this, the English lady, upon whose secrecy Poe had so implicitly relied, spoke of the letter she had received containing the above cited inquiries, and, ultimately, gave the letter itself to Mrs. Whitman.

In the ensuing September Edgar Poe sought and obtained a letter of introduction from Miss McIntosh,

and presented it to Mrs. Whitman in person. He repeated his visit, and avowed a love to which, for many reasons, the lady dared not respond. On bidding the poet farewell, however, she promised to write to him and explain many things which she could not impart in conversation. In his answer to her first letter occur these words :—

"I have pressed your letter again and again to my lips, sweetest Helen—bathing it in tears of joy, or of a 'divine despair.' But I—who so lately, in your presence, vaunted the 'power of words'—of what avail are mere words to me now? *Could* I believe in the efficiency of prayers to the God of Heaven, I would indeed kneel—humbly kneel—at this the most earnest epoch of my life—kneel in entreaty for words—*but* for words that should disclose to you—that might enable me to lay bare to you my whole heart. All thoughts—all passions seem now merged in that one consuming desire—the mere wish to make you comprehend—to make you see *that* for which there is no human voice—the unutterable fervour of my love for you :—for so well do I know your poet nature, that I feel sure if you could but look down *now* into the depths of my soul with your pure spiritual eyes you *could* not refuse to speak to me what, alas ! you still resolutely leave unspoken—you would *love* me if only for the greatness of my love. Is it not something in this cold, dreary world *to be loved?* Oh, if I could but burn into your spirit the deep—the *true* meaning which I attach to those three syllables underlined ! but, alas ! the effort is all in vain and 'I live and die unheard.' . . .

"Could I but have held you close to my heart and whispered to you the strange secrets of its passionate history, then indeed you would have seen that it was not and never could have been in the power of any other than yourself to move me as I am now moved—to oppress me with this ineffable emotion—to surround and bathe me in this electric light, illumining and enkindling my whole nature—filling my soul with glory, with wonder, and with awe. During our walk in the cemetery I said to you, while the bitter, bitter tears sprang into my eyes, 'Helen, I love now—now—for the first and only time.' I said this, I repeat, in no hope that you could believe me, but because I could not help feeling how unequal were the heart riches we might offer each to each :—I, for the first time, giving my all at once and for ever, even while the words of your poem were yet ringing in my ears.

" Ah, Helen, *why* did you show them to me ? There seemed, too, so very especial a purpose in what you did. Their very beauty was cruelty *to me.*" . . .

The poem alluded to was one entitled "April Nights," and had just been returned to Mrs. Whitman by the editor of the *Columbian Magazine,* with a request that she would alter a line in the manuscript. The lines were not shown for the special purpose Poe would seem to indicate. The poet's own passionate words will, however, best portray the influence their fair author's personal appearance had upon his mind :—

" And now, in the most simple words I can command, let me paint to you the impression made upon me by your personal presence. As you entered the room, pale, hesitating, and evidently oppressed at heart; as your eyes rested for one brief moment upon mine, I felt, for the first time in my life, and tremblingly acknowledged, the existence of spiritual influences altogether out of the reach of the reason. I saw that you were *Helen*—*my* Helen—the Helen of a thousand dreams. . . . She whom the great Giver of all good had preördained to be mine—mine only—if not now, alas ! then hereafter and *for ever* in the Heavens.—You spoke falteringly and seemed scarcely conscious of what you said. I heard no words—only the soft voice more familiar to me than my own. . . .

" Your hand rested within mine and my whole soul shook with a tremulous ecstacy : and then, but for the fear of grieving or wounding you, I would have fallen at your feet in as pure—in as real a worship as was ever offered to Idol, or to God.

" And when, afterwards, on those two successive evenings of all-heavenly delight, you passed to and fro about the room—now sitting by my side, now far away, now standing with your hand resting on the back of my chair, while the preternatural thrill of your touch vibrated even through the senseless wood into my heart—while you moved thus restlessly about the room — as if a deep sorrow or a most profound joy haunted your bosom—my brain reeled beneath the intoxicating spell of your presence, and it was with no merely human senses that I either saw or heard you. It was my soul only that distinguished you there. . . .

" Let me quote to you a passage from your letter :—. . . ' Although my reverence for your intellect and my admiration for your genius make me feel like a child in your presence you are not perhaps aware that I am many years older than yourself.' . . . But grant that what you urge were even true. Do you not feel in your inmost heart of hearts that the ' Soul love ' of which the world speaks so often and so idly is, in this instance, at least, but the veriest—the most absolute of realities ? Do you not—I ask it of your reason, *darling,* not less than of your heart—do you not perceive that it is my diviner nature—my spiritual being which burns and pants to commingle with your own ? Has the soul age, Helen ? Can Immortality regard Time ? Can that which began never and shall never end consider a few wretched years of its incarnate life ? Ah, I could *almost* be angry with you for the unwarranted wrong you offer to the sacred reality of my affection.

" And how *am* I to answer what you say of your personal appearance ? Have I not *seen* you, Helen ? Have I not heard the more than melody of your voice ? Has not my heart ceased to throb beneath the magic of your smile ? Have I not held your hand in mine and looked steadily into your soul through the crystal Heaven of your eyes ? Have I done all these things ?—Or do I dream ?—Or am I mad ?

" Were you indeed all that your fancy, enfeebled and perverted by illness, tempts you to suppose you are, still, life of my life ! I would but love you—but worship you the more. But as it is what can I—what *am* I to say ? *Who* ever spoke of you without emotion—without praise ? Who *ever* saw you and did not love ?

" But now a deadly terror oppresses me; for I too clearly see that these objections, so groundless—so futile. . . . I tremble lest they but serve to mask others more real, and which you hesitate—perhaps in pity—to confide to me.

"Alas ! I too distinctly perceive, also, that in no instance you have ever permitted yourself to say that you love me. You are aware, sweet Helen, that on my part there are insuperable reasons forbidding me to urge upon you my love. Were I not poor—had not my late errors and reckless excesses justly lowered me in the esteem of the good—were I wealthy, or could I offer you worldly honours—ah then—then—how proud would I be to persevere—to *plead* with you for your love. . . .

"Ah, Helen ! my soul !—what is it that I have been saying to you ?—to what madness have I been urging you ?— I, who am *nothing* to you—*you* who have a dear mother and sister to be blessed by your life and love. But ah, darling ! if I *seem* selfish, yet believe that I truly, *truly* love you, and that it is the most spiritual love that I speak, even if I speak it from the depths of the most passionate of hearts. Think —oh, think for *me*, Helen, and for yourself. . . .

"I would comfort you — soothe you — tranquillize you. You would rest from care—from all worldly perturbation. You would get better and finally well. And if *not*, Helen— if you *died*—then, at least, I would clasp your dear hand in death, and willingly—oh, *joyfully—joyfully* go down with you into the night of the grave.

"Write soon—soon—oh soon !—but not *much*. Do not weary or agitate yourself for *my* sake. Say to me those coveted words that would turn Earth into Heaven."

The correspondence thus inaugurated was continued by equally characteristic communications from Poe. In a letter dated the 18th October, occur these passages :—

"You do not love me, or you would have felt too thorough a sympathy with the sensitiveness of my nature, to have so wounded me as you have done with this terrible passage of your letter :—

"'How often I have heard it said of you, "He has great intellectual power, but no principle—no moral sense."'

"Is it possible that such expressions as these could have been repeated to me—to me—by one whom I loved—ah, whom I *love !* . . .

"By the God who reigns in Heaven, I swear to you that my soul is incapable of dishonor—that, with the exception of occasional follies and excesses which I bitterly lament but to which I have been driven by intolerable sorrow, and which are hourly committed by others without attracting any notice whatever—I can call to mind no act of my life which would bring a blush to my cheek—or to yours. If I have erred at all in this regard, it has been on the side of what the world would call a Quixotic sense of the honorable—of the chivalrous. The indulgence of this sense has been the true voluptuousness of my life. It was for this species of luxury that in early youth I deliberately threw away from me a large fortune rather than endure a trivial wrong. Ah, how profound is my love for you, since it forces me into these egotisms, for which you will inevitably despise me ! . . .

"For nearly three years I have been ill, poor, living out of the world ; and thus, as I now painfully see, have afforded opportunity to my enemies to slander me in private society without my knowledge, and thus with impunity. Although much, however, may (and, I now see, must) have been said to my discredit, during my retirement, those few who, knowing me well, have been steadfastly my friends, permitted nothing to reach my ears—unless in one instance of such a character that I could appeal to a court of justice for redress.

"I replied to the charge fully in a public newspaper —afterwards suing the *Mirror* (in which the scandal appeared), obtaining a verdict and recovering such an amount of damages as, for the time, completely to break up that journal. And you ask me *why* men so *misjudge* me—*why* I have enemies. If your knowledge of my character and of my career does not afford you an answer to the query, at least it does not become *me* to suggest the answer. Let it suffice that I have had the audacity to remain poor that I might preserve my independence—that, nevertheless, in letters, to a certain extent and in certain regards, I have been 'successful'—that I have been a critic—an unscrupulously honest and no doubt in many cases a bitter one—that I have uniformly attacked—where I attacked at all—those who stood highest in power and influence — and that— whether in literature or society, I have seldom refrained from expressing, either directly or indirectly, the pure contempt with which the pretensions of ignorance, arrogance, or imbecility inspire me. And you who know all this—*you* ask me *why* I have enemies. Ah, I have a hundred friends for every individual enemy, but has it ever occurred to you that you do not live among my friends?

"Had you read my criticisms generally, you would see why all those whom you know best know me least and are my enemies. Do you not remember with how deep a sigh I said to you. . . . 'My heart is heavy, for I see that your friends are not my own?' . . .

"But the cruel sentence in your letter would not—*could* not so deeply have wounded me, had my soul been first strengthened by those assurances of your love which I so wildly —so vainly — and, I now feel, so presumptuously entreated. That our souls are one, every line which you have ever written asserts—but our hearts do *not* beat in unison.

"That many persons, in your presence, have declared me wanting in honor appeals irresistibly to an instinct of my nature—an instinct which *I feel* to be honor, let the dishonorable say what they may, and forbids me, under such circumstances, to insult you with my love. . . .

"Forgive me, best and only-beloved Helen, if there be bitterness in my tone. Towards *you* there is no room in my soul for any other sentiment than devotion. It is Fate only which I accuse. It is my own unhappy nature." . . .

Before Mrs. Whitman had answered this indignant protest, Poe went to Providence and entreated her to forgive his waywardness and his reproaches, and to remember only the reasons which he had urged why she should confide her future welfare and happiness to him. Finally, he urged her to defer her decision for a week, and exacted a promise that she would write to him at Lowell, previous to his return to New York, implying that his return *viâ* Providence would depend upon the tenor of her letter. Unwilling to say the word which might separate them for ever, and unable to give him the answer he besought her to accord him, Mrs. Whitman delayed writing from day to day. At last she sent a brief and indecisive note which perplexed Poe; by return he wrote to say that he should be at Providence the following evening. Thither he went, but instead of going to Mrs. Whitman's returned in a terribly depressed state to Boston, and, by an abortive attempt at suicide—particulars of which will be elsewhere given *—reduced himself to a truly deplorable condition. Early the following Monday the hapless poet again arrived in Providence, and on the morning of that day called on Mrs. Whitman. Agitated and unnerved on account of his having failed to call on the Saturday evening, as promised in his letter, she had passed a restless night and was then quite unable to see him, but sent word by a servant that she would see him at noon. He returned a message to the effect that he had an engagement and must see her at once. Eventually he asked for writing-paper and sent her the following note :—

"DEAREST HELEN—I have *no* engagement, but am *very* ill —so much so that I must go home if possible—but if you say 'Stay,' I will try and do so. If you cannot see me— write me *one word* to say that you *do* love me and that, *under all circumstances*, you will be mine.

"Remember that these coveted words you have never

* *Vide* p. 393.

yet spoken—and, nevertheless, I have not reproached you. If you can see me, even for a few moments, do so —but if not, write or send some message which will comfort me."

Mrs. Whitman wrote that she would positively see him at noon. He called, and on that and the following day "endeavoured with all the eloquence which he could exert with such matchless power," to persuade her to marry him at once and return with him to New York. When Poe called on the second day Mrs. Whitman showed him some letters she had received, in which her correspondents strongly expostulated with her for receiving the poet's addresses. One of these communications contained the passage that called forth the words of indignant protest which have already been cited from his letter of the 18th of October. Directly he had read the letter some casual visitors arrived, and he arose to take his departure. "I saw by the expression of his countenance," said Mrs. Whitman, "as he held my hand for a moment, in taking leave of me, that something had strangely moved him. I said, 'We shall see you this evening?' He merely bowed without replying."

That evening, as was but natural to have foreseen, Poe sent Mrs. Whitman a note of renunciation and farewell, therein remarking that if they met again it would be as strangers.

Instead of returning to New York immediately, as in his note he had avowed his intention to do, Poe passed a night of wild delirium at the hotel in Providence. In the morning he arrived at Mrs. Whitman's residence, in a state of delirious excitement, calling upon her and imploring her to save

him from some terrible impending doom. The tones
of his voice rang through the house and were most
appalling. "Never have I heard anything so awful,"
records Mrs. Whitman, " awful even to sublimity. It
was long before I could nerve myself to see him. My
mother was with him more than two hours before I
entered the room. He hailed me as an angel sent to
save him from perdition. . . . In the afternoon he
grew more composed and my mother sent for Dr. Okie,
who, finding symptoms of cerebral congestion, advised
his removal to the house of his friend, Mr. Pabodie,
where he was kindly cared for.

" Of course," continues Mrs. Whitman, " gossip held
high carnival over these facts, which were related,
doubtless, with every variety of sensational embellish-
ment. You will see, therefore, that Griswold had
ample material to work on; he had only to turn the
sympathising physician into a police officer, and the
day before the betrothal into the evening before the
bridal, to make out a plausible story."

The ultimate result of this terrible scene was that
Mrs. Whitman decided upon becoming the wife of
Poe, in the hope of being enabled to preserve him
from his impending doom. Some days after the
recovery from his delirium, when he again urged his
suit, she permitted him to extract from her a promise
that she would become his wife, upon condition that
he never touched intoxicants again, declaring that
nothing save his own infirmity should cause her to
recede from her plighted troth. It was in commemoration of this, and of the terrible trial through which
she had just passed, that Mrs. Whitman composed
her lines to " Arcturus," beginning,—

> " Star of resplendent front ! thy glorious eye
>   Shines on me still from out yon clouded sky—
>   Shines on me through the horrors of a night
>   More drear than ever fell o'er day so bright,"—

and ending,*—

> " I see the dawn of a diviner day,
>   A heaven of joys and hopes that cannot die—
>   Immortal in their own infinity."

Notwithstanding the heartrending representations of her mother and friends, Mrs. Whitman resolved to adhere to her promise, and in reliance upon it Poe returned to New York, to make arrangements for his marriage. On his homeward journey, by means of the Long Island Sound Boat, he sent the following note to prove that he was keeping *his* word :—

" November 14, 1848.

" MY OWN DEAREST HELEN,—*So* kind, so true, so generous— so unmoved by all that would have moved one who had been less than angel :—beloved of my heart, of my imagination, of my intellect—life of my life—soul of my soul—dear, dearest Helen, how shall I ever thank you as I ought.

" I am calm and tranquil, and but for a strange shadow of coming evil which haunts me I should be happy. That I am not supremely happy, even when I feel your dear love at my heart, terrifies me. What can this mean ?

" Perhaps, however, it is only the necessary reaction after such terrible excitements.

" It is five o'clock, and the boat is just being made fast to the wharf. I shall start in the train that leaves New York at 7 for Fordham. I write this to show you that I have not *dared* to break my promise to you. And now dear, dearest Helen, be true to me.". . .

During the brief period of visionary anticipations which now intervened, Poe confided his hopes and fears, his expected triumphs or foreboded troubles, to

* In version given to me by Mrs. Whitman.—J. H. I.

Mrs. Whitman, in a series of idiosyncratic epistles, which, says their recipient, "enable one to understand, as nothing else could, the singular and complex elements of his nature. The intense superstition, the haunting dread of evil, the tender remorseful love, the prophetic imagination—now proud and exultant, now melancholy and ominous—the keen susceptibility to blame, the sorrowful and indignant protest against unjust reproach."

In one of the letters to Mrs. Whitman appertaining to this epoch the following passages occur :—

"Without well understanding *why*, I had been led to fancy you ambitious. . . . It was then only—then when I thought of *you*—that I dwelt exultingly upon what I felt that I could accomplish in Letters and in Literary influence —in the widest and noblest field of human ambition. . . . When I saw you, however—when I touched your gentle hand—when I heard your soft voice, and perceived how greatly I had misinterpreted your womanly nature—these triumphant visions melted sweetly away in the sunshine of a *love* ineffable, and I suffered my imagination to stray with you, and with the few who love us both, to the banks of some quiet river, in some lovely valley of our land.

"Here, not *too* far secluded from the world, we exercised a taste controlled by no conventionalities, but the sworn slave of a natural art, in the building for ourselves of a cottage which no human being could ever pass without an ejaculation of wonder at its strange, weird, and incomprehensible yet most simple beauty. Oh, the sweet and gorgeous, but not often rare flowers in which we half buried it ! the grandeur of the magnolias and tulip-trees which stood guarding it—the luxurious velvet of its lawn—the lustre of the rivulet that ran by the very door—the tasteful yet quiet comfort of the interior—the music—the books—the unostentatious pictures, and, above all, the love—the love that threw an unfading *glory* over the whole ! . . . Alas ! all is now a dream."

In this letter was shadowed forth the ideal pastoral home that, subsequently, was more fully depictured in "Landor's Cottage." In the next extract from the correspondence Poe is seen striving to arouse Mrs. Whitman's temperament into accordance with another mood of his impulsive nature. Writing on Sunday, the 22nd of November, he says :—

"I wrote you yesterday, sweet Helen, but through fear of being too late for the mail omitted some things I wished to say. I fear, too, that my letter must have seemed cold—perhaps even harsh or selfish—for I spoke nearly altogether of my own griefs. Pardon me, *my* Helen, if not for the love I bear you, at least for the sorrows I have endured—more I believe than have often fallen to the lot of man. How much have they been aggravated by my consciousness that, in too many instances, they have arisen from my own culpable weakness or childish folly ! My sole hope now is *in you*, Helen. As you are true to me or fail me, so do I live or die. . . .

"Was I right, dearest Helen, in my first impression of you ?—you know I have implicit faith in first impressions—was I right in the impression that you are ambitious ? If so, and *if you will have faith in me*, I can and will satisfy your wildest desires. It would be a glorious triumph, Helen, for *us*—for *you and me.*

"I dare not trust my schemes to a letter—nor indeed have I time even to hint at them here. When I see you I will explain all—as far, at least, as I dare explain *all* my hopes even to you.

"Would it *not* be 'glorious,' darling, to establish, in America, the sole unquestionable aristocracy—that of intellect—to secure its supremacy—to lead and to control it ? All this I can do, Helen, and will—if you bid me—and aid me."

But these aerial *chateaux d'Espagne* of the poet were even more transient than the few brief interludes permitted him of undisturbed happiness.

Those who have thus far followed the history of
Poe's career will fully comprehend the force of his
allusions in the following letter—a letter that really
contains the basis of Griswold's degrading fabrication
of the poet having "borrowed fifty dollars from a
distinguished literary woman of South Carolina," and
when asked for the money's return, or a written
acknowledgment of his indebtedness, for the satisfaction of the lady's husband, "denied all knowledge of
it, and threatened to exhibit a correspondence which
would make the woman infamous." The woman
referred to is dead, but the story has recently been
unearthed, and her name dragged before the public
by certain papers of New York, in which city, however, still resides one who knew and can testify to
Poe's veracity in this affair. All the wrong *he* did
was—when goaded by her imputations as to the impro-
priety of his corresponding with a married lady—with
his wife's dear friend, Mrs. Osgood—to hastily exclaim,
"She had better look to her own letters ! " Only that
and nothing more.*

This communication is dated two days later than
the one last quoted :—

"In little more than a fortnight, dearest Helen, I shall
once again clasp you to my heart :—until then I forbear to
agitate you by speaking of my wishes—of my hopes, and
especially of my fears. You say that all depends on my own
firmness. If this be so, all is safe—for the terrible agony
which I have so lately endured—an agony known only to
my God and to myself—seems to have passed my soul through
fire and purified it from all that is weak. Henceforward I
am strong :—this those who love me shall see—as well as
those who have so relentlessly endeavoured to ruin me. It

* *Vide* pp. 293, 294.

needed only some such trials as I have just undergone, to make me what I was born to be, by making me conscious of my own strength.—But all does *not* depend, dear Helen, upon my firmness—all depends upon the sincerity of your love.

"You allude to your having been 'tortured by reports which have all since been explained to your entire satisfaction.' On this point my mind is fully made up. I will rest neither by night nor by day until I bring those who have slandered me into the light of day—until I expose them, *and their motives* to the public eye. I *have* the means and I will ruthlessly employ them. On one point let me caution you, *dear* Helen. No sooner will Mrs. E—— hear of my proposals to yourself, than she will set in operation every conceivable chicanery to frustrate me:—and, if you are not prepared for her arts, she will *infallibly* succeed—for her whole study, throughout life, has been the gratification of her malignity by such means as any other human being would die rather than adopt. You will be sure to receive anonymous letters so skilfully contrived as to deceive the most sagacious. You will be called on, possibly, by persons whom you never heard of, but whom she has instigated to call and vilify me—without even *their* being aware of the influence she has exercised. I do not know *any* one with a more *acute* intellect about such matters than Mrs. Osgood— yet even she was for a long time completely blinded by the arts of this fiend, and simply because her generous heart could not conceive how any woman could stoop to machinations at which the most degraded of the fiends would shudder. I will give you here but one instance of her baseness, and I feel that it will suffice. When, in the heat of passion" . . .

[Here follows the narrative given at pp. 293, 294, chapter the sixteenth.] The letter then proceeds:—

"If you value your happiness, Helen, beware of this woman! She did not cease her persecutions here. My poor Virginia was continually tortured (although not deceived) by her anonymous letters, and on her deathbed declared that Mrs. E—— had been her murderer. Have I not a right to hate this fiend and to caution you against her? You will now comprehend what I mean in saying that the *only* thing for which I found it impossible to forgive Mrs. Osgood was her reception of Mrs E.

"*Be careful of your health, dearest Helen,* and perhaps all will yet go well. Forgive me that I let these wrongs prey upon me—I did not so bitterly feel them until they threatened to deprive me of you . . . but for your dear sake I will endeavor to be calm.

"Your lines 'To Arcturus' are truly beautiful."

This letter was speedily followed by the poet himself. He arrived in Providence full of the most sanguine hopes; he had proposed to himself a career of literary success, dwelling with enkindling enthusiasm upon his long-cherished scheme of establishing a magazine that should give him supreme control of intellectual society in America. His dreams of love and triumph were rapidly destroyed. In a few days he was to be married; he had advised his aunt, Mrs. Clemm, to expect his and his bride's arrival in New York early the following week, when information was given to Mrs. Whitman and to her relatives that he had violated the solemn pledge of abstinence so recently given. Whether this information was true no one living, perchance, can say. When he arrived at the dwelling of Mrs. Whitman, "no token of the infringement of his promise was visible in his appearance or manner," says that lady, "but I was at last convinced that it would be in vain longer to hope against hope. I knew that he had irrevocably lost the power of self-recovery. . . . Gathering together some papers which he had intrusted to my keeping I placed them in his hands without a word of explanation or reproach, and, utterly worn out and exhausted by the mental conflicts and anxieties and responsi-

2 B

bilities of the last few days, I drenched my handkerchief with ether and threw myself on a sofa, hoping to lose myself in utter unconsciousness. Sinking on his knees beside me, he entreated me to speak to him—to speak *one* word, but *one word*. At last I responded, almost inaudibly, 'What can I say?' 'Say that you love me, Helen.' '*I love you.*' These were the last words I ever spoke to him."

In company with his friend, Mr. Pabodie, Poe left the house, and for ever. The rupture of the much-commented-upon engagement gave rise to the wildest and most scandalous reports. The cause of the separation was almost universally ascribed to the poet. Unable to rest under the ridiculous and humiliating charges, which obtained such general currency that even some of his dearest friends at last gave credence to them, Poe wrote to Mrs. Whitman earnestly entreating her to send him a few words, for the satisfaction of those dear to him, in denial of the vile rumours about their separation.

"No amount of provocation," he wrote to her, "shall induce me to speak ill of *you*, even in my own defence. If to shield myself from calumny, however undeserved, or however unendurable, I find a need of resorting to explanations that might condemn or pain you, most solemnly do I assure you that I will patiently endure such calumny, rather than avail myself of any such means of refuting it. You will see, then, that so far I am at your mercy—but in making you such assurances, have I not a right to ask of you some forbearance in return? . . . That *you* have in any way countenanced this pitiable falsehood, I do not and cannot believe—some person, equally your enemy and mine, has been its author—but what I beg of you is, to write me at once a few lines in explanation—you know, of course, that by reference either to Mr. Pabodie or . . . I can disprove the facts stated in the most satisfactory manner—but there can be no need of disproving what I feel confident was never asserted *by you*—your simple disavowal is all that I wish—You will, of course, write me immediately on receipt of this. . . . Heaven knows that I would shrink from wounding or grieving you! . . . May Heaven shield you from all ill! . . . Let my letters and acts speak for themselves. It has been my intention to say simply that our marriage was postponed simply on account of your ill-health. Have you really said or done anything which can preclude our placing the rupture on such footing? If not, I shall persist in the statement and thus this unhappy matter will die quietly away."

"His letter I did not dare to answer," said Mrs. Whitman.

Evidently Edgar Poe did not know the real cause of the rupture of the engagement, and for upwards of thirty years his character has suffered under charges he was powerless to refute.

CHAPTER XX.

"*ANNIE.*"

IT will now be necessary to turn back some months, to resume the poet's story where it was broken off in order to complete the episodical narrative of his engagement to Mrs. Whitman. In the early summer of 1848 Poe, as already stated, lectured at Lowell, on " The Female Poets of America." Some months later he again visited the city and lectured upon " The Poetic Principle." During this sojourn in the "American Manchester," the poet was the guest of the Richmonds, a family whose acquaintance he had made upon the occasion of his former visit. The friendship which Poe formed with this amiable family, although, unfortunately, so near the close of his sad career, was one of its brightest incidents: they aided him in the darkest days of his "lonesome latter years;" they believed in him when he was calumniated; they received him as an honoured guest when the world contemned him; they remained faithful to him through all adversity; and, when death released his wearied spirit, afforded a lengthy and hospitable shelter to his broken-hearted mother, Mrs. Clemm.

Miss Heywood, a member of this generous family, has favoured us with some fresh and charming recollections of Edgar Poe, as he appeared to her girlish but appreciative ken :—

"I have 'in my mind's eye,'" she remarks, "a figure somewhat below medium height, perhaps, but so perfectly proportioned, and crowned with such a noble head, so regally carried, that, to my girlish apprehension, he gave the impression of commanding stature. Those clear sad eyes seemed to look from an eminence, rather than from the ordinary level of humanity, while his conversational tone was so low and deep, that one could easily fancy it borne to the ear from some distant height. I saw him first in Lowell, and there heard him give a Lecture on Poetry, illustrated by readings and recitations. His manner of rendering some of the selections constituted my only remembrance of the evening : it fascinated me, although he gave no attempt at dramatic effect. Everything was rendered with pure intonation and perfect enunciation, marked attention being paid to the rhythm : he almost *sang* the more musical versifications. I recall more perfectly than anything else, the modulations of his smooth baritone voice, as he recited the opening lines of Byron's 'Bride of Abydos'—'Know ye the land where the cypress and myrtle'—measuring the dactylic movement as perfectly as if he were scanning it : the effect was very pleasing. He insisted strongly upon an even metrical flow in versification, and said that hard and 'unequally stepping poetry' had better be done into prose. He made no selections of a humorous character, either in his public or parlour readings ; indeed, anything of that kind seems entirely incompatible with *his* personality. He smiled but seldom and never laughed, or said anything to excite mirth in others. His manner was always quiet and grave—'John Brown of Edinboro'' might have characterised it as 'lonely !' In thinking of Mr. Poe in later years, I have often applied to him the line of Wordsworth's Sonnet (on Milton), 'Thy soul was like a star and dwelt apart.'

"I did not hear the conversation at Mrs. Richmond's after the lecture, when a few persons came in to meet him, but I remember that my brother spoke with great enthusiasm of Mr. Poe's demeanour and the grace of his conversation. In alluding to it he always says, 'I have *never* seen it equalled.' A lady in the company differed from Mr. Poe, and expressed her opinions very strongly. His deference in listening was perfect, and his replies were models of respectful politeness. Of his great satirical power his pen was generally the medium; if he used the polished weapon in conversation, it was so delicately and skilfully handled that only a quick eye would detect the gleam. Obtuseness was always perfectly safe in his presence, although in his capacity of literary critic he gave his victim many a 'palpable hit!'"

"A few months later than this," resumes Miss Heywood, "Mr. Poe came out to our home in Westford. My recollections of that visit are fragmentary, but very vivid. During the day he strolled off by himself, 'to look at the hills,' he said. I remember standing in the low porch with my sister, as we saw him returning, and as soon as he stepped from the dusty street on to the green sward which sloped from our door, he removed his hat, and came to us with uncovered head, his eyes seeming larger and more luminous than ever with the exhilaration of his walk.

"I recall his patiently unwinding from a nail a piece of twine that had been carelessly twisted and knotted around it, and then hanging it back again on the nail in long straight loops. It was a half-unconscious by-play of that ingenious mind which deciphered cryptographs, solved enigmas of all kinds, and wrote the 'Gold Bug,' and the 'Balloon Hoax.'

"My memory photographs him again," the lady continues, "sitting before an open wood fire, in the early autumn evening, gazing intently into the glowing coal, holding the hand of a dear friend—'Annie'—while for a long time no one spoke, and the only sound was the ticking of the tall old clock in the corner of the room. (I wish I could tell you what he was thinking about during that rapt silence !)

"Later in the evening he recited, before a little Reading Club, several of his own poems; one of Willis's commencing, 'The shadows lay along Broadway' (which he said was a special favourite with him), and one or two of Byron's shorter poems. To *me* everything seemed perfect, though some said more effect might be given to his own unique poems. I suppose his voice and manner expressed the 'Runic rhyme' better than the 'tintinnabulation of the

Bells—bells—bells.' That poem was then fresh from the author's brain, and we had the privilege of hearing it before it was given to the world.

"The next morning I was to go to school, and before I returned he would be gone. I went to say 'Good-bye' to him, when, with that ample gracious courtesy of his which included even the rustic school-girl, he said, 'I will walk with you.' He accompanied me to the door, taking leave of me there in such a gentle, kingly manner, that the thought of it now brings tears to the eyes that then looked their last upon that finished scholar and winning, refined gentleman."

The " dear friend" above alluded to was the lady to whom the poet indited his most melodious poem of "For Annie." "Annie" was one of those "rare and radiant" spirits it was Poe's happiness—amid all his woe—to meet with in his journey through life. With her he carried on a most voluminous and characteristic correspondence during the last year of his eventful life, but, as a considerable portion of it refers to persons who have not yet followed the writer into the "Hollow Vale," only detached portions can be quoted. Poe's letters, as Mrs. Osgood phrased it, "were divinely beautiful," but their tenor is often liable to be miscomprehended, and misrepresented, by those accustomed only to the coldly-conventional manufactured epistles of everyday folk. A spirit kindred to the poet's is, almost, necessary to a thorough comprehension of the passionate gratitude, burning affection, and intense sympathy which Poe felt—for the time at least—for those who "sorrowed for *his* fate," and sought to aid him as he passed by on his life's journey. During the latter years of his career he appeared utterly unable to exist apart from the sympathy and encouragement of some friend—some unselfish person to whom he could turn for advice—upon whom he might depend for consolation, and to whom he might unveil the darkest mysteries of his mind. After his wife's death he appeared always seeking for such a friend; for Mrs. Clemm, whatever may have been her affection for her son-in-law, was utterly unsuited, both by age and intellect, to supply such a *desideratum.* Mrs. Osgood, Mrs. Shew, and Mrs. Whitman attempted, as has been seen, more or less to befriend the helpless poet, but, as they, one after the other, deemed it necessary to let him go his ways, he sank deeper and deeper into the "Slough of Despond."

At the time when his cravings for sympathy were, doubtless, most urgent, he became acquainted with "Annie," and to her and her family he clung for consolation and guidance more tenaciously than to any other of his many friends. Unfitted, at least in his "lonesome latter years," to take an active part in the world's work, he sought more naturally the society of refined women than that of his own sex, and, like nearly all men of a poetic temperament, being feminine (though not effeminate) in his tastes, therein found his firmest and most congenial friends. The fervour and passion of his impulsive nature may well be gleaned from these extracts of a characteristic letter, dated :—

"FORDHAM, *Nov.* 16, 1848.

"Ah, Annie, Annie ! *my* Annie ! what cruel thoughts . . . must have been torturing your heart during the last terrible fortnight in which you have heard *nothing* from me—not even one little word to say that I still lived. . . . How shall I explain to you the *bitter, bitter* anguish which has tortured me since I left you ?

"You saw, you *felt* the agony of grief with which I bade

you farewell—you remember my expression of gloom—of a dreadful horrible foreboding of Ill. Indeed—*indeed* it seemed to me that Death approached me even then and that I was involved in the shadow which went before him. . . . I said to myself, ' It is for the last time, until we meet in Heaven.' I remember nothing distinctly from that moment until I found myself in Providence. I went to bed and wept through a long, long, hideous night of Despair—When the day broke, I arose and endeavoured to quiet my mind by a rapid walk in the cold, keen air—but all *would* not do—the Demon tormented me still. Finally, I procured two ounces of laudanum, and without returning to my hotel, took the cars back to Boston. When I arrived I wrote you a letter, in which I opened my whole heart to you—to *you*. . . . I told you how my struggles were more than I could bear. . . . I then reminded you of that holy promise which was the last I exacted from you in parting—the promise that, under all circumstances, you would come to me on my bed of death. I implored you to come *then*, mentioning the place where I should be found in Boston. Having written this letter, I swallowed about half the laudanum, and hurried to the Post Office, intending not to take the rest until I saw you—for, I did not doubt for one moment, that Annie would keep her sacred promise. But I had not calculated on the strength of the laudanum, for, before I reached the Post Office my reason was entirely gone, and the letter was never put in. Let me pass over—my darling *sister*—the awful horrors which succeeded. A friend was at hand, who aided and (if it can be called saving) saved me, but it is only within the last three days that I have been able to remember what occurred in that dreary interval. It appears that, after the laudanum was rejected from the stomach, I became calm, and to a casual observer, sane—so that I was suffered to go back to Providence.* . . . It is not *much* that I ask, *sweet sister Annie*—my mother and myself would take a small cottage —— oh, *so* small—so *very* humble—I should be far away from the tumult of the world—from the ambition which I loathe—I would labor day and night,

---

* Where and when he engaged himself to Mrs. Whitman.—J. H. I.

and with industry, I could accomplish *so* much. Annie! it would be a Paradise beyond my wildest hopes—I could see some of your beloved family *every* day, and you often. Do not these pictures touch your inmost heart? . . . I am at home now with my dear mother, who is endeavoring to comfort me—but the sole words which soothe me are those in which she speaks of 'Annie'—She tells me that she has written you, begging you to come on to Fordham. Ah, Annie, *is it not possible?* I am so *ill*—so terribly, hopelessly *ill* in body and mind, that I feel I *cannot* live. . . . Is it not *possible* for you to come—if only for one little week? Until I subdue this fearful agitation, which, if continued, will either destroy my life or drive me hopelessly mad.

"*Farewell*—here and hereafter—for ever your own

"EDDY."

With this heartrending epistle of the impulsive poet was sent the following note from Mrs. Clemm :—

"MY DEAR ANNIE,—God has heard my prayers and once more returned my poor, darling Eddy to me. But *how changed!* I scarcely knew him. I was nearly distracted at not hearing from him. I knew *something* dreadful had occurred. And oh! how near I was losing him! But our good and gracious God *saved* him. The blood about my heart becomes cold when I think of it. I have read his letter to you, and have told him I think it very selfish, to wish you to come ; for I know, my darling child, it would be inconvenient. . . . Eddy has told me of all your kindness to him. God bless you for it, my own darling. *I beg* you will write often. He raved all night about you, but is now more composed. I too am very sick, but will do all I can to cheer and comfort him. How much I felt for you, *dearest*, when I read the awful account of your poor cousin's death. Have you heard anything of Mrs. L—— since her tragic performance? I never liked her, and said so from the first. Do tell me all about her.—Good-bye, dearest, your own   M. C.

"*Nov.* 16, 1848."

A week later, and the poet is found sending this impassioned appeal to his dear friend's sister :—

"FORDHAM, *Nov. 23,* 1848.

"If there is any pity in your heart, reply immediately to this, and let me know *why* it is I do not hear from 'Annie.' . . . I fancy everything evil: sometimes I even think that I have offended her, and that she no longer cares for me. I wrote her a long letter eight days ago, enclosing one from my mother, who wrote again on the 19th. Not one word has reached us in reply. If I did not love your sister with the *purest* and most unexacting love, I would not dare confide in you—but you do know how truly —how *purely* I love her, and you will forgive me. . . . You know also how impossible it is to see and not to love her . . . *so good—so true—so noble—so pure—so virtuous.* Her silence fills my whole soul with terror. Can she have received my letter? If she is angry with me, say to her, that on my knees, I beseech her to pardon me—tell her that whatever she bids me do, I will do—even if she says I must never see her again, or write to her. Let me but hear from her *once more,* and I can bear whatever happens. . . . You would pity me, if you knew the agony of my heart, as I write these words. *Do not fail to answer me at once.* God bless you, my sweet sister—

"EDGAR."

The next letter would appear to have been written on December 28th, but it is not fully dated. It was accompanied by a letter from Mrs. Clemm, in which she remarked, "I feel so happy in *all* my troubles. Eddy is not going to marry Mrs. W. How much will I have to tell you. . . . All the papers say he is going to lead to the altar the *talented, rich,* and *beautiful* Mrs. W. . . . but I will tell you all in my next." Poe's note reads :—

"*Thursday Morning* ——28.

"ANNIE,—My own dear Mother will explain to you how it is that I cannot write to you in full—but I *must* write only a few words to let you *see* that I am well, lest you suspect me to be ill. *All* is right ! . . . I *hope* that I distinguished myself at the Lecture—I *tried* to do so, for your sake. There were 1800 people present, and such applause ! I did so much better than I did at Lowell. If *you* had only been there. . . . Give my dearest love to all— EDDY."

Before continuing this correspondence with " Annie " into 1849, it will be as well to take a short glance at the literary work Poe had been performing during the last few months of the expiring year. To *Graham's Magazine,* and the *Southern Literary Messenger*, he continued to contribute his suggestive " Marginalia," and, besides revising and arranging his critical sketches for republication, laboured ceaselessly at his projected journal, the *Stylus.* As a specimen of the lengthy letters he wrote upon this subject, and of his tireless industry—when not disabled, mentally and physically, for work—may be cited the following epistle to the late Mr. Edward Valentine, a relative of his adoptive mother, the first Mrs. Allan :—

" NEW YORK, *Nov. 20th,* 1848.

" DEAR SIR,—After a long and bitter struggle with illness, poverty, and the thousand evils which attend them, I find myself at length in a position to establish myself permanently, and to triumph over all difficulties, if I could but obtain, from some friend, a very little pecuniary aid. In looking around me for such a friend, I can think of no one, with the exception of yourself, whom I see the least prospect of interesting in my behalf—and even as regards yourself, I confess that my hope is feeble. In fact I have been *so long* depressed that it will be a most difficult thing for me to rise—and rise I never can without such aid as I now entreat at your hands. I call to mind, however, that, during my childhood, you were very kind to me, and, I believe, very fond of me. For this reason and because I really do *not* know where else to turn for the assistance I so *much* need at this moment, I venture to throw myself upon your generosity and ask you to lend me $200. With this sum I should be able to take the first steps in an enterprise where there can be no doubt of my success, and which, if successful, would, in one or two years, ensure me fortune and very great influence. I refer to the establishment of a Magazine for which I have already a good list of subscribers, and of which I send a Prospectus. If for the sake of ' auld lang syne ' you will advance me the sum needed, there are no words which can express my gratitude.—Most sincerely yours,   EDGAR A. POE.

" EDWARD VALENTINE, Esq."

Mr. Valentine, whatever feelings of affection he may have still retained for his handsome little favourite of yore, is scarcely likely to have complied *in toto* with the poet's appeal. Much as Poe was admired and beloved by those in immediate contact with him, by those to whom he was personally unknown, or not known through years of estrangement, his public reputation was not of the kind to cause a stranger—as Mr. Valentine now was—to open his purse-strings very wide. However, some help was, probably, rendered him in this case.

To the September number of the *Literary Messenger* Poe contributed an enthusiastic critique on the writings of " Stella " (Mrs. Lewis), a lady from whom both he and his aunt, Mrs. Clemm, had received much kindness, as their many letters testify. In the two following numbers of the same magazine, appeared the long-promised " Rationale of Verse." In this work, amongst much that was, in many ways, quite characteristic of its author, were not wanting signs of his intellectual decadence. Whilst his readers will, doubtless, conclude with him, that as yet, none of the grammars have written much, or anything, on the subject of verse worth reading, it is to be feared they will, also, arrive at the conclusion that Poe has, if possible, in this instance, made " confusion worse confounded." The study of his own harmonious verse will afford better instruction than all the prosodies ever published.

For the forthcoming year the poet agreed to contribute a further series of " Marginalia" to the *Southern Literary Messenger* and *Graham's Magazine,* and to write the literary notices for a projected publication, to be called the *American Metropolitan.* Of the last named magazine only two numbers were published, and to one of them Mrs. Whitman sent a poem entitled "Stanzas for Music." * From these verses, which were intended to meet Poe's eyes and, in all probability, did come under his notice, their authoress firmly believed the poet was induced to write, as some kind of a response, his beautiful ballad of " Annabel Lee." Mrs. Whitman's lines are as follows, the words italicised being those supposed to have more directly suggested Poe's presumed reply :—

> " Tell him I lingered alone on the shore,
>   Where we parted, in sorrow, to meet never more ;
>   *The night wind blew cold* on my desolate heart,
>   But colder those wild words of doom, ' Ye must part ! '

> " O'er the dark, heaving waters, I sent forth a cry ;
>   Save the wail of those waters there came no reply.
>   I longed, like a bird, o'er the billows to flee,
>   From our lone *island home and the moan of the sea.*

> " Away—far away—from the dream-haunted shore,
>   Where the waves ever murmur, ' No more, never more ; '
>   When I wake, in the wild noon of midnight, to hear
>   That lone song of the surges, so mournful and drear.

---

* Subsequently enlarged and published as "Our Island of Dreams."— J. H. I.

" When the clouds that now veil from us heaven's fair light,
 Their soft, silver lining turn forth on the night ;
 When time shall the vapors of falsehood dispel,
 He shall know if I loved him ; but never how well."

With whatever feelings Poe may have regarded
these lines, he certainly evinced no desire to respond
to them, unless " Annabel Lee " be deemed a reply,
and during the short remainder of his career omitted
all mention of their writer's name. About this time he
sent a somewhat revised version of "The Letter found in
a Bottle," published in "Eureka," to Mr. Godey's *Lady's
Book,* in which publication it appeared in February 1849,
as a tale, under the title of " Mellonta Tauta." It was
accompanied by the following letter :—

" *To the Editor of the ' Lady's Book :'*—

" I have the honor of sending you, for your magazine,
an article which I hope you will be able to comprehend
rather more distinctly than I do myself. It is a translation
by my friend Martin Van Buren Mavis (sometimes called
the ' Toughkeepsie Seer '), of an odd-looking MS. which I
found, about a year ago, tightly corked up in a jug floating
in the *Mare Tenebrarum*—a sea well described by the
Nubian geographer, but seldom visited, nowadays, except
by the transcendentalists and divers for crotchets. Truly
yours, EDGAR A. POE."

It is now necessary to return to the correspondence
with " Annie," to whom Mrs. Clemm is found writing
on the 11th of January (1849) :—

" The match is entirely broken off between Eddy and
Mrs. Whitman. He has been at home *three weeks* and has
not written to her once. . . . Dear Eddy is writing most
industriously, and I have every hope that we will, in a short
time, surmount most of our difficulties. He writes from ten
till four every day. . . . We have found out who wrote those

verses that we attributed to Grace Greenwood: they were written by Mrs. Welby, of Kentucky. Have you a copy of them? If so, Eddy says he will be so much obliged to you for them. . . . Eddy wrote a tale and sent it to the publisher, and in it was a description of *you* with the name of the lady, 'Darling Annie.' * It will be published about the 20th. of next month, and then I will send it to you. Did you see the lines to Eddy in a new magazine just come out, called the *Metropolitan?* They are by Mrs. Osgood, and very beautiful. . . . Have you seen Lowell's satire, and Mrs. Osgood's letter about the lines? Something about Eddy in both."

Enclosed in Mrs. Clemm's letter was a lengthy epistle from Poe himself, and from it the following extracts may be made:—

" It seems to me *so* long since I have written you that I feel condemned, and almost tremble lest you should have evil thoughts of Eddy. . . . But no, you will never doubt me under *any* circumstances—will you? It seems to me that Fate is against our meeting *soon*. . . O ' Annie,' in spite of so many worldly sorrows—in spite of all the trouble and *misrepresentation* (so hard to bear) that Poverty has entailed on me for so long a time—in spite of *all* this— I am *so, so* happy. . . . I need not tell you, ' Annie,' how great a burden is taken off my heart by my rupture with Mrs. W. ; for I have fully made up my mind to break the engagement. . . . *Nothing* would have deterred me from the match but—what I tell you. . . .

" Write to me whenever you can spare time, if it be only a line. . . . I am beginning to do very well about money as my spirits improve, and soon—*very* soon, I hope, I shall be *quite* out of difficulty. You can't think how industrious I am. I am resolved *to get rich*—to triumph. . . . When you write tell me something about Bardwell. Has he gone to Richmond? or what is he doing? Oh, if I

---

* Apparently the tale referred to, "Landor's Cottage," did not appear until after Poe's death.—J. H. I.

could only be of service to him in *any* way ! Remember me to *all*—to your father and mother and dear little Caddy, and Mr. R. and Mr. C. And now good-bye, sister 'Annie!'"

Again, on or about the 23rd of January (the letter is not dated), Poe is found inditing the following communication to his friend :—

"*Faithful* 'Annie!' How shall I ever be grateful enough to God for giving me, in all my adversity, so true, so beautiful a friend! I felt *deeply* wounded by the cruel statements of your letter—and yet I had anticipated nearly all. . . . From the bottom of my heart I forgive her all, and would forgive her even more. Some portions of your letter I do not fully understand. If the reference is to my having violated my promise *to you*, I simply say, Annie, that I have not, and by God's blessing never will. Oh, if you *but* knew how happy I am in keeping it for *your* sake, you *could* never believe that I would violate it. The reports—if any such there be—may have arisen, however, from what I did, in Providence, on that terrible day—you know what I mean :—Oh—I shudder even to think of it. That . . . her friends will speak ill of me is an inevitable evil—I must bear it. In fact, 'Annie,' I am beginning to grow wiser, and do not care so much as I did for the opinions of a world in which I see, with my own eyes, that to act generously is to be considered as designing, and that to be poor is to be a villain. I must get rich—rich. Then all will go well—but *until* then I must submit to be abused. I deeply regret that Mr. R. should think ill of me. If you can, disabuse him—and at all times act for me as *you* think best. I put my honor, as I would my life and soul, implicitly in your hands ; but I would *rather* not confide my purposes, *in that one regard,* to any one but your dear sister.

"I enclose you a letter for Mrs. Whitman. Read it — show it only to those in whom you have faith, and then *seal* it with wax and mail it from Boston. . . . When her answer comes I will send it to you : that will convince you of the

2 c

truth. If she refuse to answer I will write to Mr. Crocker. By the by, if you know his exact name and address send it to me. . . . But as long as you and yours love me, what need *I* care for this cruel, unjust, calculating world ? . . . In all my present anxieties and embarrassments, I still feel in my inmost soul a *divine joy*—a happiness inexpressible—that nothing seems to disturb. . . .

"I hope Mr. C. is well. Remember me to him, and ask him if he has seen my 'Rationale of Verse,' in the last October and November numbers of the *Southern Literary Messenger*. . . . I am *so* busy, now, and feel so full of energy. Engagements to write are pouring in upon me every day. I had two proposals within the last week *from Boston*. I sent yesterday an article to the *Am. Review.* about 'Critics and Criticism.' Not long ago I sent one to the *Metropolitan* called 'Landor's Cottage:' it has something about 'Annie' in it, and will appear, I suppose, in the March number. To the *S. L. Messenger* I have sent fifty pages of 'Marginalia,' five pages to appear each month of the current year. I have also made permanent engagements with every magazine in America (except Peterson's *National*) including a Cincinnati magazine, called *The Gentlemen's*. So you see that I have only to keep up my spirits to get out of all my pecuniary troubles. The *least* price I get is $5 per 'Graham page,' and I can easily average 1½ per day—that is $7½. As soon as 'returns' come in I shall be out of difficulty. I see Godey advertises an article by me, but I am at a loss to know what it is. You ask me, Annie, to tell you about some book to read. Have you seen 'Percy Ranthorpe' by Mrs. Gore ?* You can get it at any of the agencies. I have lately read it with deep interest, and derived great *consolation* from it also. It relates to the career of a literary man, and gives a just view of the true aims and the true dignity of the literary character. Read it for my sake.

"But of one thing rest assured, 'Annie,'—from this day forth I shun the pestilential society of *literary women.* They are a heartless, unnatural, venomous, dishonorable *set*, with no guiding principle but inordinate self-esteem.

---

* By G. H. Lewes ?—J. H. I.

Mrs. Osgood is the *only* exception I know. . . . Kiss little Caddy for me, and remember me to Mr. R. and to *all.*

"I have had a most distressing headache for the last two weeks.". . .

The above unsigned letter was succeeded, early in February, apparently, by the following communication simply dated Thursday ——8th :—

"DEAR 'ANNIE,'—My mother is just going to town, where, I hope, she will find a sweet letter from you or from Sarah ; but, as it is so long since I have written, I *must* send a few words to let you see and *feel* that Eddy, even when silent, keeps you always in his mind and heart— I have been so busy, 'Annie,' ever since I returned from Providence—six weeks ago. I have not suffered a day to pass without writing from a page to three pages. Yesterday, I wrote five, and the day before a poem considerably longer than the 'Raven.' I call it 'The Bells.' How I wish 'Annie' could see it ! Her opinion is so dear to me on such topics—on *all* it is everything to me—but on poetry in especial. And, Sarah, too. . . . I told her when we were at W——, that I hardly ever knew any one with a keener discrimination in regard to what is *really* poetical. The five prose pages I finished yesterday are called—what do you think ?—I am sure you will never guess—'*Hop-Frog !*' Only think of *your* Eddy writing a story with *such* a name as 'Hop-Frog !' You would never guess the subject (which is a terrible one) from the title, I am sure. It will be published in a weekly paper, of Boston. . . . not a very respectable journal, perhaps, in a literary point of view, but one that pays as high prices as most of the magazines. The proprietor wrote to me, offering about $5 a ' Graham page,' and as I was anxious to get out of my pecuniary difficulties, I accepted the offer. He gives $5 for a sonnet, also ; Mrs. Osgood, Park Benjamin, and Mrs. Sigourney are engaged. I think 'The Bells' will appear in the *American Review.* I have got no answer yet from Mrs. Whitman. . . . My opinion is that her mother has intercepted the letter and will never give it to her. . . .

"Dear mother says she will write you a *long* letter in a day or two, and tell you *how good* I am. She is in high spirits at my prospects and at our hopes of soon seeing 'Annie.' We have told our landlord that we will not take the house next year. Do not let Mr. R., however, make any arrangements for us in ——, or W——, for, being poor, we are so much the slaves of circumstances. At all events we will both come and see you, and spend a week with you in the early spring or before—but we will let you know some time before. Mother sends her dearest, dearest love to you and Sarah and to *all*. And now good-bye, my *dear* '*Annie.*'—Your own EDDY."

On the 19th of the same month the poet is found writing sadly, but proudly, to this esteemed correspondent, to repel some cruel accusations which had been made against him by certain mischief-makers:—

"FORDHAM, *Feb.* 19, *Sunday.*

"MY SWEET FRIEND AND SISTER—I fear that in this letter, which I write with a heavy heart, you will find much to disappoint and grieve you—for I must abandon my proposed visit, and God only knows when I shall see you, and clasp you by the hand. I have come to this determination to-day, after looking over some of your letters to me and my mother, written since I left you. You have not *said* it to me, but I have been enabled to glean from what you *have* said, that Mr. R—— has permitted himself (perhaps without knowing it) to be influenced against me by the malignant misrepresentations of Mr. and Mrs. ——. Now, I frankly own to you, dear 'Annie,' that *I am proud*, although I have never shown myself proud to you or yours, and never will. You know that I quarrelled with the L——s *solely* on your account and Mr. R.'s. It was obviously my interest to keep in with them, and, moreover, they had rendered me some services which entitled them to my gratitude up to the time when I discovered they had been blazoning their favors to the world. Gratitude, then, as well as interest, would have led me not to offend them; and the insults offered to me individually by Mrs. L——

were not sufficient to make me break with them. It was only when I heard them . . . (speak against) your husband . . . it was only when such insults were offered to *you*, whom I so sincerely and most purely loved, and to Mr. R——, whom I had every reason to like and respect, that I arose and left their house and ensured the unrelenting vengeance of that worst of all fiends, ' a woman scorned.' Now feeling all this, I cannot help thinking it unkind in Mr. R——, when I am absent and unable to defend myself, that he *will* persist in listening to what these people say to my discredit. I cannot help thinking it, moreover, the most unaccountable instance of weakness—of obtuseness—that ever I knew a *man* to be guilty of: women are more easily misled in such matters. In the name of God, what else had I to anticipate in return for the offence which I offered Mrs. L——'s insane vanity and self-esteem, than that she would spend the rest of her days in ransacking the world for scandal against me (and the falser the better for her purpose), and in fabricating accusations where she could not find them ready made? I certainly anticipated no other line of conduct on her part; but, on the other hand, I certainly did not anticipate that any man *in his senses* would ever listen to accusations from so suspicious a source. . . . Not only must I *not* visit you at L——, but I must discontinue my letters and you yours. I cannot and *will* not have it on my conscience, that I have interfered with the domestic happiness of the only being in the whole world, whom I have loved at the same time with truth and with purity—I do not *merely* love you, ' Annie '—I admire and respect you even more—and Heaven knows there is no particle of selfishness in my devotion—I ask nothing for myself, but your *own* happiness—with a charitable interpretation of those calumnies which—for your sake, I am now enduring from this vile woman—and which, for your dear, *dear* sake, I would most willingly endure if multiplied a hundredfold. The calumnies, indeed, ' Annie,' do not materially wound me, except in depriving me of your society—for of your affection and respect I *feel* that they never can. As for any injuries the falsehoods of these people can do *me*, make your mind easy about that. It is

true that 'Hell has no fury like a woman scorned,' but I
have encountered such vengeance before, on far higher
grounds—that is to say, for a far less holy purpose, than
I feel the defence of your good name to be. I scorned
Mrs. E——, simply because she revolted me, and to this
day she has never ceased her *anonymous* persecutions.
But in what have they resulted? She has not deprived
me of one friend who ever knew me and once trusted me—
nor has she lowered me one inch in the public opinion.
When she ventured too far, I sued her at once (through
her miserable tools), and recovered exemplary damages—as
I will unquestionably do, forthwith, in the case of ——, if
ever he shall muster courage to utter a single *actionable*
word. It is true I shrink with a nameless horror from
connecting my name in the public prints, with such un-
mentionable nobodies and blackguards as L—— and his
lady—but they may provoke me a little too far—You
will now have seen, dear Annie, how and why it is that
my Mother and myself cannot visit you as we proposed. . . .
I could not feel at ease in *his* (her husband's) house, so long
as he permits himself to be prejudiced against me, or so
long as he associates with such persons as the L——s. It
had been my design to ask you and Mr. R—— (or, perhaps,
your parents) to board my Mother while I was absent at
the South, and I intended to start after remaining with
you a week, but my whole plans are now disarranged—
I have taken the cottage at Fordham for another year—
Time, dear Annie, will show all things. Be of good heart,
I shall never cease to think of you—and bear in mind the
two solemn promises I have made you. The one I am now
religiously keeping, and the other (so help me Heaven!)
shall sooner or later be kept.—Always your dear friend
and brother,   EDGAR."

From the next communication, unsigned but dated,
it is seen that the traducers are still at work. From
it these passages may be cited:—

                              "March 23, 1849.
"Will not 'Annie' confide the secrets about Westford?
Was it anything *I* did which caused you to 'give up hope'?

Dear Annie, I am so happy in being able to afford Mr. R. proof of something in which he seemed to doubt me. You remember that Mr. and Mrs. L—— strenuously denied having spoken ill of you to me, and I said 'then it must remain a simple question of veracity between us, as I had no witness—' but I observed afterwards—'Unfortunately I have returned Mrs. L—— her letters (which were filled with abuse of you both), but, if I am not mistaken, my mother has some in her possession that will prove the truth of what I say.' Now, Annie, when we came to look over these last, I found, to my extreme sorrow, that *they* would not corroborate me. I say ' to my extreme sorrow ; ' for, oh, it is so painful to be doubted when we *know* our own integrity. Not that I fancied, even for one moment, that *you* doubted me, but then I saw that Mr. R—— and Mr. C—— *did*, and perhaps even your brother. Well! what *do* you think ? Mrs. L—— has again written my mother, and I enclose her letter. Read it! you will find it thoroughly *corroborative of all I said.* The verses *to me* which she alludes to, I have not seen. You will see that she admits having cautioned me against you, as I said, and in fact admits all that I accused her of. Now you distinctly remember that they both loudly denied having spoken against you :—this, in fact, was the sole point at issue. I have marked the passages alluded to. I wish that you would write to your relation in Providence and ascertain for me *who* slandered me as you say—I wish to prove the falsity of what has been said (for I find that it will not do to permit such reports to go unpunished), and, especially, obtain for me some *details* upon which I can act. . . . Will you do this ? . . . I enclose also some other lines ' For Annie '—and will you let me know in what manner they impress you ? I have sent them to the *Flag of our Union.* By the way, did you get ' Hop-Frog'? I sent it to you by mail, not knowing whether you ever see the paper in ——. I am sorry to say that the *Metropolitan* has stopped and 'Landor's Cottage' is returned on my hands unprinted. I think the lines ' For Annie ' * (those I now send) much

* Beginning, " Thank Heaven ! the crisis—the danger—is past."—J. H. I.

the *best* I have ever written; but an author can seldom depend on his own estimate of his own works, so I wish to know what 'Annie' *truly* thinks of them—also your dear sister and Mr. C——.

"Do not let the verses go *out of your possession* until you see them in print—as I have sold them to the publisher of the *Flag*. . . . Remember me to all."

The tale of "Hop-Frog" above referred to was founded by Poe upon a terrible tragedy related by Froissart, as having occurred in the court of Charles the Sixth of France. The poet appears to have derived his knowledge of the incident from Lord Berner's quaint old English version of the chronicler's story, and in his rendering of the tale he has contrived to attract more sympathy for "Hop-Frog"—for the poor crippled dwarf, notwithstanding his awful revenge, who had no fondness for wine as it excited him "almost to madness"—than Poe's ideal heroes generally obtain.

As regards the lines "For Annie," spoken of and enclosed in the foregoing communication, this letter to N. P. Willis will be of interest:—

"FORDHAM, *April* 20, 1849.

"MY DEAR WILLIS:—The poem which I enclose, and which I am so vain as to hope you will like, in some respects, has been just published in a paper for which sheer necessity compels me to write now and then. It pays well—as times go—but unquestionably it ought to pay ten prices; for whatever I send it I feel I am consigning to the tomb of the Capulets. The verses accompanying this, may I beg you to take out of the tomb, and bring them to light in the *Home Journal?* If you can oblige me so far as to copy them, I do not think it will be necessary to say 'From the *Flag*,'—that would be too bad:—and, perhaps, 'From a late —— paper' would do.

"I have not forgotten how a 'good word in season' from you made 'The Raven,' and made 'Ulalume,' (which, by-the-way, people have done me the honor of attributing to you)—therefore I *would* ask you (if I dared), to say something of these lines—if they please you. Truly yours ever, EDGAR A. POE."

Those unacquainted with the intensely grateful nature of the poet towards all those whom he deemed himself indebted to, would be inclined to consider some portions of the above note intended for sarcasm: Poe, however, doubtless did believe that Willis had assisted in making "The Raven" famous, although he could hardly have considered it an honour for himself that "Ulalume" had been fathered upon the author of "Hurrygraphs."

The letter following that last cited is undated and unsigned; it gives a vivid picture of the horrors the unfortunate Poe was exposed to in his attempt to live by the work of his pen, and of the melancholia by which he was so often oppressed:—

"ANNIE,—You will see by this note that I am nearly, if not quite, well—so be no longer uneasy on my account. I was not so ill as my mother supposed, and she is so anxious about me that she takes alarm often without cause. It is not so much *ill* that I have been as depressed in spirits—I cannot express to you how terribly I have been suffering from gloom. . . . You know how cheerfully I wrote to you not long ago—about my prospects—hopes—how I anticipated being soon out of difficulty. Well! all seems to be frustrated—at least for the present. As usual, misfortunes never come single, and I have met one disappointment after another. The *Columbian Magazine*, in the first place, failed—then Post's *Union* (taking with it my principal dependence); then the *Whig Review* was forced to stop paying for contributions—then the *Democratic*—

then (on account of his oppression and insolence) I was obliged to quarrel, finally, with —— ; and then, to crown all, the " —— —— " (from which I anticipated so much and with which I had made a regular engagement for $10 a week throughout the year) has written a circular to correspondents, pleading poverty and declining to receive any more articles. More than this, the *S. L. Messenger*, which owes me a good deal, cannot pay just yet, and, altogether, I am reduced to Sartain and Graham—both very precarious. No doubt, Annie, you attribute my " *gloom* " to these events—but you would be wrong. It is not in the power of any mere *worldly* considerations, such as these, to depress me. . . . No, my sadness is *unaccountable*, and this makes me the more sad. I am full of dark forebodings. *Nothing* cheers or comforts me. My life seems wasted — the future looks a dreary blank : but I will struggle on and 'hope against hope.' . . . What do you think ? *I* have received a letter from Mrs. L——, and such a letter ! She says she is about to publish a detailed account of *all* that occurred between us, under guise of romance, with fictitious names, &c.,—that she will make me appear noble, generous, &c. &c.—nothing bad— that she will 'do justice to my motives,' &c. &c. She writes to know if ' I have any suggestions to make.' If I do not answer it in a fortnight, the book will go to press as it is —and, more than all this—she is coming on immediately *to see me at Fordham*. I have not replied—shall I ? and what ? The 'friend' who sent the lines to the 'H. J.' was the friend who loves *you* best—was myself. The *Flag* so misprinted them that I was resolved to have a true copy. The *Flag* has two of my articles yet—'A Sonnet to my Mother,' and 'Landor's Cottage.' . . . I have written a ballad called 'Annabel Lee,' which I will send you soon. *Why* do you not send the tale of which you spoke ? "

Appended to the above epistle are these few pathetic lines from Mrs. Clemm :—" Thank you a thousand times for your letter, my dear ' Annie.' Do not believe Eddy ; he has been very ill, but is now better. I thought he would *die* several times. God knows I wish we were both in our graves—it would, I am sure, be far better."

An intervening communication to "Annie" has been lost, wherein the poet announced his intention of once more visiting the Southern States, in order to obtain aid for his projected magazine—the *ignis fatuus* of his life—both by lectures and by procuring subscribers' names. The next letter, written on the 16th of June, shows Poe on the eve of departure, but—although not unhopefully worded—detained from day to day by some disappointing circumstances, probably of a pecuniary nature.

"FORDHAM, —— *June* 16.

"You asked me to write before I started for Richmond, and I was to have started last Monday (the 11th)—so, perhaps, you thought me gone, and without having written to say 'good-bye'—but indeed, Annie, I *could not* have done so. The truth is, I have been on the point of starting every day since I wrote—and so put off writing until the last moment—but I have been disappointed—and can no longer refrain from sending you, at least, a few lines to let you see *why* I have been so long silent. *When* I can go now is uncertain—but, perhaps, I may be off to-morrow, or next day:—all depends upon circumstances beyond my control. Most probably, I will not go until I hear from Thompson (of the *S. L. Messenger*), to whom I wrote five days ago—telling him to forward the letter from Oquawka, instead of retaining it until he sees me. The reason of the return of my draft on *Graham's Magazine* (which put me to such annoyance and mortification while I was with you) was, that the articles I sent (by mail) did not come to hand. No insult (as I had half anticipated) was meant—and I am sincerely glad of this; for I did not wish to give up writing for *Graham's Magazine* just yet—I enclose the publisher's reply to my letter of enquiry. The Postmaster here is investigating the matter, and, in all probability, the articles will be found, and the draft paid by the time you get this. So all this will be right. . . .

"You see I enclose you quite a budget of papers : the letter of Mrs. L—— to Muddy—Mrs. L——'s long MS. poem—the verses by the 'Lynn Bard,'* which you said you wished to see, and also some lines to me (or rather about me), by Mrs. Osgood, in which she *imagines me writing to her.* I send, too, another notice of 'Eureka,' from Greeley's *Tribune.* The letter of Mrs. L—— you can retain if you wish it.

"Have you seen the 'Moral for Authors,' a new satire by J. E. Tuel?—who, in the name of Heaven, *is* J. E. Tuel? The book is miserably stupid. He has a long parody of the 'Raven'—in fact, nearly the whole thing seems to be aimed at me. If you have not seen it and wish to see it, I will send it. . . . No news of Mrs. L—— yet. If she comes here I shall refuse to see her. Remember me to your parents, Mr. R——, &c.—And now Heaven for ever bless you—   EDDIE.

"I enclose, also, an autograph of the Mr. Willis you are so much in love with. Tell Bardwell I will send him what I promised very soon. . . . My mother sends you her dearest—most devoted love."

Some days later the poet indited the following interesting epistle to an old literary correspondent :—

"NEW YORK, *June* 26, 49.

"On the principle of 'better late than never' I avail myself of a few moments' leisure to say a word or two in reply to your last letter—the one from Brunswick.

"You have had time to form an opinion of 'Eureka.' Let me know, frankly, how it impresses you. It is accomplishing all that I prophesied—even more.

"In respect to D——. By a singular coincidence, he is the chief of the very sect of Hogites to whom I refer as 'the most intolerant and intolerable set of bigots and tyrants that ever existed on the face of the Earth.' A

---

* "Lines to Edgar A. Poe," in the *Lady's Book*, April 1847.—J. H. I.

merely perceptive man, with no intrinsic force—no power of generalisation—in short, a pompous nobody. He is aware (for there have been plenty to tell him) that I intend *him* in 'Eureka.'

"I do not comprehend you about my being the 'auto-biographer of *Holden's Magazine.*' I occasionally hear of that work, but have never seen a number of it.

"'The Rationale of Verse' appeared in the last November and December numbers of the *Southern Literary Messenger.* In the February number I published (editorially) a review of 'The Fable for Critics'—It is not much. Lowell might have done better.

"I have never written any poem called 'Ullahana.' What makes you suppose I have? I enclose the last poem (of any length) which I have published (*i.e.*, 'For Annie'). How do you like it? You know I put much faith in your poetical judgments. It is from Willis's *H. Journal.* Do you ever see the *Literary World?*

"Touching the *Stylus :* Monk Lewis once was asked how he came, in one of his acted plays, to introduce *black* banditti, when, in the country where the scene was laid, black people were quite unknown. His answer was : 'I introduced them because I truly anticipated that blacks would have more *effect* on my audience than whites—and if I had taken it into my head that, by making them sky-blue the effect would have been greater, why sky-blue they should have been.' To apply this idea to the *Stylus*—I am awaiting the *best opportunity* for its issue ; and if by waiting until the day of judgment I perceive still increasing chances of ultimate success, why until the day of judgment I will patiently wait. I am now going to Richmond to 'see about it '—and *possibly* I may get out the first number next January.

"Write soon and more frequently. I always receive your letters with interest. Cordially your friend,

"EDGAR A. POE.

"Please re-enclose the verses."

Among the friendships Poe made during his last days was that with "Stella," the authoress of "Records of the Heart," and other popular works. She says, "I saw much of Mr. Poe during the last year of his life. He was one of the most sensitive and refined gentlemen I ever met. My girlish poem — 'The Forsaken' — made us acquainted. He had seen it floating the rounds of the press, and wrote to tell me how much he liked it: '*It is inexpressibly beautiful,*' he said, 'and I should like much to know the young author.' After the first call he frequently dined with us, and passed the evening in playing whist or in reading to me his last poem."

On the 21st of June the poet wrote to this friend with reference to a projected publication of hers :—

"I have been spending a couple of hours most pleasantly . . . in reading and re-reading your 'Child of the Sea.' When it appears in print—less enticing to the eye, perhaps, than your own graceful MS.—I shall endeavor to do it critical justice in full; but in the meantime permit me to say, briefly, that I think it well conducted as a whole—abounding in narrative passages of unusual force—but especially remarkable for the boldness and poetic fervor of its sentimental portions, where a very striking *originality* is manifested. The descriptions, throughout, are warmly imaginative. The versification could scarcely be improved. The conception of Zamen is unique—a *creation* in the best poetic understanding of the term. I most heartily congratulate you upon having accomplished a work which will *live*.—Yours most sincerely, EDGAR A. POE."

"The day before he left New York for Richmond," continues Stella, "Mr. Poe came to dinner, and stayed the night. He seemed very sad and retired early. On leaving the next morning he took my hand in his, and, looking in my face, said, 'Dear Stella, my much beloved friend. You truly understand and appreciate me—I have a presentiment that I shall never see you again. I must leave to-day for Richmond. If I never return, write my life. You can and will do me justice.'

"'I will!' I exclaimed. And we parted to meet no more in this life. *That* promise I have not yet felt equal to fulfil."

Mrs. Clemm was with her ill-fated nephew on this occasion, and spent her last few hours with him at "Stella's" house. Notwithstanding the gloomy presentiments which oppressed him he attempted to cheer his poor "mother" and friends, by drawing hopeful pictures of his ultimate success: "Cheer up, darling mother," he said, "your Eddy will yet be a comfort to you. I now see my future before me." But for all this, Mrs. Clemm records, he "left in such wretched spirits. Before he left home he arranged all his papers, and told me what to do with them *should he die.* When we parted on the steamboat, although he was so dejected, he still tried to cheer me: 'God bless you, my own darling mother,' he said; 'do not fear for Eddy! See how good I will be while I am away from you, and will come back to love and comfort you.'" And with these last words they parted.

CHAPTER XXI.

LAST DAYS.

EDGAR Poe parted from his mother-in-law on the 30th of June, and on the 9th of July the desolate woman wrote to a friend in these terms :—

"Eddy has been gone ten days, and I have not heard one word from him. Do you wonder that I *am distracted ?* I fear everything. . . . Do you wonder that he has so little confidence in any one? Have we not suffered from the blackest treachery ? . . . Eddy was obliged to go through Philadelphia, and how much I fear he has got into some trouble there; he promised me *so* sincerely to write thence. I ought to have heard last Monday, and now it is Monday again and not one word. . . . Oh, if any evil has befallen *him*, what can comfort me? The day after he left New York, I left Mrs. Lewis and started for home. I called on a rich friend who had made many promises, but never knew our situation. I frankly told her. . . . She proposed to me to leave Eddy, saying he might very well do for himself. . . . Any one to propose to *me* to leave my Eddy—what a cruel insult! No one to console and comfort him but me; no one to nurse him and take care of him when he is sick and helpless ! Can I ever forget that dear sweet face, so tranquil, so pale, and those dear eyes looking at me so sadly, while she said, ' Darling, darling Muddy, you will console and take care of my poor Eddy — you will *never*, *never* leave him ? Promise me, my dear Muddy, and then I can die in peace.' And *I did promise.* And when I meet her in heaven, I can say, ' I have kept my promise, my darling.' . . . If Eddy gets to Richmond safely and can succeed in what he intends doing, we will be relieved of part of our difficulties ; but if he comes home in trouble and sick, I know not what is to become of us."

The most reliable account of Poe's deeds for some time after his leaving his Fordham home is that derived from Mrs. Clemm's letters and papers. It was the poet's misfortune that he had to visit Philadelphia on his journey south. There he was either beguiled into taking stimulants, or sought relief from pain in narcotics ; whatever may have been the active agent, its influence upon his debilitated frame was most deplorable. For a few days he was utterly insane, and had he not fallen into the hands of friends, would, probably, have ended his days then and there. There is no need to repeat the details of this episode, as they were furnished to Mrs. Clemm ; it suffices to repeat her assurance that during his frenzied wanderings, while he deemed himself pursued by some fearsome foes,—" while he was so deranged, he never did aught that was ungentlemanly, much less, that was disgraceful."

The unfortunate man speedily recovered his reason, and resumed his journey to Richmond. Mrs. Clemm states that she received a letter from him on the 23rd of July, and she remarks, " He writes he is better in health, and rather better in spirits. He is going from Richmond in a few days, to stay with a friend in the country for a short time. A very dear friend in Richmond, Mrs. Nye, wrote to me last week, and promised me to make him stay at her house, and says she will take every care of him ; she is a dear kind-hearted creature. But I meet with so little sincerity in this world that I can scarcely trust any one."

When Poe reached Richmond he renewed his acquaintanceship with many old friends, by whom he was introduced to several new ones. He was generally the guest, it is stated, of Mrs. McKenzie, by whom and her husband his sister Rosalie had been adopted. Among the new acquaintances he made at this time was a Mrs. Weiss ; who has published some interesting particulars of the "Last Days of Edgar Poe," * but, in some instances, where not dependent upon her own personal knowledge for facts, she has been greatly misled by erroneous report.

"I was surprised," writes Mrs. Weiss, "to find that the poet was not the melancholy person I had unconsciously pictured. On the contrary, he appeared, except on one occasion, invariably cheerful, and frequently playful in mood. He seemed quietly amused by the light-hearted chat of the young people about him, and often joined them in humorous repartee, sometimes tinged with a playful sarcasm. Yet he preferred to sit quietly and listen and observe. Nothing escaped his keen observation. . . . Though in the social evenings with us, or at Duncan's Lodge, Poe would join in the light conversation or amusement of the hour, I observed that it had not power to interest him for any length of time. He preferred a seat on the portico, or a stroll about the lawn or garden, in company with a friend. . . .

"Among other things, Poe spoke to me freely of his future plans and prospects. He was at this time absorbed in his cherished scheme of establishing his projected journal, the *Stylus*. Nearly all his old friends in Virginia had promised to aid him with the necessary funds, and he was sanguine of success. He intended to spare no pains, no effort, to establish this as the leading literary journal of the country. The plan of it, which he explained in detail, but of which I retain little recollection, was to be something entirely original ; and the highest 'genius, distinctive

---

* In *Scribner's Monthly* for March 1878.

from talent,' of the country was to be represented in its pages. To secure this result, he would offer a more liberal price for contributions than any other publisher. This would, of course, demand capital to begin with, which was all that he required ; and of that he had the promise. To establish this journal had been, he said, the cherished dream of his life, and now at last he felt assured of success. And in thus speaking he held his head erect, and his eyes glowed with enthusiasm. 'I must and will succeed !' he said. . . .

" Poe, among other plans for raising the funds so sorely needed, decided to give a series of lectures in Richmond. The first of these ('The Poetic Principle') brought him at once into prominent notice with the Richmond public. The press discussed him and the élite of society fêted him. With the attention and kindness thus shown him he was much gratified. Yet he did not appear to care for the formal parties, and declared that he found more enjoyment with his friends in the country.

"I can vividly recall him as he appeared on his visits to us. He always carried a cane, and upon entering the shade of the avenue would remove his hat, throw back his hair, and walk lingeringly, as if enjoying the coolness, carrying his hat in his hand, generally behind him. Sometimes he would pause to examine some rare flower, or to pluck a grape from the laden trellises. He met us always with an expression of pleasure illuminating his countenance and lighting his fine eyes.

" Poe's eyes, indeed, were his most striking feature, and it was to these that his face owed its peculiar attraction. I have never seen other eyes at all resembling them. They were large, with long, jet-black lashes,—the iris dark steel-grey, possessing a crystalline clearness and transparency, through which the jet-black pupil was seen to expand and contract with every shade of thought or emotion. I observed that the lids never contracted, as is so usual in most persons, especially when talking ; but his gaze was ever full, open, and unshrinking. His usual expression was dreamy and sad. He had a way of sometimes turning a slightly askance look upon some person who was not observing him, and, with a quiet, steady gaze, appear to be mentally taking the calibre of the unsuspecting subject. 'What *awful* eyes Mr. Poe has!' said a lady to me. 'It makes my blood run cold to see him slowly turn and fix them upon me when I am talking.'

"Apart from the wonderful beauty of his eyes, I would not have called Poe a very handsome man. He was, in my opinion, rather distinguished-looking than handsome. What he had been when younger I had heard, but at the period of my acquaintance with him he had a pallid and careworn look,—somewhat haggard, indeed,—very apparent except in his moments of animation. He wore a dark moustache, scrupulously kept, but not entirely concealing a slightly-contracted expression of the mouth, and an occasional twitching of the upper lip, resembling a sneer. This sneer, indeed, was easily excited—a motion of the lip, scarcely perceptible, and yet intensely expressive. There was in it nothing of ill-nature, but much of sarcasm."

Among the old friendships Poe now renewed was that with Mrs. Shelton, the Miss Royster of his boyhood's love. He had not been long in Richmond on the occasion of this last visit, before he called upon Mrs. Shelton, now become a widow.

"I was ready to go to church," says Mrs. Shelton, "when a servant entered and told me that a gentleman in the parlor wished to see me. I went down and was amazed at seeing Mr. Poe, but knew him instantly. He came up to me in the most enthusiastic manner and said, 'O *Elmira*, is it you?' . . . I then told him that I was going to church; I never let anything interfere with *that*, and that he must call again. . . . When he did call again he renewed his addresses. I laughed; he looked very serious, and said he was in earnest, and had been thinking about it for a long time. When I found out that he was quite serious, I became serious also, and told him that if he would not take a positive denial, he must give me time to consider. He answered, 'A love that hesitated was not a love for him.' . . . But he stayed a long time, and was very pleasant and cheerful. He came to visit me frequently, and I went with him to the Exchange Concert Room, and heard him read."

Twice the poet appeared in public on this final visit to Richmond, and delivered lectures on "The Poetic Principle," to large and appreciative audiences. Professor Valentine, brother of the famous sculptor, well remembers the profound impression made by Poe's recitations—especially of Hood's "Bridge of Sighs,"—on these occasions, as well as by his personal appearance. He speaks of the pallor which overspread his face, as contrasted with the dark hair that fell on the summit of his forehead. "His brow," he says, "was fine and expressive; his eye, dark and restless; in the mouth, firmness mingled with an element of scorn and discontent. His gait was firm and erect, but his manner nervous and emphatic. He was of fine address and cordial in his intercourse with his friends, but looked as though he rarely smiled from joy, to which he seemed to be a stranger: *that* might be partly attributed to the great struggle for self-control, in which he seemed to be constantly engaged. There was little variation and much sadness in the intonation of his voice, yet this very sadness was so completely in harmony with his history, as to excite on the part of this community a deep interest in him both as a lecturer and a reader."

This lecture on "The Poetic Principle" was a worthy setting for the sun of Poe's genius: in it he embodied the theories and *dicta* on Poetry that he had preached and practised ever since his boyhood, illustrating the one and demonstrating the other by recitation of some of the finest specimens of the verse of Shelley, Tennyson, Byron, Hood, Longfellow, Mother-well, and others. It is one of the best of his critical productions, containing the condensation of his most noteworthy remarks on Poesy, and those most worthy preservation.

Twice during this stay in Richmond the poet is said to have succumbed to the temptation which embittered the "lonesome latter years" of his life. Upon each occasion, it is declared that he was tenderly watched over and waited upon, especially upon the second occasion, when, says Mrs. Weiss, "during some days his life was in imminent danger." Assiduous attention saved him, but it was the opinion of the physicians that *another such attack would prove fatal.* This they told him, warning him seriously of the danger.

"Dr. Carter relates how, on this occasion, he had a long conversation with him, in which Poe expressed the most earnest desire to break from the thraldom of his besetting sin, and told of his many unavailing struggles to do so. He was moved even to tears, and finally declared, in the most solemn manner, that this time he *would* restrain himself,— *would* withstand any temptation. He kept his word as long as he remained in Richmond."

The unfortunate man did, indeed, strive to emancipate himself from the terrible thraldom in which he was held, even to the extent of subscribing to the rules of a local Temperance Society. He sent the printed slip which was given him on that occasion to Mrs. Clemm, and the poor desolate woman, on the day following its receipt, wrote to an ever-steadfast friend, "The dark, dark clouds, I think, are beginning to break. . . . God of His great mercy grant he may keep this pledge."

Bravely and earnestly the poor fellow strove to keep to his determination, spending his time chiefly among such friends of his childhood as were willing and happy to enjoy his society. " Especially did he enjoy his visits to the Sullys," says Mrs. Weiss, " where, he remarked, ' I always find pictures, flowers, delightful music and conversation, and a kindness more refreshing than all.' " Robert Sully, the well-known American artist, and Edgar Poe had been schoolfellows, and the artist remarked of his old friend, that he " was one of the most warm-hearted and generous of men. In his youth and prosperity, when admired and looked up to by all his companions, he invariably stood by me and took my part. I was a dull boy at learning, and Edgar never grudged time or pains in assisting me. It was Mr. Allan's cruelty in casting him upon the world, a beggar, which ruined Poe. Some who had envied him took advantage of his change of fortune to slight and insult him. He was sensitive and proud, and felt the change keenly. It was this which embittered him. By nature no person was less inclined to reserve or bitterness, and as a boy he was frank and generous to a fault."

Amid old friends, who not only remembered the past, but who could think of him, and act towards him, so sympathetically in the present, Poe naturally felt happier than he had done for a long time, but that he, constituted as he was, should frequently suffer from recurring fits of melancholia, seemed unavoidable. His letters at this time were inexpressibly sorrowful in tone, but Mrs. Weiss, in her Recollections, says:—

" The only occasion on which I saw Poe really sad or depressed, was on a walk to the 'Hermitage,' the old deserted seat of the Mayo family, where he had, in his youth, been a frequent visitor. On reaching the place, our party separated, and Poe and myself strolled slowly about the grounds. I observed that he was unusually silent and preoccupied, and, attributing it to the influence of memories associated with the place, forbore to interrupt him. He passed slowly by the mossy bench called the 'Lovers' Seat,' beneath two aged trees, and remarked, as we turned towards the garden, 'There used to be white violets here.' Searching amid the tangled wilderness of shrubs, we found a few late blossoms, some of which he placed carefully between the leaves of a note-book. Entering the deserted house, he passed from room to room with a grave, abstracted look, and removed his hat, as if involuntarily, on entering the saloon where in old times many a brilliant company had assembled. Seated in one of the deep windows, over which now grew masses of ivy, his memory must have borne him back to former scenes, for he repeated the familiar lines of Moore :

> " 'I feel like one who treads alone,
>   Some banquet-hall deserted '—

and paused, with the first expression of real sadness that I had ever seen on his face."

Poe now having to visit New York, in connection with the editing and publication of a lady's forthcoming volume of verse, wrote to Mrs. Clemm to inform her of his anticipated marriage to Mrs. Shelton, and also desired her to be prepared to return with him to Richmond, to reside there permanently. Notwithstanding his projected marriage, Poe's two last letters to Mrs. Clemm were very, very sad, and seemed to have been written with a foreboding that they would be his last. They were replete with anxious expressions for his relative's future happiness, and contained words of tender remembrance for " Annie."

Although Mrs. Shelton does not appear to have definitely engaged herself to Poe, there was, undoubtedly, an understanding between them sufficient to warrant the poet in his belief that he was once more an accepted suitor of his boyhood's love. Previous to leaving Virginia on his journey north, he called on the lady and told her that he was going to New York to wind up some business matters, but that he would return to Richmond as soon as he had accomplished it, although, at the same time, says Mrs. Shelton, he said he had a presentiment he should never see me any more. And in this he was right, for they never met again.

"The evening of the day previous to that appointed for his departure from Richmond," says Mrs. Weiss, "Poe spent at my mother's. He declined to enter the parlours, where a number of visitors were assembled, saying he preferred the more quiet sitting-room; and here I had a long and almost uninterrupted conversation with him. He spoke of his future, seeming to anticipate it with an eager delight, like that of youth. He declared that the last few weeks in the society of his old and new friends had been the happiest that he had known for many years, and that when he again left New York he should there leave behind all the trouble and vexation of his past life. On no occasion had I seen him so cheerful and hopeful as on this evening. 'Do you know,' he inquired, 'how I spent most of this morning? In writing a critique of your poems, to be accompanied by a biographical sketch. I intend it to be one of my best, and that it shall appear in the second number of the *Stylus*,'—so confident was he in regard to this magazine. Poe expressed great regret in being compelled to leave Richmond, on even so brief an absence. He would certainly, he said, be back in two weeks. He thanked my mother with graceful courtesy and warmth for her kindness and hospitality, and begged that we would write to him in New York, saying it would do him good.

"He was the last of the party to leave the house. We were standing on the portico, and after going a few steps he paused, turned, and again lifted his hat, in a last adieu. At the moment, a brilliant meteor appeared in the sky directly over his head, and vanished in the east. We commented laughingly upon the incident; but I remembered it sadly afterward.

"That night he spent at Duncan's Lodge; and, as his friend said, sat late at his window, meditatively smoking, and seemingly disinclined for conversation. On the following morning he went into the city, accompanied by his friends, Dr. Gibbon Carter and Dr. Mackenzie. The day was passed with them and others of his intimate friends. Late in the evening he entered the office of Dr. John Carter, and spent an hour in looking over the day's papers; then taking Dr. Carter's cane he went out, remarking that he would step across to Saddler's (a fashionable restaurant) and get supper. From the circumstance of his taking the cane, leaving his own in its place, it is probable that he had intended to return; but at the restaurant he met with some acquaintances who detained him until late, and then accompanied him to the Baltimore boat. According to their account he was quite sober and cheerful to the last, remarking, as he took leave of them, that he would soon be in Richmond again."

Early in October, on the 2nd apparently, Poe left Richmond for New York. He proceeded by boat to Baltimore, which city he reached safely on the morning following his departure. Upon his arrival he gave his trunk to a porter to convey it, it is stated, to the cars which were timed to leave in an hour or so for Philadelphia, whilst he sought some refreshment. What now happened is still shrouded in mystery: before leaving Richmond the poet had complained of indisposition; of chilliness, and of exhaustion, and it is just possible that the increase of these symptoms may have enticed him into breaking his pledge, or into resort-

ing to some deleterious drug. Be the cause whatever
it may, it now appears to have become the fixed belief
of the Baltimoreans, that the unfortunate poet, while
in a state of temporary mania or stupor, fell into
the hands of a gang of ruffians who were scouring
the streets in search of victims. Wednesday, the 3rd of
October, was election day for Members of Congress, in
the State of Maryland, and it is the general supposition that Poe was captured by an electioneering band,
" cooped," * drugged, dragged to the polls, and then,
after having voted the ticket placed in his hand, was
ruthlessly left in the street to die. For the truth
of this terrible tale there appears to be too great a
probability.

According to the account furnished by Dr. Moran,
resident physician of the Washington University
Hospital, Baltimore, the unfortunate poet was brought
to that institution, on the 7th of October, in a state of
insensibility. He had been discovered in that condition, lying on a bench by a wharf, and having been
recognised by a passer-by, had been put into a convey-
ance and taken to the hospital.

"I had meantime learned from him," says Dr. Moran,
"and afterward from the porter at the hotel on Pratt Street,
then Bradshaw's, now called the Maltby House, that he
arrived there on the evening of the 5th ; was seen to go to
the depôt to take the cars for Philadelphia, and that the
conductor, on going through the cars for tickets, found

---

* It was by no means unusual in those days for unprotected strangers
to be seized by electioneering agents, confined in a cellar till wanted, or
" cooped," as it was termed, and then drugged and dragged about from
poll to poll to vote, the superintending officials registering the votes,
apparently quite regardless of the condition of the person personifying
a voter.

him lying in the baggage car insensible. He took him as far as Havre de Grace, where the cars then passed each other, or as far as Wilmington, I forget which, and placed him in the train coming to Baltimore. He had left his trunk at the hotel in Baltimore. Arriving on the evening train he was not seen by any person about the hotel when he returned to the city. The presumption is he wandered about during the night, and found a bench sometime before morning to sleep upon on Light Street Wharf, where he was seen and taken from about nine o'clock the next morning."

His cousin, Mr. (now Judge) Neilson Poe, was sent for, and had everything done for the patient's comfort, but in vain. When his consciousness returned, the horror and misery of his condition, combined with the effects of exposure, produced such a shock to the nervous system that he never recovered, and about midnight, on the 7th of October 1849, his poor tortured spirit passed away.

On the 9th of the month—on the anniversary of " the lonesome October of his most immemorial year " —the earthly remains of Edgar Allan Poe were consigned to their resting-place in the grave of his ancestors in Westminster Churchyard, Baltimore, in the presence of a few relatives and friends.

Mr. Neilson Poe had a stone prepared to mark his unfortunate kinsman's tomb, but, by a strange fatality, the monument was destroyed before it could be erected, and, in consequence, for upwards of a quarter of a century the spot remained unnoted and almost unknown. At last, public attention having been strongly drawn to the neglected condition of the poet's grave, a public committee was formed to collect subscriptions towards the erection of a suitable memorial, and, through the exertions of Miss Rice, Mr. Paul Hayne, and others, a marble monument was procured, and, on the 17th of November 1875, unveiled in the presence of a large concourse of people.*

Poe's story, his faults and misfortunes, cannot be better summarised than in these words of Byron's " Manfred " :—

> " Look on me ! there is an order
> Of mortals on the earth, who do become
> Old in their youth and die ere middle age,
> Without the violence of warlike death ;
> Some perishing of pleasure—some of study—
> Some worn with toil—some of mere weariness—
> Some of disease—and some insanity—
> And some of withered or of broken hearts ;
> For this last is a malady which slays
> More than are numbered in the lists of Fate,
> Taking all shapes, and bearing many names.
> Look upon me ! for even of *all* these things
> Have I partaken—and of all these things
> One were enough ; then wonder not that I
> Am what I am."

It is impossible to conceive the horror and heart-rending grief of Mrs. Clemm, when the intelligence of Poe's death was conveyed to her. She was awaiting his arrival, to bear her away to her native South, and instead of welcoming an affectionate son—happy in the prospect of anticipated marriage and a prosperous future—she received the tidings of his terrible and mysterious death. In the first moments of her loneliness and anguish she wrote to her best friend, for sympathy, in these terms :—

" *Oct. 8*, 1849.

"ANNIE, my Eddy *is dead.* He died in Baltimore yesterday. Annie ! pray for me, your desolate friend.

---

* *Vide* Appendix E.

My senses *will leave me.* I will write the moment I hear the particulars. I have written to Baltimore. Write and advise me what to do. Your distracted friend,

"M. C."

Writing again on the 13th of October to the same faithful friend, Mrs. Clemm says :—

"MY OWN DEAREST ANNIE,—I am not deceived in you, you *still* wish your poor desolate friend to come to you. . . . I have written to poor Elmira, and have to wait for her answer. They are already making arrangements to publish the works of my *darling lost one.* I have been waited on by several gentlemen, and have finally arranged with Mr. Griswold to arrange and bring them out, and he wishes it done immediately. Mr. Willis is to share with him this labour of love. They say I am to have the *entire* proceeds, so you see, Annie, I will not be entirely destitute. I have had many letters of condolence, and one which has, indeed, comforted me. Neilson Poe, of Baltimore, has written to me, and says he died in the Washington Medical College, not the Hospital, and of congestion of the brain, and not of what the vile, vile papers accuse him. He had many kind friends with him, and was attended to the grave by the literati of Baltimore, and many friends. *Severe excitement* (and no doubt some imprudence) brought this on ; he never had one interval of reason. I cannot tell you all now. . . . They now appreciate him and will do justice to his beloved memory. They propose to raise a monument to his memory. Some of the papers, indeed, nearly all, do him justice. I enclose this article from a Baltimore paper. But this, my dear Annie, will not restore him. Never, oh, never, will I see those dear lovely eyes. I feel *so desolate, so wretched, friendless, and alone.* . . . I have a beautiful letter from General Morris ; he did, indeed, love him. He has many friends, but of what little consequence to him *now.* I have to go out home—to *his* home to-day, to arrange his papers. Oh, what will I not suffer." . . .

On the 17th Mrs. Clemm writes to say that she has now heard *all* the particulars of Poe's death, and that she has " been very much engaged with Mr. Griswold in looking over his (Poe's) papers," and that Mr. Griswold says, " he must have *all* until the work is published. He thinks I will realise from two to three thousand dollars from the sale of these books, there is so much sympathy and good feeling towards him, except by a few low envious minds. . . . What do you think I must have suffered when in one of the letters I found some hair of my *lost one !* . . . *His* hair, taken from that dear head when cold and insensible. . . . I received a letter from poor dear Elmira: oh, how you will pity her when you read it." Then, in alluding to the proffered services of Griswold, the poor befooled woman continues; " How nobly they have acted ! all done gratis, and you know to literary people that is a great deal. . . . Those gentlemen who have so kindly undertaken the publication of his works, say that I will have a very comfortable income from them."

Within a few days after these and many similar letters equally pathetic were written, Mrs. Clemm went on a lengthy visit to "Annie's" hospitable home. Writing to her step-daughter's husband, Mr. Neilson Poe, on the 1st of November, she acknowledges a kind letter from Willis, that had been forwarded to her ; begs Neilson to forward her the trunk containing Poe's papers, as in it were articles of "great importance to the publishers of his works ; " inveighs bitterly against the poet's sister, Rosalie, for her claim to share in the anticipated proceeds of the projected publication; furnishes instances of the friendly attentions paid her by well-known literati, and declares that she is " with the kindest friends, who do all in their power to comfort her." Several months passed

on smoothly enough, and Mrs. Clemm was comforted
and gratified by the kindly attentions of friends and
strangers, who all vied with each other in aiding the
poet's "more than mother."

In September 1850, the third volume of Poe's
works when published was found to be prefaced by
the anxiously looked-for "Memoir"—the "labour of
love" of Rufus Griswold. The secret of the man's
disinterested aid was soon manifest; never before had
so slanderous a collection of falsehoods and libels—so
calumnious a product of envy, hatred, and malice—been
offered to the public as this "Memoir" of an ill-fated
child of genius. The distress and indignation of Mrs.
Clemm were intense, and she continually, when alluding
to Griswold, writes of him as "that villain." Poe's
literary friends gathered round her and promised to expose and refute the slanderous fabrications. "I have
received a kind letter from that noble fellow, Graham,"
she writes at this period, "telling me to *remain quiet*,
that he had a host of my Eddie's friends prepared to
do him justice, and that he intends to devote nearly
half of the December number to the memory and defence of my injured Eddie."

Mr. Graham, and many others who had been personally acquainted with Poe, took up cudgels in his
defence, but, as Griswold's "Memoir" prefaced the
poet's works, and all refutations and objections were
published in the ephemeral pages of periodicals, until
1874 this veritable *scandalum magnatum* remained
unexpunged.

Mrs. Clemm continued as a guest at "Annie's" house
for some years, when she was invited to "Stella's,"
where she also spent several years, befriended and

introduced to all notable persons. Among distinguished visitors to America who remembered and greeted the poet's venerable mother-in-law, was Charles Dickens, and he generously entreated her acceptance of one hundred and fifty dollars, accompanying the gift with the assurance of his sympathy. Ultimately, the old lady found a retreat in a charitable institution of Baltimore, the " Church Home and Infirmary," and expired there on the 16th of February 1871, having lived long beyond the allotted years of sorrow. In accordance with her own request, her papers and records were placed in the hands of Mr. Neilson Poe, whilst her poor worn-out body was interred beside her beloved Eddy's, in the old ancestral grave of her father, General Poe.

APPENDIX A.

POE'S ANCESTRY.

IN her charming little book on *Edgar Poe and his Critics*, the late Mrs. Whitman contended that the Poe family was of Italian origin. The progenitors of this race, according to the lady's idea, after successive migrations through France, England, and Wales, ultimately settled in Ireland. This theory was based upon the supposition that the Poe and the Le Poer families were identic in origin; but later researches, whilst recognising the great probability, have failed to establish the certainty of this identity, the only *datum* adduced in proof of it being, apparently, similarity of sound—that least trustworthy of all philological evidence. For those, however, who may like to see the testimony proffered by Mrs. Whitman in support of her hypothesis of the Poe and Le Poer families being descended from the same ancestor, the particulars furnished by her said work—together with a few additional items on the same theme, gathered by ourselves for our 1874 Memoir of the poet—shall be given. Edgar Allan Poe, says our authority, was descended from an ancient Norman family which settled in Ireland in the reign of Henry II., and "those who are curious in tracing the effects of country and lineage in the mental and constitutional peculiarities of men of genius, may be interested in such facts as we have been enabled to gather in relation to the ancestry of the poet. The awakening interest in genealogical researches will make them acceptable to many readers; and in their possible influence on a character so anomalous as that of Edgar Poe, they are certainly worthy of note."

The family of the Le Poers, or De la Poers, was founded by Sir Roger le Poer, one of the companions-in-arms of the famous Strongbow, and of him it was remarked by Geraldus Cambrensis, "It might be said, without offence, that there was not a man who did more valiant acts than Roger le Poer." The race which sprang from this knightly adventurer made itself conspicuous in the annals of Ireland for heroic daring and romantic deeds, as well as for its improvidence and reckless bravery. The chivalrous conduct of Sir Arnold le Poer, seneschal of Kilkenny Castle, "a knight, and instructed in letters," in interposing, at the ultimate sacrifice of liberty and life, to rescue Lady Alice Kytler from the clutches of the ecclesiastics who accused her and brought her to trial for witchcraft, is fully detailed by Geraldus and other chroniclers. "The disastrous civil war of 1327," says Mrs. Whitman, "in which all the great barons of the country were involved, was occasioned by a personal feud between Arnold le Poer and Maurice of Desmond, the former having offended the dignity of the Desmond by calling him a rhymer," little deeming, indeed, that the most famous scion of his own knightly race would glorify the family more by his rhymings than any other member of it would by his swordsmanship.

The Le Poers were involved in the Irish troubles of 1641, and when Cromwell invaded the country they did not escape his pursuit; their families were dispersed, their estates confiscated, and their lands forfeited to the Commonwealth. Of the three leading branches of the family at the time of Cromwell's invasion, Kilmaedon, Don Isle, and Curraghmore, the last only escaped the vengeance of the Lord Protector, and that, according to Burke, solely by the ingenuity and courage of Alice, daughter of the Lord of Curraghmore. The romantic story of Cromwell's siege of the sea-girt castle of Don Isle, as told by Burke, in his *Romance of the Aristocracy*, is replete with interest. The isolated stronghold was bravely defended by a female descendant of Nicholas le Poer, Baron of Don Isle, and this heroine is always styled, in the traditions of the Power family, "the Countess."

"The family of the Le Poers," remarks Mrs. Whitman, "like that of the Geraldines, and other Anglo-Norman settlers in Ireland, passed from Italy into the north of France, and from France, through England and Wales, into Ireland, where, from their isolated position and other causes, they retained for a long period their hereditary traits with far less modification from intermarriage and association with other races than did their English compeers. Meantime the name underwent various changes in accent and orthography. A few branches of the family still bore in Ireland the old Italian name of De la Poë." "The beautiful domain of Powerscourt," adds this same authority, "took its name from the Le Poers," and through her father, Edmund Power, the late Lady Blessington claimed descent from the same old family. Some branches of the Power family, it may be remarked, have obtained heraldic sanction for resuming their more ancient patronymic of Le Poer.*

Thus far we have ventured to follow the line of argument suggested by Mrs. Whitman, but it must be confessed that the earliest reliable records do not carry the paternal ancestry of Edgar Allan Poe further back than the middle of the last century; but if his ancestors were descended, as is extremely probable, from the Poës of Riverston (County Tipperary, Ireland), the race may be traced back nearly two centuries earlier. The Poës of Riverston are said to have come from the Upper Palatinate of the Rhine, and for upwards of two centuries have held positions of importance, and have intermarried with various families of the aristocracy. Thomas and William Poë were officers in Cromwell's army, and Captain Thomas Poë, one of these brothers, "obtained grants of lands which were confirmed to him by Charles II. The greater number of his descendants can be traced, and one of them, Parsons Poë, went to America about one hundred and twenty years ago. He was heard from, for a few years after his arrival, but, after a while, nothing further was known of, or heard from him, so his family supposed he had died. He was descended maternally from the 'Percys' and the 'Parsons' of Birr Castle."†

"There is no good reason," says John P. Poe, Esq., of Baltimore, "to suppose that the ancestors of Edgar A. Poe were descended from the Le Poers. John Poe, the

---

* Mrs. Whitman was by birth a Power, and liked to consider herself as descended from the same ancestry as Poe.—J. H. I.

† Letter from James Jocelyn Poë, Esq., representative of the Riverston Poës. November 17th, 1875.—J. H. I.

progenitor of the family in America, emigrated from the north of Ireland, a number of years before the Revolution, and purchased a farm in Lancaster County, Pennsylvania, whence he afterwards removed to Cecil County, Maryland. At the time of the Revolution he was residing at Baltimore. His wife was Jane McBride, believed to be a sister (not a daughter, as frequently stated) of James McBride, Admiral of the Blue, and M.P. for Plymouth in 1785." * John Poe's age is not given, but his wife is said to have died in Baltimore, at the age of one hundred and six, and to have been buried in Westminster Churchyard.†

In an account furnished by Mrs. Clemm (Edgar Poe's aunt) of the poet's ancestry, she states, "My father was born in Ireland, but his parents left there when he was only six weeks old, and he was so patriotic that he never would acknowledge he was any other than an American. He lived in Baltimore from the time of the Revolution ; he took my mother there from Pennsylvania, a bride."

David Poe, the son of John, is stated by Mrs. Clemm to have married a Pennsylvanian beauty of the name of Cairnes, and to have removed with her to Maryland, where he settled in Baltimore, and became a prominent citizen, taking part in various patriotic labours, as may be seen by reference to Colonel Scharf's " Chronicles of Baltimore," and other works of research. During the War of Independence David Poe greatly distinguished himself, and received the appointment of Quartermaster of the American forces in Baltimore. Mr. Didier states that in this position Poe, when the State funds were exhausted, frequently advanced money from his own private means, and, indeed, rendered such pecuniary aid to the State that he was ultimately ruined through it. Be this as it may, in 1780, and the next few years, he is found to have purchased several lots of land in Baltimore, and to have been, apparently, a man of considerable wealth. Portions of the correspondence of General Poe—as he was usually styled after the war—with various distinguished Americans of the period, have been preserved in the archives of Maryland, and will be found

---

* In letter dated May 1st, 1875.—J. H. I.
† E. L. Didier. " Life of Edgar A. Poe," p. 21.

in Colonel Scharf's work. General Poe, despite his foreign birth, was a most ardent patriot, and omitted no opportunity of manifesting his zeal for his adopted nationality. In 1781, when La Fayette halted in Baltimore, on his way to join the army of the South, a ball was given in his honour. During the festivities, it is related that the French general appeared melancholy, and upon being asked the reason of his depression, said that he could not enjoy the gaiety whilst his men were suffering so much for want of clothing. The hint was taken, and the next morning the ball-room was converted into a work-room; the citizens furnishing the needed materials, and the ladies making them up. Mrs. David Poe, it is said, personally cut out and superintended the manufacture of five hundred garments, and her husband gave $500 towards their cost. For this graceful act of the Baltimorean ladies, La Fayette sent them a letter of thanks, dated July 3rd, 1781, which is duly given in full in Colonel Scharf's "Chronicles." When revisiting Baltimore in 1824, La Fayette referred in grateful terms to the kindness he and his troops had received from the Poe family, and on learning that General Poe was dead he paid a visit of respect to his widow.

General Poe had several children, the eldest of whom was David Poe, junior, father of the future poet; the second, George, whose descendants still live in Maryland; Stephen, who died on the Jersey Prison Ship during the War of Independence; William, who emigrated to the State of Georgia, where his descendants, one of whom is the Hon. Washington Poe of Macar, have filled many important posts;* and to these may be added, Maria, who became the second wife of William Clemm, a well-known citizen of Baltimore, and mother of Virginia, Edgar Allan Poe's cousin and bride.

Samuel Poe, a notable oddity of Baltimore nearly half a century ago, is also said to have been a son of General Poe. Many of this youth's vagaries are still remembered, and some have even found their way into print. Of one of his practical jokes, a much-esteemed correspondent sends the following amusing account:—" At the time Samuel Poe

---

* Letters from John P. Poe, Esq., of Baltimore.—J. H. I.

was a youth, the Baltimorean Germans, who were not many in number, and were rather despised, raised a volunteer company they called '*Die Jäger*,' which was generally referred to as 'the Dutch Yagers.' These honest 'Dutchmen' Poe selected as his especial butts. When they went out parading Poe would muster a lot of mischievous *gamins*, and march in their rear, sometimes giving orders in broken English, and sometimes chanting a doggerel canticle of his own composition, of which these are two couplets :—

> " ' Ven you hears te great pig trum,
> Den you sees te Yagers come ;
> Ven tey turns te corner apout,
> Den you schmells te sauer kraut.'

"This doggerel the boys used to sing in chorus, Poe strutting at their head like a drum-major, to the great mirth of the public. When they reached the place of parade Poe would halt his troop (followed by hundreds of spectators), and would burlesque the call of the roll, with the answers or excuses for absence; would inspect the company, would command manœuvres, &c., all in the wildest burlesque, to the infinite delight of his boys and a malicious public, but to the inexpressible anguish of the poor 'Dutchmen.' At last they could stand it no longer, and had Poe up to court. The charge was preferred, and the court asked Poe what he had to say. The youth, with the greatest gravity, said he was only indulging in a little innocent mirth that harmed nobody and did not disturb the peace ; that the boys liked to see the 'Yagers' parade, and he put himself at their head to infuse a little military spirit into them ; that as for his song, it was quite inoffensive, as their Honours could judge for themselves when he repeated it. And he then began intoning his famous chant, at which the court fairly broke down with laughter, and dismissed the case."

APPENDIX B.

WILLIAM HENRY LEONARD POE.

INCIDENTS as romantic and contradictory as those related of his illustrious brother are told of William Henry Leonard Poe. The facts known of his life are few : he was the earliest born child of David Poe, junior, and Elizabeth his wife. The date of his birth is uncertain, but Mrs. Clemm states that he was the first grandchild born to her parents, and that it was for his sake that they became reconciled to his father, their eldest son, with whom they had quarrelled on account of his imprudent marriage and theatrical pro-clivities. It is very probable that the boy's grandparents adopted the child from its earliest infancy, as is stated by Mrs. Clemm and some of the poet's biographers ; but Mr. E. L. Didier, in his " Life of Edgar A. Poe," says, when " Henry's " parents died, he " was taken to Baltimore, and educated by his godfather, Mr. Henry Didier, whose counting-room he subsequently entered."*

" William," writes Mr. John P. Poe, his cousin, " died early. He was a man of taste and genius, and wrote many fugitive verses, which have been lost, but which are said to have exhibited poetical power of a high order." And again, " The verses of William Poe are said to have had great merit, but we fear there is no prospect of recovering any of them. He died very early." †

Mr. R. H. Stoddard, in a sketch of Edgar Poe's life, states that William Henry Leonard, " is described by those who knew him as possessing great personal beauty, *and as much genius as Edgar !*" (The italics are ours.) " He wrote

---

* Henry was his second Christian name ; he was, apparently, named William, after his father's brother.—J. H. I.

† Letters of May 1st and October 2nd, 1875.—J. H. I.

verses," continues Mr. S., "which were printed in the *Minerva*, a small weekly paper published in Baltimore; he was a clerk in a lottery office in that city; and he was not averse to the flowing bowl. This last circumstance, joined to his rejection as a lover, was probably the cause of his going to sea, and his subsequent 'sailor's scrape' at St. Petersburg — for it was no more — out of which the dangerous and desperate adventure of his famous brother was manufactured." This last allusion is to a story told by Griswold, and his copyists, of Edgar Poe having to be rescued by the American Minister to Russia, "from penalties incurred in a drunken debauch" at St. Petersburg. The entire legend is a fair sample of those fabricated about the famous poet: he never was in Russia, nor, in all probability, was his brother William. Mr. Eugene Schuyler, the well-known author, and formerly Secretary to the American Legation at St. Petersburg, kindly undertook to have the books and papers of the Legation and Consulate in the Russian capital, referring to the only possible period in which the incident could have occurred,* searched for us, and reports, with reference to the alleged ministerial intervention, "I find no record whatever of that circumstance."

But William Poe was in the navy, and *might*, therefore, have been to Russia, so it is fairly safe to transfer the anecdote to his shoulders, accordingly, Mr. Didier says of him, "He was very clever, but wild and erratic. Having quarrelled with his patron, Henry (*sic*) Poe determined to go to Greece, and fight for the cause to which the death of Byron had attracted the attention of the world. Young Poe arrived in time to participate in the last battles of the war. On the 14th of September 1829, the Sultan acknowledged the independence of Greece. . . . Poe accompanied the Russian troops to St. Petersburg, where he soon got into trouble and into prison. He was released by the interposition of the Hon. A. Middleton, the American Minister, who had him sent to the port of Riga, and placed on a vessel bound for Baltimore. Six months after returning

* From 1820 to 30. During the time that Mr. Middleton was minister.—E. Schuyler.

home, Henry Poe died, at the early age of twenty-six,* leaving behind him the reputation of great but wasted talents."

* Mr. Didier avers that Poe's parents were not married until "the spring of 1806," and within six months after the decease of a former husband of the lady. If such were the case, William Henry Leonard Poe must have been born from two to three years *before* his putative parents' marriage, and could scarcely have had David Poe as his father: it would appear not improbable that Mr. Didier has mistaken some other scion of the family for William H. L. Poe, the poet's brother.— J. H. I.

APPENDIX C.

ROSALIE M. POE.

OF Edgar Poe's sister, Rosalie M. Poe, little need be said. Left by her mother's death a mere baby she was adopted by a Richmond merchant, a native of Scotland, named McKenzie, and brought up in his family. Mr. McKenzie having been ruined by the sudden peace that followed the battle of Waterloo, his sister, described as a most accomplished lady, opened a school in Richmond. This seminary was attended by members of the best families in Virginia, and thither Rosalie Poe was sent, but, although she is averred to have had similar advantages to the other young ladies, she was so hopelessly dull, that she could never attain proficiency in anything, even her handwriting, which is said to have been her strongest point, having been but indifferent. After leaving school Miss Poe continued to reside with various members of the McKenzie family till, at the conclusion of the Civil War, they became unable, or unwilling, to further befriend the unfortunate lady. Miss Poe was utterly incapable of procuring her own maintenance, and, during the last five or six years of her life, was a confirmed invalid. After having endured for some years a precarious existence, dependent upon the assistance of friends, a shelter was ultimately obtained for her in Washington, D. C., where she was admitted into the Epiphany Church Home, an Episcopalian charitable institution. She appears to have been very fond of her brother Edgar, and proud of his reputation, although, as she stated to us, in a correspondence we had with her a short time previous to her decease, it was not until she "was a good sized girl" that she "knew she had a brother or brothers;" and it was only during the last years of his life that she had any real personal knowledge of Edgar. Some slight record of her eccentricities are contained in Mrs. Weiss's paper on "The Last Days of Edgar A. Poe." Miss Poe died July 1874, aged sixty-four.

APPENDIX D.

LADY FRIENDSHIPS.

DESPITE all the sorrow and misfortune of his brief career it was the frequent good fate of Poe to encounter, and be associated with, high and self-sacrificing women, and, probably, no higher testimony could be cited in favour of his goodness than the enduring and friendly sympathy manifested for him by these ladies. Besides the life-long love of his wife, and the never-wavering affection of Mrs. Clemm, it has been seen during various portions of his story, that he inspired the truest and most disinterested friendship of Mrs. Stannard (the " Helen " of his youth) ; Mrs. Shelton, his first and last love ; Mrs. Shew (" Marie Louise ") ; Mrs. Osgood ; Mrs. Whitman ; " Annie "; " Stella," and others.

The reader of Edgar Poe's history cannot but feel interested in the fate of these ladies. Some of them, happily, still dwell among us, whilst others have gone before, and of these latter, Mrs. Osgood, Mrs. Shew, and Mrs. Whitman, it behoves us to speak a few words additional. The career of Frances Sargent Osgood, a lady whom Poe admired with intense and long-lasting affection, has already been adverted to in the preceding pages, it suffices, therefore, to say that although they did not meet for some years prior to the poet's death, her friendship for him suffered no abatement. Shortly before her decease, which occurred on Sunday, 12th of May 1850, just seven months after Poe's, she wrote the charming recollections cited in this work. About the same time her last and nearest complete volume of verse was published, and its final poem was this :—

> " The hand that swept the sounding lyre
>   With more than mortal skill,
> The lightning eye, the heart of fire,
>   The fervent lips, are stil! !

No more, in rapture or in woe,
With melody to thrill,
Ah! Nevermore!

" Oh! bring the flowers he cherished so,
With eager childlike care;
For o'er his grave they'll love to grow—
And sigh their sorrow there:
Ah me! no more their balmy glow
May soothe his heart's despair,
No! Nevermore!

" But angel hands shall bring him balm
For every grief he knew,
And Heaven's soft harps his soul shall calm
With music sweet and true,
And teach to him the holy charm
Of Israfel anew,
For evermore!

" Love's silver lyre he played so well
Lies shattered on his tomb;
But still in air its music spell
Floats on through light and gloom;
And in the hearts where soft they fell
His words of beauty bloom
For evermore!"

The inspiration of these pathetic lines cannot be mis-understood. Portraits of their authoress, and of *her* "Israfel," both painted by Mr. S. Osgood, are on the walls of the New York Historical Society's Library.

Few and simple words are needed to tell Mrs. Shew's subsequent story, for her life has left no ostentatious or monumental emblems, and her memory survives only in her children's love; her friends' affection; and in the grati-tude of those whose afflictions she comforted, and whose needs she supplied. After having been some years the wife of the Rev. Dr. Roland S. Houghton, she followed her husband rapidly to the grave, " entering into rest," as she herself had aptly styled it, on the third of September 1877.

Mrs. Whitman's name has, probably, been more closely connected with Poe's than that of any lady mentioned in this biography, and yet their personal acquaintanceship was the shortest, and, doubtless, her influence on his career the slightest, of any of those noble women whose

names have been grouped around his. The details, as full
as could be furnished, have been given of their short-lived
intercourse. After the rupture of their engagement, and up
till the time of his death, Poe does not appear to have
alluded to Mrs. Whitman again, save in the most conventional manner; but the lady always cherished, with unfading affection, the memory of her connection with the poet.
In her delightful correspondence and conversation, in her
melodious song, and, above all, in her truly beautiful little
monograph on "Edgar Poe and his Critics," Mrs. Whitman invariably contrived to bring more prominently
forward the brighter *traits* of her hero's character than has
been accomplished by any other person—by any other
means.

Mr. Thomas Wentworth Higginson, in a paper on Poe,[*]
thus pleasantly alludes to this lady as she appeared to her
friends in the autumn-tide of her life. She had, he says,
"outlived her early friends, and loves, and hopes, and
perhaps her literary fame, such as it was : she had certainly
outlived her recognised ties with Poe, and all but his
memory. There she dwelt in her little suite of rooms,
bearing youth still in her heart and in her voice, and
on her hair also, and in her dress. Her dimly-lighted
parlour was always decked, here and there, with scarlet;
and she sat, robed in white, with her back always turned
to the light, thus throwing a discreetly tinted shadow over
her still thoughtful and noble face. She seemed a person
embalmed while still alive ; it was as if she might dwell for
ever there, prolonging into an indefinite future the tradition of a poet's love : and when we remembered that she
had been Poe's betrothed, that his kisses had touched her
lips, that she still believed in him, and was his defender,
all criticism might well, for her sake, be disarmed, and her
saintly life atone for his stormy and sad career." Mrs.
Whitman expired on the 27th of June 1878, in the seventy-
sixth year of her age.

The two sonnets which follow are among the latest
tributes to the departed poet; and are by "Stella" (Mrs.
E. A. Lewis); one of the friends above mentioned :—

[*] The Boston *Literary World*, March 15th, 1879.

I.

FIRST MEETING.

WHEN first the sad notes of my youthful lyre
Attracted thee unto my tuneful way—
That up life's rugged steep before me lay,
By fancy fashioned to my young desire,
And made alluring by Hope's beacon fire—
I dare not lift to thine my timid gaze,
But, open-eared, my soul took in thy praise,
And spread its pinions for a region higher
Than Fame or Fate had taught it to aspire;
And when, to teach to me poetic art,
Thy " Raven," piecemeal, thou didst take apart,
With eloquent discourse that could not tire,
I felt how much of Heaven there was in thee—
The chalice of my soul o'erflow'd with melody.

II.

BENEATH THE ELM.

BENEATH the elm before thy cottage door
At Fordham—whilst the sun his slanting beams
Shot through the dark green boughs in golden gleams,
And all around respectful silence wore—
I've listened to thy song and classic lore;
Followed thee in thy wild, poetic dreams
Over Parnassus and Olympian streams;
Where Phœbus and the Muses dwelt of yore,
Making melodious all the Grecian shore;
Through Dante's "Hell" of writhing souls that teems
With thoughts that later bards have made their themes,
Midst Virgil's storms and Homer's battle roar,
Until thou didst not seem of mortal birth,
But some lone spirit sent from Heaven to earth.

STELLA.[*]

LONDON, *December* 1879.

---

[*] New York *Home Journal*, February 11, 1880.

APPENDIX E.

ALTHOUGH most people appear to have felt that Edgar Allan Poe, of all his countrymen, least needed a marble monument to perpetuate *his* name, the feelings which prompted the erection of one by his fellow-citizens were, doubtless, generous and praiseworthy; and as evidence of such public appreciation, apart from the fact that it was the first memorial ever raised to a poet in America, the Baltimore monument deserves something more here than passing mention. On the 17th of November 1875 the long-talked-of cenotaph was unveiled, amid a large concourse of people who had assembled to witness, or to take part in, the ceremonies connected with the event. The proceedings were inaugurated by music, after which Professor William Elliott, Jr., delivered the following address, recounting the history of the movement that culminated in that day's celebration:—

"LADIES AND GENTLEMEN,—I purpose, in discharging the duty assigned me on this occasion, to give a brief historical sketch of the movement which culminates to-day in the dedication of a monument to the memory of the great American poet, Edgar Allan Poe, the first and only memorial expression of the kind ever given to an American on account of literary excellence.

"This extraordinary and unique genius, born in Boston, January 20th,* 1809, during a brief sojourn of his parents in that place, died on the 7th of October 1849, in this city, which is undoubtedly entitled to claim him as one of her distinguished sons. Two days thereafter, on the 9th of October, his mortal remains were interred in the cemetery attached to the Westminster Presbyterian Church, adjoining the building in which we are now assembled.

* Edgar Allan Poe was born on January 19th, 1809.—J. H. I.

2 F

"In this connection, acting as a truthful chronicler, I deem it proper to state some facts in relation to the circumstances of the interment. The reliability of the statement I shall now make is sufficiently attested by the evidence of at least three of the gentlemen present on that occasion —possibly the only three who yet survive.

"I have been informed that the day was, for the season, more than ordinarily unpleasant, the weather being raw and cold ; indeed, just such a day as it would have been more comfortable to spend within than without doors.

"The time of the interment was four o'clock in the afternoon ; the attendance of persons at the grave, possibly in consequence of the state of the weather, was limited to eight, certainly to not more than nine, one being a lady.

"Of the number known to have been present were the Hon. Z. C. Lee, a classmate of the deceased at the University of Virginia ; Henry Herring, Esq., a connection of Mr. Poe ; Rev. W. T. D. Clemm, a relative of Mr. Poe's wife ; our well-known fellow-citizen Neilson Poe, Esq., a cousin of the poet ; Edmund Smith, Esq., and wife, the latter being a first cousin of Poe, and at this time his nearest living relative in this city ; and possibly Dr. Snodgrass, the editor of the *Saturday Visiter*, the paper in which the prize story written by Poe first made its appearance. The clergyman who officiated at the grave was Rev. W. T. D. Clemm, already mentioned, a member of the Baltimore Conference of the Methodist Episcopal Church, who read the impressive burial service used by that denomination of Christians, after which all that was mortal of Edgar Allan Poe was gently committed to its mother earth.

"Another item, which it may not be inappropriate to record in this historical compend, I will now mention, namely, that George W. Spence, who officiated as sexton at the burial of Mr. Poe, is the same person who, after the lapse of twenty-six years, has superintended the removal of his remains, and those of his loving and beloved mother-in-law, Mrs. Clemm, and their reinterment in the lot in which the monument now stands.

"For a number of years after the burial of the poet no steps seem to have been taken toward marking his grave, until at length a stone was prepared for this purpose by order of Neilson Poe, Esq. Unfortunately, however, this stone never served the purpose for which it was designed. A train of cars accidentally ran into the establishment of Mr. Hugh Sisson, at which place the stone was at the time, and so damaged it as to render it unfit to be used as intended.

"Another series of years intervened, but yet no movement to . mark the grave. True, articles almost innumerable, *ad nauseam*, made their appearance at short intervals during that time in different newspapers, but the authors of those articles were mostly of that class of persons who employ their energies in finding fault with others, totally oblivious of the fact that they themselves no less deserved the censure they so liberally meted out.

"'Poe's neglected grave' was the stereotyped expression of these modern Jeremiahs. Nor were they content to indulge in lamentations; not unfrequently our good city was soundly berated because of its alleged want of appreciation of the memory of one whose ashes, they intimated, had he been an Englishman, instead of filling an unmarked grave in an obscure cemetery, would have had accorded to them a place in that grand old abbey which England has appropriated as a mausoleum for her distinguished dead.

"But the 'neglected grave' was not always to remain such. At a regular meeting of the Public School Teachers' Association, held in this hall October 7, 1865, Mr. John Basil, Jr., principal of No. 8 Grammar School, offered a paper, of which the following is a copy :—

"'*Whereas*, It has been represented to certain members of the Association that the mortal remains of Edgar Allan Poe are interred in the cemetery of the Westminster Church without even so much as a stone to mark the spot ; therefore,

"'*Resolved*, That a committee of five be appointed by the President of this Association to devise some means best adapted in their judgment to perpetuate the memory of one who has contributed so largely to American literature.'

"This resolution was unanimously adopted, and a committee, consisting of Messrs. Basil, Baird, and J. J. G. Webster, Miss Veeder, and Miss Wise, appointed to carry out the purpose named.

"This committee reported in favour of the erection of a

monument, and recommended that measures be at once taken to secure the funds necessary to accomplish this object. This recommendation was heartily endorsed by the Association, and without delay the committee entered upon the work of raising the funds.

"In this work the young ladies of the Western Female High School took an active and, as will be seen, a successful part. An entertainment of select readings by the pupils of that school, held in this hall on the evening of October 10, 1865, under the superintendence of Miss S. S. Rice, yielded the handsome sum of $380. A literary and musical entertainment, held in Concordia Hall, December 7, 1865, in which the pupils of the Eastern and Western Female High Schools and those of Baltimore City College took part, increased the fund by the addition thereto of $75.92. May 15, 1866, a contribution of $50 was received from Professor Charles Davies, of New York, and on the 19th of the same month a donation of $54 was received as an offering of the young ladies of 'Troy Female Seminary.' These sums, with interest added, amounted, as per report of Thomas D. Baird, treasurer, submitted March 23, 1871, to $587.02. The enthusiasm that characterised the undertaking at the outset seemed now to have greatly abated, and serious thoughts were consequently entertained of abandoning the project. At this juncture a new committee, consisting of Messrs. Elliott, Kerr, and Hamilton, Miss Rice, and Miss Baer, was appointed to consider the matter.

"After mature deliberation, this committee reported, April 15, 1872, as follows : 'First, resolved, that the money now in the hands of he treasurer of the "Poe Memorial Fund" be appropriated to the erection of a monument, the same to be placed over Poe's remains. Second, that a committee of five be appointed by the President, with power to act as stated in the first resolution.' These resolutions were adopted, and the committee therein provided for appointed as follows : Wm. Elliott, Jr., A. S. Kerr, Alexander Hamilton, Miss S. S. Rice, and Miss E. A. Baer. September 2, 1874, this committee received from the estate of Dr. Thomas D. Baird, deceased, the late treasurer of the 'Poe Memorial Fund,' $627.55, the amount of principal and interest to that date, which was immediately deposited in the Chesapeake

Bank of this city. Believing that this amount could be increased to $1000 by donations from some of our fellow-citizens who favoured the project, the committee applied to Mr. George A. Frederick, architect of the City Hall, for the design of a monument to cost about that sum.

"Mr. Frederick in due time submitted a design 'at once simple, chaste, and dignified,' but requiring for its realisation much more than the amount included in the expectations of the committee. Moreover, a new feature was now introduced, that of placing a medallion likeness of the poet on one of the panels of the monument, which would still further increase the cost. With a view of determining whether the amount necessary to complete the monument, according to the proportions it had now assumed, could be raised, applications were made to a number of our citizens for contributions. From one of acknowledged æsthetic taste a check of $100 was promptly received. Two other gentlemen contributed $50 each, while Miss. S. S. Rice, a member of the committee, collected in small sums $52 more.

"A knowledge of the 'world-wide' known liberality of Mr. George W. Childs, of Philadelphia, formerly one of our fellow-townsmen, induced the Chairman of the committee to drop him a note on the subject. Within twenty-four hours a reply was received from that gentlemen expressive of his willingness to make up the estimated deficiency of $650.

"The necessary amount having now been secured, the committee proceeded to place the construction and erection of the monument in the hands of Mr. Hugh Sisson, his proposal being the most liberal one received. How faithfully he has executed his commission will be seen when the covering that now veils the monument is removed. No one so well as the Chairman of the committee knows how anxious Mr. Sisson has been to meet even more than the expectations of those most concerned. To his generous liberality are we largely indebted for the reproduction of the classic lineaments of the poet in the beautiful and highly artistic medallion that adds so much to the attractiveness of the monument.

"To most of those present, I presume, it is known that

the lot in which the monument is now located is not the one in which it was first placed. In deference to what was considered by the committee the popular wish, the monument was removed from its first location to its present one. The remains of Mr. Poe and also those of his mother-in-law were, as before intimated, removed at the same time. The new lot was secured mainly through the efforts of Mr. John T. Morris, President of the School Board, to whom, and to all others who have in any way contributed to the consummation of this undertaking, I wish here, on behalf of the committee, to render thanks.

"In conclusion, allow me to congratulate all concerned that Poe's grave is no longer a neglected one."

Upon the conclusion of Professor Elliott's address, which was listened to with deep attention, Miss Sarah S. Rice was introduced to the audience. To this lady, well known to the public from her elocutionary attainments, the greatest possible credit is due for the successful completion of the enterprise. The first money raised for the erection of the monument was through her personal efforts, and the entire monument, from its inception to the close, has enjoyed the benefits of her unremitting attention and effort. Miss Rice then read several letters from authors who had received invitations to be present on the occasion.

To the unveiling of Poe's long-looked-for cenotaph most of his country's best-known bards had been invited, but the only one, of more than local reputation, who found time to attend in person was Walt Whitman. His venerable head, with long white hair flowing over his shoulders, and his majestic figure, made him the observed of all observers.

After the letters had been read, the following poem, contributed by the well-known dramatic critic and littérateur, Mr. William Winter, was read by Miss Rice "with exquisite delicacy and utterance, and received with a burst of applause : "

AT POE'S GRAVE.

Cold is the pæan honour sings,
    And chill is glory's icy breath,
And pale the garland memory brings
    To grace the iron doors of death.

Fame's echoing thunders, long and loud,
   The pomp of pride that decks the pall,
The plaudits of the vacant crowd—
   One word of love is worth them all.

With dews of grief our eyes are dim ;
   Ah ! let the tear of sorrow start,
And honor, in ourselves and him,
   The great and tender human heart !

Through many a night of want and woe
   His frenzied spirit wandered wild ;
Till kind disaster laid him low,
   And Heaven reclaimed its wayward child.

Through many a year his fame has grown,—
   Like midnight, vast, like starlight, sweet,—
Till now his genius fills a throne,
   And nations marvel at his feet.

One meed of justice long delayed,
   One crowning grace his virtues crave :—
Ah, take, thou great and injured shade,
   The love that sanctifies the grave !

God's mercy guard, in peaceful sleep,
   The sacred dust that slumbers here :
And, while around *this tomb we weep*,
   God bless, for us, the mourner's tear !

And may his spirit, hovering nigh,
   Pierce the dense cloud of darkness through,
And know, with fame that cannot die,
   He has the world's affection too !

The Philharmonic Society then rendered the grand
chorus, " He Watcheth over Israel," from the " Elijah " of
Mendelssohn, with fine effect ; after which, Professor Henry
E. Shepherd proceeded to deliver the following address :—

"LADIES AND GENTLEMEN,—It is my purpose to speak
of Edgar Allan Poe principally as a poet and as a man
of genius. I shall abstain, for the most part, from personal incidents or biographical details. These, though not
devoid of interest, pertain properly to the historian of
literature, or to the biographer. Let his 'strange, eventful history' be reserved for some American Boswell,
Masson, or Morley.

"Edgar A. Poe was born in 1809, the same year with
Alfred Tennyson, the present Poet-laureate, and with Mrs.
Browning, the most gifted poetess of any age. The third

great era in English literature had then fairly commenced. The glory of the elder day was revived. The delusive splendour that had so long gilded the Augustan age of Anne paled before the comprehensive culture, the marvellous intellectual expansion, that distinguished the first thirty years of the present century. The spirit of poesy, no longer circumscribed by the arbitrary and enervating procedures of Dryden's contemplated academy, ranged in unchecked freedom over seas and continents, arousing the buried forms of mediæval civilisation, the lay of the minstrel, the lyric of the troubadour, the ancient glory of the Arthurian cycle.

" One day was as a thousand years in the growth and advancement of the human mind. Edgar was in his childhood when the Georgian era had attained the meridian of its greatness. He spent five years at school in England, from 1816 to 1821. During this interval little is known of his personal history, save what he has left us in the story of ' William Wilson,' in which he depicts with a power of vivid delineation, worthy of the best days of De Quincey, his impressions of the school and its surroundings. We may feel assured, however, that his mind was rapidly unfolding, and with that keen susceptibility to external impressions, characteristic of the dawning intellect of youth, acquiring a permanent colouring from the wonderful drama that was enacting around him. The term of Edgar's school life in England was a period of intense poetical activity and creative power, heroic emprise, knightly valour, and brilliant achievement. The atmosphere was echoing with the strains of songsters, whose notes make as sweet music as when they fell for the first time upon the ears of our youthful poet and aroused him to the consciousness of poet power. Alfred Tennyson was seven years of age when Edgar arrived in England, and, during the time of Edgar's school life at Stoke Newington, was spending his play hours with Mallory's ' Morte D'Arthur ' upon his knees, musing upon the faded splendours of the Table Rounde, and perhaps looking with prophetic vision to the time when Lancelot, Arthur, Percival, and Galahad should regain their ancient sway, with more than their ancient renown, as the mythical heroes of the British race. Mrs. Browning and

Arthur Hallam, the hero of 'In Memoriam,' were in their childhood : Byron, Scott, Shelley, and Keats were in the zenith of their fame, and the English tongue had not been illustrated by so brilliant a constellation of poets since 'the spacious times of great Elizabeth.' It were difficult to imagine that this constellation did not exert an inspiring influence upon the genius and temperament of our youthful poet, an influence which must have determined in some degree his future career. He must have listened with that exquisite sympathy, of which the poetic temperament alone is capable, to the mournful story of Keats, 'the young Lycidas' of our poetic history.

"A strange resemblance in mental constitution may be discerned between these wayward children of genius; the same deep taint of Celtic sadness, the same enthusiastic worship of supernal beauty, the same relentless struggle with the immutability of fact. The delicately wrought sensibilities of Keats, who could 'feel the daisies growing over him,' strikingly recalls the memory of our own poet, who imagined that he could 'distinctly hear the darkness as it stole over the horizon.' 'A thing of beauty is a joy for ever,' was the animating principle of the genius of the one and the art of the other. In 1822 Edgar, then in his fourteenth year, returned to his native land. He attained to manhood at a time when by a revolution, familiar in the history of every literature, the supremacy was reverting from poetry to prose.

"The romantic fervour, the Spenserian symphonies of our last great poetic era, were gradually yielding to the steady advance of philological investigation, critical dissertation, and scientific analysis. A new reflective era, more brilliant than that of Pope or Bolingbroke, was dawning. The cold generalisations of reason, the relentless inductions of philosophy, chilled the glowing ardour of the preceding era. The publication of Macaulay's Essay on Milton in 1825 marked the translation from the sway of the imaginative faculty to the present unsurpassed period in our prose literature. From this desultory outline of nearly contemporary literature, you will observe that our poet's intellectual constitution was formed under peculiar conditions. He does not belong chronologically to the Georgian era; his position was, for the most part, one of comparative isolation, like that of Sackville, Wyatt, or Collins, in the midst of an unpoetic generation, unsustained by the consolations of poetic association or the tender endearments of poetic sympathy. When Poe attained to the full consciousness of his great powers, none of these quickening influences existed save as matters of history or poetic tradition. Tennyson, in England, was viewing nature in perspective, and involving his critics in webs as tangled and hopeless as that which enveloped the fatal lady of Shallot. Wordsworth had abjured the teachings of his early manhood. Shelley, Keats, and Byron were dead, Morris and Swinburne were yet unborn, and the thrones of the elder gods were principally filled by 'the idle singers of an empty day.' American poetry had then accomplished little that future ages will not willingly let die.

"The succession of sweet songsters is never broken; the silver cord that binds in perennial union the spirit of Chaucer and the muse of Spenser is never severed, however slight and impalpable may be the filaments that bind it together. There are always some who retain the echoes of long-gone melodies, upon whom descends something of the inspiration of those grand epochs around which is concentrated so much of the glory of the English tongue. Such a position is not an anomaly in our literary history; such a relation was sustained by the chivalrous Surrey, who introduced into the discordant English of his time that peculiar form of verse which was attuned to the harmonies of Milton, and by means of which Shakspeare, after a long and painful struggle with 'the bondage of rhyming,' rose to the supreme height of poetic excellence. A similar relation was sustained by Sackville, the sombre splendour of whose 'Induction' proved him the worthy herald of Spenser's dawning greatness, and the gentle Cowper, who marks the transition from the school of Jonson and of Addison to the advent of the Gothic revival. Such is in some essential respects the position that Poe occupies among American poets in the order of poetic succession. Having traced somewhat in detail the conditions of the age during which our poet's intellectual constitution was developed, we are now prepared to appreciate the distinctive characteristics of his genius as revealed in his prose, but more especially in his poetry. It is known to students of our literary history, that in all periods of our literature, from the time that our speech was reduced to comparative uniformity, by the delicate discrimination and rare philological perception of Chaucer, there have existed two recognised schools of poetry—the native or domestic, and the classical. In some poets the classical element constitutes the animating principle, as in Milton, whose pages, sprinkled with the diamond dust of ancient lore 'thick as autumnal leaves that strew the brooks in Vallombrosa,' furnish the most impressive illustrations of its beauty and its power. A wonderful impulse was communicated to the development of literary poetry by that 'morning star of modern song,' the poet Keats, and since his advent our poesy has tended more and more to divest itself of domestic sympathies, and to assume an artistic or classical character. Our poetry may have lost pliancy, but it has gained in elaboration and perfection of structure. Genius and imagination are not repressed, but are regulated by the canons of art, and from their harmonious alliance arises the unsurpassed excellence of Poe's maturer productions. In the school of classical poets, he must be ranked in that illustrious succession of bards which includes the names of Surrey, Spenser, Ben Jonson, Herrick, Milton, Shelley, and Keats. Having assigned to Poe an honourable eminence in the school of literary poets, I proceed to speak of the originality, the creative power displayed in his poetry, as well as his brilliant achievements in metrical combination. Specific points of resemblance may be discovered between his poetry and that of his contemporaries and predecessors, but no general or well-defined likeness ; and few poets have displayed a more surpassing measure of creative power. Some of his maturer poems are almost without precedent, in form as well as in spirit.

"The legend of the Raven, related by Roger de Hoveden, and referring to the era of the Latin conquest of Constantinople, nor the legend of Herod Agrippa, cited by De Quincey in his celebrated Essay on Modern Superstition, furnish an adequate foundation for the text of Poe's masterpiece. The raven has constituted a prominent character in English poetry for many ages. In Macbeth, in Hamlet, in Sir David Lindsay, in Tickell's exquisite ballad of Colin and Lucy, and in Coleridge, the appearance of this ' ominous bird of yore' will readily suggest itself to all lovers of our dramatic and lyric poetry. But none of these can be considered as the precursor of Poe's poem. The nearest approach to any distinctive feature of the 'Raven' is to be found, I suspect, in the dramas of Shakspeare, those unfailing sources of intellectual nutriment. The one word, *Mortimer*, of Harry Percy's starling, presents a marked phonetic resemblance to the one word *Nevermore* of Poe's raven, whose melancholy refrain seems almost the echo of the starling's unvarying note.

"No poem in our language presents a more graceful grouping of metrical appliances and devices. The power of peculiar letters is evolved with a magnificent touch ; the sonorous melody of the liquids is a characteristic feature, not only of the refrain, but throughout the compass of the poem, their 'linked sweetness long drawn out' falls with a mellow cadence, displaying the poet's mastery of those mysterious harmonies which lie at the basis of human speech. The alliteration of the Norse minstrel and the Saxon bard, the continuity of the rhythms, illustrating Milton's ideal of true musical delight, in which ' the sense is variously drawn out from one verse into another,' the power of sustained interest and graphic delineation, are some of the features that place the ' Raven ' foremost among the creations of poetic art in our age and in our land.

" But perhaps the especial glory of the 'Raven ' is the novelty as well as the skill of its metrical forms. In the originality of his metrical combinations, Poe has surpassed almost every poet of our era except Tennyson. The invention of new metres, or new dispositions of those in existence, is a task upon which few poets have ventured for centuries. From Surrey to Cowley was an era of transition and experiment. Under the ascendancy of the conventional school our poetry glided smoothly along in the orthodox tensyllabled couplet, until Cowper broke through the consecrated measures of Pope and Dryden with a boldness and originality to which our literature had long been a stranger. Few poets of the Lake School ventured into the enchanted

ground of metrical experiment. They were inclined rather
to discard the restraints of verse, or to render it subordi-
nate to the spontaneous expression of the thought. With
the advent of the new poetic school, the increased attention
to beauty of form and perfection of structure, the expanding
of our metrical forms, became a question of serious import.
The possible combinations of metre are infinite, ' but for
centuries,' to use Poe's own language, ' no man had thought
of doing an original thing in verse.' The 'Raven,' which
is a novel blending of trochaic octometres, is one of the
most brilliant achievements that our era has witnessed,
and marks an epoch in the history of the metric art.

" In no respect is the genius of our poet more signally
displayed than in his essay upon the 'Poetic Principle,' in
which the æsthetics of poetry are discussed with a masterly
comprehension, and a felicity of illustration that entitle the
author to be ranked among the finest critics that have ever
lived. I have often thought that a dissertation upon poetry
by a great poet would constitute an invaluable addition to
the critical resources of our literature. Oh ! that Shakspeare
had left us but one line indicating the processes of his mind
in the creation of Lear or Cymbeline, or that Milton had
bequeathed the rich legacy of a single item respecting the
composition of ' L'Allegro ' or the ' Masque of Comus.' It is
one of the inestimable benefits conferred upon our literature
by Edgar A. Poe, that he has transmitted to us a critical
exposition of the principles of his art, which in perspicuity
and correctness of conception is unsurpassed in the English
language. A diligent reading of the Essay will reveal the
fact that in his theory of poetry the mind of Poe was in
perfect sympathy with the greatest masters, and the most
discriminating expositors of the art of criticism. His theory
of poetry is in thorough accord with that of Shakspeare, as
indicated in the 'Midsummer Night's Dream,' and in a
single line in the play of 'As You Like It.' It is repeated,
in terms almost identical, by Shakspeare's contemporary,
Lord Bacon, in his 'Advancement of Learning.' 'When
I am asked for a definition of poetry,' Poe wrote to a
friend, 'I think of Titania, of Oberon, of the "Midsummer
Night's Dream " of Shakspeare.'

" The next distinguishing characteristic of Poe's poetry is

its rhythmical power, and its admirable illustration of that mysterious affinity which binds together the sound and the sense. Throughout all the processes of creation a rhythmical movement is clearly discernible. Upon the conscious recognition of this principle are based all our conceptions of melody, all systems of intonation and inflection. In this dangerous sphere of poetic effort he attained a mastery over the properties of verse that the Troubadours might have aspired to emulate.

"I would next direct your attention to the classic impress of Poe's poetry, its felicitous blending of genius and culture, and to the estimation in which his works are held in other lands. The Athenian sculptor in the palmiest days of Attic art wrought out his loveliest conceptions by the painful processes of continuous diligence. The angel was not evolved from the block by a sudden inspiration or a brilliant flash of unpremeditated art. By proceeding upon a system corresponding to the diatonic scale in music, the luxuriance of genius was regulated by the sober precepts and decorous graces of formal art. No finer illustration of conscious art has been produced in our era than the 'Raven.' In all the riper productions of our poet there is displayed the same graceful alliance of genius, culture, and taste. He attained the mastery over the most subtile metrical forms, even those to whose successful production the spirit of the English tongue is not congenial. The sonnet, that peculiarly Italian form of verse, immortalised by the genius of Petrarch, has been admirably illustrated in Poe's poem of 'Zante.' Indeed, much of the acrimony of his criticism arose from his painful sensitiveness to artistic imperfection, and his enthusiastic worship of the beautiful. The Grecian caste of his genius led to an idolatrous love of beauty, embodied in palpable or material types.

"This striving after sensuous beauty has formed a distinctive characteristic of all those poets who were most thoroughly imbued with the Grecian taste and spirit. It has left its impress deep upon the texture of our poetry, and many of our most silvery symphonies owe their inspiration to this source. In addition to the classic element, his poetry is pervaded by that natural magic of style, that strange unrest and unreality, those weird notes like the refrain of his own 'Raven,' 'so musical, so melancholy,' which are traceable to the Celtic influence upon our composite intellectual character. The quick sensibility, the ethereal temper, of these natural artists have wonderfully enlivened the stolid character of our Anglo-Saxon ancestors, and much of the style and constructive power that have reigned in English poetry since the age of Walter Map, of Layamon, and of Chaucer, may be justly attributed to the Celtic infusion into the Teutonic blood. Conspicuous examples may be discovered in Shakspeare, in Keats, in Byron, and in Poe.

"I have thus endeavoured to present to you the intellectual character of Edgar A. Poe, as it has revealed itself to me from the diligent study of his works, and from many contrasts and coincidences that literary history naturally suggests. I have attempted to show the versatility of his genius, the consummate as well as conscious art of his poetry, the graceful blending of the creative and the critical faculty — a combination perhaps the rarest that the history of literature affords—his want of deference to prototypes, or morals, the chaste and scholarly elegance of his diction, the Attic smoothness and the Celtic magic of his style. Much of what he has written may not preserve its freshness or stand the test of critical scrutiny in after times, but when subjected to the severest ordeal of varying fashion, popular caprice, 'the old order changing, yielding place to new,' there is much that will perish only with the English language. The maturer productions of Poe have received the most enthusiastic tributes from the sober and dispassionate critics of the older world.

"I shall ever remember the thrill of grateful appreciation with which I read the splendid eulogium upon his genius in the London *Quarterly Review*, in which he is ranked far above his contemporaries, and pronounced one of the most consummate artists of our times, potentially the greatest critic of our era, and possessing perhaps the finest ear for rhythm that was ever formed. You are doubtless familiar with the impression produced by the 'Raven' upon the mind of Mrs. Browning, 'Shakspeare's daughter and Tennyson's sister.' It is but recently that Algernon Swinburne, one of the master-spirits of the new poetic school, has accorded to Poe the pre-eminence among American poets.

Alfred Tennyson has expressed his admiration of Poe, who, with true poetic ken, was among the first to appreciate the novelty and delicacy of his method, and, at a time when the Laureate's fame was obscured by adverse and undiscriminating criticism, plainly foresaw the serene splendour of his matured greatness.

" An appreciative and generous Englishman has added to the literature of our language a superb edition of Poe's works, in which ample recognition is accorded to his rare and varied poems, and the calumnies of his acrimonious biographer are refuted by evidence that cannot be gainsaid or resisted. No reader of English periodical literature can fail to observe the frequent tributes to his genius, the numerous allusions to his memory, the impressive parallelisms between Poe and Marlowe, the contemporary of Shakspeare and Greene, the rival of the great dramatist, that have appeared in the columns of the *Athenæum*, the *Academy*, the British *Quarterlies*, and the transactions of the new Shakespeare Society. Nor is this lofty estimate of his powers confined to those lands in which the English language is the vernacular speech ; it has extended into foreign climes, and aroused appreciative admiration where English literature is imperfectly known and slightly regarded.

" Let us rejoice that Poe's merits have found appropriate recognition among his own countrymen, and that the Poets' Corner in our Westminster is at last rescued from the ungrateful neglect which, for a quarter of a century, has constituted the just reproach of our State and metropolis. I recognise in the dedication of this monument to the memory of our poet an omen of the highest and noblest import, looking far beyond the mere preservation of his fame by the 'dull, cold marble' which marks his long-neglected grave. The impulse which led to its erection coincides in spirit and in character with those grand movements, which the zeal and enthusiasm of patriots and scholars in Great Britain and in America have effected, within the past ten years, for the perpetuation of much that is greatest in the poetry of the English tongue. At last we have the works of Geoffrey Chaucer restored to their original purity by the praiseworthy diligence of Furnival, Morris, and Bradshaw. At last we are to add to the golden treasury of our literature genuine editions of Shakspeare, in which the growth of his genius and his art will be traced by the graceful scholarship and penetrating insight of Tennyson, Ingleby, Spedding, Simpson, and Browning. Ten years have accomplished what centuries failed to achieve, in rescuing from strange and unpardonable indifference the masterpieces of our elder literature, the Sibylline leaves of our ancient poesy.

"This graceful marble, fit emblem of our poet, is the expression, perhaps unconscious, undesigned, but none the less effective, of sympathy with this great intellectual movement of our era. I hail these auspicious omens of the future of our literature with gratitude and delight. But while we welcome these happy indications, while we rejoice in the critical expansion of our peerless literature, let us not disregard the solemn injunction conveyed by this day's proceedings. While we pay the last tributes of respect to the memory of him who alone was worthy, among American poets, to be ranked in that illustrious procession of bards, around whose names is concentrated the glory of the English tongue from Chaucer to Tennyson, let us cherish the admonition to nurture and stimulate the poesy of our land, until it ascend 'with no middle flight' into the 'brightest heaven of invention,' and the regions of purest phantasy."

During the delivery of his address, Professor Shepherd was frequently interrupted by applause. When he had concluded, Poe's "Raven" was recited, followed by a rendering of the *Inflammatus*, from Rossini's *Stabat Mater*, by the local Philharmonic Society. Mr. J. H. Latrobe then gave some personal reminiscences of the poet, and, upon the conclusion of his remarks Mr. Neilson Poe, Sr. a cousin of the poet, was introduced by Professor Elliott, and said: "The relatives of the late poet would indeed be wanting in sensibility, as well as gratitude, if they let this occasion pass without some acknowledgment of their special obligation to those who have reared the memorial soon to be unveiled over the grave of their kinsman. It is impossible that they can be indifferent to the increasing fame of one whose ancestry is common to themselves, and who share his blood. They cannot but look with gratification at the fact that the imputations on the personal character of Poe, which envy has invented and malice magnified, can now, under a closer investigation and an impartial criticism, be judged with charity and justice. Personal animosity may have created slanders which a kindlier spirit is now rejecting, and the good and noble traits of character of the dead are being recognised by an impartial public."

Those present then repaired to Westminster Churchyard, where all that is mortal of Poe now reposes. The remains have been removed from their first resting-place, in an obscure corner of the churchyard, to the corner of Fayette and Greene Streets, where the monument now covering the grave can be seen from Fayette Street.

While the Philharmonic Society rendered the "Sleep and Rest" by Barnby, adapted for the occasion from Tennyson's "Sweet and Low" by Mrs. Eleanor Fullerton, of Baltimore, the Committee on the Memorial and others gathered around the monument.

While the dirge was being sung, Professor Elliott and Miss Rice removed the muslin in which the memorial was veiled, and it was then for the first time presented to the gaze of the public. The monument was crowned with a wreath composed of ivy, and another of lilies and evergreens. After the dirge, Poe's "Annabel Lee" was recited, and selections from "The Bells" were given by Mrs. Dillehunt. This concluded the ceremonies, and the crowd which had collected in the graveyard came forward to view the monument.

During the unveiling a large throng was gathered in the vicinity of Fayette and Greene Streets, unable to gain admission to the Female High School or the churchyard.

The monument is of the pedestal or cippus form, and is eight feet high; the surbase is of Woodstock granite, six feet square, the other portions being of white-veined Italian marble. The pedestal has an Attic base three feet ten inches square; the die block is a cube three feet square and three feet two inches high, relieved on each face by a square-projecting and polished plane, the upper angles of which are broken and filled with a carved rosette. On the front panel is the bas-relief bust of the poet, modelled by Frederick Volck from a photograph in possession of Mr. Neilson Poe.

On the opposite panel are inscribed the dates of the poet's birth and death. The die block is surmounted by a bold and graceful frieze and cornice four feet square, broken on each face in the centre by a segment of a circle. The frieze is ornamented at the angles by richly-carved acanthus leaves, and in the centre by a lyre crowned with laurel. The whole is capped by a blocking three feet square, cut to a low pyramidal form. "The monument is simple and chaste, and strikes more by graceful outline than by crowding with unmeaning ornament." Mr. Geo. A. Frederick was the architect.

A TRIBUTE FROM THE STAGE.—"A pleasing feature of the ceremonies was the placing upon the monument of a large wreath of flowers, made up principally of camelias, lilies, and tea roses. Together with this was deposited a floral tribute in the shape of a raven, made from black immortelles. The large petals of the lilies suggested the 'bells' immortalised by Poe's genius, the significance of the other emblems being obvious. These were tributes from the company at Ford's Grand Opera House, Mrs. Germon being mainly in-strumental in getting them up. Poe's mother had been an actress at Holliday Street Theatre, which fact had been preserved in the traditions of the stage, and had something to do with inspiring this tribute."

APPENDIX F.

To furnish a full and analytic account of the biographies of Edgar Allan Poe would be a task almost equal to that of rewriting his entire life. The history of this poet's biographies might, indeed, fill a fresh chapter, and that by no means the least memorable, in the Curiosities of Literature. Naturally, only a concise and cursory summary of these sketches can be given here. Previous to the poet's death, several slight biographical notices were published in various forms, and more or less diluted by speculative criticism. Griswold's works on American Poets and Prose Writers, contained a certain number of correct and of incorrect *data*, to which Mr. J. R. Lowell added his *quantum*, in *Graham's Magazine* for February 1845, in a clever but unsympathetic paper on "Edgar Allan Poe." Poe died on the 7th of October 1849, and two days later a somewhat lengthy and bitterly hostile paper on his life and character appeared in the New York *Tribune*, over the signature of "Ludwig." N. P. Willis, commenting in the *Home Journal* upon this posthumous hostility, revealed the fact that the pseudonymous reviler of the dead was Rufus Griswold. John Neal immediately denounced the calumniator's sketch as "false and malicious," and other friends and admirers were equally disgusted with it; whilst Mr. George R. Graham—that "noble fellow," as Mrs Clemm styles him—knowing more of the connection between the dead lion and his dissector than any one else, published a long and eloquent reply in *Graham's Magazine* for March 1850, in which he justly termed the characterisation by the *soi-disant* "Ludwig," "the fancy sketch of a jaundiced vision," "an immortal infamy," and other similar appellations.

Meanwhile, Mr. Powell, an English author resident in New York, had just completed a work on "The Living Authors

of America," in which a pleasant, unprejudiced, biographical
sketch was given of Poe's career. The book, however, did
not appear until after the poet's death ; its *data* are very
flattering to Poe, but do not appear very reliable.

In March 1850 was published, in the *Southern Literary
Messenger*, what Griswold styles an "Eulogium" on Poe, but
what really was a still more dastardly attack on the dead
man than the unsavoury "Ludwig" article. It had evidently been written and printed in hot haste, and was so
disgraceful and cowardly that the editorial proprietor of
the magazine, Mr. John R. Thompson, deemed it necessary to append a short printed note, to the effect that had
it not been inserted during his absence, and not seen by
him until too late to stop it, it should not have appeared
in the *Messenger*. Who wrote this article? It is generally
ascribed to Mr. J. M. Daniel ; yet, strange to say, it not
only uses lengthy passages of "Ludwig's" sketch without
inverted commas, or other signs of quotation, but, when
Griswold's long "Memoir of Poe" appeared in the Boston
International Magazine, he also made use of long extracts
from the "Eulogium" without acknowledgment. Certainly
he does refer to it as his authority for one of the blackest
crimes he charges Poe with, and which he himself not un-
aptly styles unfit for "any register but that of hell." Was
not this miscalled (by Griswold) 'defender,' then, Griswold
himself, or some one acting under his inspiration?

In 1850 appeared the third volume of Poe's works, prefaced by the so-styled "Memoir" of the poet, a concentration
of hatred and malice that had already done duty, as pointed
out above, in the *International Magazine*. It is quite impossible to comprehend the immense injury this publication did to Poe's memory. Its author appeared to be in
possession of the facts—as editor of the poet's works he
was in possession of the field—and, therefore, all the
numerous writers, friendly or hostile, who essayed biographical sketches of Poe, resorted to Griswold for their *data*.
And, notwithstanding intermittent bursts of indignation,
no new life of Poe, founded upon evidence independent
of that proffered by this initial biographer, was published
until the present writer's sketch, introductory of the first
complete edition of the poet's works, appeared in October

1874. During this quarter of a century, however, several noteworthy "memoirs of Poe" saw the light. The best known of these was the essay of Baudélaire, and it is chiefly remarkable as the attempt, by a man of genius, to explain Poe's character *as described by Griswold*, by an ingenious theory of his own. Of course he failed in *that*, however valuable his essay otherwise may be and truly is. Baudelaire, it should be added, had read the "Eulogium," and, probably, Powell's account of Poe already referred to.

Next in importance to the French critic's characterisation of Poe, is that by James Hannay, prefixed to the 1853 English edition of the Poetical Works. It is a charming and appreciative sketch, but having no biographical details other than Griswold's to go by, and being as instinctively attracted to Poe as was Baudelaire, Hannay also started a theory as ingenious and as unsatisfactory as his, to account for the poet's presumed misdeeds. A writer in the *British Quarterly Review* for July 1875, now understood to be Dr. A. H. Japp, in a clever and impartial article on "Edgar Allan Poe," has very thoroughly sifted the errors promulgated by the two writers, and thus disposes of the latest offspring of a remarkable group : "Owing to influences precisely similar, Mr. Curwen, in his 'Sorrow and Song,' errs in the same direction as Baudelaire and Hannay ; and *his* sympathy seems wholly misplaced, because he *will* drive against society, instead of acknowledging frankly Poe's faults and perversities."

The above writers, as intimated, did not dispute Griswold's premises, only his inferences, but others, more or less known in the literary world, doubted the trustworthiness of both. The editor of Chambers' "Handbook of American Literature," writing in 1854, mildly expressed doubts of several of the allegations made against Poe by his biographer. Nemesis began to loom in the distance. In April 1857 Mr. Moy Thomas drew attention to the fact "that Poe's miserable story rested wholly upon Griswold's Memoir ; that all since him have followed Griswold, with the exactness of a Hebrew copyist, trembling at the prophet's curse upon all who should add to or take away one tittle of the text." "It did appear to me to be an important and an interesting point," he remarks, "to learn what explanation, if any, Griswold himself had given of the reasons which had determined him to fulfil his painful task." Mr. Moy Thomas then proceeded to show, "what even American readers appear to have forgotten, that when Mr. Griswold's Memoir was first published, its assertions were denied by many who had known Poe, that no person corroborated the worst parts of his story, that some went so far as to impugn his motives; and that others, who had known and had closer relations with the poet, gave accounts differing materially from Griswold's." Finally, after alluding to the enmity existing between the poet and his biographer, Mr. Moy Thomas concludes his highly suggestive paper, by reminding English readers that there are "portraits of Poe less repulsive than that one which is best known." In November 1857 appeared in *Russell's Magazine*, Charleston, S.C., a still more remarkable vindicatory article, by Professor James Wood Davidson; in this defence of Edgar Poe's fair fame, many of Griswold's imputations were proved to be false, whilst others were rendered extremely improbable. This important step was contemporaneous with similar efforts made by Captain Mayne Reid, Mr. T. C. Clarke, and other personal acquaintances of the deceased poet, in the magazines and newspapers, and by Mr. L. A. Wilmer, in his book called "Our Press Gang." The slow progress made by these justificatory pieces may be comprehended when reading the last named author's words respecting an article he had published on "Edgar A. Poe and his Calumniators." "I do not know," he states, "that this vindication was copied by a single paper ; whereas the whole press of the country seemed desirous of giving circulation and authenticity to the slanders."

But the ball had been set rolling, and in 1860, when Mrs. Whitman published her beautiful little monograph on "Edgar Poe and his Critics," several influential literati were prepared to add the impetus of their words towards aiding the cause of truth and justice. Mrs. Whitman's defence of her dead friend dealt almost entirely with his literary character, "leaving to some later writer the task of giving to the world a more impartial memoir of the poet than Griswold's," but at the same time she pointed out that

that author's "perverted facts and baseless assumptions had been adopted into every subsequent memoir and notice of the poet," and therefore she published her book as an earnest protest against such a "great wrong to the dead."

Harper's *New Monthly Magazine* for September 1872, contained an article on "Edgar Allan Poe" which, although showing animus against the poet, was noteworthy as affording evidence of original research. In 1875 this article, revised and enlarged, and for some occult reason "submitted" to English readers, did duty as "an original memoir," as the introduction to a new American edition of the Poetical Works. In the *British Quarterly Review* it is disposed of thus: "The last addition to the Poe biography is 'An *Original* Memoir,' by R. H. Stoddard, a gentleman of New York, who denounces Griswold, and then proceeds simply to surpass him in his own line; raking together such a mass of irrelevant gossip as we never read before."

During the last fifteen years the writer of the present biography has published papers in vindication of Poe's memory, but it was not until the beginning of 1874 that he was enabled to adduce more than a few isolated items in support of his theory of Griswold's untrustworthiness. In January of that year he commenced a series of articles in the *Mirror*, on "New Facts" about the poet; in June the same year he contributed a still more exculpatory sketch to *Temple Bar Magazine*, and in the following October published a thorough vindication of Poe, as an introduction to the first volume of a complete edition of his works. In March 1875, he revised and abridged this sketch of "Edgar Allan Poe," for the *International Review*, and in 1877 contributed a further revision of it, as an introduction to the *Baltimore Memorial*, a *livre de luxe* in every respect most creditable to the "Monumental City:" this handsome volume, besides other interesting and original matter, contained Colonel Preston's pleasant reminiscences of his famous school-fellow.

In 1877, a New York edition of Poe's poems was prefaced by "a New Memoir" by Mr. E. L. Didier, a gentleman who appears to have been collecting "Poeana" for some time past, and who, ultimately, came into possession of the present writer's life of the poet: by aid of this he was enabled to compile " a New Memoir," forgetting, however, in the hurry of publication, to acknowledge the chief source of his "much fresh and interesting information." Mr. Francis Gerry Fairfield, a New York journalist, and the author of an innumerable number of " queer " papers on, *from*, and about Poe, thus briefly summarised his opinion on Mr. Didier's book :—

> "Dear D——, in your biography of Poe,
> The real cause for rue is,
> That what is true was published years ago,
> And what is new not true is :
> And the new poems that you tell about
> Upon the title-page, are all left out."

"The Last Days of Edgar Poe," by Mrs. S. A. Talley-Weiss, was a noticeable contribution towards the poet's biography that appeared in *Scribner's Magazine* for March 1878. The present writer has ventured to avail himself of some portions of this account of Poe's last few weeks life.

Numerous other books and sketches bearing upon the subject of this biography might be mentioned, but beyond those already referred to here, or in the body of the work, few or any are of biographical value, although several might be cited as of critical worth, such as Dr. Landa's "Noticias Biograficas de Edgard Poe," prefixed to the 1858 Spanish collection of Poe's tales, and Dr. W. Hand Browne's clever analysis of " Eureka," in the *New Eclectic Magazine* for 1868, remarkable as the only known attempt to examine that scientific work scientifically.

APPENDIX G.

THE BIBLIOGRAPHY OF EDGAR ALLAN POE.

The following record of the bibliography of Edgar Allan Poe is scarcely likely to prove complete, or exhaustive, although no pains have been spared to make it both. It has now been brought down to date and should be accurate as far as it goes, as copies of most of the works mentioned are in possession of the present writer. Doubtless many translations have appeared, and disappeared, without leaving any discoverable traces in the imperfectly-kept book registers of the past, whilst even several American and English distinct publications—anonymous and pseudonymous—as well as various editions of Poe's known works, are no longer recognisable. Only separate book publications are herein referred to, and no notice has been taken of various works wrongly ascribed to Poe : magazine, newspaper, and such-like ephemeral issues have also been ignored. It may be mentioned that the poet's name and works are well known in most European countries (as well as in the British colonies), but whether by means of native or foreign versions, or by journals or books, cannot always be ascertained. In France and other countries, translations of Poe's tales have frequently been published in the journals, *en feuilleton*.

AMERICAN.

PUBLISHED DURING POE'S LIFETIME.

Tamerlane and Other Poems. Boston. 1827. 16mo.
Al Aaraaf, Tamerlane, and Minor Poems. Baltimore. 1829. 16mo.
Poems. (Second edition.) New York. 1831. 16mo.

The Narrative of Arthur Gordon Pym. New York. 1838. 12mo.

Tales of the Grotesque and Arabesque. Philadelphia. 1840 (printed 1839). 12mo. 2 vols.

The Conchologist's First Book. Philadelphia. 1840 (printed 1839). (Second edition same year.)

Tales of the Grotesque and Arabesque. (Second edition.) New York. 1845. 16mo. 2 vols.

Tales. New York. 1845. 12mo.

The Raven and Other Poems. New York. 1845. 12mo.

Eureka. A Prose Poem. New York. 1848. 8vo. (Second edition is said to have been issued, but cannot be traced.)

POSTHUMOUS.

The Works of Edgar Allan Poe. New York. 1850. 12mo. 2 vols.

The Literati. (Memoir by R. W. Griswold.) New York. 1850. 12mo. (Issued as vol. iii. of the *Works*.)

The Works, &c. New York. 1850. 12mo. New edition. 3 vols.

The Works. New York. 1853. 12mo. 4 vols. (Vol. iv. contained "Arthur Gordon Pym," and other hitherto uncollected tales.)

The Works. New York. 1858. 12mo. Fifteenth edition. (All later editions of *The Works* were merely reprints of this collection until 1876, when additional pieces from the Edinburgh collection of 1874–75 were included.)

The Poetical Works. (With Memoir, founded on Griswold's, and ascribed to C. Briggs.) New York. 1858. 8vo.

Editions of the *Poetical Works*, in all sizes, with or without memoir, illustrated or not, continued to issue from the Press of New York. The poems were merely reprints of those published in volume ii. of the 1850 collection, unaltered and unadded to, until 1875, when the early lines "To Helen" were omitted, and eight juvenile pieces (which had recently been reprinted by J. H. Ingram from the 1831 edition) were included. In the "Memorial" edition of the *Poems and Essays* (New York. 1876. 8vo. Memoir by J. H. Ingram) "To Helen" reappeared, and seven of the 1831 pieces were again omitted. Other variations, of more or less importance, occur in the different editions now in circulation.

Select Works. Poetical and Prose. (Memoir by R. H. Stoddard. "Household" edition.) New York and London. 1884. 8vo.

The Raven. (Illustrated by G. Doré. Commentary by E. C. Stedman.) New York and London. 1883. Folio.

The Works. (Introduction and Memoir by R. H. Stoddard.) New York and London. 1884. 8vo. 6 vols.

British. (Prose.)

The Narrative of Arthur Gordon Pym. London. 1838. 8vo. (A reprint of the New York edition, issued by the London branch of the American firm.)

The Narrative of Arthur Gordon Pym. London. 1841. 4to. (In the "Novelist's Newspaper.")

The Narrative of Arthur Gordon Pym. London. 1859. 8vo.

The Narrative of Arthur Gordon Pym. London. 1861. 8vo. (No. 3 of "The Shilling Series.")

Several other reprints of this romance have appeared in England, but cannot now be traced.

Tales. London. 1845. 8vo. (Reprint of the New York collection.)

Mesmerism. "In Articulo Mortis." London. 1846. 8vo. (Pamphlet reprint of "M. Valdemar's Case.")

Eureka. A Prose Poem. London. 1848. 8vo. (Apparently the New York edition with another title-page.)

Tales and Sketches. London. 1852. 8vo.

Tales and Poems. London. 1852. 8vo.

Tales of Mystery, Imagination, and Humour. London. 1852. 8vo. Illustrated. 2 vols. (Two series, being vols. i. and ix. of the "Readable Books" Library.)

Tales of Mystery, Imagination, and Humour. London. 1853. 8vo. 2 vols.

Tales of Mystery, Imagination, and Humour. Halifax. 1855. 16mo. (In the "Cottage Library.") Various

editions of this collection appeared in 1856 and
subsequently, in London and elsewhere.

Tales and Poems. London. (Ward, Lock & Co.) 1864.
12mo.

The Works. London. 1872. 8vo. (This so-called collection
of *The Works* does not contain more than a third of
Poe's writings. It is believed to have had a very large
circulation.)

The Complete Works. (Edited, with Memoir, by John H.
Ingram.) Edinburgh. 1874-75. 8vo. 4 vols. (This
has passed through various editions.)

The Mystery of Marie Roget, and Other Stories. Illustrated.
London. No date. 8vo.

Tales of Mystery and Imagination. London. 1883. 8vo.
("Sixpenny Novels" Series.)

The Tales and Poems. Including "The Journal of Julius
Rodman." (Edited, with Essays, by J. H. Ingram.
Illustrated with original etchings, &c.) London.
1884. 8vo. 4 vols. (150 large paper copies printed.)

Tales. (Edited, with Note, by J. H. Ingram.) Leipzig.
(Other editions in London.) 1884. 8vo. (Tauchnitz
"Collection of British Authors.")

Selections. Prose and Poetry. London, &c. 1885. 8vo.
("The Red Library.")

Tales of Mystery and Imagination. Selected. (Introduction by H. R. Haweis.) London. 1886. 16mo. ("The
World Library.")

Tales and Other Prose Writings. Selected. (Introduction
by E. Rhys.) London. 1889. 8vo. ("The Camelot"
Series.)

Tales of Adventure, Mystery, and Imagination. (Introduction by G. T. Bettany.) London, &c. Illustrated.
1890. 8vo. ("Minerva Library of Famous Books.")

BRITISH. (POETRY.)

The Raven, and Other Poems. London. 1846. 16mo. (A
reprint of the New York edition, 1845.)

The Poetical Works. London. 1852. 12mo.

The Poetical Works. (Life by J. Hannay.) Illustrated. London. 1853. 8vo. (Many editions of this collection have appeared.)

The Poetical Works. (Poems by R. H. Dana in same volume.) Illustrated. London. 1857. 12mo.

The Poetical Works. (With Memoir.) London. 1858 (printed 1857). 8vo.

The Poetical Works. London. 1858: 12mo. 1859: 8vo. 1860: 18mo.

Many reprints of these collections have been published, some with memoir, some with illustrations, but only those hereafter specified call for separate mention.

The Poems. London. 12mo. or 8vo. 1862, &c. Illustrated. ("The Emerald" Series.) The thirteenth thousand was announced some years ago.

The Poetical Works. (With Life, and Selections from his Sketches and Reviews.) London. 1866. 8vo. ("The Library of Popular Authors.")

The Poetical Works. ("Original Memoir," derived from Griswold.) Edinburgh. 1869. 8vo.

The Poetical Works. Illustrated. Edinburgh. 1869. 4to.

The Raven. Penny edition. Glasgow. 1869. 24mo.

The Poems. (Ward and Lock's edition.) London. 1870. 4to.

The Poems. Edinburgh. 1871. Small 4to. Ditto 8vo. Ditto 12mo. (Variously reprinted at London and Edinburgh, and many other editions more or less important issued.)

Poems. (With Essay by A. Lang.) London. 1881. 8vo.

The Poetical Works. (Memoir by F. M. H.) Illustrated. London. 1882. 8vo. ("Moxon's Popular Poets.") With new Preface, 1887.

The Raven. (Illustrated.) London. 1883. 8vo.

The Raven. (Illustrated by W. L. Taylor.) London. No date. 4to.

The Raven. (Commentary by E. C. Stedman. Illustrated by G. Doré.) London. 1883. Folio.

Tamerlane and Other Poems. (Preface by R. H. Shepherd.) London. 1884. 16mo.

Poems and Essays. (Memoir by J. H. Ingram. Leipzig.

Also in London.) 1884. 16mo. (Tauchnitz " Collection of British Authors.")

The Raven. (Literary and Historical Commentary by J. H. Ingram.) London. 1885. 8vo.

Poetical Works. (Prefatory Notice by J. Skipsey. "The Canterbury Poets.") London. 1885. 8vo.

Poetical Works. (With Memoir.) New York and London. 1886. 12mo.

Poems. London. 1887. 16mo. ("The Pocket Library.")

Complete Poetical Works. (With Memoir, and edited, annotated and arranged by J. H. Ingram.) London and New York. 1888. 8vo. ("The Chandos Classics.")

The Bells. Illustrated. London. (Nuremberg printed.) 1888. 8vo.

French.

Histoires Extraordinaires. Paris. 1856. 12mo.

Nouvelles Histoires Extraordinaires. Paris. 1857. 12mo.

Aventures d'Arthur Gordon Pym. Paris. 1863. 12mo.

Euréka. Paris. 1863. 12mo.

Histoires Grotesques et Sérieuses. Paris. 1865. 12mo.

The above five are Baudelaire's world-famed translations of Poe's works. They have gone through numerous editions, and have circulated by tens of thousands, culminating in the following superbly illustrated volumes :—

Histoires Extraordinaires. (La vie par C. Baudelaire), and *Nouvelles Histoires Extraordinaires.* (Notes nouvelles par C. Baudelaire.) Paris. 1884. 8vo.

Les Contes d'Edgar Poe. Paris. 1846. 12mo.

Nouvelles Choisies. Paris. 1853. 12mo.

Contes Inédits. (Traduits par W. L. Hughes.) Paris. 1862. 12mo.

Mille et Deuxième Nuit. Illustré. Coulommiers. 1869. 4to.

Le Corbeau. (Traduit par S. Mallarmé. Illustré par E. Manet.) Paris. 1875. Folio.

A magnificent *chef d'œuvre,* worthy of all concerned.

Contes Grotesques. (Traduction avec Vie par É. Hennequin.
Vignette par Odilon Redon.) Paris. 1882. 8vo.
Œuvres Choisies. (Traduction Nouvelle par W. L. Hughes.)
Paris. 1885. 8vo.
Derniers Contes. (Traduits par F. Rabbe, &c.) Paris. 1887.
Le Scarabée d'Or. (Traduit par C. Simond. Illustrè.)
Paris. 1887. 8vo.
Le Scarabée d'Or. (Illustrations de Brossi-le-Vaigneau.)
Paris. 1888. 8vo.
Aventures d'A. G. Pym. (Traduction de C. Simond.) Paris.
1888. 8vo.
Les Poèmes. (Traduction de S. Mallarmé, avec notes.
Portrait et fleuron par E. Manet.) Bruxelles. 1888.
4to.

GERMAN.

Novellen von E. A. Poe. Illustrated. Leipzig. 1855–58. 2
vols. pp. 192, 192. (Issued in the "Familien-Biblio-
thek.")
Ausgewählte Werke. Leipzig. 1853–58. 3 vols. pp. 200,
214, 197. (Issued in the "Amerikanische-Bibliothek,"
as vols. xxxvii., xxxviii. and xcix.)
Tales of Mystery, Imagination, and Humour. Leipzig.
1855–56. 2 vols. (Vols. vi. and vii. of "The English
Library.")
Select Works of E. A. Poe. (With Memoir.) Leipzig. 1854–
58. 2 vols. (Vols. xiii. and xiv. of "Dürr's Collection of American Authors.") pp. 246, 280.
Unbegreifliche Ereignisse und geheimniszvolle Thaten. Stutt-
gart. 1861. pp. 580. 8vo.
Erstaunliche Geschichten und unheimliche Begebenheiten.
Stuttgart. 1859. pp. 456.
Unheimliche Geschichten. Jena. 1879. pp. 164. 8vo.
Der Rabe, die Glocken, und Lenore. Philadelphia. 1864.
16mo.
Der Rabe. (Mit einer biographischen Skizze.) Philadelphia.
1869. 8vo. Illustrated.

Spanish.

Historias Extraordinarias. (Noticias por el Doctor Landa.)
    Madrid. 1858. 16mo.
Historias Extraordinarias. (Two Series.) Madrid. 1859.
    16mo. 2 vols. (In the "Biblioteca de Viaje.")
Aventuras de Arturo Gordón Pym. Barcelona. 1863. 8vo.
Aventuras de Arturo Gordón Pym. Madrid. 1887. 16mo.
    (In the "Biblioteca Universal.")

Italian.

Racconti Incredibili. Illustrated. Milan. 1876. 8vo.
Racconti. Milan. 187? (No. 38 of the "Biblioteca
    Nuova.")
Nuovi Racconti Straordinari. Milan. 1885. 8vo. (No.
    143 of the "Biblioteca Universal.")

Australian.

Poetical Works. Melbourne. 1868. 8vo.

INDEX.

———o———

WARD, LOCK, BOWDEN & CO., LONDON & NEW YORK.